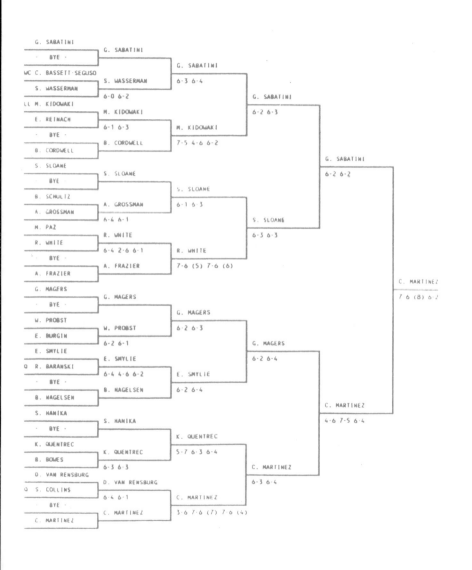

G. SABATINI
- BYE -
G. SABATINI
WC C. BASSETT-SEGUSO
S. WASSERMAN
S. WASSERMAN
6-0 6-2
G. SABATINI
6-3 6-4
LL M. KIDOWAKI
E. REINACH
M. KIDOWAKI
6-1 6-3
- BYE -
B. CORDWELL
B. CORDWELL
M. KIDOWAKI
7-5 4-6 6-2
G. SABATINI
6-2 6-3

S. SLOANE
- BYE -
S. SLOANE
B. SCHULTZ
A. GROSSMAN
A. GROSSMAN
6-4 6-1
S. SLOANE
6-1 6-3
M. PAZ
R. WHITE
R. WHITE
6-4 2-6 6-1
- BYE -
A. FRAZIER
A. FRAZIER
R. WHITE
7-6 (5) 7-6 (6)
S. SLOANE
6-3 6-3

G. SABATINI
6-2 6-2

G. MAGERS
- BYE -
G. MAGERS
W. PROBST
E. BURGIN
W. PROBST
6-2 6-1
G. MAGERS
6-2 6-3
E. SMYLIE
Q R. BARANSKI
E. SMYLIE
6-4 4-6 6-2
- BYE -
B. NAGELSEN
B. NAGELSEN
E. SMYLIE
6-2 6-4
G. MAGERS
6-2 6-4

S. HANIKA
- BYE -
S. HANIKA
K. QUENTREC
B. BOWES
K. QUENTREC
6-3 6-3
K. QUENTREC
5-7 6-3 6-4
D. VAN RENSBURG
Q S. COLLINS
D. VAN RENSBURG
6-4 6-1
- BYE -
C. MARTINEZ
C. MARTINEZ
C. MARTINEZ
3-6 7-6 (7) 7-6 (4)
C. MARTINEZ
6-3 6-4
C. MARTINEZ
4-6 7-5 6-4

C. MARTINEZ
7-6 (8) 6-2

TOUGH DRAW

TOUGH DRAW

THE PATH TO TENNIS GLORY

ELIOT BERRY

A JOHN MACRAE BOOK

HENRY HOLT AND COMPANY

NEW YORK

Library of Congress Cataloging-in-Publication Data
Berry, Eliot.
Tough draw : the path to tennis glory / Eliot Berry.—1st ed.
p.   cm.
Includes index.
1. Tennis—Tournaments.   2. Tennis players.   3. Berry, Eliot.
I. Title.
GV999.B47   1992   91-4831
                                                           CIP

ISBN 0-8050-2314-3

Henry Holt books are available at special discounts
for bulk purchases for sales promotions, premiums,
fund-raising, or educational use. Special editions
or book excerpts can also be created to specification.

For details contact:
Special Sales Director,
Henry Holt and Company, Inc., 115 West 18th Street,
New York, New York 10011.

First Edition—1992

Printed in the United States of America
Recognizing the importance of preserving the
written word, Henry Holt and Company, Inc.,
by policy, prints all of its first editions
on acid-free paper. ∞
1   3   5   7   9   10   8   6   4   2

For my father,
who taught me to drop shot,
And my mother,
who taught me to lob,
For Gloria,
whose kindness saw me through the book,
And for our son,
who is two and such fun to hug.

ACKNOWLEDGMENTS

To Robert Lucid and Herbert Warren Wind for their kindness, time, and thoughts about the manuscript. To Katherine Bryan for her keen eye and laughter. Carole Berglie for her common sense and uncommon sensibility.

To my agent, Carl Brandt.

To Ed Fabricius at the U.S. Open and more: deep thanks. Vic Seixas in Philadelphia. Jim Tevis and Temple Pouncey in Miami. Mr. Richard Berens and Mr. Brian McMahon for the Wimbledon fortnight. A special thanks to the ATP media representatives, Greg Sharko, Loren Goldenburg, and George Rubenstein. To Robin Reynolds and Leslie Allen of the WTA. Bill Henry for twenty years' support. To Renzo Baldaccini for his spirit and deep kindness. To Jim Levy. To former U.S. Davis Cup captain George McCall, and to the Australian greats, Newcombe, Roche, and Rosewall, who spoke to me as if we were equals with that great Australian inner ease. To Coach Chuck Kriese of Clemson. Martina Navratilova, Stefan Edberg, and Jay Berger for their lack of pretension in conversation. And to Arthur Ashe, who is living proof that athletes can also be thinkers.

For the players I grew up with: Dick Stockton. Hugh Curry. Tico Carrerro. Sandy and Eugene Mayer. The memory of Louis Glass. Jeff Podesta. Steve Siegel. Doubles partner Bill Powell. The heart and soul of Bill Harris.

For the industrious tennis agents, among them Bob Kain, Gavin Forbes, Sara Fornaciari, Karen Piner, Fabio Della Vida, Bonnie Hagerman, Ivan Blumberg.

For the Virginia Center for the Creative Arts.

Teachers who encouraged me and made a difference: Ben Long, Emily Dalgarno, John Barth, Eric Mottram, and John Wideman.

Five outstanding player-coaches from whom I learned the game: Elwood Cooke, Doris Hart, John Nogrady, Fred Botur, and Eddie Moylan.

Al Molloy, Hall of Fame coach, who helped me immeasurably as coach and friend.

And finally, to Jack Macrae, for his skill, humor, and hard work.

PROLOGUE

For the past couple of years I followed a trail that many tennis aficionados dream about. I followed the tennis tour, and then some.

When I was six, my parents took me to see my first major tennis match. Pancho Gonzales was facing Lew Hoad, one of the great Australians of the 1950s, at Madison Square Garden. The New York Rangers were to play hockey that same night, and a thin green rubber court was stretched out over the ice with long ropes that held the court down tightly to the hockey ice, as Gulliver was held down by the ropes of the Lilliputians. The arena was suddenly plunged into total darkness. A single spotlight was turned on to the flags of America and Australia, and in the darkness the crowd sang the national anthems of the two countries. The lights burst on, and I found myself roaring with the crowd. Gonzales and Hoad played a three-set match, their final match of the year-long Jack Kramer head-to-head pro tour. Gonzales won the struggle with great volleys and plenty of dark looks and shouts of anger. But in the warm-up, Gonzales and Hoad looked half like angels, half like gods, and it was that warm-up, not the match, that thrilled me, stuck in my mind, and years later made me want to follow the tour in search of a similarly powerful delight.

During the warm-up, Pancho Gonzales, my first tennis hero, noticed that the nets had already been set up for that night's hockey game. He asked blonde-haired Hoad for some lobs, and for several minutes Gonzales bounced his overheads off the hard surface and over the high, loose backstop around the court, sending the tennis balls skidding across the ice right into or just to the side of the hockey nets. Hoad and Gonzales were both smiling like kids as they hit those lobs and overheads. That was pleasure, that was laughter and beauty, that was great physical release and skill—and that was part of what I was after in writing this book.

Tennis is a game of sensation. The first sensation is effort, without which you never get to the other feelings. Tennis is played and watched for its sensations, and the major, final sensation—the outcome—often feels like love. Team games hurt less. The lone tennis player lives or dies on his or her own. In writing *Tough Draw* I was after both the source for the drive top players have and the tremendous, pure appeal of the action itself.

Tennis is two games, a competitive game and a social game. The question I most wanted to answer is key to any competitive endeavor: What makes some people win and others come in a close second? There is a point in every match, Stefan Edberg told me, when a match can be had. Even if a player is down, there is usually one chance, one moment, in a close battle to get back into it—or fade. I was interested in what leads certain players—sometimes the most beautiful to watch, sometimes not—to seize that moment.

Eliot Berry
New York City
March 1992

TOUGH DRAW

THE LIPTON INTERNATIONAL

Florida, March 1990

Like a good cup of tea, the Lipton tennis tournament in Miami has a leisurely pace to it, the way Forest Hills did in the old days. If the U.S. Open at Flushing Meadow in September is the World Series, and Wimbledon in June is the All-Star Game, then the Lipton in March looks and feels just like spring training.

Seeded players like Boris Becker, Stefan Edberg, and Jay Berger wandered through crowds of people who seemed to be in varying stages of undress in the hot Florida sun, a welcome change to someone like myself who had been suffering through a northern winter. A number of spectators were dressed like players. One thin, athletic fifty-year-old man with a waterfall of blonde hair, blue Fila shorts, and color-coordinated shirt looked like an aging Vitas Gerulaitis. A woman in her late thirties wearing a pink Ellesse outfit came to the matches every day with a stack of four Black Max Dunlop rackets under her arm and a twenty-year-old tennis-pro boyfriend in tow. She wore her hair pulled back in a ponytail like Steffi Graf, and her young tennis pro held her hand as she walked around the Lipton concession village, looking everywhere. Her husband must have taken too many volleys down the center of the doubles court.

The old green wooden stadium comfortably held nine thousand people, and the grandstand could seat another six hundred spectators, max-

imum. Near the grandstand, built into tall, flamingo-pink gazebos, stood
four large white draw sheets, singles and doubles, with hundreds of
hopeful names pyramiding toward a final, solitary line.

The bright Florida sun had put a smile on everyone's face. Anticipation was high. The closed, blue-carpet glare of the winter indoor season
in Toronto, Philadelphia, Memphis, and Frankfurt had given way to high
sunlight over palm trees, ocean, swimming pools, convertible cars, and
the lush vegetation on the first of South Florida's string of islands, Key
Biscayne. Tennis is a sun game, and Florida is where many players come
from and train, but rarely where they get to play a big-money tournament.
The players were blinking and happy that first day when the draw sheet
was virginal, all names and no numbers. But travel often is a means of
self-discovery, and the players who do not make discoveries about themselves are lost.

"All right," said the tall Florida highway patrolman working the tournament in battle regalia: brown shirt, badge, sunglasses, and black boots,
"take a step back, please." He held taut two thin yellow nylon ropes
running to his female sidekick, also in jodhpurs and black boots, creating
a narrow path out the back of the old stadium. Andre Agassi was emerging
after a win. There were more security guards and walkie-talkies on Key
Biscayne that morning than on early episodes of "Star Trek."

"There he is! There's Andre!" shouted a thirteen-year-old girl in a
white halter top and cutoff shorts. She and four other girls in varying
stages of adolescence surged forward to touch the winner.

Agassi was smiling from ear to ear. He looked like he was walking
on air. "Andre! Give us your shirt!" one of the girls shouted, curling up
in nervous laughter against the side of one of her girlfriends.

The fifth seed, Andre Agassi turned to grin at the youngsters calling
for his shirt. He had left grade school in Las Vegas when he was their
age, twelve. He never finished high school in Florida—St. Stephen's,
the Catholic high school from which Jim Courier did graduate. At nineteen, Agassi was a multimillionaire, supporting at least five adults, to say
nothing of today's vast tennis establishment; he also owned three $90,000
sports cars.

"I already threw my shirt into the stands," Agassi insisted, holding
the front of his baggy new shirt as if threatening to rip it off too, and
expose the circles of black hair that covered his chest and stomach. His
unshaven face grew pudgy as he grinned.

This boy, marketed as a rebel, was just the opposite. His hair was
black at its roots, but he had grown it to pop-star length, then frosted it

American blonde, hiding his Iranian identity. Andre Agassi did not want to rebel. He desperately wanted to conform—not to the country club world to which his father once aspired but to some youthful, more accurate vision of America. Agassi's grin was not exactly innocent. He knew what the young girls were giggling about: sex and money, traditional American victory.

Agassi was the son of an Iranian ex-boxer, Mike Agassi (lightweight, 1948 and 1952 Olympics, no medal), who emigrated to America, landing on his feet in Las Vegas. Working first as a waiter and then as a maître d' in a Las Vegas casino restaurant, Mike Agassi discovered tennis. It was the game the corporate presidents and Las Vegas singers played. It was everything that boxing was not: an attacking game without visible bloodshed, a game of social acceptance played more often by people who bet at the casinos than by those who worked there.

Tennis—in all its social and physical appeals and disorders—soon engulfed the entire family. Andre Agassi's sister was introduced to, and then later married, the tennis legend Pancho Gonzales, a considerably older man. For Mike Agassi, tennis had a Gatsby-like allure. But then the immigrant and his family had to face the American country club where membership was out of reach. The waiter's son could play sanctioned tournaments at the Spanish Oaks Country Club in Las Vegas, but his family could not afford to join the club and was never asked to. A Zoroastrian fire grew in the Persian-American father. He was disappointed and mad. He would show them all with his son, and damned if he did not.

Mike Agassi's boxing past occasionally surfaced at his son's junior tournaments. Short, stocky, going bald as both his sons would, Mr. Agassi became so incensed with events that could block Andre's progress in America that the ex-boxer turned casino waiter sometimes physically threatened other parents and tournament directors. Not pleased with the draw his son got at a junior tournament, Mr. Agassi told the pro at the Spanish Oaks Country Club that he would "send someone to break your legs," a threat the Las Vegas pro said he did not take seriously because Mike Agassi was always threatening people. A lightweight turned middleweight on American food, Mike Agassi wanted success so badly for his family that when Andre was four, the father arranged for Jimmy Connors to hit with Andre during Alan King's tournament at Caesars Palace. At nine, Andre had his first lesson from Pancho Gonzales. Tennis was going to be his son's salvation, a way to get to the top in America, without going to college.

Sidney Franklin, Agassi's former principal at Cashman Junior High in Las Vegas, said of the prodigy's dropping out of school to go back East to Bollettieri's Tennis Academy, "I thought he should get in at least the eighth grade. That's the most important socialization year." Larry Leavitt, then guidance counselor at the school on West Desert Inn Road, said that Agassi was essentially a good boy who was never sent to his office for bad behavior, and that Andre shared with other casino and night club children the same educational problem: nearly one third of Las Vegas's school children moved away each year.

Given the hard form his father's love took, perhaps it was best that Agassi got away from his father. Still, Andre was terribly homesick at first at Bollettieri's Tennis Academy in Bradenton, Florida. A thousand miles from home, Agassi smashed dozens of his free Prince tennis rackets on the cement courts and did not make many friends among the other young stars.

The Bollettieri camp started with only a handful of prodigies in the early 1980s. They were housed and did their homework at an old motel Nick Bollettieri had purchased. Though they rarely practiced together at the now-renowned tennis academy, as a fourteen-year-old, Jim Courier—the son of a citrus executive from Dade City, Florida—roomed with Agassi at Bollettieri's motel.

"Andre was a bit of a punk at the academy," recalled Courier. "If he had continued the way he was heading, he would have gone down the toilet." Agassi and Courier would be antagonists for the rest of their careers. Courier was a pragmatist, and the stronger person physically, even mentally, but Andre had a streak of magic.

Although he still loved to cruise the Las Vegas strip in his blue Lamborghini when he was home, Agassi had become a born-again Christian. He and Michael Chang both let it be known that they dedicated every match to the Lord Jesus Christ. Agassi clung to the Bible as his port of last resort. Chang was more assertive about the religious connection. But each young man seemed to need to fill the gap inside himself that came from making a living based on the principle of beating his fellow man hollow each time he faced him. Of course, only the best natural fighters survive, and like boxers, the best tennis players are almost always those who have something to prove to themselves or to the world. Mike Agassi's son had something to prove.

Once dismissed by Ivan Lendl as nothing more than "a haircut and a forehand," Andre Agassi bore an uncanny resemblance to Tom Hulce's Mozart in the movie version of *Amadeus*. As the Lipton started, Agassi was unmistakably the player the other players resented. Agassi's talent seemed not only difficult to explain but almost unfair to the larger, stronger boys. Next to Agassi, there were many tennis Salieris incapable of beating the wretched little prodigy. But the damndest thing about America's 7-Eleven Store Amadeus was that he could really play. He was no fluke.

In Florida, the mere sight of the Ten Million Dollar Teenager had the press people thinking of their families and first mortgages, wondering how they could skewer the millionaire high school dropout on his own racket. Agassi made it pretty easy: nearly every time he opened his mouth, he put his foot in it. The kids cheered Andre's play anyway, and the loudest cheers were from his sponsors, Nike and Canon camera. While most of the press mocked Agassi and waited for him to fall, Agassi regularly took big money to the bank. He made in an afternoon what few writers make in a year, sometimes in a lifetime.

There was an aura of great lightness about Agassi. He was almost like a dancer. He was so light, his reflexes so quick, his ability to pull the trigger on a return of serve so stunning, that the older people who generally could not stand him could not reach Agassi to hurt him. Signing autographs after his first-round match at the Lipton, Andre kept his second shirt on and glanced up at the Florida highway patrol officers in tan uniforms and Smokey-the-Bear hats. Tennis and security seemed to go hand in hand. With one final wave of his hand and a seemingly confident smile, Agassi—scruffy-cute like the pop singer George Michael—made his exit as a chorus of young girls' voices called out for articles of his clothing. The entry flap of the green-and-white press tent opened to let Andre through and then fell shut behind him, guarded intensely by a patrolman who had done two tours in Vietnam.

The Lipton press room was buzzing cheerfully. The reporters' stage was very much part of the tennis world. Where once pencils pushed and typewriters crackled, portable computers the size of electric harmonicas now clicked almost silently, sending a quick plastic noise into the general bustle and whir of reporters meeting newspaper deadlines in six different time zones. In the far corner by himself, media director Temple Pouncey, who had a fine Faulknerian name and a Mississippi accent, was trying to arrange for a French sportswriter to get use of a telephone.

The ring of phones, a sudden swear word in Swedish, a polite *bonjour*, the turning of bodies trying to avoid each other, and the sound of a dozen foreign accents were exciting at first. If you wanted a typewriter, you could request one of three old giants, but if you had your own laptop, it was a lot easier to plug you in. French, Italian, German, Swedish, and Japanese press were all assigned spaces on the long white tables clustered with complimentary airline bags, newspapers, telephones, and empty Perrier bottles and Diet Coke cans. It is the same at tennis tournaments around the world. The "press" is a movable feast. If it is digestible, it is news, and tennis players give press conferences just like senators. The press food at the Lipton went a long way toward explaining the basic adversarial relationship between most journalists and the people they cover. Huge trayloads of lasagna, salad for two hundred served in one large stainless-steel bowl, fistfuls of rolls and butter, sponsorship diet sodas and canned Lipton Iced Tea were brought in twice a day for the lunchtime and evening press feedings. Breakfast was rolls, jam, coffee and creamer.

"Pass the butter please, mate."

I looked up and smiled broadly. It was Fred Stolle, the commentator and former Australian great whose service motion I could imitate—along with those of Roy Emerson and Chuck McKinley—when I was a boy. Too shy to introduce myself, I ate incredibly fast and hurried back outside.

When the last point was over and Aaron Krickstein bowed his head in defeat and came to net to shake hands with the handsome Czech, Jakob Hlasek, whose father had skated for the Czech Olympic hockey team, the colorful crowd began to file over to the Becker match in the small Florida stadium. The old wooden stands on Key Biscayne were smaller than the concrete stadium at the U.S. Open in Flushing Meadow, but the players' emotions were close enough to touch. Aaron Krickstein's first-round disappointment filled the green hard court under the hot Florida sun. In almost five minutes the grandstand was empty. The players collected their rackets, packed their large travel bags, and moved away from the court they had grunted and flung themselves on in the heat for three sets and over two hours. The bare green court with its white lines lay basking in the sun.

For Aaron Krickstein, the disappointment was the slow, painful kind—a match within his grasp lost in front of his parents, who were among the last to leave the stands. Krickstein had been a prodigy ranked eighth in the world at age seventeen, and now four years older he was trying to prove he deserved that ranking again.

You could get close to the players in Florida, the way it is at the small ball parks baseball teams use for spring training. And you could feel the hurt inside Aaron Krickstein as he left the court with his huge racket bag tilted back over his shoulder. It was noon on the first day, and the Lipton's eighth seed was gone.

Earlier in the morning, on the practice court, everyone had been smiling. The sun was already bright, and the Florida sky was an ocean blue. Two rising young stars, Petr Korda and Goran Ivanisevic—lefties from Czechoslovakia and Yugoslavia, respectively—were practicing with their shirts off. Pale boys with washboard stomachs, they blasted left-handed forehands at each other and traded friendly barbs in Slavic languages. On the neighboring court, Aaron Krickstein, already brown and shirtless in the sun, and his coach, Tom Gullikson, had hit for nearly an hour to get the player ready for the Hlasek match. They huddled by the back fence out of voice range, talking strategy and seeking a little privacy. There was a ritual to their day.

Psychologically, it is always easier to attack than to defend. Ranked eighth in 1988, now fifty-sixth, Hlasek attacked poorly at first, then with increasing confidence. Aaron Krickstein—ranked nearly fifty places higher—won the first set 6–1. The second set went to a tie-breaker, which Krickstein lost. Krickstein had been named to replace Andre Agassi in Davis Cup play two weeks later, and in the third set he played as if he were not actually playing Hlasek, whom he might have beaten, but was really playing against Agassi and the fear that he might let the country down at the Davis Cup. The match could not have been much closer, but in the end the slender Michigan boy played as if he had more to lose, more to protect. Jakob Hlasek had played with the ease and sureness of a man happy to be climbing back up a mountain.

Now at the post-match interview in the press tent, the winner, Hlasek, would be happy and modest. The loser, who sometimes interested me more, would try to hide his disappointment and look ahead to other matches. But I had someone else in mind to interview: the losing player's father. It was certainly an awkward moment, but Dr. Herb Krickstein had a reputation as one of the most articulate and educated parents on the pro tour.

The grandstand court, which had held maybe four hundred people, was empty. Two wheelchair players were hitting a ball high, back and forth across the net with all they had, their rubber wheels moving softly over the green cement. Arms and faces contorted happily as they swung

at the ball and pushed frantically to get into position. There is something
so basic to effort itself, something that brings people pleasure.

A man climbed a tall ladder in front of the big white draw sheet and
recorded the Hlasek–Krickstein scores in black paint:

Hlasek, 1–6, 7–6, 6–3

Three points in the tie-breaker and the match would have been over,
and Aaron Krickstein would have been the victor in straight sets. I went
looking for Dr. Krickstein. Kids at umbrella stands were giving out free
sunblock, and ice cream and hot dogs were being sold at exorbitant
Florida prices that seemed pretty fair to a New Yorker. A troop of teenage
girls on the lookout for Stefan Edberg came rushing away from the entrance to the press tent. They had spotted Gabriela Sabatini, who was
warming up her legs on the porch of the low, flamingo-pink building
where the players changed. A crowd gathered quickly, standing not more
than four feet away and staring at Sabatini like racing fans watching a
stallion in the paddock. She was seeded first because Martina Navratilova
had decided to rest and point to Wimbledon, and Steffi Graf had broken
her thumb trying to ski away from a crowd of photographers. Sabatini
slowly stretched her long legs and performed some warm-ups, running
in place for about five minutes.

Then the young Latin American woman with the long black hair,
turned-up nose, and beautiful lips made her way toward the court. Sabatini's shoulders were square: she had developed a confident sideways
saunter that masked her insecurity.

There was a guard in front of her and a plain-clothes tennis official
beside her speaking into a walkie-talkie. The Florida guard had a gun
in his black holster. As I stopped to let them pass, Sabatini, who looked
trapped, half smiled as they walked her toward the grandstand court
where Aaron Krickstein and Jakob Hlasek had just completed their two-
hour battle. Tennis was tougher than it looked. It drained both men and
women players from the inside out, and that day Sabatini looked exhausted before she had begun. There were no upsets in tennis, only
time coming due. As the guards led Sabatini through the grandstand
court's gate, I turned around and spotted Aaron Krickstein's father behind
the stands.

Dr. Krickstein was with his wife and another couple. I took a deep
breath and walked toward them, looking for just the right moment. I
could hear their conversation. The two men were walking together, and

the two wives were together, and then the four came together in the bright sunlight behind the stands. People streamed by, not recognizing the parents of a top player.

"It was great to see you both," Herb Krickstein said to the other man, but I could feel pain in the father's voice. Dr. Krickstein was a strong, solidly built man with a wide forehead, glasses, a few creases from living, and an air of general intelligence about him. By profession, he was a pathologist; by circumstance, a tennis father.

"We had a great time," said the other Michigan man, clearly thrilled to have been invited. "I just hope we didn't bring Aaron any bad luck. It was awfully close."

The women stepped in, and the thanks and good-byes ended in embraces and smiles. I could not work up my courage immediately to go up to Dr. Krickstein. It was like stepping into a funeral. I could see the father had suffered in the match almost as much as the son. So I followed the Kricksteins at a distance back to the players' lounge, where I gently touched Dr. Krickstein on the arm and said, "Excuse me, Dr. Krickstein. I am doing a book on tennis. I just saw your son's match with Jakob Hlasek. I wanted to ask you a few things."

He was stunned for a moment. "What do you want to ask me?" Dr. Krickstein answered a bit gruffly. Pushed back on his broad, lined forehead was a blue University of Michigan baseball hat with a big initial *M* on it. It made him more approachable.

"Well, mostly about being the father of a great young player. That type of thing. Being the father."

He looked at me a moment. "I'll be out in five minutes," Dr. Krickstein said. And he was. We found a spot on the grass near the players' lounge.

I wanted to tread lightly. When a son loses, it is never an easy moment for the parents. By talking to me when he did not really want to, I had the feeling that Dr. Krickstein was being brave. He was saying to me that this is how his son would also react when the going got tough in a match.

"Dr. Krickstein," I asked, not knowing then that he was one of the leading pathologists in the country, "what is it like for you as a parent before a match, when your son is playing someone like Hlasek, who is capable of beating Aaron, even though Aaron is also capable of beating him? What does that feel like as a parent?"

The father, a smoothly tanned man with a 1950 baseball player's body and a quiet air of Michigan toughness, winced a little. "I knew it was going to be a really tough match. Aaron is not feeling very confident right now."

I nodded. "Why isn't Aaron feeling confident right now?"

"I don't know. You'd have to ask Aaron that."

"Is it physical, or partly physical?"

"I think it's mostly mental," said Dr. Krickstein, sighing. "You go through these things."

"You go through them in stages."

"That's right. Hlasek did not play very well in the first set. In fact, he played miserably. But he played great tennis in the third set. In the third set, he was just too good for Aaron."

"I saw Gullikson warming Aaron up this morning on the back courts. It looked like he had Aaron tuned up just right. Aaron looked real sharp and ready to go at it."

"Yeah. Yeah, he was." The father sounded proud again.

"Do you go with him to most of the matches?"

"No. Not on most occasions. We just happened to be here in Florida at this time because we have a condominium up the coast in Boca. That's why we're here."

—Sure, Dad, I thought. You and your wife just happened to be here from Michigan, so you dropped by to see your son play.

"How is it for Aaron out on the road? Does it get lonely?"

"It's lonely. But usually there's somebody with him. A friend. Somebody. A coach. He seldom goes totally alone."

"Is there any one thing Aaron needs to work on right now?"

"Yes," said the father, nodding quickly. "His serve. Aaron's serve just isn't consistent like it should be. And Aaron needs to get into the net a little more. He needs to be more aggressive." Herb Krickstein said it softly but aggressively, wincing with parental frustration. "Aaron plays too defensively."

"The serve is rhythm. That will come back. But you're right, Dr. Krickstein. Maybe Aaron is a little defensive-minded at times. It's the transition game that hurts him. The approach shot getting him into net seems to me to be the one area where Aaron is a little weak."

"Yeah, he's weak."

"Playing Davis Cup is going to be exciting for him."

"Well, it's going to be a challenge. A big challenge. Aaron's going to have to straighten himself out in a big hurry." The father's voice was concerned, even painful. Tennis fathers worry. Tennis children struggle. The game was still the game.

"Aaron shouldn't get too down on himself," I said.

"Well, he tends to do that. Aaron tends to get down on himself."

"You can't do that really. You just can't, can you?" My voice was shaking a little bit. "You've got to keep going."

"Well, you *shouldn't* do it. You shouldn't get down on yourself. But that's Aaron's biggest problem. He does that. He's always going to be that way," said Dr. Krickstein softly. "I don't think you can ever change your personality."

How could a father's voice sound so concerned and full of love and terribly critical at the same time, I wondered, knowing the answer. I found myself defending the son but beginning to be more and more interested in the father.

"Some other pretty good people get down on themselves, too," I said. "John McEnroe does it to himself over and over again." The difference, of course, was that Aaron Krickstein's demeanor on court was close to perfect. He was very quiet usually, and his anger and self-abuse took place inside, whereas Mac did it both on the outside and on the inside, committing hari-kari for everyone else to see.

"Yeah," said Dr. Krickstein, not wanting too much of the comparison with John McEnroe. "But McEnroe is a lot tougher than Aaron."

"He's tougher, you reckon."

"Oh, yeah. Yeah."

"Is toughness something you can gain through playing a lot?"

"No. Not entirely."

"I think you have to let up on yourself a little bit first," I said, "and then you can get tough. But if you hate yourself too much, you'll never get tough. You have to learn to, to . . . to like yourself a little better."

"That's right. That's well put. You have to."

"Because Aaron's got a lovely game." I tried to soften the father's disappointment.

"Well, he's got a pretty good game."

"I guess there are a lot of ups and downs for the parent of a top player."

"There are more downs," said Dr. Krickstein softly.

"Oh," I said, the father of a one-year-old myself, sensing Dr. Krickstein's many-layered love and temporary discouragement. I felt that at one time my own father might have said the same thing about me. Dr. Krickstein had a fine, tenacious competitor's heart, and his son had it, too. Aaron Krickstein had the best record on the tour for winning five-set matches. "There will be lots of *ups* to come the way Aaron plays."

"Aaron makes it awfully tough on himself," Dr. Krickstein said again, shaking his head.

The more we talked, the more I liked this burly, soft-spoken Michigan man. His thin, introverted son with the great topspin ground strokes was down momentarily, and it hurt the father to see his son feeling that way.

"One last thing, Dr. Krickstein. Does Aaron call home a lot when he's out on the road?"

"He does. He usually does."

"Once a week or so?"

"Quite often. Yeah. He does." Dr. Krickstein's face relaxed a bit. His smile widened. He felt better again. He was the father of his very talented son.

"Well, thank you," I said, "I'll look for you again, Dr. Krickstein."

I had not been to Miami in almost twenty years—not since I played college team tennis and lost to the University of Miami. Dade County. Okeechobee Road. Coral Gables, where the rich live and where the university is tucked. Moon over Miami. Palm trees silhoutted against the glass office buildings downtown. Tropical heat. Latin Miami and the best radio stations in the world, I thought. Miami Beach is a causeway island, and Fisher's Island is a club where you can't even land without an invitation and a tennis racket. Tennis is still a social game, a game of "in" and "out." Water and sun and money. Miami's Flagler Street, named for the man whose railroads rivaled those of his partner John D. Rockefeller. Flagler's genius connected the Florida Keys like dots on a map until his track got blown away by twenty years of hurricanes. On the back road into town, the sign on the long, pink one-story industrial building next to Daddy's Cash and Pawn Shop read, $5.50 PER SQUARE FOOT. 90,000 SQUARE FEET. AVAILABLE IMMEDIATELY. Asking rents. Vacant pink building. Even Miami found times tough in the 1990s.

After lunch on the first day, there was a tremendous media event at the Lipton. It was like a frenzy. Men with television cameras on their shoulders and still photographers draped with long lenses pushed into the press room, and over a hundred male and female reporters played musical chairs with sixty dark blue plastic seats. Jennifer Capriati was arriving for her first interview.

Jennifer was thirteen years old, deeply tanned, a bit chunky; she spoke with a grin and a slight lisp. Capriati was led into the press room by her father, Stefano Capriati. The Italian former movie stuntman was built like a soccer star blown up in weight from twenty years of wine, inactivity, and frustrated ambition. A hundred reporters pressed against each other trying to ignore the father and get a look at the young girl and hear her first words, which were, "Hi!"

The press corps giggled. The little girl had the reporters eating from the palm of her hand. They instinctively liked her. She was press virginal, and still free to say what she wanted. I could not take it for long. I didn't like being fed information; it was like canned carrots. One day Capriati would probably become a great player, but she did not have much natural touch, and she was never going to play like my favorite woman player of all time, Maria Bueno, the graceful Brazilian queen of touch and angled volleys. Capriati did have an uncanny presence, but despairing of the scene, I left her explaining her future to reporters in friendly, modified Valley Girl talk. There was a match worth seeing out on the grandstand: Jay Berger, ranked ninth in the world, was up against Goran Ivanisevic, ranked thirty-ninth.

Jay Berger was the tortoise to every man's hare. Thickly muscled, slightly duck-footed, Berger was an unlikely star. My wife said he had a kind face, far less arrogant than some of the other players' faces. While the Capriati interview was in progress, there was only one other person in the press section, the same writer I had sat next to at the Krickstein–Hlasek match. We looked at each other nervously, even a little competitively, the way most writers do before they crack the ice, and I stuck out a hand.

"Hi," said the man in the seersucker suit, tie, and glasses reading my press badge that said ATP PASS, "I'm Marvin Glassman. I write for a South Florida publication," he added, as if apologizing that it was not *Sports Illustrated* or *Tennis*. Otherwise confident, Marvin looked a little bit hot in his blue seersucker suit and tie under the scorching Florida sun, but he was dressed for work. Marvin Glassman knew as much about tennis as Joe Franklin knew about Bing Crosby. Tennis was his major passion. As kids, we both had seen Whitney Reed, the crazy Californian, play his great 9–7 in the fifth-set loss to Rafael Osuna on the grass at old Forest Hills, in one of the most exciting matches of all time.

Marvin and I both preferred individual sports to team games. We disliked the herd mentality. Maybe nonteam sports made athletes selfish, but most great athletes were selfish anyway. Baseball had its pace and tradition to admire; football, its conquering of fear. Tennis was more like writing or steering a ship—you were entirely responsible for whatever took place in front of you.

We waited for Jay Berger to finish practicing his impractical serve against Goran Ivanisevic, who kept blasting his fluid left-handed bombs into the back fence, and it looked like a complete mismatch. I leaned back and let the hot Florida sun beat down on my winter-white northern face.

"I'm a Jay Berger fan," I said. "What do you think of him?"

"Here," said Marvin Glassman, thirty-five years old, opening the large, aging brown schoolbag he always carried with him. "Here's my article on Jay Berger and the tournament."

The article in the Miami weekly *The Jewish World* was not trying to be sophisticated. But as I read, I realized again just how much tennis and golf were—beyond all other sports in America—the two main social sports. Tennis in a sense was America, in both whom it included and whom it excluded. Tennis and golf, the two competitive games most played after college, both had their physical beauty and their social cruelty, the side of American success and exclusivity that was rarely spoken of. But Marvin Glassman had a sense of humor, and his article, set between South Florida ads for sprinkler systems, funeral homes, and beauty salons, concluded,

Jay Berger: This 23-year-old native of Plantation, Florida, will be helped by having the home-town fans rooting for him. He has never let them down—finishing as a quarter-finalist at the Lipton twice. Despite the fact that he has been wearing a knee brace since having surgery at age 15 and having no windup to a very basic serve, Jay's results in the last year have been anything but hamburger meat.

"What do you think?" asked Marvin.

"I like it, especially the hamburger meat. You know what I like about Jay Berger, Marvin? He hangs in there. He never quits. He doesn't look like much, but he knows how to win. This match with Ivanisevic is going to be the best match of the day."

"Absolutely. But the national writers are in the air-conditioned tent taking Jennifer Capriati's temperature, and eight thousand people are in the stadium watching Andre Agassi play his second round against Gunnarsson," Marvin said disgustedly. "Andre is a great talent, but in my opinion he is a mediocre competitor. If his match is over first, watch out. Agassi's leftovers will all be coming over here to watch."

I had found a press pal. This was an imperfect world and tennis was a perfectable game. We were both hooked.

"Have some suntan oil, Marvin," I said, slopping some number-six sunblock on myself. It felt good to have company.

The referee said, "Play," and a half-second later a huge left-handed bullet was thumping into the backstop behind Jay Berger. Seventeen-year-old Goran Ivanisevic started the Berger match with an ace.

"Jay is in for a lot of trouble," predicted Marvin. "Goran's father was a university professor in Split. The family sold their house to have money to give Goran tennis lessons. The kid's first coach was almost banned by the Yugoslav tennis federation for coaching techniques the Communist party considered unorthodox. The coach said Goran was a genius, but people say the coach had a severe drinking problem. The first time Goran played, he hit the ball with the same swing as today. I'm an Ivanisevic fan," said Marvin. "The father struggled for years on a Yugoslav teacher's salary. That's worse than Dade County. But now the family owns a tennis complex—and a tennis prodigy. I pick Goran in two sets."

I smiled. I had an odd attraction to Jay Berger's game. It reminded me of some of the kids I had played against as a boy in New York, except that Berger was much better. He did not *look* like a natural. In fact, the other players called his style "playing ugly" when they referred to Jay Berger's and Brad Gilbert's style of play. And that was the beauty of it. Because tennis finally was not a game about looking beautiful, but about competing, and that meant hitting the winning shot or continuing to answer your opponent until the other person, in despair, gave up or missed, trying to make the grand gesture. Berger's beauty was that he never gave in. He was every duffer's hero, every public-court player's dream, final proof that you did not have to *look* beautiful to win big.

Goran Ivanisevic was hitting the tennis ball incredibly hard on the fast Florida cement. Slick, dark-haired, high cheekboned, and handsome like a cross between Tom Cruise and Cary Grant, Ivanisevic was the lower-ranked and younger player, but somehow in their body language Berger managed to secure for himself the underdog's role while young Ivanisevic already played like an indisputable front-runner. The squint-eyed young man from Split, the basketball hotbed of Europe, kept grunting and hitting huge two-handed backhands, lifting the ball from corner to corner as much with his legs as with his two long arms. He had Berger on the run.

It was raw talent against tenacity. It was a mismatch and a great match, Ivanisevic's prodigious natural talent banging up against Berger's inner toughness and determination. Smacking the ball with incredible intensity and pace, Ivanisevic won the first set. The question was not how young Ivanisevic could have won the first set 6–4, but how Berger had won even four games. "Jay was lucky he got that," said Marvin Glassman. "Goran is too good. He makes Roscoe Tanner's serve look like a creampuff."

Ivanisevic tossed the ball gracefully into the air with his right hand. His body language said he was going to serve the ace up the middle to Berger's backhand, but at the last second the Split teenager changed the angle of his left hand and crushed a 120-mile-an-hour serve wide off the forehand side of the court. In less time than it would take to clap your hands loudly, Berger, guessing right, hit a full-swing forehand with his old black Prince 90, and the cross-court return was an outright winner. Ivanisevic dropped his handsome head, let his racket dip to the concrete, and looked disgustedly in the direction of Berger as if to say, Who are you? You must be kidding.

If you judged Jay Berger's ability by his looks, the book by its cover, you were making a big mistake. They changed ends, and the uninitiated might have laughed. When Berger set himself to serve, he had a hitch. It was a bit like a stutter. He slowly placed his pre-graphite aluminum Prince 90—one of nearly a hundred he had stockpiled in his garage when his favorite racket was discontinued—up onto his shoulder. Once Berger's elbow was fully cocked and his racket was hanging behind him in basic "scratch-your-back" fashion, he looked up, tossed the ball skyward with his left hand, and suddenly leapt straight up after it. Off his feet, Berger's leap turned vicious, and he cracked down hard on the ball. Most pros agreed. Jay Berger's serve looked like he had had his first lesson about two weeks ago and was still working out the kinks. It didn't matter. Berger was that good a *competitor* once the points got under way. But the young Yugoslav boy he was playing against hit left-handed forehands harder than some of Berger's first serves. Slowly, though, Berger began to rally—but how could he possibly win?

Berger began to build a plateau of patience. This was not an easy thing to do at eighty to ninety miles an hour. At first Berger did not seem to care if he won the points; he just wanted to stay in the points without being blown off into the Florida scrub around the court. Ivanisevic made him look bad a dozen times without even trying. Talent was making a fool of tenacity. But once Jay Berger established that he could stay in the points, he created a plateau for himself. And once up there on the plateau, he was a totally different player. Both aggressive and defensive, above all Berger remained patient—modest at the interior, respectful of his young opponent and at the same time fiercely defiant in his play. Berger was strong and much faster than he looked, and he had the important physical ability to absorb an opponent.

At 2–all, ad-out in the second set, Jay Berger, his black eyebrows turned up like a Punchinello puppet, walked slowly back to return serve. Ivanisevic's first serve was a thundering left-handed ace that sank into the green windbreaker before Berger could pull his forehand back. Totally nonplussed, Berger looked up at the umpire to ask if the ball had been in. The referee, who hadn't seen it either, nodded, *good.* Berger shrugged. Ivanisevic scowled. It was deuce.

There was a tremendous roar from inside the stadium court. "Agassi must have won," I said.

"Straight sets," said Marvin Glassman. "Here come Andre's leftovers."

Soon there was standing room only in the grandstand court, and Ivanisevic seemed bothered by the overflowing crowd. Two young handicapped players with red Wilson racket bags maneuvered their wheelchairs with the special-angled competition wheels into a position to watch from the side of the court. Berger had finally attached himself to Ivanisevic; the umbilical cord was loose but joined. It had come down to a fight of personalities, and Berger was gaining.

"Goran's first-serve percentage is down," said Marvin Glassman. "He looks a little vulnerable." I smiled. We liked the drama of it. It was part situation comedy, part high drama, and Marvin Glassman had a healthy way of mixing up the two.

The fight intensified on court. Each point had a little angle, a little story to it. Instinctively, Ivanisevic wanted to rape and pillage like Attila the Hun. The young Slav shrieked now when he put away an overhead. Jay Berger wanted Goran to think twice about life, about every ball he hit. Ivanisevic was Mr. Instinct, not a thinker yet. Jay Berger was Mr. Hang-in-There, trying to do with thought and pure effort what his body could not always do on its own. The wall Berger threw up was made of rock-hard glass. Ivanisevic was made to look at himself in the glass wall on almost every point. And what the young Yugoslav saw began to look erratic, nervous, and increasingly furious. Ivanisevic wanted to go on a

ninety-mile-an-hour rampage, sex at the speed of sound, but even as
Berger slapped his thighs and shouted angrily at himself to be more
consistent, the delicate fulcrum of the match began to tilt.

Berger broke Ivanisevic just once in the second set but it was enough.
He quickly swept the set off the court like a poker player who somehow
beats Queens on Jacks with three threes. It was a set apiece, but Ivanisevic was the more dramatic natural actor.

"I predict a Croatian victory," said Marvin Glassman in no uncertain
terms. "The kid will turn it up a notch."

Twenty percent of the tennis court was still in the sun. The speed
and pace of the tennis balls on the shadowy late-afternoon green concrete
court was incredible. At 3–all in the third set it happened. Ivanisevic
served hard to the corner. Berger threw himself at a two-handed backhand return of serve and ripped it down the line. Racing up to net,
Ivanisevic was forced to hit a half-volley drop shot with his backhand.
Flinching with the returned ball at his feet like a matador passing close
to a bull, Ivanisevic nearly missed the very tough shot. But the tennis
ball cut up into the air, hung briefly, and angled impossibly out of reach
off the side of the line as Berger charged forward, too late for a play. It
was a great, nearly impossible winner by Ivanisevic.

"Out!" called the lineswoman at the back of the court.

"She blew that call," said Marvin Glassman immediately.

Goran Ivanisevic roared and spun around in a circle, gored by the
invisible bull. It was the third straight call in the third set that had gone
against him. He hammered the top of the net, swore in Croatian, looked
up into the beautiful red sunset-streaked Florida sky, and shouted again
at the top of his lungs for all to hear, this time in English: "Impossible!"

Jay Berger turned his back, leaving the courtroom action to Goran
Ivanisevic and the South Florida "Perry Mason" fans. The referee would
not overrule his lineswoman's call. Ivanisevic talked with his hands.

"But my ball was in! Here. Right here on the line! Stupid!" shouted
Goran Ivanisevic. "Stupid! I'll show you just where my ball landed.
Here!" And to prove his point, the handsome six-foot four-inch,
seventeen-year-old Yugoslav cleared his throat, leaned over the net, and
spat right onto the line. "You call that out!" dared Ivanisevic. Even his
spit was in.

"The referee should change the line call," said Marvin. "But they
never do. It's a loyalty thing. Goran needs John McEnroe, Sr., as his
attorney."

Goran Ivanisevic tried to storm back in anger, but his anger in the third set against Berger made him look like what he was: young, very thin, and desperate to win.

At the back of the court, Jay Berger sighed and tried to keep his own head together. He had been climbing down further and further inside himself, attacking every ball he could take a full swing at before Ivanisevic did the same thing to him. At 5–4 in the last set, Berger had to hold serve for the match. The chance of breaking a serve, which continued to look as if it could be dismantled in parts and put in the trunk of a car, seemed a real possibility for Goran Ivanisevic. But suddenly, at just the right time, the Berger serve came together. He hammered in four straight first serves, and Ivanisevic missed all four, swearing at each one. Jay Berger kept his cool. To the amazement of people who looked at tennis primarily as a function of talent and not as a combination of talent, concentration, brains, luck, and heart, Florida's Jay Berger had held off Goran Ivanisevic, who had been expecting a breakthrough against the ninth-ranked player in the world.

Jay Berger usually did not give personal interviews after the general press interviews, not because he had a hundred reporters knocking on his door but because he was superstitious about talking about himself. I agreed with him but wanted to meet him. I was fascinated with what made some players winners and others also-rans.

"Goran blew a gasket today."

Berger shrugged. "He's still learning."

"You got him, though. You're a great competitor. Where do you get that inner fight from?"

"I just try to do well the things that I know I can do well." Berger had a slightly high voice. "I don't make a lot of mental errors. I hit hard. And I try to find out where my opponents are weak."

"But where does your fight come from? You hang in there like a monkey taking a bite out of a tree."

Jay Berger laughed. He was slightly over six feet tall and huskily built with dark, hairy legs and the trim muscular upper body of someone who turns on a ball thousands of times in an afternoon. He thought for a second about the origins of his own inner fight. "It probably has something to do with my being very small as a kid. I didn't really grow until I was about seventeen or eighteen. When I was young, twelve or thirteen, my parents started taking me to the junior tournaments, but everybody was much bigger than I was and they all beat me. I fought hard because I had to. If I didn't fight in those junior matches, I would have been totally embarrassed."

It was a year of upsets and transitions in tennis as well as in the world. At the start of the outdoor season at the 1990 Lipton, there was little indication that the major themes of the tennis year would be, first, the success of American children of immigrant parents—Andre Agassi (Iranian), Pete Sampras (Greek), Michael Chang (Chinese), Jennifer Capriati (Italian and Swedish); and second, the emergence of former Eastern Bloc players like Goran Ivanisevic from Yugoslavia, Petr Korda from Czechoslovakia, and the Russian *troika*—Andrei Chesnokov, Alexander Volkov, and Andrei Cherkasov—as the Russians opened all borders, beginning a period of political freedom and economic despair that swept Václav Havel into power in Czechoslovakia and, in the same month as the French Open, led to the execution of dictator Nicolae Ceausescu and his wife against a garden wall in Romania.

Tennis matches often come down to hunger—who wants it more—and the children of first- and second-generation immigrant families often seemed to want it more. In a sense, Agassi, Chang, Sampras, Capriati, and Monica Seles all were children of parents who at some time had felt like outsiders in America. The first-generation immigrant families were digging hard to get a toehold in a country that looked so rich from the outside but was so tough a reality to live. The parents of the tennis prodigies had almost all discovered that life in America is a horizontal struggle, a long and difficult draw sheet on its side, not the vertical skyscraper they had once imagined climbing.

Sports was at the crossroads of the American Dream. Country-club children really had no chance in professional sports. It is different when you are playing for your family, and your father's survival and dignity depends on your winning. The two youngest stars, Monica Seles and Jennifer Capriati, had the biggest burden to bear. Neither of their fathers worked at anything but their child's career. Karolj Seles was a talented cartoonist without a newspaper. Stefano Capriati preferred carrying his daughter's racket bags to jumping out of moving cars for a living. And yet the first instinct of the top tennis families was not for money. It was *acceptance* these families all wanted—a feeling of being a part of this huge, rich thing called America.

The Changs had struggled mightily and clung to their prodigy possessively. The Sampras family was probably the least involved in their son's tennis, and that was a good thing. Mrs. Gloria Sampras, who came to America from Greece as a young woman shortly before she married her husband, did not "even know how to keep score," according to her son, Pete. Mr. Sotirios Sampras got so nervous when his son played that he would go for a run rather than watch the match in person or on TV. Swedish, Italian, Iranian, Chinese, Greek. The talented tennis children were all American, but the parents of these new stars would never feel quite as American as their prodigy children.

The fascination at the Lipton with thirteen-year-old Jennifer Capriati and her multimillion-dollar contract, signed before she even played in her first pro-tennis event, was incredible. Her Swedish mother and burly Italian father were very different in personality and looks, and Jennifer was their union, their American daughter.

The young girl was devoted to both parents. One sensed in the first days at the Lipton that Jennifer, built more like her father than her mother, wanted to do well in tennis for them, and that the little girl knew what she was doing. It was fun—the attention, the competing—but deep down she wanted to get them all a big house so they would never have to worry about money again.

Denise Capriati had for the moment kept her job as a Pan Am stewardess, but that was never a sure thing. The father, Stefano, appeared to have more at stake than his wife, who, although she smiled proudly up in the stands, also covered her eyes when watching her young daughter having to fight so hard for the money and the glory. The pressure went beyond the courts. The family was betting the ranch on their young daughter. They had been living for over a year on one salary: Denise Capriati's.

The more I saw Capriati play, the more I liked her and worried about her. She was very strong physically, and she had the biggest heart on court since Chris Evert, but her tennis game was certainly not all there yet. She did not have the magic hand—touch—but then neither did Chris Evert. There was an abundance of great expectations surrounding the Capriati prodigy, and when the thirteen-year-old sensation beat the tenth-ranked woman in the world, Helena Sukova, a two-time Wimbledon quarter-finalist, 6–3, 6–1, the star was born.

She was not an untrained miracle. Jennifer Capriati had learned the game from Jimmy Evert, Chris Evert's father. When she was five, and Stefano Capriati had already gone shopping for the right tennis pro, he brought his daughter to Mr. Evert because, tough as Stefano looked, he sensed that Chris Evert's father was "more gentle with the children"—and he already had a champion in the family. Jimmy Evert, wrinkled and honest as the Florida sunshine was long, taught at the public courts at Holiday Park in Ft. Lauderdale. Evert did not take on many new pupils, and he never would work in a country club because he felt freer to come and go at the public park courts, but he decided to take on the Capriati girl. The old Florida pro knew it had been hard for his daughter, and knew it was not going to be easy for the Capriati prodigy, either. Asked what he thought of the then ten-year-old Capriati, Jimmy Evert— never one to jump on a bandwagon—said noncommittally, "Jennifer hits a pretty good ball."

Jennifer Capriati's third-round match in the ninety-degree Florida heat with Nathalie Herreman of France was not supposed to be much of a challenge for Capriati after she had beaten Luanne Spadea and Helena Sukova in straight sets, but it turned out to be a dogfight. The linespeople in their khaki pants and blue-striped khaki shirts strode onto the blistering-hot green asphalt court, tugging down their white poker visors and folding their arms like Mr. Clean. The crowd was packed to see Jennifer Capriati; no one knew much about Nathalie Herreman, the stocky, deeply tanned French left-hander. In the first game, Capriati started hitting a very heavy ball with her Wilson Profile, the latest in racket technology. But Herreman was twenty-two and had heavy left-handed topspin ground strokes, incredibly strong bronzed thighs, and the determined strut of a fighter. Herreman's friz-blonde hair was pulled back in a ponytail, and her short skirt bounced on her muscular golden-brown legs. The twenty-two-year-old from Paris was at least going to make it clear to this American prodigy that she meant business.

The French left-hander's banana-angled kick serve gave Capriati problems right away. Most of all, Herreman, unlike Sukova, was not scared. The little girl was not going to win this match easily. Playing in the Florida heat for over an hour, they came to the turning point of the match—an odd moment. Capriati actually won the point. But she did so in a way that annoyed Herreman, and *that* was the turning point. Suddenly, as the thirteen-year-old girl turned away, Nathalie Herreman picked up a loose ball and smacked it hard across the court in anger. The ball missed Jennifer Capriati's head by only about two inches. The young American looked up in surprise. Herreman raised her racket a little in half-apology but stared stonily straight ahead. The stocky French player was fighting mad. The ball hit at Capriati's head seemed to unnerve Capriati, and the message from the older player was clear: I want this match just as much as you do, Shirley Temple.

The crowd *oooh*ed at the ball the talented, tough French left-hander whistled over Capriati's head. Any friendly games were all over. Press interest peaked. This tennis was for real. And when the match was over an hour later, few people in the crowd were surprised that Nathalie Herreman had won it, 7–5, 6–3. Jennifer Capriati's initiation into professional women's tennis had just begun.

My notes during Capriati's match with Herreman said of the young prodigy,

> I like her forehand, her volley and her attacking spirit when she is down, but her backhand is average and she is a little slow and may get slower if she gains weight like her father instead of growing slender like her mother. She is not that good right now. She has no touch on drop shots or volleys. Her serve has a nice natural motion. And she is fearless. She is going to see a lot of backhands when the girls get on to her. She'll do better with serve and volley types than with other baseliners like Seles and Sabatini. Maybe she is just tired, but she appears a little slow. Capriati's fighting spirit will win matches for her that the rest of her talent might not be able to win.

Jennifer Capriati, age thirteen, had taken a very tough loss. It was the ball that went whizzing right over her head between points that I'll remember. The young prodigy reacted to the aggression like a child: the twenty-two-year-old woman scared her.

For most of the year, the men's and women's tours were separate forces that competed and diverged but rarely intersected. But the best tournaments—the majors—had both men and women. The women players at the Lipton made the atmosphere more fun, more relaxed, a better place to be. The first three rounds of women's play at the Lipton was a reminder that the pro tour was not all Agassi, Edberg, Becker, Lendl, and Capriati. Off on a side court I joined seven people watching a women's doubles match. The looping topspin two-handed backhands, the big forehand volleys, the swaying elephant-trunk return of serve position, and the awkward oversized racket-head serves of the young women were fun and relaxing to watch. A clump of palm trees cast a shadow on the hot court. The barriers by the courts were low at the Lipton, and the handful of spectators hung over the side.

"Are you girls sisters?" a woman from St. Louis asked, leaning across the low fence in the middle of a game while the other doubles team went to pick up a ball on the neighboring empty court.

"Yeah," the two pretty young blonde sisters said together.

"I thought so," said the woman. "What's your name?"

"Bartlett," said the taller sister.

"From California," said the sister who volleyed better.

"Well. I'm from Missouri," said the spectator proudly.

The opposing team had returned. The two young women put their hands on their waists and looked over in disgust. "Deuce," they said snappily.

"I think they think you're coaching us," said one of the Bartlett sisters as they went back to return serve.

"Oh, I wouldn't do that." The woman from St. Louis turned to me. "I wouldn't know how to coach anyway! I just hope the two sisters from California win, don't you?"

I did, and I stayed and watched them while the sun slowly began to set. The Bartletts finally lost a close three-setter, and the four top-spinning young women shook hands and picked up their big tennis bags. The sun was now a brilliant orange over the Florida Keys, and the glare of the sunset spread over the court. Florida was a great place to be at that moment. As the sun became a huge red ball, it dipped down into the water by the Key Biscayne causeway where the two highways meet. Up north it was winter, but here the players took their warmth from the sun. I wished the Bartlett girls had won their doubles match, but not everybody was going to be Jennifer Capriati. And when the red ball fell out of sight, thin black clouds brought in the night.

The difference between winning and losing is devastating to those who feel it. The day before, Edberg had played Amos Mansdorf, a very solid player who had served in the Israeli Army. Losing is awful for the players, but to an observer it is usually more revealing of a person than winning.

Mansdorf came out into the dusty Lipton parking lot after losing his match with Edberg, 6–2, 6–1, and nobody seemed to recognize him. Short, round-shouldered, but powerful in the legs, Mansdorf had played less than his best. He was usually so workmanlike, but he could not get started against Edberg. Nothing, not even the simple things he could do most days in his sleep, seemed to work. That day, Stefan Edberg had been so light on the court, so quick to every ball. Mansdorf walked slowly through the dusty Lipton parking lot, contemplating the difference between his level and the level of Stefan Edberg. Dressed in light tan pants and a pale blue short-sleeve dress shirt with a wide, open collar, Amos

Mansdorf was twenty-four years old, but in defeat he seemed much older. Stoop-shouldered, carrying his heavy, brown European-leather tennis bag in front of him in one hand, the losing player looked like the Willy Loman of the tennis courts—death of a salesman tennis style, all effort, hope, and struggle and then no sale. In a sense they were all selling themselves, giving all they had. But Edberg won so easily, so effortlessly, that the Swede had taken all the joy from Mansdorf's effort.

A quiet, handsome ex-soldier who parted his brown hair near the middle, Mansdorf headed quietly toward the fleet of small white rent-a-car Cadillacs provided to the players while they were still in the draw. The loss was hurting him so badly in the stomach, he seemed to stoop. The gritty Mansdorf slowly opened the rental car door, tossed his heavy bag of rackets into the back seat, and quietly drove himself out to the airport for the long flight home to Israel.

One of the best matches in recent years was the Lipton quarter-final between Stefan Edberg and Jakob Hlasek, who had beaten Aaron Krickstein in the first round. Hlasek had been ranked as high as number eight in the world, and the handsome Swiss-Czech wanted to show Edberg he still belonged up there. Their three-set match lasted two hours and forty-four minutes in the blistering Florida sun. The score in all three sets was 7–6. The match was decided in the tie-breakers.

A great doubles player because of his height, reflexes, speed, and ability to get on with a partner, Jakob Hlasek served and volleyed like a champion that day. The Swede with the strong stomach muscles was so far over the ropes he was almost out of the ring. But the elasticity in Edberg's body was also part of his personality. He never panicked; he could absorb a lot of the other man. Outplayed for much of the way, Edberg held tenaciously onto a thread of hope. As the deep Florida heat, 110 degrees down on the cement court, began to bake both players, Stefan Edberg seemed a shade more fit than his larger, very fit opponent.

At 4–all deep in the third set, the six-foot four-inch Czech served a booming ace up the middle. At 15–30, with Hlasek up at net, there was a tremendous side-to-side exchange, ending with Edberg striking his long-arm backhand up the line at full force for a winner. Edberg double-pumped his fist and broke Hlasek's serve on the next point. Trailing psychologically for most of the match, Edberg was ready to serve, up 5–4 in the final set.

Now Hlasek turned on the pressure. The handsome Czech with the rough jaw leaned into the service court. All Edberg had to do was hold serve. But the Swede double-faulted on the first point, and on the last point of Edberg's service game, a twisting second serve bit the top of the net cord and flew fifteen feet out of court, a second double fault. Edberg shook his thin blonde head and swore softly at himself in Swedish. Hlasek nodded quietly. The Czech had broken back. It was 5–all in the third set. Now the test of wills began.

Challenged, the Swede immediately broke Hlasek's big serve again to lead 6–5 in the third set. Again, all Edberg had to do was hold his own serve.

"Cash in, Stefan!" an American shouted in the crowd.

But tenacious Hlasek broke Edberg's big twisting serve at love. Hlasek hit a net-cord backhand passing shot that leapt so fast past Edberg that the Swede could only look down again; 6–all. The third set. Nowhere to hide. They were deep into each other, both afraid, both unafraid, as they entered that strange valley, the last-set tie-breaker.

Edberg looked fresh and nervous, bouncing on his toes, but the first point went to Hlasek, and the son of the former Czechoslovakian hockey star began to dominate the last-set tie-breaker. At 3–2 in points for Hlasek, the two tall blonde serve-and-volleyers hit a series of reflex volleys angled to go past each other while both players were up at net. It was like watching a doubles point, but there were only two volleyers on the hard court. Hlasek won the lightning-fast volley exchange on a powerful forehand volley that Edberg lunged after futilely. Hlasek was up by 4–2, then 6–4 in the tie-breaker, double match point.

Hlasek, serving for the match into the backhand court, slowly bounced the ball down on the hot green concrete. Stefan Edberg crouched and swayed in his return of serve stance. Edberg was ranked higher. Hlasek hit a booming first serve that was just long. His second serve on match point was a nasty kicker high into Edberg's backhand side. Edberg had to leap, and he took a backhand swipe at it. Hlasek was already on top of the net. He had raced up there so fast that he seemed to have been perched there forever. Edberg hit his backhand return high and was rushing back toward the center of the court, trying to cover the open court. Seeing the crossing movement on match point, Hlasek stepped up and punched his forehand volley up the line behind Edberg. The stroke was short, and it was firm. The Swede looked back as the ball landed behind him. The crowd roared. After two hours and forty-one minutes, Jakob Hlasek lifted both arms and pumped them in triumph. Stefan Edberg's shoulders slumped in defeat, as they always did if he lost, and he trotted toward the net with his right hand coming forward. Hlasek moved in to accept the handshake, just as the baseline linesman behind the play said, "Out."

The crowd was cheering Hlasek's effort and did not hear it, but Stefan Edberg pulled his hand back.

There was turmoil in the ninety-five-degree two o'clock Florida heat. Jakob Hlasek, one of the few real intellectuals of the tennis tour, had a favorite writer, the Swiss-German writer Stefan Zweig. Zweig's best story was *Die Amok Laufer*. It was about a doctor who goes mad in the sun and tremendous summer heat in Burma, finally running amok through the streets. The heat in South Florida was a match for Burma's heat that day. The line call on double match point was wrong and excruciating. The players had been meeting to shake hands after the match. The madness of something impossibly close but irretrievably lost seemed to be racing through Hlasek's head. He implored the referee and the linesman. Hlasek, the crowd, almost everybody except the linesman thought that Hlasek's volley had been perfect, right on the line. Edberg stood by, quietly, professionally. The ball had hit the line, like a mouth bites into an apple.

But the call stood. What did Edberg do now, serving, down 5–6 match point in the last-set tie-breaker? Edberg hit a near ace to make it six points apiece. Hlasek shook his head. The players changed ends in the heat at 6–all. Making an effort to stay calm, Hlasek served a double fault. Edberg looked up at the sun and blue sky and eased himself over to the forehand side. Now up 7–6 in points, Edberg had arrived finally at his first match point. The Swede missed his first serve and Hlasek took a fearless swing at the kick second serve. The blast from Hlasek passed Edberg up the line before the Swede could even reach out to volley it. But the ball was fractionally mis-hit, and it landed half an inch long over the baseline. Jakob Hlasek had lost. Stefan Edberg, the elastic Swede, had won.

Beside himself, Hlasek came to net to shake Stefan Edberg's hand. The crowd could almost hear the rough-looking Czech screaming inside. Frantic, Jakob Hlasek raced around the net in disgust and mockingly shook the hand of the linesman who had called his winning volley out on match point.

"I should not have done that," Hlasek said afterwards in the press room. "But when I broke Stefan for the second time in the tie-breaker, I thought it was mine."

Three 7–6 sets. The tie-breakers decided 7–9, 7–5, 8–6. Edberg.

"Stefan. When Hlasek hit that big kicking second serve on his first match point, before he hit the volley behind you, were you trying to put the ball anywhere particular on the return of serve?"

"Yes," said Edberg with a dry, Swedish smile. "I was trying to put the ball back on the court." He was a champion.

There was such a fine line between winning and losing. The players had nearly been up at net congratulating each other on Hlasek's victory, and Edberg went on to win three minutes later. What separated them? What was that milli-fine difference in their competitive natures? Because in sports, there really is no such thing as *luck*. There are verdicts.

The win would have meant so much to Hlasek. He had had Edberg with both feet in the grave. A true international and an immigrant, Hlasek spoke five languages, and his personality changed in each one. In the press room, he was disappointed in English. He spoke to the French reporters very matter-of-factly in nearly perfect French, "Yes, I am a bit disappointed. But I think I am on the *bon chemin*. Stefan is a very good player, but I was not nervous in the tie-break. I felt very much at ease today." Hlasek seemed to accept the loss in French, but talking to the Swiss-German reporter as they went out at the back of the Lipton press room, the big blonde Czech with the border-guard good looks finally said what he was really thinking, in German: "*Schiese!*"

The next morning five photographers with unbelievably phalliclike zoom lenses positioned Stefan Edberg, fresh from the shower in a powder blue and white warm-up jacket, beside an orange tree under the high, hot, blue Florida sky. Edberg had the reputation among the tennis photographers as the most difficult player on tour to photograph during or after a match. The pictures never quite looked the way Edberg did in person, and his photos never looked the same twice.

The Swede had both gentle and hard streaks in him, and I was not quite sure where the two opposite sides of his nature came from or how he had managed to blend them so well.

Edberg was uncomfortable posing for the photographers, and when he caught sight of me watching the photographers taking his picture, Edberg posed for one more, jumped the low wooden fence near the orange tree, and ran out the back of the parking lot where his girlfriend, Annette Olsen, was waiting for him. One of Sweden's top models, she was very blonde, wore bright red lipstick, and had a cherub's face. Annette Olsen came from the neighboring town of Växjö, also Mats

Wilander's hometown, which was only five kilometers from Stefan Edberg's equally remote but slightly larger Swedish port town of Västervik. Edberg was taller than Wilander and different from him in the essential ways that taller and shorter people are different. Annette Olsen had been Mats Wilander's girlfriend for two years before she met Stefan Edberg. The love triangle was very Swedish and did not last five sets. Annette chose Edberg. Wilander had had a string of problems since then, including his father's death, that made him question the point of competing, but losing Annette Olsen after winning the U.S. Open had clearly hurt Wilander. Stefan Edberg never *looked* competitive, but apparently he was in things that mattered to him.

Back in the press room there was competition, too. Everybody wanted Edberg. "But I must have exclusive with Mr. Stefan!" shouted the man from Japanese TV, trying to push ahead of me. I offered to interview Edberg *with* the Japanese man, but he refused, and that is how I got to sit alone with Edberg. Lauren Goldenburg, the ATP media rep, put one hand on her hip and told the Japanese to cool their heels.

"Come on," Edberg said softly to me, and we sat down opposite each other in a far corner of the press tent.

"What about loneliness on the tour?" I asked him. "I've heard some of the players on the tour mention it."

"Loneliness doesn't happen with me," said Stefan Edberg. "Not often. Either I have my coach with me, Tony Pickard, or I have my girlfriend with me or my younger brother. And I have been around the world enough to have a few friends where I go. That makes life much easier."

"Do you go back to Sweden often?"

"Not often," he said quickly. "Sometimes to see my parents or play in Davis Cup. But, you know, I can be on my own without seeing anyone. I actually kind of like that. Because that is the kind of person that I am. I actually find it nice to be on my own."

"How much does Pickard actually do with you on court?"

"Tony is really my friend, not just my coach," Edberg said of the forty-seven-year-old former English Davis Cup player nicknamed the "Gray Fox" because he was handsome and his black hair had turned to English silver. "Before I was working out with him a lot on court. But lately, it is not possible. Tony is having one of his hips replaced."

Edberg's sing-song voice was quiet but so matter-of-fact I laughed. Somewhere deep inside Edberg—I was not quite sure where—he was much tougher than he looked.

Tennis was a game played with the legs and with the head, but most of all, particularly when the serve was used as a launching pad, with the stomach. "You're very fit. What kind of physical training do you do? Do you do a lot of running at a certain point during the year? Fifteen-mile runs?"

"No! You must be joking!" Edberg laughed and sounded amused. "I never run that far."

"I knew some Swedish squash players. And they used to go about fifteen miles."

"Ya," said Edberg, still smiling at that idea. "But that's a different game. I go maybe four or five miles. And that's good enough for me. That keeps me fit. Sometimes I do sprints. And I do knee jumps up to my chest. Training on court. And jumping rope. But I am not working out in a gym or anything. No weight lifting."

"Do you do a lot of sit-ups?"

"A lot," nodded Edberg seriously. "The stomach muscles are the most important muscles in tennis. Everything is attached to them, especially the serve. So I do many sit-ups every day, even more since I ripped my stomach muscles playing Ivan in the Australian final."

"You were down a set against Carl-Uwe Steeb, and Hlasek had the match points on you. What's happening with you right now?"

"I am struggling a little. Actually, the match with Jakob was one of the closest matches I can ever remember playing. Everything we hit for three sets was on the lines. He must have been very unhappy with the line call on match point. But if they had called the ball in, I would have shaken his hand and said nothing. I let them call the lines. It does no good to argue. But," the Swede added softly, "they did not call that ball in."

"Do you think there is a chink in Lendl's armor? He likes to dominate so much. But when he is not way ahead he becomes a much weaker player."

"Well," said Edberg, "Ivan is making the most of himself. He is the fittest one of us all. But every top player likes to play with a big lead. That's when we play our best tennis."

"And with Becker? Do you think his mental problems on court come because he gets bored out there? What is it with Becker? He seems to go off the boil sometimes."

Stefan Edberg nodded. "Sometimes he sort of goes off track. Maybe because he is physically tired. Maybe because he is not mentally prepared to go out there and work. I think that is always going to be his problem the way he plays. Boris takes a lot of chances out there on the court. And one day it is not going to work for him. And then he loses." Stefan Edberg's voice had a sudden edge of tension.

"What do you think are the strengths and weaknesses of your own game?"

"Well," said Edberg, remarkably at ease and modest talking about himself, "I am serving quite well. I think I am a very solid player. When I am playing well I'm sort of serving and volleying quite well, and I am also moving well on the court."

"You're a natural glider."

"That is really the key to my game," said Stefan Edberg. "Not the serve. But how I *move* on the court."

"If your game goes off, what goes off? Is it your forehand?" Stefan Edberg's long, elegant backhand was more consistent and more penetrating in a straight line than his forehand, which looped over and around the ball in moments of indecision.

"No," Edberg said quickly, almost defensively about his forehand. "It's the movement that goes off, not the forehand. If you are not quick enough, you are not confident enough, and then you are going to be struggling. Because there's very little that does it in this game." Stefan Edberg, seated in his tennis shorts and pale blue windbreaker, held his hands about half an inch apart.

"That isn't much," I agreed, noting how close Edberg's two hands were together, thinking of Jakob Hlasek, and the milli-difference between winning and losing.

"That distance," said Stefan Edberg, still keeping the steeple of his hands fractionally apart. "Only that much can make the difference in this game."

"And what is that difference?" I asked.

Stefan Edberg smiled and shrugged. That was his answer.

It was not a question of good or evil. Champions always have a way of winning a match when the difference between two players is narrower than the space Edberg held up between his hands.

That night, I had a terrible hunger for a steak and a baked potato. The Cuban food had not worked out so well the day before. I was staying with my Italian wife's Greek nephew in a high-rise with valet parking on Brickell Avenue, just over the bridge from Key Biscayne. The nephew had a date for a black-tie dance in Miami, but he told me where I could find a good steak in town. The waitress was about fifty-seven, and she recommended the homemade key lime pie, which made me feel like a human being again. All this beating on each other. Tennis looked like a fluff game, but these tennis people were just trying to beat the hell out of each other. Life for the players was tough. After all the press pasta and salad served in stainless-steel pans, I needed a good meal, and I got it. Steak, baked potato, salad, and key lime pie—an American meal. A cup of tea with milk along with the pie.

"Thanks," I said to the waitress, deciding not to put the meal on my credit card. "Is cash all right?"

"Sometimes," the old-time Florida waitress said with a smile. "But I haven't seen it for weeks."

Red-haired and powerful, Boris Becker made me think of the race horse Secretariat, who also took some time maturing.

The big German and his mentor, Ion Tiriac, had not been expected in South Florida, but Becker had been given a wild-card entry to the Lipton when he decided at the last minute not to play Davis Cup for Germany. Becker was having problems with the German press and public. Having almost single-handedly won the Davis Cup for Germany twice, Becker told the German tennis federation that now he was going to play for himself and try to become the number-one player in the world. The decision not to play Davis Cup was not popular in Germany, but Becker and Tiriac had a goal.

It was not going to be easy. For starters, there were personal complications. Twenty-two-year-old Becker and his girlfriend, Karen Schultz, a twenty-four-year-old studying to become a professor of Romance languages, were breaking up. A Ph.D. candidate, Schultz was both pretty *and* an intellectual. As Becker's tennis guardian, Tiriac could deal with the first (the pretty) but not the second (the intellectual) part of the Schultz factor. Tiriac thought the bright young woman was a troublemaker for Boris. She had brought out Becker's cerebral side, uncovering in him a deep hunger, even a passion, to learn. Becker's girlfriend had introduced him to the German poet Rainer Maria Rilke's deeply melancholic and beautiful poetry. And Boris was already interested in the American actor James Dean. The combination of Rilke and Dean was an intellectual cocktail that few other tennis players were interested in trying to swallow. Becker was in inner turmoil. Karen Schultz had taken Boris Becker to college, not just to bed.

Becker told Arno Luik of Germany's *Sports Magazine* about his friend, Karen Schultz:

> She finds the whole thing [tennis] ridiculous. All the fuss and the artificial life are not to her taste at all. Maybe we get along so well because she lives in a different world than I do. She is sort of a counterbalance to the world in which I normally move. She has a totally different attitude about life than the other people surrounding me; they are all programmed to achieve success. And besides, she doesn't really care about sports, which is wonderful. She had no idea about tennis and if she ever jogs five minutes she considers this a gigantic achievement. You ask me, "Who is the boss in this relationship?" I consider this a very macho question. It's so typical: The man is the boss, he comes home in the evening and the wife cooks for him. Karen can't cook and I frequently do not come home in the evening.

Asked about being faithful to his girlfriend, Becker replied, "I could have sex with many women. The same thing happens to me that, unfortunately, happens to many women: you are chased like game. But if you can have it all, you are no longer tempted. I certainly have had my one-night stands. And then you wake up in the morning and think: How could I do anything with this strange woman lying next to me? And then you lose part of your face when looking in the mirror and know that the thing was not worth doing. Am I a faithful guy? Do you mean whether I don't sleep with another woman? For me, being faithful means more I respect my partner, that I keep no secrets from her, that I am honest, that I am how I am and that my partner is how she is. That we love each other the way we are."

It was not clear if reading Rilke and admiring James Dean had affected Becker, but he certainly possessed a decided streak of German melancholy as well as honesty. "After tough tournaments," he said, "I frequently go through phases of deep depression. I walk up and down in my apartment and see no reason why I should go on. There are nightmares. And I say to myself a thousand times: '*Mensch*, what are you doing?' I feel persecuted during these days. I cannot go out and be among people who touch me and ask me how I am. I very frequently think about the meaning of life and death because I live through so many extreme moments. I thought more than once that it wouldn't be so bad if I died at that moment. And sometimes I think that I've already lived through too much. In any event, I can say that I am not afraid of death."

The sense of longing and malaise among young Germans of Becker's generation is still pronounced. Many of the Germans I taught in Germany on a Fulbright in American Literature reacted to recent German economic prosperity the way young Americans did in the late 1960s—with disgust and distrust of the system that had brought them their prosperity. In a sense, many of the young feared their economic success as an act of domination, a cover-up of darker secrets that lay not so deeply beneath the surface. Boris Becker's Davis Cup doubles partner, Eric Jelen, said bluntly of Becker's antihero idealism, "Boris talks like a communist." If so, Becker was a communist the way John McEnroe and Mats Wilander were rock musicians. Like the tennis players who wished they were rock stars, Becker's malaise had a source: deep feeling, the marks of childhood, and the scars that come from all that winning and losing. There was something grotesque about the amount of money the young pros were making, when teachers' salaries in America or Germany were a pittance. Boris Becker, like McEnroe and Wilander, all true athletes, sensed there was something out of balance in the world. Though he liked what money could buy, Becker hated the money, too.

At twenty-two, Becker was going through late adolescence. Deep in his powerful frame, Becker was very sensitive. He was perceptive and young, and he had an imagination. He *felt* what had been wrong in Germany and what was still wrong today. Faced with the past of Germany, Becker wanted to be a "rebel without a cause." He bought nine copies of the James Dean biography translated into German and gave them to his closest friends.

And yet, sometimes Becker was so frank he sounded a little cruel. He said of Yannick Noah in the Arno Luik interview, "If Yannick Noah were white and had short hair, he would only be ranked number fifty in the world. He has a good serve but that is all. No player among the top one hundred has such bad ground strokes."

Becker liked Lendl least of all, and he said of the lean Czechoslovak while Lendl was still number one on the computer, "Lendl is finished. He is the Last of the Mohicans."

The top players had a varied range of personalities and personal lives. As the season started, Edberg was accompanied by his Swedish girlfriend but not his coach. Ivan Lendl had his seven German shepherd guard dogs, mansion, and young wife back in Greenwich. Andre Agassi had his Day-Glo Las Vegas image, his Bible, and Nick Bollettieri. Boris Becker was a little different from all of them, but perhaps closest in one way to McEnroe. Becker was not just after tennis trophies, money, and happiness but actually was seeking self-understanding. Tiriac was not opposed to this in theory, but he was opposed to it in practice. Boris was spending a great deal of time in bed, and apparently not alone. Becker might have spoken for all the top players, however, when he said:

> To make it to the top, I believe one needs to be different from the norm. I believe we are formed during our childhood. We acquire scars and develop character traits and our strong and weak sides. And we live according to them as we grow older. I can't say things about the scars, things that are very, very personal. But at least this: I've always been an outsider. The only way to be together with other boys, to be accepted by them, was through sports. That's where I found my self-approval. And that's how I developed this character trait that I've always been a bit tough on myself. I'm actually not a loner like most of the other tennis players. I like to play on the team. That's why I love Davis Cup.

Becker was playing in Key Biscayne because he had just told the German authorities that he would *not* play Davis Cup for them. Boris Becker seemed confused. His relationship with Karen Schultz was on the rocks. The German media at the Lipton were waiting eagerly for their Boris to fall.

Boris Becker's second-round opponent was the handsome Frenchman Jean-Philippe Fleurian. Nobody gave Fleurian much of a chance, but the Frenchman had quite a pragmatic attitude. Before his match with Becker, Fleurian made a reservation to fly back to Paris that evening. As it turned out, he had to cancel his flight.

The Frenchman with the black Lacoste shirt, bright green shorts, and very fit legs won the first set 7–6. But it was the kind of set that marquee-name players often lose early in a tournament, almost as if they are getting the kinks out of their game for the action to follow. But down a set and 1–3 in the second set, Becker was still toying with Fleurian in such a way that one sensed the smiling, deeply tanned Frenchman would capitulate and lose when the larger German player really turned it on. But suddenly Jean Fleurian's jaw set. The Frenchman started slapping his thigh before each return of serve. Becker's hair was unsettled on his head, sticking up like a rooster's pompadour. Becker's walk had no more bounce to it. *Allez!* Fleurian roared at himself as he hit another great forehand return of serve and went up 4–1 in the second set. Fleurian was prepared to dive and scratch for everything, and he did.

"That's why Jean's beating him," said a sixty-year-old Florida lady in a tennis dress sitting next to me.

Boris Becker did not seem to mind what was happening to him. The frightening fact was that even though he was trailing a set and was down 1–4 in the second set, during the rallies Becker was still moving Fleurian around like a cat swatting a fly. But he kept missing his final openings. Becker's malaise, his unhappy overabundance of talent, was on display in Florida. On the far right-hand side of the stadium court in the shadows sat Boris Becker's manager, Ion Tiriac, the large shape of Boris Becker shifting across the front of his teardrop-shaped sunglasses. On court, Becker exuded a sense of aloneness, the McEnroe-like sensation that he was being persecuted by unseen forces. At the same time, in flashes, Becker was invincible. He seemed then truly great, like Pancho Gonzales, like a mountain lion whose prey might get away but only because the bigger animal decided to let him escape this one time. I had never seen Becker look so unsteady. One moment he was completely dominant, and in the next it looked like Becker was quitting. Down 1–4, he stopped playing a rally and let Fleurian drive through a backhand winner. Serving at 1–5, Becker hit a second serve so far out it looked as if he did not want to be on court. But then, concentrating, the big redhead rocked back and served an ace. Becker's serve was awesome, but there was something going on inside him that had nothing to do with his opponent.

"C'mon, Fleurian!" a Florida woman in pink shorts with her legs crossed shouted at the handsome Frenchman from the fifth row.

When Boris Becker sprayed a final topspin backhand ten feet wide to lose to Jean Fleurian 7–6, 6–1, the South Florida crowd roared in disbelief. A crowd loves an upset the way it loves a lynching: until it is over, and then there is a feeling of remorse. They cheered the Frenchman in Miami, but the crowd was disappointed Becker was gone. The young German put an arm around Fleurian when they shook hands, and Becker's congratulations were incredibly warm to the man who had just had the biggest win of his career.

It was a curious match. Boris Becker had flown all the way from Monte Carlo at the last moment to play, and then had almost insisted on losing. Becker was more complicated and less practical than Edberg. The young German player said he hated the notion of invincibility. Losing was proof of his vulnerability, his humanity. I sensed in the easy way that Becker lost his match to Fleurian that he did not want to be an oppressor on court like the player he disliked most, Lendl. But winning by its nature is often oppressive. Boris Becker had played like he wanted to be some version of the new Germany—imperfect, occasionally weak, but above all human.

"That's it, you know," Becker said in the press room. "I lost. I am a kind of player who all the time has a couple of lows during a year. And if they come right now, then I am glad because they are not going to be at the French Open or at Wimbledon or at the U.S. Open. I lost. That is all."

Then came the questions asked in German.

"Boris, you said your mind was not on the tennis match. Where was it?"

"Not on the tennis match," snapped Becker to the first German questioner.

"For example. Where was it? Can you tell us?"

"No I can't," snapped Becker again in German. He spoke so calmly and so intelligently in English. He reacted so strongly and negatively to the German reporters and their questions in German. Becker's answers to four consecutive German questions about the loss to Jean Fleurian were: "I don't know," "I can't say," "I don't know," and "No." Then Becker got up and left. Most of the English-speaking reporters had already left the room, but something about the German press infuriated Becker.

Standing near the flamingo-pink and white draw sheet kiosks where Fleurian's name was posted with the first-round score, 7–6, 6–1, Ion Tiriac, Becker's manager, was still chain smoking. "Disgusting," muttered Tiriac.

Tiriac was the rough side of a racket that you spin for serve. *Rough or smooth?* Spin Tiriac a hundred times, and ninety-five times he will come up rough. Tiriac looked like someone you don't go up to talk to in a bar, but I had to. He seemed like the kind of hockey defenseman who checks well into the boards but scores only twice a year off an ankle.

Tiriac was walking quickly away toward the players' lounge to pick up Becker after the shower. "I'll tell you this!" Tiriac was saying to a wisp-thin English reporter trotting by his side. Tiriac's head was down, his black mustache was tipped with gray hair. He had taken off his dark glasses, and his eyes were angry. "This loss had *nothing* to do with tennis. Nothing!"

The English reporter shadowing Tiriac stayed so close that I could not get around him to ask Tiriac a question. I hung back, trying to be polite with the English writer, angling for position for several minutes like a schoolboy trying to get up the courage to cut in at the school dance. I wanted to ask Tiriac a few dozen questions about Becker, who only talked in private for money.

"Excuse me," I finally blurted out, catching Tiriac's baleful eye. His mustache was a horseshoe around his mouth. I introduced myself with the darn English reporter hanging on Tiriac like a shrimp on the back of a shark. "I'd like to ask you a few questions, Mr. Tiriac."

"Tomorrow," Tiriac said in his still heavy Transylvanian accent, looking me directly in the eye. "I will be here tomorrow, and I will be glad to speak to you then."

"You're going to be here?" I said softly, knowing Becker had just lost.

"Oh, yes. I will be here tomorrow," said Ion Tiriac. "I will be here all week. If you are here, I will talk to you tomorrow. Definitely."

I was past the age of youthful disappointment. I did not even bother to look for Tiriac the next day. And that was a good thing, too, because South Florida was one place where Tiriac certainly was not. He had flown back to Europe, leaving Boris to play in the doubles in Florida. Becker seemed incapable of lying. Tiriac would do it for him at the drop of a hat. I cussed him out, but Tiriac's lie was just a way to create a little space for himself and Becker. Nobody knew Becker like Tiriac—perhaps not even Becker. Tiriac had got away, but I was determined to catch him. The English reporter smiled as Tiriac turned his big back on me and walked away.

Monica Seles, the third seed, was feeling very bad about herself. The media attention had swung completely to Jennifer Capriati. The even younger Capriati was "in" like the hula-hoop. Seles had been dropped by reporters like a Mickey Mouse watch. The tall Yugoslav girl had lost the week before in Boca Raton, and she was playing without confidence. In the press room, she did not smile half as much as usual—until Nathalie Herreman took out Jennifer Capriati with the ball that whizzed over Capriati's head. Seles met Herreman the very next round and beat her 6–3, 6–1, and *that* win brought the old beam back to Seles's smile.

"I was feeling a little down at the start of the week, a little disappointed in myself, but I feel much better now," said Monica Seles, beginning to bubble again.

Gabriela Sabatini, like Capriati, was gone earlier than she had expected. She was slouching down into herself as the Florida highway patrolman brought her back to the press room after her loss to Conchita Martinez. The young Argentinian looked hurt by the effort of the straight-set loss to her Spanish rival. Sabatini's brown eyes looked away as she talked. She answered the questions softly. Gabriela Sabatini was hurting inside.

"I was thinking too much about my serve. I was not really very confidence," she said in Spanish-style English. The black-haired young woman was wearing a thick gold cross and thin gold necklace. "I didn't fight enough. I was a little negative. I was not thinking well. During the tie-breaker I was feeling upset."

Sabatini looked exhausted mentally and physically. It was an accumulated fatigue, not one match but hundreds. Not one plane ride, but thousands of miles around the world. The Argentinian nineteen-year-old felt virtually like a stewardess of the tennis courts, and she had no more serve to give. Sabatini clung to her last ounce of Spanish pride. She would not acknowledge the other player.

"It was not the opponent," insisted Gabriela Sabatini, wincing. "It was me, the problem."

The press room cleared out. The head of security, a chain-smoking man with a thin black mustache and a Hispanic name, was still standing there with his back to the rear flap of the tent. He recognized me now after a week, and instead of his customary security frown, he nodded.

"How ya doin'?" I asked in my New York voice. "They're like movie stars, aren't they?"

"Absolutely," said the South Florida security chief, a Cuban American who had a potbelly and a face tough enough to have landed at the Bay of Pigs. "You won't believe this," he said, suddenly opening up to me. "A woman just came up to me outside the tent. She offered me five hundred dollars for Sabatini's wet shirt. Gabriela put on a clean one before she came into the interview room, and she must have dropped the wet one on the grass outside the tent and forgot it when she left. I can't believe this woman. She was a very well-dressed Spanish lady, about forty-five years old. She pulled out five one-hundred dollar bills. She wanted Sabatini's wet shirt."

"What did you do?"

"I gave the woman the shirt. I wasn't going to wear it." The Miami head security man shrugged. "No charge."

Pete Sampras moved toward the court like a young colt. When I first
spotted him in the second round of the U.S. Indoors in Philadelphia, it
was like seeing Dwight Gooden pitch for the first time. I had never seen
anything as smooth, fast, and effortless as the Greek-American kid's
delivery and talent. Pete Sampras started the 1990 season eighteen years
old and ranked eighty-two in the world. He had a reputation as a junior
player with a great talent but a flaky head. In the juniors, Sampras was
up one week, down the next. Now he was at the stage where no one
knew what was going to happen when he walked on court.

Philadelphia, Sampras's breakthrough tournament, had been hell for
Ivan Lendl the year before. "Ivan was all upset. He had to take his
German shepherd puppy dog to the vet," explained Philadelphia tournament director Marilyn Fernberger with a smile. "Pete handled the
pressure much better, but nobody really knew who he was."

The volley was the stroke that was the key to Sampras's personality.
When he was good, he was brave. After Sampras's second-round win at
Philadelphia, the former U.S. and Wimbledon Champion Vic Seixas,
after first ripping into John McEnroe and McEnroe's father, said of the
young Greek-American boy,

> Pete Sampras reminds me of the way we used to play. Just one volley.
> That's the sign of a great volleyer. Pete hits one volley, and it's done.
> He looks to me just the way Pancho Gonzales looked to me when I
> saw Pancho at age eighteen in a tournament in Mountain Lakes, New
> Jersey, in 1949. Pancho would hit just one volley.

Seixas still had an eye for talent. Tennis was a language, and the great
players spoke the language intimately and fluently. I loved hearing what
their rackets had to say. Although Sampras was erratic, he was brilliant,
and when he was brilliant, his game looked effortless and consistent.
McEnroe once had that same effortless quality, but it was more unusual
in a right-handed player than in a lefty. Sampras was right-handed and
had a different inner fabric. In the Greek there was something at the
interior that was so smooth, so fierce yet placid, that I felt an odd twinge
of jealousy as if I wanted to own Sampras outright like a car. Lendl was
a Volvo. McEnroe was a vintage, quick-turning MGB painted in British
racing green with left-hand drive. Becker was a big, beautiful Mercedes
convertible. David Wheaton was a little stiff, like a Lincoln Town Car

changing lanes. Pete Sampras was a blue 1956 Thunderbird in mint condition. He came with an unmarked white interior, 3,000 miles on the speedometer, bucket seats, and 468 horses under the hood.

Andres Gomez, the giant Ecuadoran left-hander whose best surface was clay and who looked like Mountain Rivera, the ex-boxer turned professional wrestler in *Requiem for a Heavyweight*, said of Sampras in a Hispanic Miami paper, "He is very underrated in America. He handles pressure well, and I'd have to say of all the young Americans, he is the best because his all-around game is strong."

Watching Sampras in Florida made me nervous. Sampras was so young and undefined—a young artist. He was not the tennis jailer, Lendl, or the furious, imaginary liberator, McEnroe, but rather Sampras was the reluctant hero who did not quite believe in himself. He produced as clean a sound as Itzhak Perlman made on a violin. And yet he was shy and did not have the outgoing flair of Andre Agassi. After each match in Florida not even three journalists—the required quorum for an interview—requested the sixteenth seed, and so we had to see him first in action, and I recalled thinking that Laver was always better on the court, too.

Pete Sampras did not get a tough draw. He was the tough draw. In the first round, the eighteen-year-old beat Paul Chamberlain, a player who had made it into the top sixty in the world after four years of struggling on the satellite tour in places like Burma, Cairo, São Paulo, Mozambique, Oklahoma City, and Casablanca. Sampras leapt over most of the satellite tour, which was a deep whirlpool for hundreds of would-be players. The travel was tough. In Casablanca, the hotel informed the tennis players they could not stay overnight at the reduced rate if they lost their afternoon matches. Chamberlain went through four years of that. Sampras had not. Sampras had too much class in the end but nearly lost to the gritty Chamberlain in straight sets 2–6, 7–6(4), 6–1.

In the third round, Sampras played the tall, left-handed, powerful, and extremely awkward Frenchman Guy Forget, who would star in the 1991 French Davis Cup victory. In the very first game, Sampras showed how he was different from McEnroe. Forget, who played with an odd, wiggle-shaped racket designed by eighty-six-year-old Rene Lacoste with a crocodile painted in the middle of the strings, hit a huge left-handed first serve that was about six inches out, a country mile in tennis. The fifty-year-old linesman missed the call completely, which made it an ace. Sampras turned quickly to the linesman and said, "Did you see that ball?"

The Greek kid's jaw was lean and straight but not tense. His dark
eyes were concentrated but not threatening. The linesman did not answer
and stared tensely straight out into the glare of the hot green cement
court, still looking for his service line. Sampras moved without another
word to the backhand side to return serve. Sampras knew he had got a
bad call. In the same situation, McEnroe would have exploded like a
defense attorney. Sampras said nothing and hammered the dangerous
Forget, 6–1, 6–3, without thinking.

But the French were becoming a force. When Pete Sampras arrived for
his night quarter-final match with Jean Fleurian, the man who had upset
Boris Becker, there were black storm clouds over Key Biscayne and a
strong wind blowing the palm trees. Sampras was wearing long white
warm-up pants and the kind of white undershirt that Pancho Gonzales
used to favor. The Fleurian–Sampras match was scheduled last. Sampras
paced in front of the players' lounge, his chin thrust forward, his large
head tucked down in concentration as he gripped the two black Wilson
rackets in soft red covers that hung loosely in his right hand like appen-
dages to his arm. A young friend with two pretty teenage girls came up
to Sampras, breaking his concentration. "Everything okay, Pete?"

Dark-haired Sampras looked up in surprise and grinned. "Yeah.
Everything's just fine," he said, squeezing one of his graphite rackets
with the brown leather grips. "I'll see you later maybe." Sampras nodded,
smiled, and burrowed back down into his shoulders to concentrate.

Jean Fleurian had hunger and intensity in his eyes after the win over
Becker. The Frenchman came out in stylish black sweats, black Lacoste
shorts, and a bright green shirt. It was a dark night. Bright lights lit up
the dark green court with its pale green border.

"Mr. Sampras to serve," announced the referee.

Sampras, as if doing what he was told, hit an ace up the middle.
Unbelievably hard! He had the easy natural snap of a great right-handed
fastball pitcher. On the next point, Sampras hit a single, flat backhand
volley deep into the forehand corner. One volley. A winner in the old-
fashioned way. Then another ace. The score was 40–love in twenty seconds. Sampras was on fire. But it was a cold Florida night.

The wind had dropped the temperature twenty-five degrees, down
into the low sixties. The match had not started until after ten o'clock.
Pete Sampras was working the night shift.

In this darkness, wind, spitting rain, and bright lights, Sampras would either lose or earn his heart's right to victories in the future. Jean Fleurian, whose attitude and confidence had matured in that single victory over Becker, was still in perfect form himself. Down love–40 in the first game of the match, Fleurian hit five straight great returns of serve and broke Sampras's serve. The Greek-American boy could not believe it. His head jutted forward on the change-over. His mouth was tight, a look that could kill. It might have been smarter to return serve in the windy first game. The ball was getting blown all over the place. Sampras started pressing.

Jean Fleurian differed from many of the French players of the fifties, sixties, and seventies. His effort, like those of his countrymen Leconte and Forget in Davis Cup, was more like the dogged efforts of the French players of the glory years of the twenties and thirties—Borotra, Brugnon, Lacoste, and Cochet, the Four Musketeers. Jean Fleurian was a Frenchman playing not just to look good and come in a close second.

The match became beautiful. Fleurian and Sampras started playing good old-fashioned bullet-serve tennis. Gonzales–Hoad, Trabert–Sedgman, McKinley–Sangster, Newcombe–Stolle–Emerson tennis: bang the serve, watch the chalk fly or the line glaze. One-volley tennis. The radar gun sign on the side of the old Florida stadium court registered the ace by Sampras at 118 miles per hour.

"I think I like Sampras more," said an old Florida gal with no make-up, a sweater, and light blue slacks. "Pete makes more aces."

But Fleurian had the upper hand, and he kept hitting great inside-out forehands that headed straight down into the corners after they crossed the net with the nasty top. Was the Frenchman who had upset Becker good enough to win? As if to answer, Sampras served a 121-mile-per-hour ace and held his service game on just five swings of his racket: three aces, one serve, and a volley.

"Root for Pete!" shouted another Florida woman. "Oh, hell! That was a pansy return he hit. Pete, you got lucky on that one. This wind's the same for both of them. But still. They don't like it, do they?"

People were talking to themselves in the stands as if they were home with their feet propped up. The Florida crowd was not self-conscious. People let it all hang out at night down in Florida, wearing windbreakers and yellow sweaters.

Conditions on court became very tough. The storm brewing over the Florida Keys had come inland, and black clouds were already funneling rain over Miami's glass office buildings but not over the palm trees on Key Biscayne. The wind gusted fiercely, blowing the serve tosses. Lendl would have been furious with nature's elements. But Pete Sampras moved along with the quiet patience of a Greek donkey and the acceleration of a well-made American sports car. At eleven o'clock, when Fleurian won the first set 7–5, thunder clouds began to spit rain. A Dartmouth sweatshirt appeared in the sponsors' boxes.

"I hope I get pneumonia instead of the flu," an elderly Florida gentleman said cheerfully to his wife.

Then it happened. At 30–all, 1–0 for Fleurian in the second set, Pete Sampras pulled up lame. It was like watching a race horse just before it was destroyed. What was it? An ankle? A broken hip like Chang's? Sampras limped to a chair. Bill Snyder, the ATP trainer, came running out onto the court. Some of the crowd began to filter out of the stadium. Five minutes later, Sampras returned, limping, and Fleurian broke Sampras's serve. It was 2–0 Fleurian in the second set. Because of his injury, Sampras stopped trying to serve and volley because it hurt too much to come to net. Instead, the Greek-American kid with the best first volley since Tony Roche stayed back on the baseline and tried to hit ground strokes. It was no more fun to watch. Sampras was hurt. His head hung down between points. Like all good players, Fleurian smelled blood and poured it on. The Frenchman broke serve again and switched ends quickly, up two service breaks and 3–0 in the second set, ready to serve.

"Jimmy," the large female security guard in brown uniform called out to her Florida girlfriend, who was sitting alone near me in a windbreaker in one section of the nearly empty wooden stands. It was eleven-thirty at night, cold and wet. "Jimmy," repeated the female Florida security guard, "do you want to wait for me in the van, hun? This one's almost over."

I could not stand to watch Sampras lose. I liked Fleurian, but I liked Sampras better and hated to watch him get finished off like that. The trainer came out again, and I drove back to Brickell Avenue, where the couch I was sleeping on was hard and only two feet wide. I had a couple of Corona beers, called my wife in New York, and went to sleep listening to the thunder ripping across the sweet Miami skyline late at night.

The next morning I thought about Sampras. Maybe the Greek kid was a little weak, like people had said, "a mama's boy," maybe a little too gentle all the way around. Undecided, I drove off to the Kraft Foods Women's Tennis Tour Breakfast. I spotted Marvin Glassman on line for the scrambled eggs and link sausage. Marvin had left the Sampras match at eleven, after the first set. But Hugo, the young writer from Portugal who came to the breakfast wearing a white shirt with a bright red bandana tied around his throat, had stayed to the end.

"Did Sampras default or finish it out?"

"No," said the young Portuguese writer. "He won."

"Sampras won? No! I don't believe it!" I was thrilled. Sampras had the stuff, the guts to win when he was down.

"Yes!" said Hugo. "After the last injury minutes, Pete decided to keep playing. He was down one set and 3–love with Fleurian serving for 4–love in the second set. He was hurt, that's for sure. But Pete stayed back, and he began to pass Fleurian with *everything*. I don't know why, but Fleurian, who beat Becker from the baseline, started to come to net on almost every ball. And Sampras passed him every time, and so hard the passing shots! Pete killed Fleurian with passing shots. Afterwards, the French press asked Fleurian why he started to serve and volley when Sampras was hurt instead of making Pete run around back on the baseline, and Fleurian said he changed his game because Pete was so much better than him from the baseline. Can you believe that? Fleurian was wrong, *but he did not know it.* What Fleurian did not know that was the difference in the match. Pete Sampras did not win until almost one o'clock at night. It was beautiful," said the young Portuguese reporter for the major paper in Lisbon.

I smiled. It was as beautiful a win as any of Hemingway's bullfighters ever had had. The Greek kid was tough inside—like the Greek islands surrounded by the blue Aegean, hard and dry. Sampras had not defaulted the way many tour players did when they were not even hurt but wanted to protect their ranking. He had played hurt and won. But he paid the price. The following announcement was on the press tables after the Kraft breakfast. Sampras's win had been a Pyrrhic victory.

PETE SAMPRAS WITHDRAWAL

Pete Sampras has suffered a tear of the left rectus muscle. That is a hip flexor muscle which raises the leg. "Sampras will be out two weeks," said tournament doctor, Charles Virgin. Sampras said this is an old injury which he suffered in Toronto. He subsequently reinjured it in Philadelphia and at the Lipton. Sampras received treatment for the injury during his match Wednesday night against Jean Fleurian, whom he defeated 5–7, 6–4, 6–1.

Because of Sampras's injury, Jay Berger of Plantation, Florida, advances to Friday's semi-finals against the winner of Thursday's Agassi-Courier match.

The above information comes from tournament referee Alan Mills at 12:45 P.M., Thursday, March 22.

A major announcement affecting women's tennis was supposed to be made that morning at the Kraft–Virginia Slims breakfast. Marvin Glassman and I found two free chairs at a table with five women photographers whose black cameras and long camera lenses were propped up in the center of the breakfast table.

"We're at a table of photographers," Marvin announced, trying to break the ice.

Nobody said a word, so Marvin continued talking. "I told the organizers out at the courts that next year they have to change the caterers for our press lunches. Italian food and tossed green salad for two hundred reporters for ten days in a row," said Marvin. "It's disgusting, really. I like Italian people very much. Also the food, but not on a daily basis. This Kraft breakfast, though, is excellent."

We went back for seconds on the English muffins, link sausage, bagels, cream cheese, and scrambled eggs.

"Eliot is from New York," Marvin announced to the photographers. He might as well have said I had just escaped from Alcatraz. New York did not play well out on the road.

"Pass the butter, please," Marvin asked one of the women across the table, and I thought she was going to throw it at him. "You know, you ought to join my organization, Eliot."

"What organization is that?"

"The South Florida Freelance Tennis Writers Organization," said Marvin, buttering some toast. "We have great lectures."

The press had come to breakfast that morning because the food was free and the WTA had a "major announcement" to make. Was Chris Evert tired of talking nicely about Jennifer Capriati because John Evert represented Jennifer? Did Chris want to attempt a comeback? Did Pam Shriver want to retire? No. A man with a car dealership in northern Massachusetts was donating a $70,000 green Jaguar to be the grand prize for the top woman player at the end of the year.

The curtains of the glassed hotel breakfast room were drawn open, and on the other side of the window sat the new luxury car. For fifteen minutes we walked around the Jaguar, appreciating it as the reason for our free breakfast. Then we ate again.

Up at the dias, Cliff Buchholz, the short blonde tournament chairman at the Lipton, once a fine junior player from St. Louis, introduced his handsome, larger, more famous brother, Butch Buchholz, the former Jack Kramer touring pro, to speak about women's tennis. Leslie Allen, a tall, shy, quiet black woman, stood in the wings wearing her long red pleated dress. She was a former women's player and a tireless worker for women's tennis, but she was overlooked in the hierarchy of things.

If women's tennis had become more interesting to watch than men's tennis—and some people thought it had—it was because the men players hid their fear of failure in their power. The women's game was slightly slower and isolated the process of applying pressure on each other and thus, quite often, it was more interesting to watch as a battle of the wills. Men caved in quicker. The women fought harder psychologically. The Buchholz brothers, hard-working tournament officials, seemed to be there to give the women's tennis scene two token handsome men, an image of the game that quite a few of the women officials resented. All in all, it was a strange Florida corporate breakfast, waffles and Betty Stove waving from the front of a $70,000 dark green Jaguar convertible.

Outside, Marvin Glassman stood at the front of the hotel waiting for the parking attendants to bring around the rental cars. Cliff Buchholz, the tournament chairman, came through the glass swinging doors deep in conversation with a sponsor, who was dressed in a dark business suit for the Florida power breakfast. His blonde hairline receding with distinguished flecks of gray, Cliff Buchholz gave the parking attendant his ticket and a dollar bill. As Buchholz's short white Cadillac was on its way back around the parking circle, Marvin Glassman spoke up.

"Oh, hi, Cliff," called out Marvin, stepping forward.

Cliff Buchholz smiled in horror with his sponsor on his arm. He did not know Marvin Glassman from a Martian.

"Good to see you again," said Marvin, shaking hands. "You know, Cliff, you don't look at all like your brother, Butch. I guess it's because he's taller. One of you must look like your father, and one of you must look like your mother. It's the same with my brother. We don't look like each other either."

Buchholz smiled uneasily, said something serious to the corporate sponsor as they got into the white courtesy Cadillac, and then drove almost directly into a telephone pole.

"That was a near miss," I said.

"Cliff never could play as well as his brother, Butch," explained Marvin with a sigh as he assessed the near accident.

"Do you need a lift?" I asked as they brought around my blue Alamo rental.

"No," said Marvin firmly. "I'm waiting for the courtesy bus. It's express back to the courts."

Ivan Lendl's deep-set eyes were so dark that they looked like they were moon craters to his Slavic soul. Lendl was a strangely lonely but powerful figure on the tour. If John McEnroe, who had been defaulted in Australia and thus was not allowed to play at the Lipton, was Mr. Chaos, Ivan Lendl in every pore of his body was Colonel Control. Nearly everything about the Czechoslovak who spent his childhood behind the iron curtain and his youth behind the baseline of the red-clay courts of Prague was associated with the control of chaos that speeding tennis balls and personalities like John McEnroe and Jimmy Connors kept trying to put over on him. Lendl by nature tried to live by the brilliant Russian chess champion Gary Kasparov's assertion that the champion is the man who ultimately "controls chaos."

A jailer as a tennis player, Lendl constantly forced confessions of weakness from his opponents. A baseline bully, a willful answerer not an initiator by instinct, Lendl created his own brand of fear not by attacking his foes at net, like McEnroe, but by staying back and insisting that others had no right to try to squeeze time down his throat in the form of volleys. Now, hoping to win Wimbledon, he had to change all that and volley.

And here was where your sympathy for Lendl might begin. Despite what his former best friend, Wotjek Fibak, and former agent, the highly skilled Jerry Solomon, said openly about the way Lendl ruthlessly dissolved friendships and business relationships, Lendl wanted so much just to be accepted.

He was comic at times, and not always intentionally. "I don't want to be the one who criticizes the tournament," said Lendl the first day at the Lipton. "But I *vil* say that I have seen better facilities. These courts and changing rooms are not the way I thought and understood they were going to be. I think they must go next year to first-class accommodations and stadium, or the tournament must move. If I am to be back next year, the facility must improve."

"What do you think of the draw, Ivan?" another reporter shouted. "Should there be thirty-two seeds instead of sixteen?"

"In a big draw," said Lendl, "like here at the Lipton are ninety-six players, or at *Vimbledon* or the other Grand Slams where there are one hundred twenty-eight players, I think there should be thirty-two seeds, otherwise with just sixteen seeds, sections of the draw could open up, and you could get a situation where the seeded players lose because it is not their best surface. There could be problems at *Vimbledon* with the seedings and with the draw. A clay-court player could be seeded in the top sixteen and if he loses, it could open up the whole side of the draw to somebody unseeded. That would be a pity."

"How do you think that French Foreign Legion hat looks on you, Ivan?" asked the sound-bite reporter from Texas, holding up his boom mike for the evening news. Everyone thought Lendl looked a cross between Ichabod Crane and Beau Geste in the white hat with flaps.

"How is it looking on me? Not too good, I would say. But it serves its purpose. I find the protection on the neck from the hat makes a very big difference to me—at least two or three degrees during the course of a match. You would wear it. You would do the same as me in this heat. Except," said Lendl, his big teeth smiling awkwardly, trying to defend himself with a joke, "except that you sit down for a living. And I run for a living."

Well said. Lendl did run for a living. But Lendl was a little bit like Richard Nixon. He could make enemies even when he was trying to be funny.

Tony Roche, the former great Australian serve and volley man, was walking by himself toward the back lane of the Lipton, wearing a red windbreaker and a pair of tennis shorts when I spotted him. I hesitated briefly, then approached Lendl's coach. The son of a butcher, Tony Roche had one of the greatest backhand volleys ever, especially on grass, where the slice took. The stocky Australian had played the game with the heart of a lion, but he had not been as tough from the baseline. Roche and Lendl, his pupil, were an odd couple. The beer-drinking Australian serve and volley lefty and the introverted right-handed baseline Czech seemed very different at first, but they shared a deep athletic respect for the aspects of the game the other had mastered. Roche had an old soccer player's legs and backside. His Australian accent was still broad, friendly, and outgoing in the great Australian way. I wanted to ask Roche about Lendl and the volley. I held my mike up to Roche in the strong Florida wind, cupping it like a match.

"I read a book you wrote a part of," I said to Roche. "It was about ten years ago. It had a chapter on the serve by Stan Smith or Marty Riessen. The backhand by Ken Rosewall. The forehand by Arthur Ashe. And you wrote the chapter on the volley. Do you remember that chapter?"

"Yeah. Sure," said Roche in his ripe Aussie accent with a smile. "But that was twenty years ago, mate, not ten."

"Okay. Twenty. It was a great chapter on the volley, and you wrote it. You indicated a couple of weeks ago that Lendl still had to improve his volley. You said, 'Has Ivan learned to volley? Yes. But he still has trouble getting up to net.' I laughed, because that is exactly what your technical chapter on the volley was about twenty years ago: getting into a position to hit it."

Roche smiled. "That's right."

"Do you work on the court with him or stand on the side?"

"Oh, yeah. I do the drills," the forty-seven-year-old Roche said a little defensively. "I go on the court with him."

"What are you doing specifically with Lendl on the court?"

"Well, first I make sure he's moving well," said Roche, "that he's one hundred percent fit and ready to last five sets."

"Do you do with Ivan any of the things that Harry Hopman did with you, Laver, Emerson, Newcombe, and Rosewall? Any of the same drills or exercises?"

"Not really," said Roche. "Because Hopman used to do mainly two-on-one drills, and we're just normally doing one-on-one. The two-on-ones certainly are good for conditioning. But what we do simulates a match more."

"And how do you do that?"

"Ah, well, there's a variety of drills. The big thing is, when Ivan is playing well, he's moving well. So we gear a lot around that. Movement."

"My big question about Ivan is, watching him on TV in Australia and seeing him here at the Lipton: Why is he still staying back on the baseline ninety-eight percent of the time?"

"Well," said Tony Roche, "when Ivan plays in tournaments, he wants to win. He doesn't like to experiment in a tournament. I mean, he wants to win every time out."

"But don't you think that Ivan has to throw a little caution to the wind and start coming in to net?"

"Well," said the Australian, whose own instincts were always to charge forward, in part because he had been brought up on rough Australian grass, not Czech red clay, "he still has three months to prepare for it."

"Structurally his volley is not terrible. He doesn't have great feel for the ball the way you or Laver did. But structurally, Lendl's volley is okay, isn't it?"

"There aren't that many great volleyers around," said Roche. "I mean, the game has changed. There's only Edberg and McEnroe who can really volley."

Roche had left out mention of Becker or Sampras's volley, but I didn't press him on it. "You talked about the *transition game* twenty years ago in your chapter on the volley. Getting from the back part of the court, the serve or the ground strokes, up to net. The transition game is where Ivan is most uncomfortable. You said that the trick is not so much *hitting* the volley as getting yourself into the *position* to hit a volley."

"That's exactly right," said Roche. "It's really the same with any shot in tennis. Unless you are in good position and have got good balance as you hit the ball, you're not going to make the shot."

"But with Ivan it seems that there's just the one big chink structurally in his game—the volley—and getting up there to hit it. The volley is the one stroke that he can't perfect, perhaps because it is more than a stroke. It's an attitude."

"Well," said Tony Roche, downplaying himself, "we haven't really had that much time before to practice after the French. And he's done really well anyway. When you make the finals of Wimbledon twice like Ivan has, you're no slouch." Tony Roche nodded for emphasis. The Australian was as loyal as they come.

I nodded. "That's for sure. He's no slouch. One question about you. Did you really go to that faith healer in the Philippines, and did he really operate on your bad left elbow with his fingernails and cure it?"

"Yeah," said Roche, raising his eyebrows sheepishly as he smiled. "He did heal me, that guy. I was finished before I saw him, and he put me right."

"Well, thanks a lot," I said, grinning. The great Australian players were childhood heroes of mine.

"All right, mate," said Tony Roche in his broad, friendly Australian accent. "See ya later."

In the quarter-finals at the Lipton, Ivan Lendl played the Spaniard Emilio Sanchez, older brother of Arantxa Sanchez-Vicario. Both men stayed back on the baseline of the hard court in the ninety-degree heat. Lendl ran on his long, bandy legs, flaps down on the white French Foreign Legion hat. The hard baseline match went to 6–4 in the third set, and the nimble yet strong Emilio won because he took more risks and attacked more successfully. Lendl did not come up to net on his serve at all.

"Why don't I play my best in South Florida?" Lendl said after the match. "Maybe the conditions. It is so humid here I can't get the clear sound of the ball on my racket. And the wind is really unfortunate. Both players have to deal with it, but the wind can help one player more than the other. It affects my service toss a lot."

Lendl was the perfectionist, the worrier, the controller of finite space, even in defeat. A Japanese company had made a special larger-headed racket for him to take to Wimbledon.

"Can we expect to see you serving and volleying more as you get closer to Wimbledon?" I asked him after the loss to Sanchez. "Serving and coming right up to net?"

"Well," said Lendl, crunching ice, "as soon as I touch the grass, I will serve and volley. That's how I've played on grass since I'm seventeen years old, and I feel that's the way to play on it."

"But you won't volley on the hard courts?"

Lendl sucked some more ice. "Wimbledon is so far away that it is not necessary."

"Ivan," asked a Spanish reporter, "now that you and Boris are both out of the draw, do you think Emilio Sanchez will win the tournament?"

Lendl squinted and answered like a match being struck. "No, I don't think so."

Lendl's reply was repeated by the same reporter to Emilio Sanchez five minutes later. "Well," the trim, handsome Spaniard said with a certain kind of smile, "I may not win. But one thing's for sure. *He* won't."

The green-and-white press tent was located directly behind the wooden stadium. There were guards in long khaki pants everywhere, even in front of the Port-a-Flush Winnebagos whose large signs accurately dubbed them "The Crowd Pleaser."

Out in the Lipton Players and Officials parking lot, as I searched in vain for my blue Alamo rental car, I ran into a Florida linesman who had just worked the Andre Agassi–Jim Courier match. Jim Courier had wanted the match against his ex-roommate at Bollettieri's Tennis Academy so badly that it had backfired on him. Courier said he had no personal animosity toward Agassi, but the tempestuous Courier had been doing all his swearing during the Agassi match—in Spanish. The South Florida linesman who worked the service line for Agassi–Courier was sixty years old and looked like an aging Clark Gable. He had a gray version of Gable's mustache, a drinker's face, and a white tennis visor.

"Some of these young players today are getting away with murder out there when it comes to verbal abuse," said the Florida linesman. "You know what they're doing? They're talking Spanish! Well, hell. Just because they say a word in Spanish doesn't mean it's not just as dirty."

"That's right. You should have heard Gomez in Philadelphia," I agreed firmly, trying to hide my smile. "*Puta* means 'whore,' but these Spanish guys use it like they mean 'fuck,' don't they? I think these Spanish guys have an unfair advantage, don't you?"

"You're absolutely right," the Florida linesman said gruffly, venting some steam from his system. Just then a Chinese woman appeared walking toward her car, but the Florida tennis linesman was so worked up he did not see her and kept talking. "This *puta* and this *fuck* stuff have *got* to stop. If I have my way, these boys are going to get fined for both *puta and* for *fuck*." The gruff Clark Gable look-alike in the white tennis visor saw the look of horror on the face of the Chinese woman as she walked by. "Oh my God!" the Florida linesman called out, covering his head with his hands. "Code violation!"

There was one person who was missing but was always there. I had always wanted to ask a tennis official about John McEnroe, so I did. "If you're a good referee, can't you just defuse McEnroe?"

"No way," said Clark Gable. "If you try to talk to McEnroe, do you know what he says? He says, 'Do your fucking job, but don't talk to me.'" The Florida linesman nodded and shook his head. "That McEnroe's a son of a bitch."

The next morning I decided to get the word from the horse's mouth, the man who defaulted McEnroe in Australia, the English referee, Gerry Armstrong. John McEnroe was the only top male player missing from the Lipton draw. The default in Australia caused him to be banned from play for three months just as his game looked in Australia as if it were coming back to its old magical form. But even when McEnroe was not there physically, he seemed to be there in everyone's mind.

I felt a certain kinship with McEnroe. He was a New Yorker. He was the son of a successful lawyer, and we also had that in common. We were both first-born sons. I had had a fierce temper when I was a kid playing tennis, and I thought at times that I understood McEnroe's fierceness. At his best, for about a year, he was the best player I ever saw, including Laver and Gonzales. But there was a self-destructive imp at play in his soul. He was not just a perfectionist. When I saw McEnroe arguing with the referee in Australia, I could not help thinking that he was bursting to overflowing with the bile of a lawyer's natural argumentative energy. But John McEnroe also fit a lawyer's definition of a fool. Great lawyers are great battlers, but their cardinal rule is that a lawyer never takes his own case. McEnroe had an insistent, dramatic, and artistic personality, but when he was tired, John McEnroe, never as skillful (because he was unschooled) as his extremely talented lawyer-father, roared at the referee like a Mafia defense attorney pleading his own case.

The referee's tent at the Lipton was located toward the rear of the Key Biscayne tennis complex, which had been designed in the style of a shopping mall, with the stadium and grandstand as the two anchor tenants at either end, and the cement in between used by the potential shoppers, the fans, to pass by the epicenter of the tennis facility, the concession village.

Toward the rear of the complex, back near where the food was unloaded, the referees were all sitting in the shade and sunshine outside their tent like Civil War soldiers in camp, waiting for their next assignment. The referees were reading *USA Today* and chatting about a variety of subjects, the baseball strike, Russia's economic woes, and the penalty points awarded against Ken Flach in Philadelphia for racket and verbal abuse. Feeling uncomfortable there, I decided to wait for Armstrong around the corner from the referees' encampment.

I had always had mixed emotions about John McEnroe. There are few people in any decade in any field who can be called a genius. I thought that anyone as scrawny, freckled, balding, irritable, and paranoid as McEnroe, anyone as grim, thin, and unhappy who could stand up to the big thunder and dislike of men twice his size and overall strength, had to be a genius.

I loved the young McEnroe of the late seventies and early eighties with the soccer player strut in his thighs and the bandana around his red, stuffed-up, Queens-housewife hairstyle. I liked the cock-sureness in his young footsteps on the grass lawn where the Queen of England saw him, where he beat Borg after first losing to him, where he beat Connors in straight sets, as Connors had done to Rosewall when Connors was the young punk on the English tea lawn. But I never much liked the nasty Mac, who seemed spoiled as well as deeply angry. It wasn't the anger in its pure rage form that I objected to as much as the way McEnroe spoke too often with no consideration for anyone but himself. A good lawyer would never make that kind of mistake. But then,

McEnroe never had to stand entirely alone on his own two feet—except on the court. Off the court, his father, who served as his business manager and was a partner in the distinguished New York law firm of Paul, Weiss, Rifkind, urged John to behave but was always ready to argue his son out of any scrap, and there were many. In Philadelphia, Vic Seixas told me, "The father behaved just as badly as the son over at Wimbledon in the early 1980s. He was ready to sue everybody."

The McEnroes were an extremely loyal, closely knit family, and their son was an exceptional champion. But now the son was thirty-one, and old enough to be a man and not just a son. Lendl, whom I considered inferior as a talent, had owned him for five years. I began to feel about McEnroe the way Vladimir Nabokov, the Russian novelist who had given tennis lessons in Berlin to survive when he first fled Russia, had felt about Luzhin, the chess prodigy in his great novel *The Defense*:

> Luzhin's present plight was that of a writer or composer who, having assimilated the latest things in art at the beginning of his active career and caused a temporary sensation with the originality of his devices, all at once notices that a change has imperceptibly taken place around him, that others, sprung from goodness knows where, have left him behind in the very devices where he recently led the way.

I was curious to meet the person who had finally defaulted McEnroe. Gerry Armstrong was a thirty-five-year-old Englishman from Sussex who had wispy blonde hair thinning fast and a pleasant English country smile. McEnroe had been a very good schoolboy soccer player at the Trinity School in Manhattan, and Gerry Armstrong was a former English professional soccer player himself. When Armstrong arrived at the referees' tent at the Lipton, I waited until he finished reading his newspaper, and then we started talking. I felt a certain sympathy with the man who defaulted McEnroe, but also for Mac, because I felt he had been hung in Australia for past crimes against himself. A sociologist from Philadelphia, Digby Baltzell, was writing a book called *John McEnroe and the Decline of Civilization*. The title made Gerry Armstrong smile.

"I would think," said the English referee, "you have to go on court thinking something might happen no matter who the players are. But I guess it wouldn't be human if you did not feel there was more of a chance of that happening when John was playing."

Gerry Armstrong had not played tennis competitively, but he had played soccer at the level of what he called "one of your minor league baseball teams." He was being modest. He had played second-division English football (soccer), which was a shade or two better than the level of the U.S. Olympic soccer team. I took that as a positive sign, because even if you were not a tennis player—and Armstrong was not—to referee a sport it helps a lot if you have at least competed in another sport to understand the ebb and flow of effort and have the reflexes and eye to absorb the speed of the ball. The thirty-five-year-old English footballer turned tennis referee did not have the thick, attacking legs of a goal scorer. Positions in a sport are often very revealing about a character, a personality. I wondered what position Gerry Armstrong had played in soccer.

"What do you guys, the referees, talk about before you leave the referees' tent and go out on court to ref a match? Do you offer each other encouragement before you go out to face the lions, that kind of thing?"

Gerry Armstrong smiled easily. "I think we've all done it enough that it's almost second nature. There are ten full-time traveling referees now. Sometimes we'll make suggestions to each other about a specific player. But it's more just situations. If things crop up in a match, how to handle them. How to answer players' questions, rule interpretations, that kind of thing."

"I used to like a referee named Frank Hammond. Do you remember him? Big, heavy guy. He had a great sense of humor, a good thing for a referee to have. He used to sit up there in the chair and boom out in that voice of his, 'Mr. McEnroe!' And just the sound of his voice was funny. It could defuse a situation. I thought that made Frank Hammond a good referee."

"Well, Frank was a bit of an entertainer," the Englishman said dryly. "Today, we feel the players, not the referees, should be the focus of attention."

"Having played sports yourself, you know that when people are really tired they are more likely to react in extraordinary ways."

"Sure. It's always the last couple of minutes in a football [soccer] match that can get a bit dicey."

"As tennis referees, you are all aware of what is going on inside these tennis players? You know how tiring it can be when a match goes over four hours?"

"Yes. We are. Obviously, there is a line, though, that you cannot cross over."

"I mention fatigue because I remember a few years ago when Larry Holmes had just been dethroned by Michael Spinks. He was exhausted, and he said after the fight, 'Rocky Marciano couldn't carry my jock strap.' " Armstrong started to laugh. "And this created a big furor back in New York, in America, because Rocky Marciano is considered a patron saint in some circles. The reporters crucified Larry Holmes. I thought they should not have expected much else, interviewing a fighter just five minutes after he went fifteen rounds. Sometimes tennis is a fight out there, too, isn't it? Each hit of the ball. Think of the grunters, Connors and Seles. It's bam, bam, like a punch, except in tennis it's all sending a ball over a net. In tennis, you never actually touch anybody, but you are hitting at them. The fighting is usually invisible, but it's all going on inside the two people."

"That's right. It is."

"Okay. Let me ask you about McEnroe."

To be the soccer player he had been, Gerry Armstrong had a certain kind of fire in him, but I could not quite place it. Refereeing had always struck me as a strange avocation and an even stranger career, but what McEnroe always seemed to forget was that all over the world the *spirit* of refereeing existed. There were a thousand angry schoolmasters ready to slap his hand with a ruler. Tennis was a game on many levels about what was called "in" and what was called "out," what was socially acceptable, the form without which there was chaos, and the referee in a match was the ultimate social arbiter, part cop, part tennis committee member at the country club. The problem with McEnroe was that he thought he was the whole party, not just part of the scene. To that extent, the default in Australia had set the record straight; still, having watched the tape over and over again, I did not think that McEnroe deserved to have been defaulted.

"There were three incidents in the match," said Armstrong. "In the first, John got a call he did not like and stood over a lineswoman."

"Yeah. That was lousy. He's a bum when he stands over the women linespeople that way. Somebody should kick him in the pants. He made her feel lousy, and she didn't miss the call, either."

"I gave John a warning for that. He didn't actually say anything to the woman, but he said it with his body, didn't he? It was pretty clearly meant to be intimidation. But I just gave John a warning. The warning was as if to say, 'Hey. You can't do that.' "

"Right. He deserved that one. It's the next stage that bothered me, when McEnroe bounced his racket on the court, and his racket broke inside. It didn't shatter, but it came right back up off the ground and hit him in the stomach like he was committing hari-kari with his own sword."

"That was racket abuse, pure and simple, and that's an automatic penalty point," said Gerry Armstrong. "The supervisor, Ken Farrar, came out then for a verification of the rule. It was John who requested Ken and the rule interpretation."

I nodded, picturing the scene. It could not have been calm waiting on court for the supervisor to come on and hear the case. McEnroe's lawyerly juices must have started to flow.

"Before we go on to the supervisor—actually two people came on court so there were three official bodies in all and just one McEnroe—couldn't you just have said, 'Okay. Cool it, John'? Did you have to award a full penalty point at that juncture? It gave away the whole service game, and probably the set. It changed the whole flow of the match."

"You have got to realize, I am responsible to two players. Imagine how his opponent, Mikael Pernfors, felt. The racket was broken even if the frame did not look broken from the outside. I could hear John's racket break inside. Everyone must be judged by the same standards. The same form. Under the procedures used, there is an automatic penalty point awarded against a player who breaks a racket. That's an absolute. John wanted to continue playing with it . . ."

"Then at ad-out, why not let him continue? If the racket really was broken, why not let him try to shovel himself out of his own grave? Why escalate?"

"Even if a racket is only broken on the inside, it is an automatic point penalty against, I'm afraid. I was just waiting for the crowd in Australia to calm down before I made my announcement." The mild-mannered Englishman smiled and raised his blonde eyebrows.

"And that's when McEnroe went berserk?"

"Right," said Armstrong. "Well, when the two supervisors came on, and they would not change my decision for him. That's when it happened."

"How?"

"Well, John very calmly, very professionally, very politely asked, and Ken came on. And Peter Bellinger came on, too, and their discussion ensued. I believe John asked how they could tell if his racket was broken. He wanted to serve with it. He wanted to continue."

"He wanted another serve."

"Probably. Yes. I think John was a little . . ."

"Embarrassed."

"Probably. I guess he was thinking—I mean," said Gerry Armstrong. "That was a huge point. It meant the service break. No doubt about that. After Ken and Peter spoke to him and said, 'That is the rule. Your racket *is* broken,' they turned right around and started to walk off the court."

"He had called for the supervisor but two men came on. That meant three officials including yourself. McEnroe started to say something to these two gentlemen. What was it?"

Gerry Armstrong smiled.

"Come on. I heard he said, 'Blank you blanks!' Or something to that effect." I asked, "Was it 'Fuck you, mother-fuckers'?"

"Very, very close," said the former English soccer player.

I had played the tape a dozen times and come to the same conclusion. A close match had degenerated into a scene from "Abbott and Costello" or out of "The Three Stooges." The tournament director, Bellinger, looked like a cross between Margaret Thatcher's husband and the landlord in "Abbott and Costello" who was always after the rent. The tennis match suddenly took on an air of farce and became a dumb, avoidable tragedy they all, including McEnroe, especially McEnroe, had let it become. It was so dumb. So avoidable. So McEnroe. But did they have to default him? The Australian crowd was furious when it happened, but the crowd hadn't heard anything. Then why default him? What exactly were McEnroe's parting words to those two gentlemen, Bellinger and Farrar?

"Actually," said Gerry Armstrong, the presiding referee, "he said to their backs, 'You mother-fuckers! Fuck you!' "

"I see."

"That kind of language," said Gerry Armstrong. "It just can't be tolerated."

Edberg, Becker, and Sampras were a lot easier to like than McEnroe. But McEnroe, like Luzhin, Nabokov's imaginary chess prodigy, like Bobby Fischer, the real-life chess master whose own personal problems made McEnroe's seem tame by comparison, was an attacking player whose brilliance could be excruciating to be around. I still thought they could have let McEnroe continue in Australia as long as he felt he could play with the same racket. But like a schoolboy who never took to discipline, McEnroe was punished for his past. Someone should have kicked McEnroe in the pants years ago, a big fellow player, a John Sadri or Chip Hooper, but cowboy justice never happened to McEnroe, and that was a shame, probably because the players and officials were all scared of McEnroe's litigious father.

"The swear words came through loud and clear on television," said Gerry Armstrong.

"We didn't hear it in America."

"No. They edited the swear words out. It was a delayed tape."

I sighed. The referee was right, I guessed. You could not say that on TV. Except it was real. It was raw. It was emotion. It was McEnroe, instead of spoon-fed TV politeness or violence. When it came to McEnroe, I could not help myself. I found myself defending him, as unpopular as that could be, because I loved what McEnroe could do with his left hand. "Well. I guess you're right. You can't say that on TV. But you know, this may be the end for McEnroe."

"It may be. I don't know people's backgrounds, but it is going to be very tough for him to come back." The English referee's voice trailed off. "When I was playing soccer," Gerry Armstrong went on in a thoughtful voice, "we would argue with the referee on occasion."

"But if you went too far, you would get the yellow card."

"Right. You could disagree, but in the end the referee was *always* right, and when it came down to it . . ."

"You just had to trot off."

"Yes," said Armstrong, getting ready to do the Agassi–Berger semifinal at the Lipton. "Exactly. You just have to trot off. I was never too much of a bad boy, really." The referee's voice was relaxed, light, happy. His Sussex disposition seemed sunny.

"By the way," I asked the English referee, "what position did you play in soccer?"

"I was the goal keeper."

The goal keeper. The final line of defense. It was almost too perfect. The goal keeper was the denial position, and it struck me that the referee who defaulted McEnroe had been a professional goalie, not just by position but by nature, for in sports nature and position are invariably one. Shot! Save! The English second division goal keeper turned referee had finally turned away McEnroe. By all the logic of the social norms, he was right to perform the deflection, to raise the red card.

But with that source of strife and occasional ugliness came such a beautiful, free, relaxed left-handed swing, a stroke with both accuracy and magic touch. What was the source of McEnroe's anger? And was the anger really necessary? I was reminded of the great southern writer Thomas Wolfe's description of his hero, young Eugene Gant from North Carolina:

He was wired like a race horse. A white storm of inchoate fury would burst in him like a rocket, and for a moment he would be cursing mad.

Like Bobby Fischer, the modern chess master mired in himself; like Tilden, who the world scorned; like Luzhin, the chess prodigy who leaps to his death, McEnroe—part fool, part brat, part genius—was in trouble again. I shook hands with the English referee who defaulted him in Australia, a much more pleasant and less talented man than McEnroe, a goalie.

The men's semifinals paired Stefan Edberg and the baseline Spaniard Emilio Sanchez, and the Swede cut off the net all day. Jay Berger reached the other semifinal against Andre Agassi.

Berger had impressed me tremendously. His semifinal effort against Andre Agassi was not McEnroe but it was very good tennis. Berger had courage and chutzpah. Against Agassi, Berger threw caution to the wind and hit the ball even harder and more toward the lines than Agassi. Refusing to acknowledge any limitations, Berger won the first set 7–5. But Andre Agassi had two more gears and won the next two sets in the ninety-degree Florida spring sunshine. Jay Berger was finally tired, but after the match he kept smiling and shrugged as if he were just starting a season-long battle.

"In the first set when I was down four–one," gasped Berger, "I just said to myself that I was going to hit everything as hard as I could, and it worked. But when Andre starts moving you from side to side, nobody on the tour does it better."

As my wife said, Berger had a kind face. Love was not easy, especially within the context of competition. Berger was scheduled to play in twelve consecutive tournaments on the European circuit, and he was going to be joined on his travels by his attractive Czechoslovak fiancée, Nadia Stastny, in Monte Carlo and Rome. There was nothing tougher than traveling, competing, and being in love. Competition and love were instincts that did not easily balance. Many of the marriages, let alone the relationships, split up on the tour. Some players became like sea captains and kept their wives or friends at home. Some learned to adapt to company. The level of concentration and focus had to be so intense, so selfish at times. I wondered how Berger, his fiancée, and love would fare on the European circuit.

The women's singles tournament at the Lipton was won by Monica Seles. That ten-day tournament was the turning point in Seles's career. The presence of a younger prodigy initially made Seles feel bad about herself, but Seles soon reacted the right way: she befriended Capriati. When she easily defeated Judith Wiesner in the final, Seles admitted she had been way down psychologically at the start of the Lipton.

"I came into this tournament and I can't say I was full of confidence," said the tall sixteen-year-old Yugoslav girl with the pulled-back blonde hair. She had long legs like both her parents. Karolj Seles, her cartoonist father turned tennis coach, was tall and thin, and Seles's mother looked particularly strong in an Eastern European way.

The common sense of the young Yugoslav girl came from traveling on the hard road. Originally from Hungary, the family had lived in three countries and spent the last four years staying at a house in a tennis camp. Almost as soon as the tournament was over, Monica Seles's father announced that the family was moving out of Nick Bollettieri's Tennis Academy. He offered no compensation to Bollettieri for their four years of food, lodging, dentist bills, and tennis lessons other than the advertising value of Monica's presence, now departing. It was a pretty cheap move. Like Navratilova, Seles had not had an easy childhood, and in the future she would benefit and suffer from that road paved with stone, not gold.

Loaded slightly less heavily than Jennifer Capriati with paternal baggage, blessed with an innate ability to hang in there mentally, possessing a two-handed backhand that could leap off the side of a court like a speeding teenager's hard right turn at a red light, Monica Seles was an original, not an assembly-line product.

Judith Wiesner, the twenty-four-year-old Austrian with the white Kneisel racket and incredible industrial-strength topspin off both sides, said of losing to Seles, "Her game is completely different than anybody else's. She hits the ball so hard you really don't have time to recover."

Seles smiled and giggled with the press, then turned serious and said after winning the Lipton, "Last year I would be thinking, 'Judith's only number one hundred in the world and she can't beat me,' and then I wouldn't be as aggressive, and I would lose. You think you're so good and then you find out you aren't as good as you think you are. I don't want to set any big goals for this year and then get scared," said Seles. "I will just try."

Nick Bollettieri, Andre Agassi's five-foot six-inch coach, had been alone and looked unhappy the day before Andre Agassi's final-round match with Stefan Edberg. Bollettieri, whom I remembered much more than he remembered me (from junior tennis), was standing in the concession village in green fluorescent sunglasses with both arms wrapped in a hug around two rackets. Nobody seemed to notice him. That was like not noticing Don King when Mike Tyson was fighting. Bollettieri smiled as I came up to ask him for an interview, but he had no clue as to who I was until I told him.

"I remember that match," he insisted when I reminded him of the 6–4, 10–8 scores in my losing match in the semifinals of the Easterns at Forest Hills with a fourteen-year-old Brian Gottfried. In 1965, I had won the New York State singles and doubles, the New York State Jaycees, and was ranked third in the east in the sixteens. I was quick and strong for my age, but when I lost to the fourteen-year-old prodigy, I knew that I was going to college, not Wimbledon, where Gottfried eventually reached the semis. "You got us at a very bad moment," remembered Bollettieri. "We were afraid Brian had a heart murmur. We spent the morning of your match taking Brian around to heart specialists in Forest Hills."

I laughed. "Shall we do the interview right here?" I asked.

"No. Let's do it over here," said Bollettieri, taking me around to the gazebos that held the draw sheets.

Nick Bollettieri had a round, leathery tanned face and a Cheshire cat's smile. Still clutching Andre Agassi's two rackets that needed stringing, he pushed his fluorescent green Ray-Bans back on his nose and leaned against a Florida palm tree for support. Fifty-two years old, wearing ankle-high Nike sneakers and no socks, black tennis shorts, and a white cotton V-neck T-shirt, Nick Bollettieri was brown as a berry and still liked to coach in just his tennis shorts with his shirt off. Bollettieri had been in the tennis business for thirty years, many of them ankle deep in soft green Florida entoutcas clay and hot sun. The son of an Italian immigrant, an ex-Marine who became disenchanted with things during a year at a Miami law school, Bollettieri's tennis camps had become a lucrative business, but only after many years of struggle and perseverance.

The tennis academy began housing students with his pros, grew into a motel, and now that an education deal had been worked out with St. Stephen's School in Bradenton, boasted seventy-five tennis courts, a famous staff sports psychologist (Jim Loehr), dozens of teaching pros, and videotape and ball-boy machines galore. There were now 350 tennis camps in America alone. Harry Hopman's widow and Rick Macci ran two of the major rival camps, but Nick Bollettieri had more top-name players, starting with Brian Gottfried.

Up close, Nick Bollettieri's hair was jet black, a tribute to his good Italian genes or to Grecian Formula. His face was lined from the sun in a slightly apelike crease of a smile. He had the irrepressive aura of a fifteen-year-old self-promoter. As an instructor of junior players, Bollettieri was accused of producing topspin clones. Yet he had produced several champions, and he was very clear to say publicly that players like Andre Agassi and Jennifer Capriati were "one in fifty thousand." I came to like Bollettieri. It was the parents, not Bollettieri, who stocked his tennis camps with "future champions." It was the parents who were the dream machines.

In fifteen years of operation, 45,000 "students" had attended his tennis academy, 30,000 children between the ages of six and sixteen and another 15,000 adults. Now 5,000 tennis players a year passed through Bollettieri camps across the country. His best advertising was the players he produced.

"You've had so many people play for you," I began. "Monica Seles, Andre Agassi, Jim Courier, Pete Sampras, and David Wheaton. What have you done to put together a program that got so many of the top men and women players following what you're saying? You've practically had everybody."

"Well, not everybody," said Bollettieri, smiling as he tilted his head. "But we certainly have had a lot. We've been very fortunate."

"You've had more of the top players in the game than any other coach in the world."

"Well," said Bollettieri, "what I've tried to do is set up a system."

"What exactly is the Bollettieri system?" It sounded dangerously like a diet.

"Working with a person's style," Bollettieri shot back. "Working with their mind, their physical make-up, how they feel about life. We're not trying to make major changes in their games."

"So what do you do? Do you get them physically stronger?"

"Right. Everything. It depends what area is needed. You see," said

Bollettieri, "everybody is an individual. And I think that next Friday—a week from next Friday—is going to be quite interesting. On that date, Agassi–Bollettieri release their worldwide video, *Attack*."

"*Attack?*"

"Right. *Attack* is going to be one of the most interesting videos ever done in this country. And what we are trying to do, the concept," explained Agassi's mentor and substitute father away from home, "is to try to say to a person who is starting to play tennis, 'Well, all right. Listen, you're not too fast on your feet. Ah, you're forty-five years old. Ah. This is what we think you should be doing instead of trying to make major changes. Because at your age, it's too late for major changes.' I think people of all ages can relate to that. The hardest thing is to change. It's the same with a boy or girl of seventeen or eighteen. They're already pretty much formed. There's not too much you can do for them. If you took them early, you would spend a lot of time looking at their background, their educational background, the physical make-up of their family. Take a look at what they've done in other sports."

"You like to get a good athlete if you can."

"Absolutely. That's an ideal thing. If you have an athlete today . . . with a mind . . . then you really have an advantage. And now if you can get a *big* athlete . . ."

"Size helps?"

"Well, it seems to."

"I thought you mostly did great things with shorter players, Jimmy Arias, Andre Agassi."

"Right. We've been very fortunate that way. But of course, I had Chip Hooper and Fritz Buehning and the Brian Gottfrieds and the Paul Annacones, the David Wheatons. And those are *big* boys. The Mike DePalmers. We also did well with—"

"Jimmy Arias?"

"Jimmy. Yeah. Well. Jimmy's married now. And Jimmy's back at the academy, living nearby. And that's where he should be." Nick Bollettieri nodded wisely. "So what we're trying to do at the academy is to develop a special system within a person's individual make-up. Of course, if I work with a youngster that I take from the very beginning, then he or she has to be taught the total game."

"The 'total game.' Does that necessarily involve a lot more topspin?"

"Well, the grips are different."

"The grips are different, and the rackets are different. Is that why you tend to teach the topspin style?"

"But I don't teach that style *per se*. *Attack* is tailored to the individual."

"So you aren't pushing the industrial-strength topspin?"

"That's right! Because—" Bollettieri's New York accent emphasized the *cause* in because.

"Because you want to go through the ball more, don't you?"

"Well, that just depends," said Agassi's coach. "If you put too much topspin on the ball, they can run it down. But if you're building up a point, perhaps a little more spin might be the thing. When you have the opening, you also have to learn how to drive the ball through it. I think the game is going to be more than just groundies. I think the game is going to hitting the ball more on the rise."

"Like Andre does."

"Right. Andre's way ahead of everybody in that department."

The idea of taking the ball on the rise was not new—every champion from Tilden to Connors did it, but the title of the new video, *Attack*, was definitely catchy. "Agassi takes the ball so early, doesn't he?"

"Right," said Bollettieri. "And Monica Seles. And Jim Courier."

"What about Pete Sampras?"

"Ah. It was too bad Andre got sick there in Philadelphia. He was playing Pete and had to default. It was a shame," said Bollettieri, who coached both Sampras and Agassi, "because Philadelphia should have been Andre's tournament. Andre ate some bad Chinese food the night before he played Pete. But that should have been Andre's tournament."

"But Sampras did win it. What does Sampras have to do now?"

"I think Pete has to look a little more to the off-court activities the way Andre has. The physical training. Last week in Palm Springs, Pete lost in the third set, and some people said he gave up, that he 'didn't want to pay the price.' Well, it's not fair of people to say that about Pete, because he's still young. He's got plenty of time. Give him two years."

Nick Bollettieri was an American original. He looked tired, like he had eaten one too many late meals with teenagers at Arby's. He had a wife and a son who wanted to become a photographer, not a tennis pro. Like Don King, Bollettieri managed more than one fighter at once, but he was not malign. Even the young kids who worked for Bollettieri did not consider him to be a great businessman. Bollettieri did not even have a contract with the Seles family, just a verbal understanding, and they walked out on him after four years of accommodations and tennis lessons. Bollettieri was not nearly as rough as Don King, but as they say in attributing a painting, you could say of Bollettieri that he was "the school of King." He coached so many players, he had to have conflicts of interest. Smiling behind his sunglasses, Bollettieri looked up at the bright blue Florida sky. A passing white cloud was spitting rain. Then large Florida rain drops began to fall.

"Well," said Nick Bollettieri, eyeing the tape machine between us, "don't forget *Attack*. From Bollettieri–Agassi. This home video is going to have a dramatic impact on the way tennis is taught in the next twenty years. *Attack!* And if you'd like a prediction, Andre is going to beat Edberg tomorrow."

The finals of the men's and women's wheelchair singles were taking place on the back courts. It made me think of Bruce Kimball, the Olympic diver who killed two Florida kids driving drunk, and of Thomas Muster, who was hit by a drunk driver going thirty miles an hour in a Florida parking lot the night before he was to play the 1989 Lipton final against Lendl. Muster was lucky to be playing again and on his feet. The women's wheelchair final was held on the grandstand court where Jay Berger had beaten Goran Ivanisevic.

The wheelchair tennis players were so strong, so damn proud—and rightly so—of what could be accomplished if one really tried. The bright sunlight made it all the more clear. It touched me. The setting was so official. The full allotment of linespeople were standing to call the lines of the wheelchair finals. The players were sitting in special angle-wheeled racing chairs with their legs strapped in tightly. They played as fiercely as Lendl or McEnroe. Something unseen had happened to each of them. Their rage was the country's rage. Their effort was based on the desire to be beautiful, to move where others could move, to be powerful where others were powerful.

The women's wheelchair match was particularly hard-fought. The struggle of the two female competitors, a large German player and a pretty young American in a sleek wheelchair, caught my attention. The players glared at each other between points, and on the change-overs they sped past each other without even looking up. They were relentless, neither yielding an inch, neither smiling. It was their Wimbledon on the hard courts of South Florida, and they both wanted it so much.

DeLonge, the young American player, held her serve after three hotly contested ad-outs. The German player, Isseche, furiously disputed the final line call on a drop-shot angle DeLonge played beautifully. The men's wheelchair match very nearly mimed the moves and disputes of

the more mobile game. My eyes started to tear in appreciation until I
recognized the triumph of bravery over pity.

The morning of the Edberg–Agassi final there were South Florida policemen and policewomen in brown uniforms all over the tennis grounds.
A French reporter, stopped at the press room to have his I.D. examined
for the hundredth time, said, *"Mais, dis-donc. C'est un prison, quoi!"*
("Say! This place is a prison!") *Secure,* as in security, was the operative
word in South Florida that week.

As Andre Agassi took the stadium court in the final against Stefan
Edberg, the crowd of teenage girls started screaming for Agassi as if he
were a singer for Menudo. Tennis was more personally judgmental than
almost any other sport. What people really liked about tennis was seeing
the flesh of the players, male and female, and interpreting it. The exposed
bodies and naked strokes added up to a human sum—a person we all
would either like to know or like to criticize. People enjoyed the dis-
approving easily as much as they enjoyed the approving. The public's
reactions to Lendl, to Agassi, to Edberg, to Becker, to Sampras were
really the public's reactions to the language of the players' bodies and
how their movement related to people's own dreams of movement and
personality. Tennis spectators are first and foremost body-language in-
terpreters, and the interpretation says as much about the viewer as about
the players.

Stefan Edberg had managed to keep his feet on the ground. As he
told Penny Crisp in the *New Age,* a newspaper in Melbourne, Australia,

> As a good Swedish man, I was brought up to believe in household
> work. Even as a millionaire, I think it is important to take respon-
> sibility for my own laundry. It is part of my philosophy . . . never
> become a prima donna.

I couldn't imagine that the Nike boys, Agassi and McEnroe, did too
many of their own socks. So who was the real rebel, McEnroe, Agassi,
or Edberg?

In Agassi's case, the rebelliousness in March seemed mainly to consist
of an oversized shirt, his wraparound sunglasses, his hairy navel, and a
willingness to show it to a camera. A rebel? Agassi was certainly a very
safe rebel. The marketing boys knew what they had in Andre perhaps
more than Agassi or Bollettieri knew themselves. They had America

itself, part immigrant, part blonde. They had the incredible success of one unlikely individual, a soap opera of talent, the kind of good looks that made Roseanne Barr unhappy as a young girl, the cavalierness of the open convertible and the teenager from Camelot driving it. The marketing boys knew. Andre Agassi *was* America, the star risen from the vast part of America, the less affluent child come good in the *Great Gatsby* sport of tennis.

In Florida that Sunday afternoon, fast-food slowly made its way up into the sunny stands. Courtside, the sponsors' boxes were full of white shirts and club ties—corporate America, Florida style. In March, there was no inkling that the highly competitive, tennis-loving president would soon be sending us to war.

Curiously, there were no Australians near the final. The Australians were having a tough time on the tennis tour, and had been for several years. It was as if today's Australian players were struggling in their minds. The former Australian greats had become psychological fathers the younger players had not been able to overcome. I found John Newcombe, still handsome in khaki slacks, a dark blue shirt, and his famous smooth brown mustache, and I asked him what had happened to Australian tennis fortunes.

"Do you think that the fact that you guys—Laver, Rosewall, Emerson, Hoad, yourself, Stolle, Roche—were so good and such legends—do you think that has put pressure on these young Australian guys today, psychologically speaking?"

"Well, it has," said Newcombe, "because they're all trying desperately to get back to the top of the rankings. The last ten years in Australia have been spent reorganizing all the junior programs, and we have some pretty good junior players now. Among the older ones, Darren Cahill is a much better player than he's showing just now. But he's tying himself up in knots trying so hard to win."

"It's almost as if your generation of Australians are the famous fathers these kids just can't overcome. Your Davis Cup captain, Bob Carmichael, said in an interview that he thought Australia was a less hard, less tough place to live these days. He seemed to imply that life in Australia had gotten more cushy, more affluent, and that was why more good players weren't coming up through the ranks in Australia. Is that true?"

"Well," said Newcombe, who spent over half the year in Texas at his tennis ranch, "I don't think Australia has gotten all that 'cushy.' We've had to move away from grass courts because they got too expensive to maintain. We've gone to hard courts like the Americans. But I do think these younger guys feel like they have to play better than we did, and that doesn't help them."

Arthur Ashe and Cliff Drysdale, the former South African Davis Cup player, did the color commentary of the finals between Stefan Edberg and Andre Agassi. They both picked the tall, incredibly lean and athletic Edberg to win in four sets. So did I. As the players came into the stadium, Stefan Edberg looked the way Gary Cooper might have if he had been a tennis player. Agassi, shorter, getting thicker through the chest from weight lifting, had on pink bicycle tights under his black Nike shorts and a baggy white shirt featuring a black-and-pink piano-key motif. Agassi looked nervous coming into the stadium, and to calm himself he put his left hand to his lips and blew a kiss to his fans. Edberg, carrying a huge tennis bag over his left shoulder, looked lean and concentrated, head down shyly, staring at the hot green cement. The Swede had something more than usual at stake. If he won the match against Agassi, Edberg would pass Becker in the rankings. It was added pressure.

From the top of the stadium I could see the Miami skyline, the high arching bridge, and the causeway leading out away from the city to Key Biscayne. Down below, Agassi looked like a teenager in with a man. But Agassi attacked the ball early, as Bollettieri said he would, and for once Agassi looked like he was in part an Iranian kid with short, dark hair, while down his neck his American blonde shag hung like he had been too concerned with Edberg to think of the peroxide bottle the night before.

On the very first point, Edberg was pulled up to net involuntarily by a net cord, and Agassi blistered a forehand passing shot by the Swede up the line. The spring sun in Florida was blisteringly hot. Agassi played with a watch on his left wrist; Edberg's pale wrists were bare. The players were having an odd dialogue, a kind of sex, with each other. Edberg wanted to be the aggressor, but Agassi was attacking the ball from the baseline, swinging Edberg from side to side as he had swung Jay Berger the day before, and doing everything, including serving slow, very high kicking sixty-mile-an-hour second serves, to keep Edberg off him and away from the dominant position, the net. Agassi's passing shots were so quick that Edberg began to stay back more and more. Agassi dominated.

Edberg's Swedish girlfriend sat watching in the players' box. Her face was tanned and smooth, her lips were red, and her slightly teased blonde hair was pulled back off her head. Her eyes and emotions were hiding behind dark glasses. Annette Olsen was a country girl beneath all her

glamor. Down on court, Edberg looked pale, uncomfortable, and unhappy with himself.

Edberg's forehand, always the barometer of his confidence, began to
float long. An hour before the final, Edberg had felt a surge of doubt as
to how to play Agassi on cement, and the Swede ran through the Florida
crowd to the stringer's trailer to get his four rackets restrung tighter.
Now the Swede felt as if the string job was too tight. Edberg looked
nervous and uncomfortable with his racket—that is, with himself. He
began to roll over the top of his forehands, cupping the top of the ball
instead of making a real impact straight through it.

Down in a sponsors' courtside box, grimacing and shaking his fist
between points, Nick Bollettieri was seated with Agassi's older brother,
Philip, whose baldness—hidden under a pink "Lipton Chmps" hat—
was a preview of Agassi's hairline at forty. Bollettieri and Agassi surprised
a lot of people. Edberg's shoulders fell, the telltale sign that the Swede
was getting ready to pack his suitcase. And even though Agassi would
tank the third set, 6–0, it was the Las Vegas boy, not the Swede, who
took home the winner's check for $180,000—about the cost of the new
Lamborghini Agassi bought after the final, not for himself but for Nick
Bollettieri as a sign of affection and appreciation. Edberg had not moved
or served well. The Swede shook his head and said something self-
recriminating before trotting up to congratulate the winner. Agassi leapt
the net. When it all was over and Edberg had turned his back, Andre
Agassi double-pumped his arms into the air, threw his shirt into the
crowd, and thanked God for the win.

I have a theory that winning in any sport deeply connects the winner
to the place where he or she wins. Florida was not such a stretch for
Agassi. A person or a team rarely wins where their essentials do not
connect strongly to the place, either matching it or overcoming it. Edberg, the Swede, was a little off in South Florida. The blistering Miami
heat and lack of air circulation inside the small green wooden stadium
was Agassi weather, Las Vegas weather, plus humidity.

In the air-conditioned press tent Agassi's girlfriend, Amy Moss, a
delicate wisp of a girl with a fair mountain of light brown hair, was
standing to one side of the packed room, wearing a very short pale blue
culotte. She was a Christian, they had felt obliged to tell the world.
Physically, she looked just right for Agassi: light, thin, quick. They would
leave the press room holding hands. Both were nineteen, and he was a
millionaire who had just won almost $200,000.

It was America, the land of impossible dreams come true.

"The critics are the critics," Agassi said softly. "They'll always find stuff to criticize. If I silence them in this way, they're going to find something else. I'm not really concerned with that too much." But you sensed he was. "I played well today, but I think we've seen a better Stefan Edberg. Either he was tired or the heat got to him, or maybe he was just feeling a little tentative. Stefan made a few mistakes. I capitalized on them."

The Las Vegas boy with the eighth-grade education sat smiling before the bank of microphones and about two hundred reporters from the seven countries that carried the television broadcast of the final: Japan, Germany, Italy, France, Sweden, Australia, and America. The cameras clicked and rolled. Why had he won? the reporters asked the nineteen-year-old millionaire. Agassi sounded unsure as he answered.

Just hard work. I have a new trainer. Gil Reyes is his name. And he just knows what he is doing. He really clicks well with me. He motivates me well, and I'm paying the price, you know. I mean, you come here and you see that I'm strong and going the distance and I'm beating these guys, but there's a lot behind the scenes. I worked for that. I'm in the weight room, and I'm doing the weights, upper body, lower body, the track, you know. Everything. And I'm basically just like a robot. You tell me what you want me to do, and I'm confident that you know what you're telling me.

Andre Agassi smiled, got up, and left with his slender girlfriend. Edberg was unavailable for comment after the match. The day belonged to Agassi, to the sultry heat, and to the wheelchair players on angled, soft-rubber tires playing their hearts out.

The Florida crowd leaving was America, its vast convenience-store carelessness, its random slaughter, its drink, its aspirations, its heart, its leisure, its loneliness, its hunger, its desire to be recognized as *outstanding*. Andre Agassi was the champion here.

Agassi was the wheelchair contestants' champion, too. The wheelchair players believed in the distant goal, the hard work, the long shot, the American Dream that Agassi had attained. The champion was of the crowd, not of the club. He was the crap table in Las Vegas, the inexpensive steak, the stand-up comic's joke, the boy from Nebraska Johnny Carson made good, the shot at the big time, Diet Coke against Diet Pepsi, the sand around Las Vegas, the wheelchair tennis championships, the blue Florida sky, the convertible car, the Bible written in dull English for comprehension, the whippet-slender, mountain-haired petite girl-friend, the long brown pants of the South Florida security forces—male and female, helmeted and visored—out to protect the crowd from itself and from the uninvited, the empty spaces that were so hard to understand. The players attacked those empty spaces with their volleys, their ground strokes, their souls. And Agassi had been best at opening and closing the empty spaces. Across the paved parking lot lay the long, wide bare Florida beach where huge palm trees grew in the sand. Beyond that lay the ocean. Well pleased, the crowd went home over the jungle-gym foot bridges above the parking lot baking in the Sunday afternoon heat, and though many of the spectators had rooted for the Swede, most of them identified with the American winner, the young Iranian boy from Las Vegas with dark roots and flowing bleached-blonde hair.

JAY BERGER

Jay Berger had a public parks tennis game. Born at the army base where his father was a dentist, as a little boy he went to Florida, where his father set up his practice in the town of Plantation. The small town is like it sounds, slightly Southern, slow but very steady in pace. Dr. Berger shares an office with another dentist, and it is the kind of periodontal practice that has a recorded message giving the after-hours home phone numbers of both doctors. In fact, the first time I spoke with Paul Berger, Jay's father, he thought I was calling about a molar that was giving me pain.

Dr. Berger was a little surprised that I was interested in his son. Although Jay Berger was ranked in the world top ten, the phone did not ring off the hook with endorsement offers or reporters' inquiries. Compared to what some of the other top players were making, Jay Berger was merely an "everyman." When he started, he did not have a major sneaker manufacturer or racket producer behind him, and in his first two years on tour nobody asked to sponsor him. But after reaching the semifinals at the Lipton, Jay Berger was ranked number seven in the world. There were five hundred players ranked in the world, and about one hundred and fifty figured in most of the important tour events. Jay

Berger was one of the few who did not have a regular coach. By and large, he tried to figure things out for himself.

The first time you saw Berger play, you could not believe he was one of the top-ranked players in the world. Jay Berger had legs like a satyr and a smaller but solid upper body. He had the kind of sympathetic face that a mother could love more than anyone else until the one right girl comes along. That one girl, Nadia, might finally have come along. They were going to find out together on the tour that spring in Europe, where Nadia came from. Berger had a fine smile off the court, but on court he looked a little unhappy, which was deceptive again, because he was enjoying himself. He looked slow, but he was not. He wore a small black support over his left knee, which made opponents think he could not move, but he was a great scrambler. Jay Berger's ground strokes looked like he never took a lesson in his life, and that was not true, but his heavy topspin forehand and two-handed backhand were what many tennis purists called plain or "ugly," and what Berger's coach from Clemson University, Chuck Kriese, called "funky."

Tennis players' strokes are like baseball players' batting stances. There are not two the same. Jay Berger was like a Rusty Staub or Joe Morgan at the plate. He looked a little funny up there, but he was very good through the ball, and that's where it counts.

Watching Jay Berger reminded most people of their own playing abilities. Berger was much better, but he did not *look* that much better. He looked vulnerable, and sometimes he was. He lacked the polished surface of Edberg, Becker, or McEnroe so that nearly everyone underestimated Jay Berger—except Jay Berger. After he beat Australian Wally Masur 6–3, 6–4 on the blue indoor carpet laid over the hockey ice at the Philadelphia Spectrum, Masur, who had a smooth, classic-looking Australian serve and volley game, came off court shaking his head and said, "He's bloody tough, mate."

The very look of his game lulled people into a false sense of superiority. They were headed down the wrong track from the time the first ball was hit. Meanwhile, Berger was climbing down into himself, figuring out what he had to do to allow the limitations in his own game to overcome the strengths of his flashier opponents. In a sense, Berger was the perpetual underdog.

Clemson University, located in South Carolina, is well known for its football team, which won a national championship in 1981. But the tennis team, coached by Chuck Kriese, the best interview since Bobby Knight, had also been a national powerhouse since almost the day Kriese arrived.

Coaches in any sport tend to know more about a boy or girl than anyone but the parents, certainly more than most of their academic teachers. It is in sports that all the strengths and weaknesses of personality seep through for all to see. The coach is the person who sees it all and tries to improve on it. Coach Kriese talked about tennis with the intense, slightly Southern voice of a man who has thought about aspects of the game from the first thing in the morning to the last of the day. The coach had the philosophical spirit of a man who had tried to figure it all out and still could not quite predict which of his players was going to be a winner.

"You see," said Chuck Kriese, "Jay Berger was so underestimated by everybody. By some people he still is. The U.S. Tennis Association asked Jay to play Davis Cup against Mexico this year, and he won both matches, but it was the first time they ever contacted him. Back then, back in his junior tennis days, the USTA was not interested in Jay Berger. They tended to look at the tinsel, the sizzle, instead of the substance, in a player. Some associations still have a tendency to look for the talent from the *outside* instead of from the inside. But that is not the way to discover talent. You have to look for real talent from the *inside* out. A lot of these young kids look great when they are junior players, but a couple of years later, you just can't depend on them to get the job done. I look for three things in every player: a great head, a great heart, and great legs. Jay Berger has all three. There are very few players out there in the world who are as good in pressure situations as Jay. He is a great crisis management player. He can be down a set and down a service break, and he'll manage that crisis and come back to win the match. That's tennis. That's *crisis management*.

"The first time I saw him, Jay was seventeen and losing in the first round of the national juniors at Kalamazoo, Michigan, to a kid his age. I saw him fight his guts out, dive for the balls on cement, scratch and dig—and lose. I found him outside the stadium at Kalamazoo under one of the oak trees old Rolla Anderson planted out there. Jay was almost crying. He was seventeen. He had lost in the first round of the national juniors. I spoke to him. I'm glad I did.

"One year later, after his freshman year of college, Jay Berger won the U.S. National Juniors, and two months after that he got to the round of sixteen at the U.S. Open. That's an amazing leap in fourteen months. I'd like to say I had a lot to do with it here at Clemson, but it was him," said the coach.

"Talent is nothing," continued Kriese, "especially when you talk about the top hundred players in the world. The difference is mostly what they have inside. Jay never won a junior tournament before he came to Clemson, but he had had the right balance between push and love from his parents. Plus, he had the legs. That's an ideal situation. That meant he did not get down on himself when he lost, and he kept pushing himself to do better. His freshman year, Jay played number four on the Clemson team, and he did not get invited to play in the NCAA tournament.

"Now this was a big point in his development. Jay had a year of eligibility left in the juniors. Most college freshmen pass up that last junior year and go off to play pro satellite tournaments. They are content to take losses in situations where they are not expected to win. I told Jay and his father to go back and play the junior tournaments again. It all has to do with being able to push the right *recall buttons*. If the best Jay had done as a junior was a first-round loss at Kalamazoo, I believe that later in his career he would accept that level. All the players push their recall buttons—or get them pushed. A recall button is your past plus your own current self-image, basically your current self-esteem. Jay needed to win something. And that was my point with Jay and his father. It is a lot tougher to go back down to the juniors and win at that level, when you would be a 'good win' for somebody else—and when you are expected to win because you are a year older—than it is to skip the last year of your age group, flash around against the pros on the satellite tour, and lose. Nobody will blame you if you lose against the pros. But I wanted Jay to get a recall button that said, 'I am not afraid to face real pressure.' I wanted him to face his peers. I told Jay and his father to forget the pros and go back and try to win Kalamazoo.

"And by God, he did. He surprised all of us. Jay won the national clay court juniors in Louisville without losing a set, and then he won the U.S. National Juniors in Kalamazoo in five tough sets over Woody Hunt, one year after I saw him almost crying out under that oak tree in Kalamazoo after losing in the first round. Jay had made an imprint for himself, psychologically speaking: he had won when he had a lot to lose and not much to gain. Because if he had lost, he might have been finished. But he was getting good at crisis management. And *crisis management* is the key to tennis at whatever level."

Coach Kriese had seen thousands of players at junior tournaments, and very few ever made it into the world top ten. "What Berger did *not* do was try to bail out of the pressure. See, most tennis players seek a comfort level. It's habit forming. There are second-round players. Other guys are happy if they reach the round of sixteen or the quarter-finals.

And then there are the finalists and the champions, who get used to winning and demand it from themselves. After Jay Berger went back to win the U.S. Juniors and then got to the round of sixteen at the U.S. Open, it was time for him to turn pro. He had established the right recall button."

"What's the recall button again?" I asked.

"It's your past history plus your current self-esteem. That's your recall button in a crisis situation." You could almost see the college coach late at night doodling the formula for winning at the kitchen table,

Own past history + current self-esteem = Your Recall Button

Coach Kriese was right—a little crazy, but right. The coach was suitably focused, like a scholar deep in his work.

"Tennis is simple really. If you don't have the self-esteem, you won't win. It's that simple. People do on court what they have done on court in the past. To my way of looking at things, tennis is a game about the head first, then the legs, and the shots are third in importance. Jay's father and mother were smart in raising him. He always had the good work ethic. But if he had turned pro a year earlier—before he started college—I think he would have burnt out by now. He wouldn't have established the right recall button."

"What kind of a kid is Jay Berger?" I asked Kriese. Jay Berger was twenty-three. He seemed fairly quiet, very confident in a young, not fully formed way. He seemed to be a player who was prepared to do battle the minute he stepped onto a court, a person most comfortable, confident, and at home on the tennis court.

"Jay is a rebel," said his former coach, surprising me. "A free thinker. Bright. The type of player you like to have on court playing for you in a crisis situation. Jay is a right-brain type."

"A right-brain type? Is that someone who does what they're told?"

"Just the opposite," said Coach Kriese. "The rebels are right-side-of-the-brain people. The left-brain kid is the one you say, 'Jump!' to, and they say, 'How many times?' It's a lot easier to coach those kids. And I'm not saying Jay did not know how to practice. But he was a rebel. He did not put out in practice like a fellow we all loved at Clemson, Lawson Duncan."

"Oh, yes. I saw Lawson lose in Philadelphia to Petr Korda."

"Well, we love Lawson at Clemson. He got to the NCAA college final for us, but Jay Berger had something else even though he never excelled in college. Jay played number four on the team. He beat Lawson in the ATP final at Charleston last year. Lawson was a fine player and easier to coach. Jay didn't practice shots or rally a lot. He just played hundreds and hundreds of sets. He didn't care how he *looked*. He was practicing from the word 'go' *to compete*. It's much easier to coach the other type of player, but by God you need those rebel right-brain kids to win with."

"What about McEnroe?"

"John McEnroe was a right-brain rebel kid and he has sort of a funky-looking game, too. But Harry Hopman, the old Australian coach, saw what was there. He took on McEnroe like a project. You take a rebel and give him a work ethic and you may have a champion there. Rebels prosper. The perfect, all-American kid we're all taught to look for, they just can't get the job done at crunch time. Unfortunately for John McEnroe, Harry Hopman died in about 1983. If he had lived, there's no telling how good McEnroe could have been, because Hopman knew how to give a rebel discipline.

"It's tricky," continued Kriese. "Some kids *look* like rebels, but they aren't really. It's all a show. Those kids with the store-bought, beautiful strokes seem so strong, but a lot of times the strokes just cover up the weakness—and that's the way they compete. In college a player can hide his weaknesses with talent—but not in the pros. On the tour you can find out how someone is getting on with their wife or girlfriend just by watching a set." Kriese chuckled. "The winners win. The thing I like about Michael Chang is the same thing I like about the Berger kid: he has a great head, great legs, and a great heart."

"The strokes are really just an accent you talk with."

"That's right."

"I've got to ask you a funny question. Are you responsible for teaching Jay Berger his serve?"

"Oh, no," said Kriese, almost laughing. "It's certainly not the kind of serve you'd expect from a player ranked number seven in the world. But that's part of Jay's mystique. He psychs the hell out of people. But no, Jay Berger did not learn that serve here at Clemson. He arrived with it on campus."

"How would you describe his service motion?"

"Well, I'd say it's like a pitcher pitching out of the stretch position instead of pitching out of a full wind-up."

"Then what makes him so tough to beat? His game *looks* vulnerable. But it's not."

"The thing with these young players is that most of them are up and down. They are all pushing that recall button, or getting it pushed for them. They are recalling what they have done in the past and they play on their current self-esteem. That's their psychological base. A fellow like Jay Berger has faced the pressure of being someone else's good win. The players who ducked the pressure or skipped it somehow have games that look like Swiss cheese to me. Jay Berger filled in all the holes. He is at the point where he has narrowed down the difference between his worst day and his best day. And *that's* a big deal. Say on Jay's best day, on a scale of one down to ten, he's a two or three. Becker or Edberg are one or twos. Well, now, on his worst day, Jay's only a five or six. He's still going to beat a lot of people on a five day. But it's the players who have a swing between a high of one or two and a low of eight or nine who never make it. Inconsistency. I wonder about this kid Pete Sampras," said the Clemson coach.

"I like Sampras," I said. "But I like Berger, too. They're so different. They're like the prince and the pauper when it comes to talent."

"Well, that's right. Talent doesn't always win," said Kriese. "You don't know for sure how Pete Sampras is going to turn out. He does have great talent, greater than Jay Berger's, except maybe when it comes to winning *consistently*. I don't know for sure about Pete Sampras's recall button, but I've got an opinion. Pete Sampras never won a national tournament in his own age division. And that bothers me. See, there's a new number-one junior player that comes along each year, but it helps psychologically out on the tour to know you were the best in your final junior year. The first time I saw Pete Sampras," said the forty-year-old coach—young enough to still have the spark and old enough to remember—"Pete was thirteen and his folks had him skip the fourteen-and-unders and played him in the sixteen-and-unders at Kalamazoo. Everybody was going crazy because he was so young. But I thought he should have been playing in his own age group and winning. It will be interesting to see how Sampras does when he comes of age and people *expect* him to win. He's still a prodigy, not quite a man. But maybe Pete Sampras's recall button will tell him for his whole career 'I'm an up and down player.' His parents always took him out of his own age group and put him way ahead of himself. Pete's tremendously gifted *physically*, but *mentally*, you need the right recall button, and you only get that by facing the music in your own age group, where it hurts most to lose." The intense coach paused to reflect.

"I definitely think some parents move the kids out of their own age group too soon. The worst travesty is this child prodigy business. Jennifer

Capriati. That's Mozart stuff, starting that early. It's freaky. And I don't think it's so good for the kids. I say give the kids three years to learn the game, because this is a game you have to *know* how to play. At age eleven to fourteen, let the kid start competing. By sixteen or seventeen, they should be winning a tournament. What kills me is how the college girls are packing it in by the time they are twenty. If they haven't made it big by then, they just quit. That's crazy. In my opinion, a young player does not reach her prime when she's fourteen or fifteen, but in the area of nineteen to twenty-five. The kids are starting too early and quitting too early. A boy should be in his prime between twenty-three and thirty. That's where Jay Berger is. Right on schedule. The boys mature a little later. But most boys are quitting by the age of twenty-three or twenty-four. Physically, the boys and girls can both do it when they are younger. They've shown that. But what *burn out* means is that the emotional and mental part of the boy or girl has not caught up to the physical development. There's no pressure in the beginning: it's all up-hill, and that's the easy part. But then they're up there—and they can't handle it, emotionally. Sooner or later, all of them want to be little boys or girls. So why not let them do it in chronological order?"

"Prodigies don't wait," I said, though I followed his reasoning for *most* young players.

"The problem with this country," said Coach Kriese, "is that it's what I call a 'microwave society.' We rush things. We want to put a T-bone steak into a microwave. And we ruin the steak. We want it right away from these kids. Instead, what's wrong with a nice stew? You put it on the back burner. You stir it now and then. You let it cook. Then, when you go to serve it, the stew is ready and it tastes real good. Now that's Jay Berger. They couldn't microwave Berger. And by taking it slow with him, but pushing at the same time, his parents gave him confidence and the feeling that he was loved. That's a real fine stew," Coach Kriese laughed warmly. "You can come back in tennis matches on that kind of stuff. I say, 'Throw out the microwave!' "

I laughed. I liked this coach. He cared about his players, and he had a sense of humor. And he understood the meaning of a *recall button* to Jay Berger and all the other players ranked in the top twenty in the world. Coach Kriese's final words from South Carolina came back to me.

"A lot of these kids look like a Mercedes when you first see them hit, but if you're going to win the Indianapolis 500—or even get somewhere in the U.S. Open—forget the paint job. You better look under the hood."

So I looked a little further under the hood of Jay Berger's tennis vehicle: himself.

"Jay was very small when he was a kid," said Paul Berger to me by phone from Florida when I called after nine one Sunday night. "Jay just picked up the racket one day. I laid it in front of him when he was about four or five years old. And the way he holds it today is the same way he picked it up back then."

I saw this pale embryo of a kid, small as a tennis ball, floating around in the imagination of his father. I saw him as a tennis player before he was born, an idea in his father's competitive mind. The father, Paul Berger, talked gently now about his son, as if somehow they were related but had been separated a bit by the circumstances whereby his twenty-three-year-old son had won more money in three years with a racket— nearly $700,000—than the father had made in ten years as a dentist. Fathers and sons. There was the source and there was the rub. But there was great love and admiration in the voice of the father, something you did not always see on the junior circuit.

"Jay always played on the public-park courts here in Florida, and when you do," laughed Paul Berger, "anything can happen. You can be ready to serve or hit an overhead, and a wino will come up behind the court and shout something at you."

"Jay has a great ability to concentrate. Is part of that fear, I mean, *respect* for the other player?"

"I think so. But at an early age, seven or eight years old, Jay was already very competitive. *Very competitive.*"

"How do you know he was competitive at age seven or eight?"

"You just know," said Dr. Berger. "You can see it in them. They start fighting with each other over the net. Jay got into a lot of arguments on the court when he was seven and eight, and even though he was always much smaller than the others, he would never back down. That's what I mean by competitive. The ones who stood up for themselves won, and the kids who didn't and were just real nice on court all the time generally lost.

"Jay's older sister, Cheri, was a player," continued Dr. Berger. "She was not that talented, but she did well enough to get a scholarship to Wisconsin. Jay's younger sister Andrea, who is twenty now, was ranked number one in the country in the sixteen-and-unders, and she played for Florida in college. Our third daughter doesn't want to play tennis. I think the youngest one was frightened off by having to live up to the expectations. The pressure was too much for her."

I nodded. Jay Berger was a second child, and second children were often very good triers. It was toughest on the youngest. I was a firstborn and had had my own struggles. I liked the way Jay Berger kept fighting and kept trying no matter how far down he was. "Jay was not a star when he was growing up."

"That's right. He won the National Juniors, and he grew a lot that year, but that was by far the best he had ever done. Jay's pattern as a kid was that he'd be ranked about number thirty or forty in the country his first year in the age division—the ten-, twelve-, fourteen-, and sixteen-and-unders—and the second year in the division he would get ranked number seven or eight, but never higher. He was inconsolable when he was seventeen and lost in that first round at Kalamazoo. Chuck Kriese was the only coach to recruit Jay after that loss and offer him a scholarship. When Jay won Kalamazoo his last year in the juniors, it gave him great confidence, really for the first time. But he was always very competitive, even when he could *not* beat anyone. Jay always took a loss very hard. To lose was like dying. That's the way the little kids are. The competitive ones feel like they are dying when they have lost. You can't console them. It's different for adults. We know better." He laughed.

"Did you have a tennis background yourself, Dr. Berger?"

"No. I took the game up as an adult. About the time Jay was four or five."

"What was it about tennis that you, as a parent, wanted for your child?"

"Prestige. A feeling of accomplishment, of excelling at something. We'd look at the top juniors of Jay's junior days, a Robbie Weiss or Aaron Krickstein or Luke Jensen, the boy who played with two forehands, and we'd say, 'Look what they're getting.' Trips all over the country, to Mexico, even to Europe. The parental motivation is to look out on the courts where all the kids are playing and be able to say, 'My kid's out there and he's number one or two.' That's it. And I think it's the same for all the parents. You feel like a big shot if your kid is number one. The parents get *very* involved. I don't care what the other parents say. The parents have a lot of expectations with their kids in tennis. If they tell you differently, that's a lot of bull," said Jay Berger's father.

"I guess it could get pretty competitive among the parents out on the junior circuit."

Dr. Berger laughed and exhaled. "It was something I will never forget. Jay was never a top kid player. The parents of the highly ranked kids walked around the tournament site as if *they* were all seeded. Some of the tournament parents would not let their kids practice with the other kids. They were afraid their children might improve the other children and be passed by them. Can you believe that? There were a few nice parents who understood what it was all about. But I remember one father in the twelve-and-unders. Jay had split sets with this man's son for the first time. Twelve-year-olds. The other boy was much higher ranked than Jay. The father grabbed the son by the neck between sets and shouted, 'How could you lose a set to this kid Berger! He's *terrible!*' Of course the other kid collapsed in the third set. Jay didn't look like much even then, and for quite a while he wasn't. I know that has helped him out now on the pro tour. He doesn't have unreasonable expectations. He doesn't put that pressure on himself."

"Did you ever do the wrong thing yourself watching Jay?"

"Once. When Jay was eight or nine, he lost to a boy I really thought he should beat. I got so upset. I frightened him. I yelled and yelled at him after that match. I realized what I'd done the next day. It was a catharsis. I promised myself never again to let him feel I was disappointed if he lost. My wife and I both got crazy at the junior tournaments, but we've learned to handle the pressure now just like Jay has, and we don't get as disappointed anymore if he loses. Some kids tried so hard to please their parents by winning. That doesn't work out, though. As parents, you have to just let the kid win or lose. They're trying so hard. Some kids felt everybody would love them if they won. But the pressure of *not losing* gets to be too great for a lot of them. Some kids cracked and rebelled against their parents and even lost on purpose. I saw lots of kids just hit the ball right down into the net while their parents were standing behind the court, dying on every point. Jay was one of the kids who got through it. He still felt loved even when he lost. Chemistry between the parents and children is the big instrument in tennis. Not the coach. Unless the coach becomes substitute parent."

"Andre Agassi really has a father-son relationship with Nick Bollettieri, doesn't he?"

"Nick is very powerful," said Paul Berger.

"How?"

"When giving a love feeling. When you're winning. Tennis is very parental with Nick."

"He's done a lot for the great young players. Maybe not so hot with the kids who are not going to the top."

"That's exactly right." Paul Berger sighed. "That's this country, I'm afraid. But I'd never say anything bad about Bollettieri. He means very well."

"Tell me. Was there quite a lot of cheating, or not, on the junior circuit? We used to call a bad line call 'getting hooked.' "

"Definitely. Absolutely," laughed Dr. Berger. "The young kids hooked each other fiercely. Usually what happened was the good players knew who the fair kids were and who the hookers—the cheaters—were. Jay got hooked quite a bit. One kid in particular, who was good as a junior but has never quite made it as a pro, was a terrible hooker and a very good junior player. It hurt him in the long run. You can't do it in the pros."

"In New York, some of the kids used to laugh and say, 'When in doubt, call it out.' But like you said, everyone knew who the cheaters were, and the best players did not cheat. Tell me this. How did your son beat Boris Becker six–one, six–one?"

"I think Boris underestimated Jay. Jay has not beaten him since then, but that day at Indian Wells, California, Boris must have come out super-confident and bored. My wife got a call from Jay that night, and he said, 'Mom. I beat Becker today, one and one.' We were all on cloud nine."

"Not too many people get to say that. Was that Jay's big breakthrough match?"

"Not really. The real breakthrough came when Jay was fifteen at the Easter Bowl Tournament in Miami. It was a very dramatic match. The kid he was playing against collapsed on court twice from heat exhaustion. Jay was limping around the court on torn cartilage, but he would not stop. The other boy finally collapsed a third time in the heat and defaulted in the third set. Jay was so competitive. After the match, he dropped down onto the court and told us to get him to the hospital fast. The other kid had heat exhaustion, but Jay's knee cartilage was really torn badly. A few hours after that match, at age fifteen, Jay had knee surgery. He still wears the black knee patch he got as a result of that surgery. That was his breakthrough match, though. He kept going, and the other kid did not."

"Why did Jay make it on the tour and some of his contemporaries not make it?"

I could almost hear Dr. Berger wince. "A lot of the kids were over-hyped as juniors. That's extra pressure. One boy we know won the U.S. Juniors at seventeen, but now in the Men's he throws up before each match. The kids are so tough on themselves. Jay is just a better competitor. I think it's because he learned early how to lose. That was the important thing. The kids who won all their matches could never handle losing. Jay lost quite a bit. When Jay's turn finally came to win, he was ready. He never *thought* he was going to win. He never *expected* it. Winning is still a great thrill for him. But Jay was never afraid to lose. He had done it so much."

"Did you ever in your wildest dreams think he would be ranked number seven in the world?"

"Never. He was not very well schooled in tennis. I didn't really know how to play."

"I saw him beat Goran Ivanisevic at the Lipton."

"You saw one of his better matches. Jay was on that day."

"He digs in, Dr. Berger. He makes the most of what he's got. Do you remember what it was like when Jay was a kid, and you got to the tournament and you went up to the draw to see who Jay was playing? Do you remember that feeling?"

"Oh, yes. I always will. The draw is always a very tense place. Jay still doesn't like to look at it. He still won't peek ahead in the draw. When he was a young kid, I'm talking about the ten-, twelve-, and fourteen-and-unders, Jay was always frightened by the draw sheet. Whenever he *thought* he would get to a certain round, he would lose. The draw sheet was always in the center of wherever the tournament happened to be held. The parents and the children would huddle around it, especially on the first day. The little kids looked scared to death of the other names. If they knew they had to play somebody tough, the kids would say, 'Gee, I got a tough draw.' The parents would come away from the same draw sheet, and they'd say, 'I've got to play so-and-so in the quarter-finals.' The kids were the realists. The parents were the optimists or the fanatics. The draw was more than trying to see who you played first," said Paul Berger. "I think we were all trying to guess how far we would get."

PORTUGAL, SPAIN, ITALY, AND FRANCE

The European red-clay court season is one of the most grueling yet enjoyable parts of the pro tour. The tennis is tough. The settings are the best of old Europe.

The athletes were glad to be back outdoors after the "perfect" neon artificial conditions indoors in Stockholm, San Francisco, and Memphis, and after the Lipton in blustery March in Florida, where Lendl in particular was displeased with the natural atmospheric conditions, the wind and the humidity. The red clay in Europe was not suited to everybody's game. It put an emphasis on athleticism, not sheer power. The larger a player's size, generally the less his overall mobility. Few American bodies had excelled over the years on the red clay. Before Chang in 1989, the last American to win the French Open was Tony Trabert in 1955. Red clay, the European surface, was always intended to be an equalizer against the more powerful American, Australian, and English players whose "big games" were better rewarded on the English grass or American cement.

Jay Berger was one of the few American players—Chang, Courier, and Agassi were the others—whose tennis game and attitude were well suited to the European red clay, a surface of strategy, legs, and guts that often gave a player time to recover between shots. The deep clay made the balls heavy and slowed an attacker's killer instincts into a long, drawn-out European battle of wills.

The red-clay court season started in Estoril, Portugal, at a beautiful, tree-lined public park with its 1930s fascist-era tennis stadium. The European season Berger faced was eight tournaments and twelve weeks long, culminating in the Grand Slam event of the red-clay season, the French Open in Paris.

In a sense, all parts of the red-clay season pointed to Paris, just as all grass roads led to Wimbledon and all concrete roads led to the U.S. Open. Paris was the big pay day and the most beautiful city in the world. But between Portugal and Paris, Jay Berger and his fiancée, Nadia, saw all the major tennis centers in Europe except Wimbledon, since grass was a surface that Berger, knowing himself, would not play on, saying, "Grass is for cows." Very few players tried to play in all eight of the major European red-clay championships, one after the other over the course of twelve weeks. Thomas Muster, the Austrian left-hander, also played all twelve weeks on the European red clay. The gutsy Muster still had a slight limp, but he was built like a gladiator everywhere except his damaged left leg, which would never be the same after being struck by a car doing thirty-five miles an hour.

Jay Berger flew to Portugal. Ranked seventh, he was accompanied for the first time by a traveling coach, José Higueras, the former Spanish Davis Cup star who used to slide so effectively on the red clay in the manner of his great countrymen, Manolo Santana and Manuel Orantes. Higueras, who would be hired by a struggling Jim Courier early in 1991, stayed with Jay Berger right across Europe. Nadia joined them in Monte Carlo. The major European red-clay stops were:

TOURNAMENT	LOCATION	1990 WINNER
Estoril Open	Estoril, Portugal	Sanchez, E.
Trofeo de Godo	Barcelona, Spain	Gomez
Philips Open	Nice, France	Aguilera
Monte Carlo Open	Monaco	Chesnokov
Madrid Open	Madrid, Spain	Gomez
German Open	Hamburg, Germany	Aguilera
Italian Open	Rome	Muster
French Open	Paris	Gomez

In Barcelona, the big Ecuadoran Andres Gomez, accustomed to the red clay at home, said that he went to pray to the Virgin Mary at the Catholic shrine of Fatima because he had been playing so poorly. His prayers apparently were answered for the well-traveled South American left-hander, demolished by Sampras on the faster hard surface in the United States, went on to win not only Barcelona but Madrid and Paris. Spain's Juan Aguilera, who is smooth and slender like a matador, beat Boris Becker in the finals of the German Open by the one-sided clay-court scores 6–1, 6–0, 7–6, proving that speed and agility counted far more on the European red clay than Becker's heavy-thighed strength. The Russian Andrei Chesnokov, the only male player with a female coach, played two great matches with Austrian Thomas Muster. The dour Russian beat Muster in the bright sun of Monte Carlo at the terraced tennis club overlooking the blue Mediterranean and then lost to the incredible Austrian in the final of Rome's great tournament, the Italian Open. The Italian crowd, which had seen the Austrian pushed onto center court in a wheelchair a month after the accident in Florida, went wild with Latin appreciation for his return just one year later in the final. The muscular blonde Austrian beat Chesnokov in their rematch, 6–1, 6–3, 6–1. Had it not been for the terrible accident, which he had partially overcome, Thomas Muster might have become the number-one player in the world. He had been lightning fast, as strong as Lendl, and a better natural athlete. But even with a damaged leg, Muster possessed the speed, stamina, and inner fight of champions.

Gomez stunned the world and Andre Agassi in the finals in Paris.

Looking like Anthony Quinn in *La Strada*, the six-foot four-inch Ecuadoran had enough time—European, South American time—on the red
clay to absorb Agassi's one-speed, blistering American attack. The Las
Vegas prodigy played as if he had been not only nervous, which is natural,
but also limited as a traveler and a person, because Andre knew only
one way to be and one way to play—the faster American way. Unable
to adapt to the European setting, Agassi argued with the French president of the International Tennis Federation, Philippe Chatrier, who said
that Agassi's Nike clothes made him look like a walking billboard. The
Las Vegas boy called the Frenchman a hypocrite, pointing to the Lacoste,
Granini, and Banque de Paris placards around every inch of the red-clay
center court.

As usual, Agassi attracted all the attention. Most French fans, including the eighty-six-year-old Rene Lacoste, embraced Andre for his
baseline game, his flair and color. But someone else *won*. The veteran
Gomez mugged Agassi on the soft red clay, taking the pace off, then
putting it back on. Nick Bollettieri did his best to console his young,
wounded player, and they hurried home. The joyous Gomez, instead of
flying to England to practice for Wimbledon, flew back to Quito and
drank French champagne for a week at fourteen thousand feet above sea
level. Seeded at Wimbledon, Gomez lost in the first round and never
won another major tournament.

Jay Berger did not win any of the major tournaments in Europe, a
result that did not surprise me as much as it surprised some of the
Europeans. Berger was the reigning U.S. clay court-champion, a title
Andre Agassi had held the year before. But no Americans won tournaments on red clay in Europe that year. Based on his number-seven world
ranking, Jay Berger was seeded number one in Estoril, Portugal. The
tournament was held in the beautiful, flowering public park where the
Portuguese government of the 1930s built their lasting tennis stadium.
In Portugal, Berger lost in the quarter-finals 7–5 in the third set to Spain's
tenacious and quick Jordi Arrese, who would crush Bjorn Borg in the
Swede's ill-fated comeback a year later. The American was seeded first
again the following week in Barcelona, but Berger lost in the quarter-
finals in straight sets to stubborn Chesnokov. Still seeded number one
the following week in Nice, the American lost on the Riviera in three
close quarter-final sets to yet another Russian, nimble little Andrei Cherkasov. The Russian's style was quintessentially European: thin legs,
speed, and lots of patience.

There were five tournaments and nine weeks to go in the red-clay European season, but somewhere between Monte Carlo and Madrid, the drain plug seemed to be pulled on Berger. He was a counter-puncher playing on the surface of counter-punchers: red clay. The American was a baseliner, but like Agassi, Berger liked to hit winners from the baseline, easier to do on an American cement court than on the European red clay where Berger, like the slender Europeans and cagey South Americans, had to move the chess pieces around on each point, fighting for an opening.

It helped his spirits when Nadia arrived in Monte Carlo. He had been struggling for a couple of weeks when she joined him in Monte Carlo before Madrid and Germany. His Spanish coach, José Higueras, a red-clay court specialist, could not entirely connect with the American player whose hard ground strokes were slightly mechanical and formal for the sliding style of the former Spanish Davis Cup player. Seeded first for the last time, Berger lost in the first round in Madrid 6–4, 6–3 to an unknown Spanish player. But Nadia was there, and losing hurt a little less because of it. In Madrid, they stayed at the hotel she liked best on the tour, the modern Limalya. It was not easy to concentrate on tennis and see Europe with your fiancée at the same time. Nadia, realizing this, left Berger and Higueras practicing in the mornings on the red clay and went off to see the Europe she had never seen while inside Czechoslovakia.

"When Jay loses," said Nadia, "I am giving it some time. I let him think about it alone, and I go on with him to the next one. I'm not distracting him. I do my own thing in the day. I go for a walk. I go to see the place where we are. I liked Rome the best because there was a lot to do in Rome. I went to the Coliseum and to see the Vatican art collection, which Jay saw the year before. He practiced in the mornings. I did my own thing. No pressure. I can take care of myself. We get together at the end of the day. After the matches. Sometimes we talk about it. Usually not. At the end of the day, we'd go to dinner together. It is so nice that way."

They went to only one big party—in Monaco. It was a bash for the players at Jimmy'z, a former haunt of both Bjorn Borg and Princess Caroline, and the most famous disco on the Côte d'Azur. Another night they ate near the heart of old Monte Carlo, the Hotel de Paris, where the bathrooms are the size of studio apartments and each has its own bidet.

Berger played well when he got to Germany. Seeded fifth with Becker and Agassi both there, Berger reached the quarter-finals in Germany, almost making the semifinals.

Twelve straight weeks of hotels and foreign food—even in Europe— was too much for a twenty-three-year-old from Florida. It was a little tougher on Berger than on Nadia. Even American tourists would tire of twelve weeks of constant travel, changed plans, new faces, and different languages—Portuguese, Spanish, Italian, and waiter-French.

Berger stuck by his plan, but he had planned too much. Eight tournaments sounded good on paper. Agassi only played in one European event, the French Open, in part to peak for the big-money event, in part because the Las Vegas boy felt best at home. Berger, by contrast, took the leap. He played every major clay court event. He had wanted to see Europe.

Berger was exhausted by the time the trip was over. Except for the brief good showing in Germany, it was pretty much downhill for eight weeks after Madrid. The slide culminated in Paris in a first-round, three-set loss to Alberto Mancini, the Argentinian who had himself been ranked tenth in the world the year before and had tumbled on self-doubt right out of the top hundred. Mancini's reprieve was the *coup de grace* for the travel-weary American. Berger wanted a rest. He could not wait to get back home. Everyone in Paris, from the hotel waiters to the tournament officials, seemed a little curt and unfriendly, even in the most beautiful city in the world. He had been away for three straight months of competing, playing both for appearance money and for the money that went with each round in the draw. Paris was a bust. He got $5,500 for losing in the first round, and he and Nadia gladly packed their bags and headed for Orly.

Berger was a player who depended on inner fire to overcome smoother talents. But in the end he had tried to do too much—and he knew it.

"I will never ever try to play this many tournaments in a row again," he told me.

"On this tour," said his father back in Florida, "as soon as you get to a level where you are happy, you aren't going to be there very long. Jay can't just stay at number seven. He has to want to be number three, or he's going to slide back out again. Some of these players are getting fifty thousand dollars just to show. Becker is getting like a hundred and fifty to two hundred thousand just to play. As soon as you're satisfied on tour, you are lost. I don't think Jay is satisfied, but I hope not. I'd like to tell this to Jay. He calls up, but I can't tell him anything anymore. He doesn't want to hear anything from me. I bet you could tell it to him easier than I could. I'm his father."

"The appearance money is a mess," I agreed. "If they're going to have it so they can guarantee the players for the television, they should make the appearance money competitive, too. If you win, you get more. In that case, maybe you've earned your appearance. It all has to be on an incentive basis. Otherwise, you take the incentive out of winning."

"I think that might have started to happen to Jay. They are starting to give him a little appearance money. It's about forty thousand an event. The top four plus McEnroe get four times that. But it worries me. If they take the incentive out of Jay's game, he is finished. The incentive of winning is everything for Jay."

"He's a trier," I said. "I've never seen him quit."

Berger gave it all he had in Europe. He took and banked the money, and the European currencies came with a fine exchange rate. But he was exhausted. He needed two weeks solid of sleep and sun and walks with Nadia in Florida—and only after that could he start running on the beach to get ready for the Canadian and U.S. Opens, which were going to be played on cement, his number-one surface. It was a business as well as a dream.

Playing the eight red-clay European tournaments, Berger made $60,405—less what he had to pay in hotels, travel, and meals for him and Nadia, and salary for himself and José Higueras. Twelve weeks in Europe for three people. He probably netted $20,000 from the money in the draw. At the Lipton on the American hard courts in Florida, by reaching the semis he made $49,580. But Berger wanted the European trip, in part to be on the road with Nadia, in part because he had been guaranteed in appearance money nearly four times what his draw earnings turned out to be. His business decision was that he was twenty-four and ranked seventh in the world, and if people in Europe wanted to pay Jay Berger $20,000–$40,000 a crack just to show up and play, he'd take it. It was more than flattery. He made nearly $200,000 taking it—not a bad summer's work with a wedding scheduled for just after the U.S. Open in September.

He lost any delusion that he might be a superstar. In Europe, as in America, the press race after the number-one seed and do not stop until he or she has lost. Berger lost. He was by nature a counter-puncher, not an Edberg or a Becker, not quite a star. Jay Berger was a person who did better with a goal, aiming for someone seeded above him, rather than defending himself against all the other players climbing at him from below. He had worked a long shift in Europe.

Berger had given all of himself to the red clay of Europe. The other Americans, less good on clay than Berger, or larger and better suited to a pure serve and volley attack, were heading over to England and the faster surface, Wimbledon's grass. Berger needed a nap. When the short season of English grass-court tournaments began, Jay Berger, completely drained by the red clay, was home in June in Florida, sleeping until ten-thirty in the morning, having coffee with Nadia and lunches at his mother's house in Plantation.

VÄSTERVIK

In Search of Stefan Edberg

The American writer Thomas Wolfe wrote in *Look Homeward, Angel* about how the home is at the center of a person, and later he would write that if you leave a place you can never really return to it. But home is the place where we all start. It is the one thing we cannot escape, even if we choose not to try to go back. Home is deeper than our surface.

Stefan Edberg was an enigma to many of the writers who covered him and to many of the tennis fans who watched and appreciated him. Almost everybody admired Edberg's high, leaping serve, his true volleys, and his appealing demeanor on court, but off the court he offered such a quiet, nearly glassy-smooth surface it was difficult to tell if he was bland and handsome or just shy and handsome in the Swedish way. Ivan Lendl snarls like a Doberman pinscher chained to his baseline. Stefan Edberg has a much longer leash and moves like a greyhound around the court. We spoke about physical things in Florida, the importance of strong stomach muscles and how his court movement was the key to his game. But like Borg before him—though Stefan's taller and plays a completely different game—Edberg seemed hard to get to know, the Greta Garbo of professional tennis.

Edberg left few visible clues, but one of them was his girlfriend, Annette Olson. The attractive Swedish model came from Växjö, eight kilometers from Edberg's hometown of Västervik. As a teenager in the mid-1980s, before becoming smitten with Edberg, she had been the girlfriend of Växjö's own tennis champion, Mats Wilander. Stefan Edberg never talked about it. Annette Olsen had seen more top tennis played around the world than anyone except Don Budge.

They lived in London, in the beautiful old Kensington section of the city, near Hyde Park and the Royal Albert Hall. Though the young Swedish couple had shared a flat together for two years, marriage was still far from Stefan Edberg's mind:

> Neither she nor I am in a hurry. To be married is not at all important to Swedes. We believe more in togetherness and mutual trust. Besides, I'm a typical Capricorn and she is a typical Taurus. When we rush, we rush slowly.

Edberg's tennis earnings had made him a rich man, but he had managed to keep his feet on the ground. At home in the London flat he still washed his own clothes, and on the road and at the matches he carried his own tennis bags, while lesser players often let their coaches carry the bags.

He was a genuine star on the courts. The 1932 Wimbledon and U.S. Champion, Ellsworth Vines, one of the hardest hitters of all time, singled out Edberg over Becker and McEnroe as his favorite player because Edberg's overall serve and volley game was so fluid, so daring, yet so sound. And yet, perhaps the key to Edberg's popularity with women— quite different from Boris Becker's appeal for many men—was that while Edberg attacked relentlessly, he did so without giving the impression of being personally aggressive.

Edberg was good young. His English coach, Tony Pickard, spotted him at a tournament in Milan when Edberg was only fifteen. He is the only player ever to have won the Junior Grand Slam (the Australian, French, Wimbledon, and U.S. Open titles all in one year as a junior player in 1985). Now only twenty-four, the responsibility he took in handling his own life had made the Swede far more mature than many of his contemporaries:

> Tennis is more emotionally draining than people think. Therefore you must not burn all your feelings privately or talk them away publicly. Time is also important. I hate it when people are not on time. I'm

extremely punctual. I don't have time to wait for people who don't respect other people's time. I wait a few seconds, then I leave.

He was a prodigy who did not remain a mere prodigy as a person. The Swede had grown into a man, something his countryman Bjorn Borg had not quite been able to do. Edberg attributed much of his success to what he had learned in Sweden from his parents. He was such a star, and yet his surface seemed so smooth and gentle it was hard to imagine where his fire came from.

"Västervik?" said the Swedish stewardess on the flight to Stockholm. "I've never heard of Västervik. Where exactly is it?"

It was a pale, cloudy day in Stockholm when we landed. Late spring in Sweden still had a touch of winter in the air, though some of the trees in the city were already starting to bloom. Stockholm's classical nine-teenth-century brownstone train station was beautiful, as were the yellow buildings of the city. Anna Karenina would have died well on the Stockholm train tracks.

The express train south from Stockholm was fast, smooth, and handsome with red crushed velvet seats and immaculate white head rests. We crossed the river and looked back at Stockholm with its elegant, northern-European mix of old and new buildings. On my Eurail map, the train from Stockholm reached Västervik only by way of an acute angle. The change was at Linköping (pronounced "Lynn chirping"). After two and a half hours on an elegant Swedish train, suddenly you are in the country, another world entirely. You step down, cross the tracks, and board a little orange country train with two local cars and soiled white head rests, and this smaller, slower train takes you the rest of the way to Stefan Edberg's hometown. Stefan Edberg had left Monaco, where he lost on the red clay in the round of sixteen to Juan Aguilera, 7–6, 7–6. He would be heading to Munich, then on to the French Open, the last red-clay court event, and to Wimbledon, the jewel of the grass-court season in England. I felt I knew him as a striker of the ball. Västervik was the last stop, nearly six hours from Stockholm by train.

The front car was about a third full with incredibly tall blonde kids. An older local woman whose black hair was streaked with gray sat down next to me and snapped her newspaper ceremoniously out in front of her. The conductor standing on the top step of the little train greeted his passengers more like a friendly old schoolteacher than a train conductor. He waved, the engine shuddered, and we were on our way.

The old country train chugged along at a good clip. In Sweden there was far more open land than people or houses on the horizon. The trip to Västervik was a trip back through time to an Ingmar Bergman–like unspoiled countryside. For long stretches of time there were no houses on the horizon. No people. A single, lone old bicycle was leaning up against a tree in the middle of a forest. The landscape between Linköping and Västervik replaced people with the quieter relationship between the trees, the ground, and the curving blue sky. A red barn sat isolated and quiet at a severe angle to the finely tilled brown field below it. Elegant Swedish pine tree branches hung like curtains and swayed in a warm northern wind on either side of the old, straight railroad tracks. It was a simpler world here, at least in appearances.

The houses that infrequently appeared reminded me of Edberg. These old yellow stone houses were not likely to go condo. I saw an immaculate house alone in the clearing of a forest, and by its side stood a flag pole with the bright blue-and-yellow Swedish flag hung for the birds to see. Sometimes Edberg's walls seemed two feet thick and impenetrable. But Edberg was not cold, just very Swedish, as if trying to keep the warmth *inside* himself, where warmth is really needed. His English coach, Tony Pickard, knew that about Edberg, but it was tough to convince the world that quiet people are not necessarily shy.

Little gray country foot paths appeared and disappeared by the side of the railroad tracks. The approach to Västervik was like the approach to a moon landing. There was lots more open land. Glacial rocks. A small lake. The land got rougher as the train approached the east coast of Sweden and Edberg's hometown. Twin power lines stood alone like a tree on a barren hill. As the little orange train gathered speed through the trees, it tooted its whistle. I smiled. We were worlds away from elegant Stockholm, from Monaco and Wimbledon. We were entering the world of Västervik and Växjö, the homes of Stefan and Annette.

Large black-and-white milk cows stood at angles to each other and lifted their heads as a rain cloud passed low over the horizon. Stefan Edberg was a country boy working in a city world. Large, tightly wrapped rolls of hay lay together in a field. Two hundred or so blue-and-orange tilling blades were stacked in an empty lot in a clearing. The train tracks curved in the pale sunlight.

Edberg and Olsen came from a beautiful—but difficult—place to reach. For the last few miles into Västervik, there was only one track in both directions. It was not easy to get to Västervik, and it could not have been easy to get out.

"Västervik! Nexte stoppe!" the conductor called out. And there, tucked up against the railroad track siding, lay a green cement tennis court.

Two large Swedish mansions flashed by at the edge of Västervik. The town had some wealth, but it had not belonged to the Edbergs. His father was a detective with the police. His mother had been a school-teacher and was a housewife. Västervik had been a nineteenth-century sailor town, a place where sea captains took houses near the church at the top of the hill, and the sailors lived farther down the three main streets that descended toward the sea. The Edbergs would have been a second mate's family. Modern two- and three-story concrete buildings now sloped toward the sea, but up above, perched on a raised grass island, sat a fabulous old red church with turrets and towers as wild and fine as any orthodox church in Russia.

There was something normal here, something very human in this seaport town. Parts of Västervik were as charming as Honfleur in France or Nantucket in America. As you walked down the hill from the church and the train station, it was soon clear that the oldest buildings were the best constructed. The Västervik Town Hall, built in 1793, had been painted yellow and dominated a wide square with huge cob-blestones.

The sea was the very end of each street, and I walked toward it. It was a cool Swedish spring day. The harbor itself was placid, calm. Wild geese glided across the surface, and a family of ducks near the old jetty dunked for food, making the only apparent ripples on an otherwise glass-smooth surface.

"*Respect*," said Penny Crisp, the Australian writer, who was also clearly taken with Edberg. "Respect is a key word when setting out to add depth to an Edberg portrait. He gives it to others and wins it effortlessly for himself."

And yet, I sensed here in Västervik the other side of Edberg's nature, his sense of order. "I save my big emotions for the tennis court," he said. "I am sorry. Order and organization are the most important things in life."

It was hard to imagine any crime in a low, hillside port town as pretty as Västervik, but Stefan Edberg's father was the police detective in Västervik in charge of violent crime.

The Edberg house was on the outskirts of town in a modest, modern development with quality white aluminum siding. His younger brother, Jan Edberg, opened the door and let me in. He was seventeen, and his tall bicycle leaned against the side of the house. When we had talked for a while, Edberg's brother brought out the family photo album, and we opened the old brown pages together. Bengt Edberg, the police chief, was a strong-jawed man with very dark hair. It was not a cruel face, nor was it a kind face. Stefan Edberg's father had a strong, no-nonsense face. When I called from the States, I discovered that the police detective spoke only Swedish.

"I thought your father might let you translate a few things for him," I said to Jan. "I wanted to ask him a bit about his detective work. I thought he might have a couple of stories, something a little funny."

Jan Edberg shook his head. "I tell you this," the tall blonde boy said without blinking, "if my father gave you an answer, it would have been a serious one."

Then where did the champion get all his gentleness around the court? The photo of Stefan's blonde mother, Barbro Edberg, was much gentler. The photo of her in the album was round. Dated 1972, it showed a young blonde woman with a smile that was full and very warm. Edberg's mother looked a lot like Donna Reed, the American TV actress of the 1950s; she had a round, classic Swedish face—gentle, kind, smiling, and beautiful. It was Edberg's mother who had first spotted the notice for a children's tennis clinic in the hometown paper. It was Mrs. Edberg who took her well-coordinated eldest boy down for a tryout at the local clay courts at age seven. By the time Stefan was eleven, the national Swedish coaches knew they had a champion. Stefan Edberg had not been a late bloomer like Boris Becker.

"Tell me about tennis in Västervik. When Stefan was growing up, were there very many indoor tennis courts?"

"Yes. And lots of different surfaces. Mostly he was playing on gymnasium floors and on plastic surfaces."

There was nothing faster than playing on boards, no surface that could make you learn to serve and volley better than a wood or plastic gym floor. The ball went so fast on those types of indoor surfaces that Edberg had to learn to put the pressure on fast, or he would have been pressured off the slick court himself. Mats Wilander had perfected the outdoor Swedish red-clay game. Edberg's was a Swedish indoor serve and volley game, smooth and fast as the wood and plastic courts he had grown up on.

"Did Borg's popularity inspire building the indoor courts in Västervik?"

"Well," said Jan slowly in his hesitant, then firm, Swedish way, "they thought about building tennis courts in Västervik for a long time. And they did so."

" 'And they did so!' "

"Yes."

I burst out laughing, and so, finally, did he. The young man was so serious. *And they did so!* The Swedes wanted to become champions at tennis even though there was snow on the ground six months a year. And they did so. The Swedes were very determined characters, especially on cross-country skis or tennis courts.

"Are the winters hard?" I asked.

Edberg's brother shook his head and sighed. "Terrible. Västervik is fine in the summer. The tourists come here from elsewhere in Sweden and from Germany. But the winter," he sighed, dropping his head and shaking it again. "The winters here are *very* cold. And very boring. We are full of gossip here. In Västervik everybody knows everybody. It is like a disease. Cold. Oh, boy!" said Jan Edberg. He started to shake. "Nobody's out and nothin' to do!"

"The wind coming up off the water?"

"The wind is okay. But not the cold. It is down to thirty degrees below zero sometimes. It's difficult to get around. The harbor always freezes over. Yes, it's really cold! Even for the cars. In the morning they don't start."

"Even the Volvos?"

"Ya! Even the Volvos. They don't start either." The seventeen-year-old Swede smiled just as he was about to laugh.

"What about crime in Västervik? Your father is in charge of violent crime. Is this a rough little town?"

"Not like New York. Sometimes there is a little drinking problem."

"I was down by the seaside. Västervik is a beautiful town," I said.

"Yes. It is beautiful," Edberg's younger brother said with a shy smile in his flat, sing-song Swedish voice. "It is so beautiful that everybody wants to leave. But it is not so easy *to* leave. After senior year in high school, all the younger people want to go away. That is for sure. Either for college or for work. But mostly for work. Me?" said the younger brother of the Wimbledon champion. "Yes, I hope to leave one day also. I don't know where I will go. But somewhere in the world. I do not play much tennis. So I will see."

We spoke a little bit longer, hoping Mr. Edberg would return, but the police detective–father was not going to come around. He was hiding like a stag in a forest. I was curious to meet Edberg's mother to see if what made Stefan great as a player was in part the gentleness I had seen in her face. "Could I speak to your mother?" I asked brother Jan.

"No."

The blunt answer was a surprise, and I did not press it.

"You cannot see my mother," Jan Edberg added softly, "because she is not here. My parents have divorced. I live now with my father."

The mother, not the father, had launched her eldest son into tennis, and often it showed in the champion's mannerisms on court, which were less outwardly macho and aggressive than those of many of the other top players. Stefan Edberg, the small-town boy from Sweden, seemed a two-sided player, sometimes flying very high and inwardly happy, sometimes dark, petulant, and moody. Though there was certainly a fierce will underlying Edberg's entire game, it was the blonde, sunny spirit that I liked most and that Edberg used to best advantage. I admired him: he kept his opposing sides so well balanced. And it was that maturity that helped make him a champion.

It was four P.M. and Sweden's beautiful natural light was falling down into the sea. The cab driver heading back into town was particularly outgoing for a Swede. "Stefan Edberg. Oh yes," said the driver with the walrus mustache. "Everybody likes him here. The girls *and* the boys, the old ones *and* the young ones, and that is not so usual."

Back in town, I walked the streets.

The store windows on Main Street had a slight scientific air about them, as small-town shop windows often do. A vacuum cleaner or a lawn mower occupied an entire store window in Västervik, as if to say, "This is not just a useful instrument. It is a scientific discovery. Buy it. Use it." The main business concern in Västervik was Electrolux, famous for its vacuum cleaners. The town was not sophisticated, but it was genuine, like a small town in North Carolina in the 1920s.

I liked the town and the people I met very much. They were friendly, helpful, and unassuming. The stores of Västervik ranged in sophistication from the friendly, well-stocked Baby Bjorn children's store, with snug and colorful winter clothes for kids, to Rune Larsson's Mode For Man, where local fashions lagged a few years behind Stockholm while trying to be a couple years ahead. A big flower store was located next to the town library. Half a block south, the town's only movie house was playing *Gremlins II*, dubbed in Swedish, no subtitles.

The best restaurant in town was the Poseidon, down near the water-front. Prices were much higher than in New York's better restaurants, so I got up from the table a bit sheepishly and walked out. The best buy in town was a Swedish pub where all the smoked salmon you could eat on crisp bread went for about twelve dollars.

There was a strange system for calling taxis in Västervik. At first it was hard to understand why it was devised. Wherever I walked, there were taxi call-boxes along the street. The convenience of it was colossal. There must have been a dozen yellow taxi call-boxes in front of Town Hall. I could not understand why there were so many call-boxes. Then I got it. The winters were long. The drinking was heavy. For snowbound, hard-drinking citizens, a call-box every fifteen feet was a pretty good idea.

Five television channels reach Västervik, and by far the most popular with the young was the "Sky Channel," an all-English channel of fantasy TV and rock 'n' roll. England, not America, was the fantasy land in this small weather-locked Swedish coast town, so pretty and green in summer, so harsh and cold in winter.

Speedy Gonzalez, Västervik's only taco restaurant, seemed a reasonable financial choice for dinner. The thought of take-out Mexican food in Sweden seemed bizarre, but it fit the bill. The kroner had quietly been eating up my dollars.

The taco place was immaculately clean, which meant the food was going to be mediocre, and it was. The young black-haired woman behind the counter put on a tape of Mexican music that sounded better than Linda Ronstadt and her *caballeros*, and prepared some tacos and enchiladas. By the time she had finished talking, I knew more about the underside of Västervik than I could have found by spending the winter there. Gossip was alive and well.

"A lot of kids in Västervik are playing tennis now," she began. "Ever since Stefan Edberg, everybody wants to become a good player. There is one girl now. They say she is going to be the Stefan Edberg of women's tennis. Most of the kids want to go away. It is so small here in Västervik. Everybody knows everybody else. The problem is work. There is no work here for young people. The best is the tourists in summer, but this generation of Västervik kids doesn't want to clean the hotel rooms. The parents used to do it, but the Swedish boys and girls won't do this kind of work anymore. So we do it. The foreigners. In the summer, it is beautiful here. The artists come for their special time, and it is like a big party for two weeks. Drinking is the big thing here." The fourteen-year-old Mexican girl sighed. "The young kids—sixteen or seventeen years old—come in here drunk at night. They are not only drunk, they are *so* drunk when they come in here they can hardly stand."

"The teenage girls, too?"

"The girls, too. Of course."

"Why do they drink so much in Västervik?"

"They are very shy," the Mexican girl said softly. "And when they get drunk, they . . . I don't know. It is easier for them to speak."

"And at school the next day?"

"They point fingers and say, 'She did that. He did that.' If you ask a grown-up man or woman in Västervik, they say, 'Oh. Such a lovely town.' But they don't see the young boys and girls get drunk. And it is not only the young people who drink here. I once saw a group of sixty-year-old women on a bus. They were all drunk. In the local newspaper the grown-ups write in to the editor and say only that it is a shame that all the *children* are drunk. But the older people here are drinking, too. Everybody drinks too much in Västervik. Every Friday and Saturday night, you see the same thing. The kids go to Disco Jackie. It is the 'in' place. At one o'clock at night it's over and they all come here to eat after being drunk. Every weekend night the same." The young Mexican shook her head. "When the Swedish girls go to town, they stop and talk with each other and say, 'Oh. That foreigner boy is looking at me. Those people from Iran and Iraq are awful. We Swedes pay taxes for them, and they drive a Mercedes.' But I know these foreign families don't have money. They live two families—twelve people—in the same apartment here in Västervik, and they buy a Mercedes to show people they have money. The Swedish people here are not so open as in Stockholm."

I thought of a small town in North Carolina in the 1920s and wondered if it was that different here.

"My family and I live on Texas Street," said the young Mexican woman, living in Sweden. "It is the best part of town. People with a little more money live in the part of Västervik called 'America.' "

I thanked her, remembering what Jan had said about all the young people wanting to leave town: "It's so beautiful that everybody wants to leave." Stefan Edberg had left, but he had retained the heart and soul of this modest, coastal town; it stoked his inner fire. Perhaps you could not go home anymore. Stefan Edberg had not. But in Annette Olsen, who came from the even smaller country town of Växjö, Edberg had taken with him the thing that was closest to him, his past.

Stefan Edberg had his mother's inner gentleness and blonde good looks. I could see her shy smile in him, and the twinkle of humor in her eyes was part of that look of confidence that often spread across his face like a mischievous wink. At other times, he seemed insulated, troubled, back inside the thick walls of a house of his own making, suspicious of people the way a police detective could be.

I took the slow two-car orange train with the worn head rests back to Stockholm the next morning. Leaving in the rising early morning Swedish light on the chugging, quaint two-car train, I looked back at the small town and the red church up on the hill, which gave the town such a pervading sense of order when you arrived. Västervik was a town of gentle politeness, quiet friendliness, good manners, and deep alcoholism. It was part of Stefan Edberg, and the champion had risen beyond it.

Look homeward, angel.

When the smooth train with the red velvet seats and clean white head rests reached Stockholm, I bought *The International Herald Tribune*, my favorite paper. They had the scores. Edberg had lost in Paris. He was heading toward London, where he now lived.

WIMBLEDON

"[This] was what she loved: life; London;
this moment in June."
　　　　—Virginia Woolf, *Mrs. Dalloway*

The walk to the All-England Club from the Southfields tube station, the stop before the actual Wimbledon town, sets one in a tennis mood. A visitor from abroad comes up the steep stairs of the brick station built before the Second World War and looks to the right and to the left to see which way the English traffic is coming. The cars seemed to be approaching from all sides, but none of them were coming at me at quite the expected angle. Waiting at the roundabout traffic light, I picked up some blockers from the crowd, looked right, and stepped.

A red double-decker London bus called a Fred Perry Special, named for the Wimbledon champion in 1934, 1935, and 1936, is available for transport from the Southfields Underground station to the Wimbledon tennis grounds if you are prepared to wait for a double-decker bus as long as it may take for another Englishman to win the tournament. Most people walked. The crowd hurried along together past the old row houses marked "For Sale," smelling the honeysuckle in front of the modern brick apartment complexes with rhapsodic English names like Briardale and Osborne House.

In the distance down the road, the muted colors of the crowd backed up at the entrance of the grounds was visible like a human river, and as

106

you walked on, black London cabs roared by on the empty High Road with the same sense of grandeur, panache, and anticipation as the black London taxis that pulled up to the house at the end of Alfred Hitchcock's movie *Dial M for Murder*, starring Ray Milland as the debonair former Wimbledon tennis star and Bob Cummings as the American detective–story writer who saves Grace Kelly from the murderous charm of the tennis player.

There are two Wimbledons: the outside where the cockney ticket touts and oddsmakers rule and inside the All-England Club, where membership is hereditary. Nothing, though, can spoil the deep beauty of the grass courts the first time you see them.

The grounds at Wimbledon are set up in a circle, a bit like the Underground Circle Line in London. The fastest way to get around London and the tennis grounds at Wimbledon is not in a straight line, the American way, but in a circle, the European way. Crowds pack the center of the club near the draw sheets during the tournament. But the edges of the club grounds provide concrete paths and foot bridges that are quiet and nearly empty except for the roses and barbed wire on top of the club's blackened brick wall, which was standing when D. H. Lawrence wrote *Women in Love* and when Winston Churchill talked on radio to a brave city during World War II. It is that sense of history that an American loves in England, and that nostalgia—pick your image of England—that is part of what Wimbledon means to an American like me.

Center Court at Wimbledon is still an impressive place, at least in part because in our modern era it remains so small and old. The little hexagonal tennis stadium with its dark seats and diamond green lawn for a stage seems more like the site of a medieval joust or an outdoor stage for an early production of *Henry IV* than a nineteenth-century reproduction of Shakespeare's Globe Theater. The Center Court is still a magnificently theatrical place, though the modernization of the footpaths and the rest of the grounds gives Wimbledon today a sensation of both the Globe Theater and the more concrete-based National Theater on the south side of the Thames.

Attached to the old Globe Theater Center Court is now a modern five-story building with state-of-the-art BBC television equipment, press rooms, photographers' lockers, and pubs. As I wandered through the thick crowds milling around the draw sheets, I heard a lady from Iowa say, "That new building is a little ugly, but will you look at their lawns!"

I laughed out loud. The grass at Wimbledon on the first day of the tournament was trim but incredibly lush, like the gardens inside the "wilderness" fence in Jane Austen's *Mansfield Park*.

All the hardest-hitting men and women were there. Ivan Lendl, who had won the warm-up tournament at the Queens Club, beating Boris Becker in the final on grass, 6–3, 6–2, after Becker had dropped Edberg in the semis, wanted Wimbledon—the one major thrill he had never had—so badly it was nearly embarrassing. At Wimbledon, Lendl was like a shy, awkward young man obsessed with a woman who was not really interested in him. The confident, aggressive man who had settled in America became again at Wimbledon the lonely, bumbling Czech country boy he had been when he first played in England ten years before. For her part, Wimbledon was the same elegant, sophisticated English woman who could be both cruel and indifferent to her would-be lovers. Wimbledon was as beautiful and as English as the actress Julie Christie, and as elegant as the silver trophy presented each year by the knowledgeable Duchess of Kent. It remained to be seen if Wimbledon would ever accept Ivan Lendl as her champion and her dance partner.

Boris Becker had conquered Wimbledon three times already. The young Greek-American boy Pete Sampras had aspirations to do the same: "My whole season has been pointing to Wimbledon. It's the one tournament I've always dreamed of winning," said Sampras. The shy but determined Swede Stefan Edberg had won once at Wimbledon, but his road of self-expression in England still led directly through Boris Becker. McEnroe had won Wimbledon three times, stirring up and amazing the crowds. Navratilova had won eight times, more than Jack Kramer, more than Bill Tilden, more than anyone but Helen Wills. As the fortnight began, the skin under Navratilova's eyes looked like beaten copper. She was rested but sleepless with desire.

Victory at Wimbledon requires great courage from the man and woman who win there. Modern lawn tennis started in the late nineteenth century and became a true world championship just after World War I. In many ways the courage of that generation of England's finest young men, the lost generation of World War I soldiers, was mimicked in the requirements of grass-court tennis. It was not enough to stay behind the lines. The winner had to vault over the baseline and rush forward across the grass to make the volley, to cut off the enemy's reply or be beaten in the effort. Those who hung back could not win at Wimbledon. To win on grass, you had to come forward into the area of pure instinct and reflex, the net.

"No, you can't always get what you wa-ant!" wailed the duo just two days before John McEnroe's opening match at Wimbledon.

John McEnroe and Vitas Gerulaitis stood on stage at the Hard Rock Cafe in the Mayfair section of London. The two old friends were performing with guitars two nights before McEnroe's first match. The tennis players were trying to get started with their song, but the reverb from Gerulaitis's amplifier would not quiet down. The pre-Wimbledon party at the American bar for homesick Americans and trendy young Londoners was packed with tennis players, wives, and girlfriends. Every year now, the star tennis players and famous rock 'n' rollers were invited to jam together before the start of Wimbledon. John McEnroe, seeded fourth at the tournament, was always there. Becker and Edberg never were. And Ivan Lendl was back at his hotel riding his exercise bike.

In 1760, James Boswell, the tousle-haired rebellious son of a highly successful Scottish lawyer, came to London full of hope, mischief, a love of pretty actresses, and a wild streak that was self-destructive and nearly uncontrollable. Boswell met Dr. Johnson and found his life's work in writing biography.

In 1990, John McEnroe, the still rebellious son of a highly successful Irish-American lawyer, came back to London to win a tennis tournament and to have a good time. But McEnroe on stage at the Hard Rock Cafe two nights before he faced Derrick Rostagno was like Boswell without Dr. Johnson. Instead of the wise and humorous Dr. Johnson, the mentor and older friend Boswell had finally found through admiration of another, McEnroe had chosen as his older friend and mentor, well . . . Vitas Gerulaitis.

McEnroe, playing guitar left-handed, nodded at Gerulaitis and Mick Jones, the plump lead guitarist for the rock band Foreigner, and the celebrity band broke into song. Where did he think he was? Delta Mississippi? Who did McEnroe think he was? B. B. King or Eric Clapton? This was Mayfair, for four hundred years the most fashionable section of London. This was not East St. Louis, and John McEnroe was never going to be B. B. King.

Mats Wilander, another tennis star who had fallen head over heels for the guitar, described McEnroe's guitar playing this way: "McEnroe's music is like his tennis: loud, screaming. I play music like my tennis, too: not loud, not flashy."

I felt a sympathy for Mats Wilander with his guitar that I sometimes was lacking toward McEnroe. It was life itself and an expression of sorrow that Wilander found in his guitar. His young father, a foreman in a Swedish manufacturing plant in Växjö, had died that spring at age fifty-two after working six-day weeks for thirty years. Mats had worked the same way on the tennis court, and after his father died, super-work-manlike tennis suddenly seemed crazy to Wilander.

Unlike Agassi, who rarely showed dark emotion, McEnroe had the anger, the imp of the perverse. Where did it come from? There was a little bit of Edward G. Robinson's *Little Caesar* in John McEnroe. He seemed to want to be a tough guy, not the son of a wealthy lawyer. I understood him. He would back down from nobody to prove he was his own man. But at thirty-one, McEnroe was still rebelling. That was his way with the tennis racket, that was his sound with a guitar. Rebellion and anger.

A tennis aficionado watching McEnroe and Gerulaitis sing the old Rolling Stones hit with a band of rock musicians at the Hard Rock Cafe off Grovesnor Square, the equivalent of New York City's Fifth Avenue at Fifty-ninth Street, could not help but wonder if John McEnroe should have been home doing sit-ups.

"What is the last thing you want to do when you wake up in the morning?" McEnroe asked Robin Finn of the *New York Times*. "Sit-ups," he exclaimed, "I know I could talk myself out of doing them."

Of course, he had. Speaking of Ivan Lendl with all the scorn that the genius has for the triumphant lesser talent, McEnroe said, "What chance do I give Lendl of winning Wimbledon? Zero. But I will say, when it comes to preparation, Lendl gets an A and I get a C."

Right again. McEnroe knew himself, a bit, but still he would not change.

The night before the match began, I arranged to have dinner with my former professor at King's College, University of London, the English poet and scholar Eric Mottram. He recommended an Indian restaurant in Holborn, near the old London theater district.

"I should think you would be interested in charisma in your book about tennis," said Mottram, eating quickly our *methi gosh, pilau, nan,* and mango chutney.

I nodded.

"Charisma is the difference between being very good at something and being a genius," snapped Mottram in his quick English way. "Charisma has nothing to do with good or evil. You can be an absolute turd and have charisma. Look at John McEnroe. Borg didn't have charisma. Billie Jean King didn't have it either, until she admitted that she was a lesbian. That Australian aboriginal girl didn't have it. She was too nice, and she got too nervous. Pancho Gonzales had charisma. McEnroe has it. Connors had it a bit. Becker doesn't have it, at least not quite yet. If he loses a bit more he may find it. Laver had heaps of charisma on court. He didn't have a lick of it off the court, but that doesn't really matter," said Mottram, dipping his *nan* into his *methi gosh*. "The interesting thing about charisma is that it can come and go. Sterling Moss, the British race car driver, had charisma. Then he lost it. That can be fatal in a race car driver. McEnroe should be more careful. Charisma is not necessarily given for an entire life. It can come and go, you know."

The draw sat like a pyramid on its side. There were no short-cuts in the big 128-name draw, no places to hide. Self-reliance was as important as skill. Technique was less glamorous than having a big heart, but in the close matches, what separated the competitors more—heart or technique, desire or fitness?

Derrick Rostagno, ranked 129th in the world, had got a very tough draw. He met John McEnroe, seeded fourth, in the first round. Rostagno had only got past the second round twice all year, but in his career he had beaten Brad Gilbert, gone five sets at Wimbledon with Jimmy Connors, and held double match point, serving, against Boris Becker. Derrick Rostagno was nearly twenty-five years old, had flowing black hair and a talent so stylish he had taken longer to develop than a mere power player.

The Wimbledon linespeople marched onto Center Court at Wimbledon, preceding the two players. The referee was up in his chair. The Wimbledon linesmen wore dark military-green pants with bright green blazers and fancy green ties. The Wimbledon lineswomen, marching onto Center Court in a single file with their male colleagues, wore olive-green dresses whose hem lines were a good eight inches below the knees. The dresses on the Wimbledon lineswomen hung like small tents from their hips, the better to smother big serves when they could not turn out of the way. The lines corps nervously assumed its bent-over ready position as John McEnroe and Derrick Rostagno finished their practice serves. Gilbert and Sullivan could have written songs for the Wimbledon linespeople; they took their duties very seriously.

On the croquet-perfect English lawn, Irish-American John McEnroe was surrounded on all sides by English schoolmaster and schoolmistress types ready to slap his hand with their rulers if the brat dared step out of line. McEnroe scowled at the sunny sky, frowned at the linespeople and his opponent. He was ready to play.

McEnroe's first serve was wide, and an official arm in a green blazer stuck dramatically out to the right of the court: *fault*. Recocking, McEnroe hit a running ace up the middle, and the Wimbledon linesman squatted low, placing both palms just above the grass, my favorite call: *ace*.

No one, including McEnroe, had given Derrick Rostagno much of a chance. But Rostagno had the makings of tennis charisma himself. Playing without a sponsor, he bought his own tennis clothes, choosing Lacoste because he thought, rightly, that the plain white with the little crocodile suited his dark tan and long legs. Derrick Rostagno had always struck me as a little weak, a little too good looking to be a champion, as if the force inside him was more charm than fury, as if down where the furnace was supposed to be there was instead a mirror. But playing McEnroe brought out a fierceness in the brown-eyed Rostagno. He played more and more like an artist. Rostagno's volleying had great touch, cleanness, and firmness on the grass that day. His father was an Argentine Italian who had played violin with the Los Angeles Philharmonic. His parents had met in Paris, where his father had been studying classical music. Rostagno was a bit of a free spirit, too, a gypsy but not a vagabond.

Boris Becker considered himself to have been very lucky against Rostagno, but players radiate their own luck. Against McEnroe, who showed his opponents no respect, Rostagno was consciously less willing to be the victim. He had let the simple reason be known: he did not like McEnroe.

During the match, John McEnroe wore a thick white bandana across his forehead. He was a frustrated actor, sometimes a great actor. Two nights before he had been imitating a guitar player. Now he looked like Stephen Crane's wounded soldier. The young soldier's strength in *Red Badge of Courage* came from looking inside himself and trying to understand his fear of failure. McEnroe looked as if he was trying to understand himself, but he was playing tennis as if in the middle of psychoanalysis. He was thinking instead of reacting. Professor Mottram was right. Charisma was the difference between being very good and being a genius. It was a spark. It was part confidence, part massive self-doubt ignited to produce something that was strong, bright, and triumphant. Charisma was the temporary illusion of complete self-assuredness. A champion once, McEnroe now looked very unsure of himself. His child's psyche was meeting his body's older self.

"It's not like I'm a punch-drunk fighter who had too many fights," McEnroe said before the tournament. "In tennis we fight over a net, so we never get hit like a boxer. I have plenty left."

But John McEnroe's legs had lost their chiseled look and their exuberance. He had stopped playing doubles with Peter Fleming years before and had lost his only easy (thus likely) method of physical training. Fitness was always key to McEnroe's ability to concentrate. Doubles had relaxed him and sharpened his reflexes for singles. John McEnroe was one of the best singles players since World War II, but he was probably the greatest doubles player of all time. Now his battles were all his own. It was all singles for John McEnroe. In Florida, I had taken his side with the English referee. In Philadelphia, I watched him lose to Richey Reneberg, a very competent player—and it had been like watching someone who painted by numbers defeat a player who could carve up a grass court like a sculptor. If you were a McEnroe fan—and I was still on McEnroe's side of the border—you were disappointed because, to the tennis lover, McEnroe's life and Wimbledon were part of the same thing.

Out in Hollywood, in the West Coast lap of luxury during the mid-late 1980s, surrounded by family, recognized in L.A. as being both rich and a true star, McEnroe lost some of his essential unhappiness. Life became easier for him, but there was an irony to it: he had lost his edge.

McEnroe played Rostagno like a wounded, red-headed killer now dangerous only to someone willing to give him something for nothing. Rostagno did not make the offer. The cellist's son beat McEnroe 7–5, 6–4, 6–4. John McEnroe trotted to net, shook hands, and scowled.

"John McEnroe was a yard slow," said Mark Cox, the burly left-handed former British Davis Cup player commentating that night on the rebroadcast for the BBC.

And yet in that scowl, that look of perfunctory, tight-lipped, mocking congratulations that McEnroe extended with his hand across the net to the relieved and happy Rostagno, McEnroe showed a glimmer of his old nastiness, a glow from his shadowy but deep charisma.

"It wasn't Rostagno," McEnroe would say in a sneering fashion after his loss. "It could have been anybody." If McEnroe could only have taken a small lesson from the player he had admired most—Borg, who held the beast back for many years—I suppose he would not have been McEnroe. Instead, McEnroe reminded us of the side of humanity many people wished they could deny, the rage.

Two rounds later, somehow gentle again after his win over McEnroe, Derrick Rostagno lost in straight sets to the tall, thin eighteen-year-old Yugoslav Goran Ivanisevic, who three months earlier Jay Berger had taken apart mentally on the hot Florida hard courts at the Lipton. The draw was starting to narrow.

Goran Ivanisevic ran hot and cold. He was a young fury, a Slavic McEnroe with a tremendous initial desire to beat other people. Rostagno looked so fresh and calm after the match, I was sure he had won, but he had lost completely: 6–2, 6–2, 6–4. The young Yugoslav was capable of crushing people. On the path back to the changing rooms, Don Budge, the Grand Slam winner in 1938, was stopped by Rostagno's coach, who shook Budge's hand as if it belonged to a king. Still tall, his bright red hair now white and his freckled face beet-red from the surprising English sun, Budge still traveled the circuit to every Grand Slam event. It was better than a hot springs for the retired champion.

"We played well, as well as we played against McEnroe," Derrick Rostagno's coach tried to explain to Budge. "But this Ivanisevic kid did not miss a return of serve the whole match. And his first serve is the hardest I have seen in thirty years."

Don Budge smiled but said nothing. He enjoyed all the losses almost as much as he had enjoyed all his wins.

Suddenly everyone wanted to know more about Goran Ivanisevic. I had more than a clue. I had seen him spit over the net against Jay Berger to show a Florida linesman where a drop volley had actually landed. A loser in mid-March, Ivanisevic had blossomed in the interim in Europe. Wimbledon was his breakthrough tournament. The English grass rewarded speed, aggression, power, and bravery.

This is what Ivanisevic's friendly manager from Milan, Fabio della Vida, told me. Goran Ivanisevic was Croatian, not Serbian, a difference that caused wars in Europe. Young Goran was a hot-blooded, emotional boy brought up in the beautiful old Adriatic town of Split. Yugoslavia, as it existed then, had a dual personality. It was a repressive, militaristic but Western-leaning regime. Dubrovnik and Split were in Croatia, and Belgrade, the political and military capital of Yugoslavia, was in Serbia. It was in Bosnia that Archduke Ferdinand of Austria was assassinated, igniting World War I. The Serbs and the Croatians mixed like oil and fire, as we learned once again a year later. The country was long on discipline and rebellion. The Serbs stood for military order and power; the Croats for nine hundred years of paprika and independent thinking.

Ivanisevic's father, Sdrjan, taught mathematics at the University of Split. His mother, Gorana, taught chemistry at a school in Split. By Western standards, the Ivanisevic family was poor; by Yugoslav standards, they were middle class.

Fifteen minutes from the local red-clay tennis club, the family could play tennis outdoors even in winter, basking in the sunshine near the Adriatic. But when Goran was young and they had to pay travel expenses to go to junior tournaments elsewhere in Europe, it was difficult for the family to pay his way in Western European currencies. The Yugoslav government in Belgrade did not give the young star from Croatia much assistance.

Yugoslav communist authorities wanted the young prodigy to conform to their training methods. But Ivanisevic's coach, a tough old man who spoke no English and taught at a single red-clay court in the Croatian countryside, would not do what the communist authorities told him to do. Everyone was supposed to play like Bjorn Borg, but the old Croatian preferred serve and volley.

"He told them all to go to hell," laughed Fabio della Vida, the agent. "And that is how Goran started to learn his tennis."

The first breakthrough for Goran Ivanisevic came at an exhibition match in Lausanne a few weeks after his loss to Berger at the Lipton. Tiriac was a friend of della Vida's, and Tiriac had arranged that the exhibition money be split in Switzerland. The opponent was Boris Becker. Ivanisevic's Italian agent for ProServ was with Ivanisevic behind the curtain in Switzerland. "Just before going on court for the Lausanne exhibition with Boris, Goran was extremely nervous. Back stage I thought he was going to throw up, but once Goran stepped onto the court, he was all right. He played like he had nothing to lose. And he did not lose! I tell you, Goran was thrilled when he won. He had beaten Boris in their first meeting."

But in Nice and Monte Carlo, it was a different Ivanisevic. He lost to Jim Courier in straight sets on the red clay at Monte Carlo, and after that match the gritty Courier said of the more naturally talented Ivanisevic, "When you play Goran, you don't know which Goran is going to show up. I was lucky the other guy showed up today." Courier won the match on clay 6–3, 6–1. The promise shown in beating Becker in the exhibition match in Lausanne had not been duplicated. The young Yugoslav had expected it to happen again automatically. But it did not. Then suddenly at Wimbledon the other Ivanisevic showed up, beating everybody in sight. He was serving left-handed aces and volleying as if he had played all his life on the grass.

"How did he break through?" I wanted to know, having seen him lose the tough one to Jay Berger just twelve weeks earlier.

"Talent is sudden," said the agent. "Plus, he worked very hard. When you are talented like Goran is, suddenly, after much work, you wake up one morning and your game is two or three steps ahead of the others."

Angelica Gavaldon, the Gussie Moran of 1990 women's tennis, came down the wooden stairs to give her interview following her seesaw win over England's lone hope, the six-foot four-inch left-hander, Sara Gomer. I had never seen Angelica Gavaldon before, but when the other reporters said she played in loop earrings so big you could stick your feet through, I decided to stay.

The late Ted Tinling, dress designer, tennis expert, and relaxed eccentric in a tennis world that admired what it also scorned, said of young Angelica Gavaldon, "She is half Madonna, half Lolita." The Mexican-American girl was accompanied into the interview room by an elegant, late middle-aged Wimbledon male press presenter who introduced himself like a third former to the press by saying, "Hello. My name is Anthony. This is my first year as a presenter." The busty five-foot four-inch sixteen-year-old American with blonde Spanish highlights came in wearing large gold loop earrings, smiling widely, and speaking English with a Spanish accent a bit like Charo's.

"Hi!" Angelica said to the press as she sat down, tossing her head. She was sixteen going on twenty-six.

"Did you ever play anyone as tall as that?" someone asked.

"No." The angel grinned. "She was like a giant, but I just hung in there."

The scores were strange. Gavaldon won 7–5, 0–6, 7–5. All of England had been rooting for Sara Gomer, who had upset Manuela Maleeva the day before. For the first time ever, no English man or woman made it into the third round at Wimbledon. It was not Angelica Gavaldon's problem. She was erratic at times but rock steady in the crisis points, and the very tall English player with the sliced left-handed backhand fell apart under pressure.

"We understand you have many superstitions," the reporter next to

Bud Collins said to Angelica Gavaldon. "Could you tell us about your superstitions?"

"Yes. Sure. Well I have many. My earrings are one. I wore these gold loops at the Australian Open and I got to the quarters there, so I am wearing them again here. They are my luckiest pair. And also, here at Wimbledon I have a new superstition. Every night, my girlfriend and I kneel on the edge of the bathtub before I get in."

"Kneel on the edge of the bathtub?"

"Yes. On the edge of the tub. I kneel there before I get in. It's bringing me good luck at Wimbledon," said Angelica Gavaldon, smiling happily.

On court, Angelica Gavaldon was a tough baseline player. She hung in there and fought hard against her much taller English opponent. The Gavaldon family maintained homes in Coronado, California, and twenty minutes south in Tijuana, Mexico, where their daughter was born. Angelica came back later than her nine o'clock curfew once, and her father was waiting in the driveway for her date with a gun. The daughter told the story to the Wimbledon press and added, "Now that's strict."

"She *looks* like a champion," her mother, also named Angelica, exclaimed later. "She tries so hard. She fights."

Outside the interview room, the English player, Sara Gomer, was momentarily alone. She was so tall she stooped to hide it. She was a big girl in her powder-blue track suit, but she had a kind, gentle smile, even in defeat. A crowd of English boys and girls her age and younger surrounded her, asking her for an autograph, and smiling with a mixture of pleasure and embarrassment, she obliged. She was taller than all of them. Sara Gomer was taller than Christine Truman, another shy, big English girl who had won the French Open one year. The first night of Wimbledon, the BBC featured Sara Gomer's win over Manuela Maleeva, and did a long interview with her that played all over England. For a night, she was a star. The next day, with all of England on her large but young shoulders, she lost to Angelica Gavaldon. John Lloyd, Chris Evert's former husband, prettier than he was useful, said on the BBC the night Sara Gomer lost, "I'd suggest she lose some weight." Watching her shy, kind face as she signed autographs after losing to Angelica Gavaldon, it was almost as if she had heard the unkind remark before it was said.

The English could not understand why they were not doing better, when it was they who held Wimbledon. There were several reasons beyond the English weather: the attitude of players content to be big fish in a little pond, the lack of quality coaches, and the pressure to live up to the legend, Fred Perry. But the weather in Sweden was no better, and there was at least one excellent English coach, Tony Pickard. Above all, it was the lingering class system that was to blame. The best English athletes never got onto a tennis court.

I went for a run one night in Bushey, a modest North London suburb where I was staying with friends. I ran past some old council flats (public housing) that had tennis courts attached to them. A father and son were on one of the courts. The father had his back to the fence and his young son was standing on the "T" of the service box taking penalty kicks at his father from the middle of the court. They were playing soccer.

That image—soccer players on the empty tennis courts—stuck in my mind. In England, the game never opened up as it did in Australia and America. Fred Perry, now a hero, was the son of a leather tanner and, although the All-England Club had recently erected a bronze statue of Perry in long white pants at the entrance to the club grounds, back in the 1930s when he was playing, Perry was considered to have come from the wrong side of the tracks. It was a lingering hurt even for a gentleman like Fred Perry. In 1990, after they erected the statue at Wimbledon, the English press voted Perry an award. At the black-tie awards dinner, Perry thanked the press for the honor, but said to the gathered English press, who had once been so cruel about his modest origins, "It's very nice, but it would have meant much more to me in nineteen thirty-three." Strong words from a true gentleman, one born not wealthy but a gentleman of the soul.

Great athletes are often born in resentment—from Fred Perry and Bill Tilden to Pancho Gonzales, Rod Laver, and even John McEnroe. Stefan Edberg seemed to be the exception, but beneath the easygoing surface lay Västervik, Sweden.

England has produced only a handful of really good players plus Perry, the only truly great one. In the modern era, Roger Taylor, Mike Sangster, Mark Cox, Christine Truman, Anne Jones, and Virginia Wade were outstanding. But tennis in England has remained exclusive, essentially a club game not open socially or economically to blacks or moderate-income whites. Tennis in England is frozen in time, a game like it was played in America in the 1930s. The promising English players need to get to America or Australia if tennis is really their love. And that was exactly what tall, shy Sara Gomer was going to do. After Wimbledon, she would rent a van in Florida with another English woman, and they would play the tough small events around the United States.

At Wimbledon, one of the primary sights is the elegant, heavily guarded Members Enclosure, essentially the entrance to the club proper, which allows its facilities to be used for the tournament the way Forest Hills was once used for the U.S. Open. They call Wimbledon the "All-England Club," but that is exactly what it is not. Barbed wire tops the old brick walls that surround the club. If something is enclosed here, something else is closed out. Wimbledon, an American's dream, rubbed many English people the wrong way.

"If the tickets were free," said a forty-five-year-old Englishman, "I still wouldn't put a foot in the place."

But he would have missed the kind, tired smile on Sara Gomer's face as she stooped to sign autographs after her loss to Angelica Cavaldon. He would have missed a lot. Center Court was as fine a natural stage as any in the world.

Young Pete Sampras faced a dilemma at Wimbledon. He had reached the stage in his career where he and others had begun to expect a great deal from him. Sampras usually played doubles with his good friend from Nick Bollettieri's Tennis Academy, Jim Courier. But Sampras and Courier had agreed before the French Open that they would not play doubles together either at the French, where the tenacious Courier was supposed to shine, or at Wimbledon, which Sampras had dreamed of winning since he was fourteen and used to watch hours of tape of his hero, Rod Laver.

Pointing his whole season toward Wimbledon, Sampras had in effect put all the weight on his own shoulders. There had been some deep distractions in the Sampras camp. After winning in Philadelphia, Sampras was suddenly desirable, like a wine future from a very good year. No one thought Sampras would mature right away, but both IMG and Pro-Serv, two of the major sports representation groups, wanted to have Sampras on their shelves. The competition was not only tough inside the draw. The agents for ProServ contacted Sampras late one night in his hotel room. Sampras was already represented by IMG, but the late-night pitch convinced him that he should change agents. He was not the first player "stolen" in the management skirmishes. But it was unsettling. It made young Sampras feel a little guilty, as if he had betrayed a loyal friend. And he had. His injury at the Lipton had kept Sampras recovering down at Nick Bollettieri's Tennis Academy for three months. The one match he played was a 6–1, 6–0 loss on clay to the very coordinated Swede Jonas Svensson at the BMW Open in Munich. After that loss, Sampras flew back to Florida for more rehab. Thus, before going off to England, Sampras had changed management and taken a bad loss when he was hurt. But the change in management initially nagged at him worse than the physical injury. Young Sampras had a conscience.

A decision was made by the new management group, ProServ, to try to help Sampras get his confidence back. He lost to the young Australian Richard Fromberg on grass at the Stella Artois event at the Queens Club before Wimbledon, and then he went up to Manchester, where he worked his way through a relatively weak field, winning five matches and the final from Gilad Bloom, 7–6, 7–6. Sampras flew back to London on the 24th. On June 25, after five straight matches in Manchester, Sampras played his first round at Wimbledon against the experienced South African grass-court player and doubles specialist Cristo van Rensburg.

Van Rensburg, his hair cut in a weirdly modern Afrikaans style, was a friend of Lendl's and very experienced on grass. The underdog, van Rensburg, always played well at Wimbledon and did not get nervous. Sampras, on the other hand, had put all his eggs in one basket—winning the singles at Wimbledon. There are many ways to explain a loss to someone you can beat, but in Sampras's case the explanation was probably just that he wanted Wimbledon so much that he got nervous. The grass was dry but getting dark late in the afternoon. It was close. Pete Sampras lost to van Rensburg 7–6(7–4), 7–5, 7–6(7–3). He played badly on the big points. Back at the hotel room after the match, packing his bags before most of the draw had even got through to the seeded players, young Pete Sampras called home. He felt like crying. Sampras was experiencing what it felt like to be a minor step in the big pyramid of the draw. It was a long flight back to Los Angeles.

The grass was not for everybody. Andre Agassi ducked it, putting off the potentially unpleasant experience that Jim Courier, also a baseliner, chose to face. Agassi felt he needed muscle more than he needed the experience of losing on grass. Back in America, Andre was lifting weights and getting ready for the U.S. Open. It was a conscious choice, a business choice, but—in my mind—yet another Agassi educational mistake.

Several Americans whose best surface was not grass—Brad Gilbert, Michael Chang, and Jim Courier—came to Wimbledon and performed beyond expectations. Gilbert put an end to David Wheaton's great string of five-set wins. Gilbert was a lot like Jay Berger. He didn't look beautiful; all he did really well was win. At Wimbledon there are no fifth-set tie-breakers, and Gilbert beat David Wheaton 13–11 in the fifth set. Having

watched every minute of David Wheaton's five-set wins over Paul Annacone and the athletic but self-destructive Swede Jonas Svensson, I had
expected Wheaton to beat Gilbert, but he lost the fierce personality test
by a shadow. Despondent over having been beaten by the herky-jerky
Gilbert, who shaved his swarthy face down to his neck line, Wheaton,
the tall blonde classic serve and volleyer, said, "Brad just played the big
points better. Damn it. He has no chance tomorrow against Becker."

Wheaton was right. Gilbert would have been a major scalp for Wheaton if he could have got it, but he just could not. Brad Gilbert's tennis
game was like an old car that worked. He even called his own game
"ugly." Gilbert was a Rene Lacoste–type player. Describing his own
game in 1927 in his beautiful, long out-of-print book, Rene Lacoste clearly
knew himself:

> I have not the genius of Tilden, nor the physical qualities of a Borotra
> or of a Cochet. If I have sometimes succeeded in beating them, it is
> because I have willed with all my force to win, to utilize the means
> which were within my reach.

Brad Gilbert was a better natural athlete than Jay Berger, but they
shared the same kind of self-knowledge that Lacoste had. They had
themselves in perspective, and that was rare on the tour. Their confidence, unlike Yannick Noah's, ran deep. A player like Noah, a first-round
loser at Wimbledon, knew only his strengths. After beating Wheaton by
a whisker, Gilbert said with a relaxed smile in the Wimbledon interview
room, "Sure. I skipped the French Open. But it's not like they were
going to miss me in Paris. I've never gotten past the second round at
the French. I'm a Northern California hard-court player who likes to
hang out on the baseline. But I know when to come in."

Gilbert had got into the round of sixteen on grass. He had made the
most of what he had. Michael Chang would make a career of doing just
that. Recovering from his broken hip at the start of the year, and having
lost in the first two rounds of a half-dozen tournaments on his preferred
surface—clay—as he launched his comeback, Chang was a picture of
composure and fight at Wimbledon. Chang was so polite he would bite
your shoe laces off. Down two sets to love to the Australian left-handed
fast-court specialist Mark Kratzman, Chang looked like he was learning
something from the grass on each point and he solved the Australian in
five sets. After the match Chang was reminded that he had beaten his

round-of-sixteen opponent, Stefan Edberg, in the final of the French Open in 1989. It was a major recall button for both players.

"I know he will be favored on grass, but I have a pretty good record against Stefan," Michael Chang said very calmly. "I will be playing to win tomorrow."

Listening to Michael Chang's quiet confidence, you could almost expect it to happen. But Stefan Edberg was playing at his home away from home. In the morning he woke up in his apartment near the Royal Albert Hall and had breakfast with Annette Olsen. The Swede's outwardly quiet but tenacious personality was ideally suited to the English grass and temperament. That afternoon, the cool, lanky Swede beat Chang 6–3, 6–2, 6–1 on the fast green grass.

Jim Courier, the baselining Florida boy with the tight-fisted forehand and topspin backhand, was not a natural on the surface, but he had come to learn. Seeded higher than he should have been for his second time on grass, Courier played well but lost in four tough sets to Mark Woodforde, the left-handed Australian who sometimes partnered McEnroe in doubles. Woodforde had grown up on grass courts, Courier on clay and cement.

Jim Courier played almost the entire match on grass as if he were Harold Lloyd hanging onto the arm of the Times Square clock, and the left-handed Woodforde finally shook off the higher-ranked but less-experienced grass-court player. "I won the second set, and I had set points in the first set," said Courier in the BBC radio interview room, talking to four of us alone, his tight, freckled face still wincing after the 7–5, 5–7, 7–5, 6–4 loss. "That's where I lost it. The first set when I had set point. Two sets to love up is entirely different than one set all."

Courier was not easy with himself. I liked that in a competitor. "In what way do you think you must improve to become a complete player, a better player on grass?" I asked Courier softly.

"Well," Courier nodded his head thoughtfully, "my volley is improving. And it needs to."

"Do you think you can become a complete serve and volleyer?"

"I'll never be a Mayotte. My ground strokes are too good to abandon them. Not to be cocky, but I'll never play a Paul Annacone–style game. He's all volleys, no ground strokes."

Winning for Courier was instinctual, but losing was a learning process. I put great store in the fact that Jim Courier was there, and Andre Agassi was not.

"When you had break point on Woodforde's serve in the third set, you and he were both up at net. All you had to do to win the point was angle the ball away, but you took a full-swing volley and hit the ball right at him. He reflexed it away."

"Yeah. I should have just angled it off instead of trying to put the ball through him. My reaction was, 'Who's stronger than who?' It was kind of stupid of me."

"What did you do after the French before Wimbledon to get ready?"

"I went home to Florida and got my batteries recharged," said Courier, smiling at the thought. "Now I've got Stad and Stuggarten [Gstaad and Stuttgart] on clay before Cincinnati. I'll stay in England and practice on clay over at Queens next week. See a few sights. I'd rather be in an English-speaking country. London's almost like being in America except they drive on the wrong side of the road here."

I smiled. Courier did not yet seem capable of beating Agassi regularly, but he had grit and hated himself just the right amount, and often that was worth more than pure talent. As compared to Agassi, Courier had three things in his favor: he was built like a high school running back, he was learning that only part of his obstinacy was useful, and, above all else, he was not afraid of losing. The difference between Agassi and Courier really came down to a difference in their attitude about losing. Courier was prepared to face defeat, to climb down into the lion's mouth, whereas Agassi, sticking to a five-year master plan for greatness, picked the tournaments where he would feel most secure. "You want to beat me?" the Floridian's body language seemed to say. "Then you better bring your lunch, 'cuz I'm going to keep you for a while."

Jim Courier had kept Woodforde on court almost four hours, and he still seemed fresh. The night before, Dave Stewart, the black Oakland Athletics pitcher, had thrown a no-hitter back home, and Courier, who had been a high school baseball star, responded to another reporter's question about the feat by grinning widely and doing an impression of the high-pitched Stewart's voice. "Hi!" squeaked Courier. "Ahm Dave Stewart." The strong Florida boy came from a town of five thousand people, and the more he traveled, the deeper he understood who and what he was.

"You even chipped and charged a few times off a slice backhand," I said.

"Hey!" said Courier, grinning and pushing the Cincinnati Reds hat back on his freckled face. "How about that!"

The food at Wimbledon was better in the press dining room than around the grounds, unless you reckoned the strawberries and cream (and not even cream at that) at two pounds fifty was worth the thrill. Upstairs from the interview bunker in the new building, I got on line with reporters from around the world. The elderly Indian reporter from the New Delhi paper nodded my way, grinned, and said to me in passing, "They have issued me a brown striped press card, which refuses me entrance to Center Court and to the Jennifer Capriati match this afternoon on the grandstand. For twenty years they gave me the other card, but now they call me a 'Rover,' and I have to wear around this damn brown card. Damn them. Will you be watching Boris Becker later? Perhaps we can watch together. It's so hot I think I'll stay inside a while and hear what the BBC has to say."

It was lunchtime on the sixth day. The photographers, large men with sloping bellies, had sidled up to the English pub bar for a little lunchtime imbibing, conversation, and respite from the heat. At the Lipton, the reporters were fed like high school students from huge stainless-steel bowls of salad and trays of lasagna. At Wimbledon, you could order a meal, but it sure was not free.

"I'm really hungry!" I heard myself say out loud. "What's good today?"

"A bit of fried bread and chips?" the counterwoman suggested.

"Not today, thanks." As a student at the University of London, I used to go to a workingman's "caf" for lunch when I was out of fifty-pence pieces to put in the electric meter of my Pimlico flat. I could never understand how the English working class stomached fried bread. It was the same general idea as French toast, but it was not the same thing at all. A piece of bread dropped into boiling grease or sizzled in grease on the grill. Caw! Blimey.

"Eggs up, broiled tomatoes, well-done sausage, baked beans, and a buttered slice," I said, just the way the spry old cockney lady used to say at the caf.

"Cup of tea, luv?" asked the young woman behind the counter at Wimbledon.

"I'd love one. Milk and sugar, please."

"Ta," said the heavily made-up young woman, ringing up the pound notes which held the face of the Queen of England.

England could be a little cold on the outside, but the hot tea always reminded me of how warm the English could be inside. The reporters were not standing with the jovial photographers at the pub bar but were scattered alone at tables or crowded silently in front of the television screen watching the World Cup soccer matches in an air of competitive, impending work. I found an empty table over by the far window. The window was open, and there was a bit of a cool English summer breeze. The hot weather of the first week had faded, but the sun was still bright. From the window up two stories from the grass one could see the Wimbledon grounds, the betting touts, and the crowds of happy tennis fans. Wimbledon seemed at times like an English horse race meeting, and Becker and Edberg were the favored horses.

At the table next to mine, a Japanese woman was drawing squarelike figures in small boxes. Her hand was moving quickly from right to left, drawing the words. She was meeting a deadline in Japanese. I waited for her to put down her pencil for a moment, and I went over. "Are you covering Wimbledon for a Japanese newspaper?"

"Tennis magazine," said the Japanese woman, smiling.

Japan was becoming a favorite stop for tennis professionals like Becker, Edberg, Lendl, and McEnroe as well as rock stars like Madonna.

"Is tennis very popular with the Japanese people?"

"Mmm," said the Japanese reporter. "Women play tennis in Japan, very much tennis. I write for a tennis magazine for women. Men do not play so much tennis. In Japan, men play golf. Women play tennis."

"Is it very expensive to play tennis in Japan?" Japan was the ultimate dollar- (or yen) per-square-foot world, and tennis courts took up space.

"Oh, yes. Expensive. Very expensive. Not like you say, *public* courts. In Japan, tennis only in clubs. Golf club is for men, and golf clubs more expensive. Golf *so* expensive. In Japan," she explained, "tennis is woman's game."

I thanked the Japanese reporter, and she went back to drawing her picture-letters in the little boxes, moving her hand firmly from right to left across the page. I headed out to watch Jennifer Capriati.

The Wimbledon guard on the outside court told me and my writer friend from New Delhi that we had the wrong press passes for that match. But the weather was on our side. It was so hot that week in England that most of the press remained in the new air-conditioned press facility watching Capriati's match live on TV. The man from India and I didn't mind the sun, and after a bit of negotiation, we were seated happily at courtside baking in it.

At least one spectator did not seem to be as interested in the tennis as we were. There was a small grassy hill near the court, and a crowd of people stood on it, their heads turning from side to side with the ball. In the middle of this crowd lay an Englishman, face down in the grass, snoring, his white skin bright pink from sunshine, his beer drinker's stomach like a cushion mostly covered by his blue checked shirt. He was quite asleep. The man was wearing hiking shorts, and the back of his calves turned bright red in the sun. He woke up with a start midway through the third set. The crowd had cheered a shot by Robin White, the tall, elegant California blonde who had once played at Wimbledon in a tight white body stocking. She was twenty-six now and was giving fourteen-year-old Jennifer Capriati more than she wanted.

The Capriati prodigy was different in one major way from when she made her first appearance in Florida. She had gotten tougher. Her right arm was thicker. Her low-slung torso, powerful like her father's, had become leaner from all the play and struggle since the Lipton. Her tan, baby face was much thinner. Her bright eyes were more intent, more fixed, and less frivolous when she spoke about her tennis. She was still fourteen, but she was tougher.

Jennifer Capriati was like an Ever-Ready battery. Knock her down, as Nathalie Herreman had at the Lipton, and Capriati just kept getting up. She was tough that way. Tennis careers are different from business careers: it is always much easier going up the mountain than it is staying at the top. Capriati was still on the upslope. If she lost, she still knew where she was going. Pete Sampras had found himself a bit too far up the slope, and the height scared him a little. In a way, his loss at Wimbledon was a relief. There was less pressure if a player backslid a bit before he had to confront his expectations and the public's. Pressure had started to mount for Jennifer Capriati. She was still the most sought-after interviewee among the American press. Desperate to do the right thing but caring so much about his daughter that almost everybody but his daughter thought he overdid it, father Stefano carried her big pink and purple tennis bag and dressed up in pale blue Sergio Tacchini tennis warm-ups. His daughter was in a pressure cooker but she retained some innocence. After her second-round win, she told the press that she and her younger brother got into a fight back at the hotel as to which London play they were going to see that night. The fourteen-year-old and her twelve-year-old brother traded a few gentle punches before their mother broke up the argument. Her younger brother landed one to her right arm. It seems Jennifer wanted to see *Cats* again, and the brother did not. Eventually, as she told it, their parents took them to see *Cats*.

Out on the grass courts, Capriati was a force to be reckoned with even though she was still learning to play the grass-court skid bounces. Young Capriati looked twenty percent better than she had at the Lipton in Florida. Her serve had more snap in it, less push from the elbow, more crack at the top of a more fluid backswing. She came forward now on the grass, the force of her young personality behind her all the way. She had great resolve, which finally is more important than experience, but she still did not have anything like Maria Bueno's great touch. Maybe it was the way she held the racket in the butt of her hand. Like Chris Evert, Capriati was awkward on the volley. But against long-legged Robin White on grass, her hand began to look more comfortable on the racket, and Capriati began to hit her volleys with stunning flashes of confidence.

Capriati and Evert did share the single most important tennis asset: they were both fearless competitors. When the chips were down, willpower was always more important than having a beautiful-looking game. Even under pressure Evert and Capriati had few hitches in their strokes. They hit all the way through the ball. The top women players took immediate advantage of any excess motion or affectation in their opponents' ground strokes. If they spotted any excesses or weaknesses of personality in overly looping forehands or undercut backhands, they went right there to punish the affectation or expose the weakness. In this way, Capriati and Evert went straight through women who looked prettier or fancier on court. Their tennis games were revenge on those players who might be more stylish or more fortunate in other ways. That's what toughness is. But long-legged Robin White was a lot tougher than she looked at a distance.

The young California woman was up 3–0 in the third set. Robin White looked like a winner. Jennifer Capriati wore a tennis dress that was long over her legs the way Doris Hart's tennis dress was when she won Wimbledon in 1951. Yet Capriati looked thoroughly modern in other ways, including her new Wilson racket, which she used like a cudgel.

"I don't want to hear about fourteen-year-olds any more," Robin White said with a smile after she lost her 3–0 third-set lead. Robin White was half-laughing. The tall California woman's hair was blonde and smooth, and her voice was incredibly deep and cheerful. After thirteen deuce points on her own serve, including five ad-outs, Robin White finally held serve to go up 3–0 in the third set. But the effort in that

service game finished Robin White. Holding serve killed her, and the
3–0 lead meant nothing. Capriati won the next six games and the final
set, 6–3.

"I would like to see how strong she gets physically in a couple of
years," said the twenty-six-year-old White. "Because I have never seen
a fourteen-year-old hit the ball that hard. I mean, it's the balls that you
are reaching for on the stretch when you really feel the power." White,
from San Diego—tall, strong, and unashamedly attractive—clearly did
not like losing to someone twelve years younger. "My game plan was to
attack her at all possible times, on every short ball to keep the pressure
on. And I don't care who you are, it's a lot of pressure to make the
passing shot. And I have a lot of confidence in my net play. It's just that
she really cracked the ball awfully well when she was deep in the court.
She came up with the passing shots."

"How does Jennifer Capriati compare with Steffi Graf at that same
age?"

"I'd say Jennifer is much stronger physically," said Robin, reflecting.
"Capriati is already a pretty good-size girl. I'm not saying she moves
poorly by any means. She covers the court pretty well. But that would
be the big difference. Movement. Steffi had power, not like they do
now, but she was so darn quick. And actually that puts more pressure
on you than someone who hits the ball hard."

Robin White, a loser to Capriati 7–5, 6–7, 6–3, looked tired and
upset. She wished she could play the end of her match with Capriati
over again. And don't we all? She was old enough to be philosophical,
young enough to be disappointed: "I got in two or three matches last
week down in Eastbourne before the rain came. But then it started
bucketing. We ended up sitting around a lot waiting. You'd rather be in
the gym working out or doing something than waiting for grass to dry.
I mean, it was *pouring* down in Eastbourne. I think," said the California
woman, "the English must be the most optimistic people in the world.
It's raining cats and dogs, and the English say, 'Now, girls, let's just wait
a couple more minutes. It's clearing.' I mean, really! And the players,
we're like, '*Please!* Let us go.' It kept raining, but they kept us. Maybe
next time."

"What chance do you give Jennifer Capriati against Steffi Graf,
Robin?" an English reporter asked.

Robin White frowned. She did not like being turned into an odds-
maker for the fourteen-year-old who had just beat her. "Well, Capriati
will be the underdog, and that will be different for her. Steffi, she's . . . I

don't want to say it's fifty-fifty. Jennifer probably has a twenty percent chance—twenty percent. Jennifer likes the pace, and that's what Steffi plays. She won't play many people who will hit the ball harder than Steffi."

Twenty-one-year-old Steffi Graf and nineteen-year-old Gabriela Sabatini both had sex scandals break around them during the fortnight. In Sabatini's case, it was her own love affair; for Steffi Graf, it was her father's.

Sabatini had got involved with a young German stringing machine shop owner named Frank Unklebach, who fancied himself the local ladies' man. Heavily chaperoned by Betty Stove, her coach, and by her family, Sabatini had apparently fallen heavily for the young German man; Frank, like the young German playmate who slept with Steffi Graf's father, sold the story of their lovemaking to the German rag press.

Sabatini was still young sexually—and most every other way—and she deserved to meet nicer people than a racket stringer from Ulm named Frank Unklebach, a cheap, good-looking guy from the local disco. The adverse publicity upset Sabatini, and twice she skipped her post-match singles interviews to "get ready for doubles." It was a tribute to the Argentinian that she was able to focus on her tennis at all. Gabriela Sabatini had photographers running after her and taking pictures up her legs and from the rear from low on the court since she was fourteen and a prodigy like Capriati. Sabatini was a beautiful young woman, but if she turned out to prefer the company of other women to the company of men, it would not be a total surprise. The men around her had for the most part behaved like porno photographers. At Wimbledon, there was some justice for Sabatini. Though every day the English tabloids dragged her through her "scandal," which was really just a young woman being human, Sabatini had by luck got a really good draw. She faced and beat Burgin, Huber, Tanvier, Tauziat, and Zvereva—all long shots—before meeting Martina Navratilova in the semifinals.

Steffi Graf's story was far crueler and more sordid because she had done nothing at all. Her father, Peter, who tripled as his daughter's coach, manager, and confidant, was always so positive about tennis and so obsessed about good form on the court and off it. But at the famous Jimmy'z discotheque in Monte Carlo, Peter Graf introduced Steffi to a young woman her age who he said was to be a friend for his daughter. The three of them had danced in Monaco until way after midnight, and Steffi thought the young woman, who had been a model for the German *Playboy*, was *her* friend. The deception came at a time when Steffi Graf was starting to mature into a young woman. She was already the greatest mover of all time on a tennis court, the game's most coordinated player, with the possible exceptions of Maria Bueno, Martina Navratilova, and Suzanne Lenglen. But though Steffi Graf held herself like an aristocrat and would pose in the German edition of *Vogue* to prove how grown up she had become, she was still socially undeveloped. She put so much trust in her father, yet Peter Graf let her down in a crushing way.

The woman Steffi had been dancing with in Monte Carlo, whom her father subsequently hired as a traveling secretary, sold the German papers a story saying that Peter Graf was now the father of her child, a "love *kind*," as *Das Bild* called the baby boy. While paternity was never proved, the damage was done. The young champion's confidence was severely, some say permanently, shaken.

After her win over Claudia Kohde-Kilsch—a 6–0, 6–4 victory Graf was capable of winning from memory—the German woman with the sandy blonde hair, bobbed as in Picasso's 1954 Greek-like portrait in profile of Mademoiselle D., came down the wooden stairs into the interview room, but only after an announcement was made to the assembled press by the chief Wimbledon official, a somber man with shoulders that pinched. As Danny Kaye would have said, the Wimbledon official "was beside himself, his favorite position." In a voice usually reserved for matters of state, he said in impeccable BBC English, "This is a health warning. The Club would not like to see the lady champion upset by questions which are not directly concerned with her tennis and what has happened on court. Regretfully, if *any* questions are asked outside this framework, I shall immediately end this interview. Buzzer Haddingham will repeat this warning in German before our German language interview begins. Please, for Steffi's sake, cooperate with us and respect our wishes."

Steffi Graf slid down quietly into her chair behind the microphones. Her face was pale and a little tight. Her nose was red and large, following surgery to relieve a chronic sinus condition. She no longer looked invincible. The charisma had been tainted. After her losses to Monica Seles in the consecutive finals on clay of the German Open, when the wound of her father's indiscretion appeared, and the French Open, where the wound festered, Steffi Graf—a loyal daughter—continued to defend her father and play tennis on memory and form. But tennis is played from the heart. Watching her struggle with herself, one suddenly felt how strong Martina Navratilova was back in the days when nearly the whole world was saying nasty things about her. Martina Navratilova had cried many times over the years. In the Wimbledon interview room, Steffi Graf's face looked composed but red, like she had been crying too. And yet, certain members of the press still tried to get in a question about her father—it was lack of imagination masquerading as duty and honesty. The Wimbledon official had been fair.

"Do we attack her?" Bud Collins had joked blackly before Graf came into the room. But Collins did not. In fact, when his turn came, Bud Collins spoke extra gently to Graf.

Not all the press were as kind. What was interesting was the way Graf described the match she had just played against Claudia Kohde-Kilsch, the lanky West German with the severely sloping shoulders, big serve, and attackable psyche. "It was," said Graf, "like playing from my memory in the first set. I did not think about anything, only my tennis, and everything went well that way. But in the second set I became distracted. I lost the desire to win. I was up four-love, but I nearly lost the set."

The young German woman who had so completely dominated Martina Navratilova, Monica Seles, and the rest of the world just the year before was suddenly very vulnerable. Steffi Graf could not afford to get sentimental in the next round. Fourteen-year-old Jennifer Capriati said of her next opponent, "I think Steffi is a great champion. That is why I want to play her so badly."

Center Court at Wimbledon is a club within a club. My Indian friend with the brown Rover pass was back in the interview bunker, but I felt there was a way to get into Center Court if you persevered. Security at Wimbledon was heavy; the art of craning one's neck between games on the steps at Flushing Meadow was not permitted at Wimbledon. If you do not make it back to your Center Court seat on time between games, the English guards make you stand at the very bottom of the stairs, listening to the ball. When I questioned a stadium guard about this policy, he smiled from under his hat with its thin red stripe around the band and said in a friendly, chatty way, "I'm sorry, mate, but we're full up for the moment."

"Did you hear they stopped Navratilova trying to get in through the players' gate?"

"Yeah. Well, they're a bit unbelievable about rules here," said the Wimbledon guard. "S'pose they have to be with this IRA mob up again. But they're definitely getting stricter here every year. Right over the top, mate. Right over the top. 'Course the young fellow at the players' entrance had no clue who Martina was. 'E must have been away at college," smiled the handsome English guard.

By the time Jennifer Capriati had stepped onto Center Court, I had arranged a press ticket and was seated in the old press seats with their green wooden writing tables. Boxed flowers ringed the court. Young Capriati and Steffi Graf curtseyed to Princess Fergie, as the Florida player would later call Prince Andrew's strawberries-and-cream, red-haired bride, the former Sarah Ferguson. The Royal Box was spacious. Apparently, the definition of "royal" had been expanded.

English royalty was now much more like American royalty. It consisted largely of entertainers, ex-athletes, and—the primary difference— vestiges of the aristocracy and the Raj. The former cricket star and his wife Mr. and Mrs. Graham Gooch were in the box near Chris Evert. Among those few lucky enough to be invited to the box for more than one day was H. R. H., the Duchess of Kent. The lesser English royalty in attendance was part of the program of the afternoon's matches, and they changed, like a menu, each day. The cast of characters this day included Brigadier and Mrs. Jeremy Phipps, the Earl and Countess of Dalkeith, Mrs. Ian Peacock and guest, Sir Francis Renouf and Mrs. Marion Gore (great-granddaughter of the 1908 men's champion), Mr. and Mrs. Barry Edwards, Mr. and Mrs. David Soul, Lord and Lady Iliffe, and Sir Geoffrey de Bellaigue and guest.

It was fun to try to discover the pecking order. The press was given the daily guest list for the Royal Box, and on the back of the page, written in longhand before copying for the press, were the actual seat placements for those invited. There were six rows in the Royal Box, but some rows apparently were more royal. The front row had only nine large seats. Rows two through five each held a dozen seats, and the sixth row accommodated eighteen guests in sardine fashion. Still, it was the Royal Box. The chairman of the All-England Club sat front-row-center, unless the queen was there, and the pecking order was established around and beside him. For example, Earl and Lady Dalkeith were front-row fare, as were Lord and Lady Romsey and Brigadier and Mrs. Jeremy Phipps. The high commissioner for Pakistan and Mrs. Sharyar Khan were in the second row, as were Lord and Lady Iliffe. The mayor of Eastbourne and his wife were in the fourth row next to Sir Geoffrey de Ballaigue, whose family was traceable to the Norman Conquest. The English comedian Barry Edwards and his wife were in the fifth row, while American actor David Soul and his wife were back in the sixth row next to Mrs. Ian

Peacock and guest and Captain and Mrs. A. Rogers, equestrians I guessed.

Jennifer Capriati tried to stop laughing about the curtsey. The American teenager played as if she had come to learn, not necessarily to conquer. Capriati had spunk. Her body language was not as graceful as that of her German opponent, but she ran for everything. Steffi Graf, though, was still a champion. In a most difficult personal situation, Steffi Graf showed the champion's steel she had inside. Everyone had been ready for the prodigy to beat the champion, but Graf repeatedly whipped forehand cross-court winners with her sharp, rapid, almost angry precision and gracefulness. Between games, Graf marched across the grass in short, quick paces. She was arrogant above her insecurity. And she was thoroughly engaged. Graf chipped her backhand and angled her volleys down and away off the grass against the Florida baseline girl's topspin blasts. It was a "learning loss" for Capriati—the type that Andre Agassi had denied himself by not showing up at all. Steffi Graf won 6–2, 6–4, and the scores were a proper measure of the match.

"Well," said Jennifer Capriati, grinning afterwards, "I had a lot of fun and I thought she was really great. I finally got to hit against that forehand, and now I know why they call it *that forehand*. It was just a bullet."

Said Graf, shy, coquettish, subdued but smiling a few minutes later, "I thought she would be more nervous than I."

The most telling match of the first week was Stefan Edberg's great match with Amos Mansdorf. The last time I saw Mansdorf he was carrying his heavy racket bag out to the Lipton parking lot in Florida after a crushing 6–2, 6–1 loss to Edberg. At Wimbledon, nobody gave Amos Mansdorf a chance of beating Edberg. But this time the former Israeli soldier met the tall, lanky Swede on Center Court.

Mansdorf, whose father was an engineer and whose mother was a schoolteacher, had looked in Florida like he was ready to retire to the baking heat of Tel Aviv. But somehow, in the cool wind in England, Amos Mansdorf came alive.

Wind in England is the gray sky's scenery changer. If it is raining in London, the wind can bring better things—flashes of sunshine through the clouds, the hope of light. But the wind that summer day was carrying a storm from Dover. Both players came out onto the old Globe Theater Center Court in sweaters. Edberg kept his sleeveless sweater on throughout the match; Mansdorf took his off when he broke Edberg's serve in the first game.

The serve is the key to victory in grass-court tennis, and in a heavy wind, the toss can be blown off course. Edberg was a passenger to his serve. It carried his personality with it. The Swede tossed the ball high, climbed to reach it, and as he went over the top of it with all that torque and determination, he leapt forward in a crazy controlled dash to the net, not so much foot-faulting as flying. Against Mansdorf, Edberg's service toss, his point of origin, was getting blown all over Center Court. The shorter man had a lower, quicker toss, like Bill Talbert's, and the quiet, determined Israeli was as on that day as he had been off in Florida.

It was Mansdorf's day. Every volley he hit skidded away for a winner, the lower bounce on grass not giving Edberg a chance to run the balls down. And yet as always, the Swede had character. He had hung on by a thread at the Lipton down two match points on Jakob Hlasek's serve. Edberg knew how to win from a desperate losing position. Though he trailed Mansdorf two sets to one, 6–4, 5–7, 3–6, Edberg kept clawing. He raced through the fourth set, 6–2, with a champion's disdain and appetite, but the former Israeli soldier nodded, as if to say, "I am not going away."

The fifth set was a death fight. Edberg went down a service break and 3–1. The Israeli soldier seemed relaxed yet concentrated, and that happy condition made him so clean through the ball. Mansdorf showed only one moment of hesitation, one moment of self-doubt, but the slender Swede turned to one side and squeezed through that narrow opening in the door, winning 9–7 in the fifth set. In four hours, Edberg had won 160 total points, Mansdorf 157.

"There's a slight mental difference," Amos Mansdorf said after losing. "Deep inside you know it in the back of your mind. You have the feeling all the time that the top guy is going to play well. And he did play well on the big points, you know. You feel the pressure all the time that he is not going to *give* you the match—that you must win it. And I had to say to myself, 'Win this match because he's not going to give it to you.' I had to come up with the big shots to break his serve again in the fifth set. And I didn't."

Edberg, smiling and shaking his head in relief, acknowledged that he had made a great volley in the last game of the match, a volley he moved forward on and took in a reflex at the very top of the net with Mansdorf ten feet away taking full aim at him with a forehand. Mansdorf blasted, Edberg reflex-volleyed standing right on top of the net, and the ball fell over dead, a winner on the grass, with Edberg down break point at 7–all in the fifth set.

"I was a bit lucky," said Edberg. "That only happens once in a lifetime almost. But I thought I had to go as close to the net as I could. It was lucky to get over, but, I mean, those sort of things happen in tight situations."

It was a fourth-round match that Edberg almost lost but won. But every great player, like a matador, can brush closely with defeat and survive it. Edberg managed to slip sideways through Mansdorf's narrow opening of self-doubt. Those who most believe they will win often do so.

"I think," said Edberg, "a match like this is probably going to do me a lot of good. When I got to deuce in the eight–seven game, that's when you really feel you have a chance to win it, and I said to myself, 'Try to make every return,' and that's virtually what I did. He hit some good shots, and I finally hit that backhand down the line, which gave me the break. It really feels good to get into this situation and then to come out of it."

The Israeli press in the interview bunker gave Mansdorf a hard time for being beaten, but he had played beautifully, bravely. Crushed at the Lipton three months earlier, Amos Mansdorf had played to the limits of his considerable heart. The match was so close. It was like madness. The wind, the sun, the fine line between them. The balance could have gone either way. In the end, it was Edberg who let out the scream of joy.

Edberg's coach, Tony Pickard, called the remaining handful of Swedish reporters together after the group press questions in English and Swedish, and he said to them in relative private, "I was not worried in the fifth set. Because all the way through the match, Stefan had done nothing stupid. The chance was just not there all the way through the fifth set. Every time Stefan had a near chance, Amos aced him. When the wind blows, you go to hit a forehand and suddenly it's a backhand. Big fellows always have more trouble with the wind. But at the end, the chance came. Just *one* chance. Stefan had had to wait five sets for his one chance. At seven-all in the fifth set, it came. He had hung in there all the way and took it."

The match was a thing of beauty, a Hitchcock movie about a man named Hannay, a thriller with 39 steps, a win like Mr. Memory on the old English vaudeville stage as he croaks for the last time in his heavy cockney accent, "Am I right, sir? Am I right?"

THE SEMIFINALS

The draw sheet on the yellow scoreboard at Wimbledon, once a barren family tree, was now almost entirely full of names. The draw at Wimbledon was ultimately a game of musical chairs, and when the music stopped there were always several fewer chairs left on which to sit. Different players had different goals. But those good enough to make it to the semifinals at Wimbledon had felt themselves under great pressure and had responded.

Martina Navratilova was the fiercest of the women players at Wimbledon in 1990. The Czechoslovak living with her blonde companion and business partner, Judy Nelson, in the luxury of Aspen, Colorado, had been brought up red-clay dirt-poor in communist Europe. On the exterior, she appeared to be a steel-hard champion. Inside, she was the little girl from outside of Prague who never knew her real father and was raised by her mother and a strict stepfather who swept clay courts for a living. The stepfather eventually adopted the girl and gave her his name. Her older brother, also adopted, was a stage set designer still in Prague.

On the first day of her fifteenth Wimbledon, the second seed and eight-time Wimbledon winner was stopped at the player's entry gate and refused admission to the grounds by a young male Wimbledon guard because she did not have her player identification card with her. Dressed to play, Navratilova was forced to wait twenty minutes at the front gate to be identified by a tournament official. Martina alternately fumed and laughed in disgust.

(It reminded me of a story about mistaken identity I once heard about General Eisenhower: There was an international meeting of famous people being held at the White House shortly after Eisenhower left office. The White House guards had been warned that there might be gate-crashers pretending to be famous people. Pablo Casals, the cellist, appeared at the front gate of the White House and said, "I am Pablo Casals. Let me in!"

"Sorry, sir. We've had several cases of mistaken identity," the White House guard told the world-famous cellist. "How do I know you are Pablo Casals?" The great cellist pulled out his instrument, played a few notes, and the guard let him in.

Next, Picasso turned up at the White House gate and said to the guard, "I am Picasso! Let me in."

The guard said, "Sorry, Mr. Picasso, we've been having some cases of mistaken identity around here. Please identify yourself." Picasso pulled out his invitation, drew a sketch on it, and the guard said, "Go right in, Mr. Picasso."

About an hour later, former President Eisenhower showed up at the gates of the Kennedy White House and said to the guard on the gate, "I'm Ike. Let me in!"

"I'm sorry, General. We've had several cases of mistaken identity this afternoon. But the two gentlemen who arrived just before you, Mr. Casals and Mr. Picasso, were both able to prove their identities."

"Who the hell are Casals and Picasso?" growled the tall, balding older man.

"Oh. Go right in, General Eisenhower," the guard said.)

Navratilova was one of the greatest players of all time—male or female—but she had to keep proving who she was. In a sense, that was what kept her going, kept her fighting. She deserved to be "let in," but the public somehow always kept Navratilova waiting at its front gate, reserving judgment on her identity. The scene at the Wimbledon players' gate was potentially quite comical. "I am Navratilova!" she said, but they did not believe her. Like Picasso and Pablo Casals, Navratilova offered to use her skill to identify herself. She said she would bounce a ball into the air off her racket a hundred times without missing, but the young guard still would not believe her without seeing her player badge.

After her first two victories Navratilova was too angry about the incident at the gate to laugh about it. Like McEnroe, Martina had a trip-wire personality, but on court she turned her anger back on herself. Navratilova was a finely tuned piece of physical and emotional equipment, rarely at peace with herself. She felt everything. Her voice shook with indignation and disbelief. Navratilova sounded so hurt and disgusted that her voice cracked almost as if she wanted to cry. It was a case of another man being unfair and stupid to her.

Navratilova and John McEnroe had the two most complicated personalities on the tennis tour. In becoming champions, they had become exaggerations of what they were inside, having to insist on themselves more and more with each match. Their identities grew swollen with victories and hard with losses. The problem for them both was that the public was never quite willing to grant them full approval.

It was a matter of sexual preference with one and anger with the other. The "public" is often the sum not of what is said but of what a few individuals may think but never say. Spectators like to see themselves in the great players. For different reasons, Navratilova and McEnroe were never the mirrors most people wanted.

Chris Evert and Stan Smith were both *very* good players, and they seemed safe—they were reassuring. Stan Smith got the million-dollar Adidas sneaker contract, while Martina Navratilova got the Thor-lo socks ad. Chris Evert always had the Wilson sponsorship, while for years McEnroe could not get a racket company to sponsor him because, like a destructive child, he kept breaking whatever they gave him. One year, Navratilova won the U.S. Open and Wimbledon with no contract from the company whose racket she was using. To get clothing sponsorship, Navratilova had to found her own company. McEnroe and Navratilova were selling themselves on court, but most companies felt they were sending the wrong message. Chris Evert and Stan Smith had both played tennis with great courage and skill, but they did not belong at the same party with Casals, Picasso, Navratilova, McEnroe, or William Tilden.

Navratilova and McEnroe are forever linked in my mind, and not just because they marched to their own drummer. Both left-handers wanted total acceptance and needed enormously to be loved by the public, and yet, like Bill Tilden, they did things as individuals that assured they would never receive the full warmth of the public's undivided love.

In Navratilova's case, her journey to come to terms with herself was underpublicized and particularly touching. Her soul was so visible on court. She wanted acceptance so badly. Chris Evert understood her better than anyone else, because she had felt it all from the other side of the net, and Chris was consistently kind to Martina off the court. Navratilova had had so much to deal with. She never knew her real father. By two accounts, he drank heavily, was a wild man, and left her mother when Martina was just a year old. He died when she was only seven years old, never having come to see her. Her adopted father, Mr. Navratilova, the court sweeper, was a tyrant but had a deep but difficult love for his daughter. The two most important men in Martina's life— the father she knew and the father she never knew—hurt her self-confidence before she ever headed out on the tennis tour.

Martina took her role as a champion a step further each year. An insatiable winner, she eventually became a physical phenomenon, but from the outset she was not quite as natural an athlete as Steffi Graf nor as tough inside as Chris Evert. Navratilova's muscles were a cover-up. She was physically strong in direct proportion to how much she had been hurt. But the public reacted to Navratilova as it had seventy years before to Tilden. Tennis ultimately was a game of domination. Was it surprising that two of the very best, Bill Tilden and Martina Navratilova, were dominant in a particular way?

Navratilova harnessed her drive better than McEnroe did his. She did not blame others as often, for instance. McEnroe was intense, but he had never suffered like Navratilova. She would turn on herself with a vengeance whenever she let a match slip away. McEnroe, who equated winning with being right, hated himself at times, but he rarely—with the exception of Lendl in the 1980s—hated his opponents.

Sometimes the most talented people have the most beast. The meek do not like to see angry people or want to try to understand how they got that way. But silence on a tennis court does not mean that a person is nice off the court, though it helps create that often attractive illusion. Borg and Laver's silences created a semblance of stability, but they were no more stable than race car drivers. Martina Navratilova had the champion's beast in her, and she rode it well. It kept her insides on fire when many younger players were already thinking of retirement.

After her third-round win over Austria's Judith Wiesner, the Lipton finalist, I asked Navratilova what she thought of the prodigy process that had almost fully overtaken women's tennis the way it had women's gymnastics. "Martina," I said, "a Hollywood talent agent once remarked that, 'Young movie stars who become the full-time employee of the family have a hard time knowing where they stop being the product and become themselves.' That sounds a lot like tennis to me. . . . I'm talking about the sixteen-and-under involvement of the parent with the child as it relates to the top girls."

"Wow," said Martina, breaking into a smile behind the Wimbledon microphones, "I could get in some hot water there."

"Oh, go ahead," I urged her.

Navratilova took a deep breath. Her glasses and headband were still on after her victory. She was silent for a few seconds, looking up at the lights. She was no longer a kid. Navratilova was thinking. "I'm thirty-three years old," said Martina softly. "And I still have a hard time dealing with my father. When it comes to playing tennis, I mean, he's telling me one thing, and I say, well, maybe, yes. How do you argue with your parents? You can't. You have to be able to talk to a coach on a one-to-one basis, and you can't always do that with your parents. You know, you're always their little girl. I am still my father's little girl. You can't keep your parents out of it altogether. But I definitely don't think they should be involved with coaching, because for one thing parents are not that good as coaches. Okay. They think they're great players and they have read every book, and they—you just can't talk to them. Coaches can be very helpful. Hopefully, the father will stay in the background. Peter Graf was the exception to the rule, where it actually worked with the parent as the coach. But I think for the most part that starting so serious so young will be very detrimental to them later."

As the draw opened up over the two weeks of play, it turned out that Navratilova had got a very good draw. She was someone who made her own luck. She did not beat her opponents; she crushed them. She came on like a big wave crashing onto the beach. Having been trounced by Monica Seles 6–1, 6–1 in the final of the Italian Open in Rome on red clay just six weeks earlier, she had the pressure off. Navratilova was able to go about her grass-court business in relative peace. The hungry English tabloid reporters were more attracted to the heat of sexual publicity around Graf and Sabatini and the young brilliance of Monica Seles, who had won the Italian, German, and French Opens. But when Seles lost on the baseline to Zina Garrison, a volleyer, 9–7 in a third-set quarter-final thriller, the door was ajar for Navratilova. For once, she distributed the pressure without letting it land like a vulture on her own shoulders.

Navratilova played Gabriela Sabatini in the semifinals, and the coltish Argentinian did not seem to mind being dispatched by a legend in the round of four. Sabatini had been on the tour since she was fifteen, and she seemed to still subscribe to the pecking order of women's tennis. The Argentinian was content to be third or fourth best and had never won a Grand Slam final. Navratilova was one step away from her dream of surpassing the great Helen Wills's eight Wimbledon singles wins. Navratilova had to beat just one more woman player. It was not Steffi Graf.

The German lost 6–3, 4–6, 6–4 to the American Zina Garrison—the first black woman to reach the finals at Wimbledon since Althea Gibson won Wimbledon in straight sets in 1957 and 1958. Garrison's career had ridden an emotional roller-coaster. Less talented in the hand, less technically correct than Martina, Garrison had suffered for several years from the eating disorder bulimia. In the recent past, the black woman from the same tough Houston neighborhood that produced the boxer George Foreman had alternated among hope, uncontrollable appetite, nausea, fasting, and disappointment.

Zina had managed to get her eating under control, and at Wimbledon she wound up wearing Navratilova's angular "MN" clothing logo until she faced her in the final. Zina had not had clothing sponsorship before Martina and Judy Nelson gave her one before the tournament. As Arthur Ashe put it, "Zina was not exactly the little blonde girl next door."

In the past, Zina Garrison was not known for having a positive recall button. She had a reputation for *choking* in close matches. But in the semis she played bravely and Steffi Graf cracked under the pressure.

The sleek-moving German liked to dominate completely, and like Navratilova, when she did not do so Graf got nervous. Steffi Graf's nerves showed against Garrison in the place where they had been appearing all season, her undercut backhand. Graf's backhand was the repository of all her self-doubt, and Zina Garrison kept chipping away at it, coming forward to volley down on Graf's floating, undercut responses. The gradual change in Graf's backhand stroke was key to the match and her metamorphosis from world champion to unhappy daughter. At first, Graf played Zina Garrison with disdainful confidence. But as Zina kept attacking her, Graf's entire personality became isolated in her backhand, and it ached. The case of nerves spread to Graf's brilliant forehand. In the end, Graf played as if she could depend on nothing, least of all her father.

Zina Garrison recognized doubt when she saw it and repeatedly went into Graf's weaker side. But apart from her opponent's uncertainty, why did Garrison, a notorious choker in the past, win?

Confidence. And the source of Zina Garrison's confidence was love. Black, five feet four inches tall, faster around the court than any woman on tour except Steffi Graf, Zina Garrison was in the best mental and physical shape of her life. That might sound conventional, but not to Zina Garrison, whose mother had raised her children all by herself.

Garrison had the type of inward pain and drive you cannot manufacture by taking tennis lessons at the country club. When Zina was eleven months old, her father, Ulysses, a postman, died of a stroke. Less than a year later, her much older twenty-one-year-old brother, Willie Garrison, a minor league catcher for the Milwaukee Braves, was hit by a foul ball in his left eye, developed a tumor, and died. Her life sounded like a scene from Bernard Malamud's "The Natural." And it got tougher. In 1983, when she was just starting to travel on the pro tennis tour, Zina Garrison's mother died from complications of diabetes, leaving Zina completely alone. After her mother's death she became bulimic. "My mother was the one thing I had," remembered Zina. "She was the one person I could talk to, the person who could understand me. She was there when I needed her. When my mother died, all of a sudden I felt alone."

Garrison threw herself into her tennis and was a hard fighter, except when she had a lead and was overcome by fits of nerves. When it got close in a tennis match, the young black woman did not seem to have a very high opinion of herself. Not many of the white women on the tour had befriended her. Zina found lots of ways to lose close matches, especially to great players like Navratilova, Evert, Graf, and Seles. Off court, she began to go on wild eating binges, followed by nausea and fasting. "I had an empty space in my life," she admitted to Houston writer Lloyd Gite in an interview for *Essence* magazine. "The only way to fill that space was with food. And then I'd force myself to throw up. I was throwing up blood. I was destroying myself as a person and a player. Bulimia does not just destroy your insides. It starts messing with your mind, because you are depressed all the time."

It was during this time that Garrison gained the reputation for being moody off the court and inconsistent on the court. All that changed at Wimbledon in 1990. Zina Garrison had finally found the love of her life and her confidence.

It was not an easy search. The first thing she did at the urging of friends was seek help from a psychiatrist. It helped a lot. "The therapist made me deal with everything in my life," she said. "The bulimia. My mother's death. The men in my life. My tennis game."

Ten months after starting her therapy, with her ranking still sliding, she met the love of her life, handsome Willard Jackson, who owned a waste-management company in Texas. "He's helped a lot," Garrison admitted with love in her eyes and a shy smile. "I'm more relaxed, much more positive. And now I'm not worried about what my boyfriend is doing back home. Willard travels with me a lot."

"It was not love at first sight for her," Willard Jackson explained to Lloyd Gite in his gentle way. "I was very attracted to Zina when I first saw her, but I didn't think I had a chance of getting a date with her. I thought for sure she'd be taken. I don't mind being the husband to the star. Hey. I enjoy it. We're a team. She's out in front, and I'm more in a support role," said Zina's young husband.

Garrison also had a new coach with her at Wimbledon—the doubles specialist from Houston, big Sherwood Stewart, an excellent volleyer and coach who kept urging her to come forward.

"Willard's starting to coach now, too," laughed Garrison. "Me and Sherwood straightened that out real quick. I said, 'Sherwood, get on him!' "

"It's hard *not* to coach," said Willard sheepishly. "I'm up there watching. My stomach's churning, too." At Wimbledon, Zina Garrison finally had two people rooting for her, a coach and a husband.

"I know I'm inconsistent," admitted Garrison. "But I'm good." She had always felt acutely black in a predominantly white sport. The year before at Wimbledon she called Althea Gibson to ask for help, not because she had any desire to be the "next Althea Gibson," but because Garrison wanted technical help. Zina's ground strokes were not fluid. She choked up on her grip and tended to chop down on the ball, a stroke best suited to only one kind of court: grass. At Wimbledon, Garrison acknowledged the help she had received from two older women players. Contemporaries rarely help each other.

"Last year at Wimbledon, I called Althea Gibson back in America. I felt suddenly like Althea was the only one who could really understand. Actually, Billie Jean King helped me a lot this year. Billie told me that sometimes you feel like you don't deserve to win because of something that has happened in the past. In my case, back even to the slavery days. I started to understand it. I wasn't afraid of it anymore. Billie Jean's conversation with me really helped. See, you get in a position to win or lose a match, and you have to feel like you *deserve* to win. Then you can win."

Something had worked. The scrappy black woman from Houston beat Monica Seles 9–7 in the third set and Steffi Graf 6–4 in the third set. In the final, with Althea Gibson flown over by NBC especially for the match, Zina faced a player who understood and shared the young black woman's loneliness and her tough life perhaps more than any other player but Lori McNeil.

Navratilova and Garrison walked across the bright green lawn together, curtseyed to Princess Diana and the Duchess of Kent and the other royals, and began warming up on the most famous court in the world. They were both very nervous, especially Navratilova, who nearly lost her serve in the second game of the match. The key for Garrison, as it had always been for Chris Evert, was to get Martina so precariously balanced between her physical talent and her emotional vulnerability that she cracked. If Garrison had won one of the several break points she held in Navratilova's opening service game, the outcome might have been different. Other women, especially Evert, but also Billie Jean King, knew how to get past Navratilova's hard body and get into her sensitive head and throw a going-away party. But Garrison could not do it. She was carrying too much mental weight and was too tired from getting through her half of a very tough draw. History repeated itself. Her recall button was hit, but to Martina's advantage. Their bodies and minds both remembered. Navratilova beat Zina Garrison 6–4, 6–1 for the twenty-seventh time in their twenty-eight meetings.

Zina Garrison smiled gently and trotted up to net. Martina Navratilova thrust both her arms into the air and smiled in something like the relief, the pain, and absolute joy of the orgasmic moment of winning Wimbledon. Navratilova had broken the Helen Wills record. She had won Wimbledon nine times.

In her previous eight victories, Navratilova had met and beaten Chris Evert five times (1978, 1979, 1982, 1984, and 1985), Hana Mandlikova once (1986), Steffi Graf once (1987), and the nearly forgotten child prodigy Andrea Jaeger once (1983). She was certainly the greatest player of her era and possibly the greatest of any era.

Typically, Navratilova did not have long to enjoy the pleasure of her victory. The blow came from the only woman player who had more career Grand Slam victories than Navratilova, Margaret Smith Court. The big Australian woman, the most physically powerful woman ever to play tennis, said in Australia three days after Navratilova's victory, "Martina is a poor role model for young players like my daughter because she is a lesbian."

It was a cruel remark. Margaret Smith had been such a great player herself. Something in the Australian woman was still competing. If she had seen Martina Navratilova struggle and weep through the years, if she had seen the Czechoslovak woman try to come to terms with herself and finally find temporary peace and a strong happiness that Bill Tilden never found, perhaps a great champion like Margaret Smith—who happened to find love in another way—would not have taken a potshot at what Martina Navratilova had just accomplished.

Bill Tilden, seven times U.S. champion and winner of Wimbledon in 1920, 1921, and 1930, three of the six times he crossed the ocean by boat to play at Wimbledon, died in 1953 in a Hollywood motel, trying to become a playwright, recovering from a jail term for soliciting young boys. Charlie Chaplin, who knew that great people do not always conform, tried to help Tilden by getting him to take a coaching job at the club in Monte Carlo. Tilden refused. He had lost his stage, the competitive tennis court, and thought he could write plays in Hollywood. Martina Navratilova was as great a player as Bill Tilden, and modern times were slightly more tolerant.

Navratilova kept trying. Anyone who admires effort for its pureness had to admire what she had done. What she did off the court was her own business. She paid a price in sponsorship popularity. But the crowd finally grasped the greatness of Navratilova's accomplishment. After her victory the entire Wimbledon stands rose as one to applaud Martina

Navratilova. Her path to glory had not been an easy one. She stood on court, basking in her moment. The toughness of her draw in life had made it all the more probable that she would finally get what she wanted. The fans in England cheered her until Martina Navratilova, overcome with emotion, took off her glasses, rubbed her eyes, waved, and grinned like a little girl.

The women's draw, like the men's draw sheet, had started with 128 names, and at the end of two weeks there was only one name remaining. Just one seat left in musical chairs. The players Martina Navratilova beat were:

ROUND	OPPONENT	SCORES
(128)	S. Amiach	6–1, 6–1
(64)	A. Smith	6–2, 6–3
(32)	K. Kschwendt	6–1, 6–1
(16)	J. Wiesner	6–3, 6–3
(8)	K. Maleeva	6–1, 6–1
(4)	G. Sabatini	6–3, 6–4
(2)	Z. Garrison	6–4, 6–1

She did not lose a set in the entire tournament. The draw sheet Navratilova went through at Wimbledon looked like this when she had played the finals:

(1)
Martina Navratilova
WINNER
6–4, 6–1
Navratilova
6–3, 6–4
Navratilova
6–1, 6–1
Navratilova
6–3, 6–3
Navratilova
6–1, 6–1
Navratilova
6–2, 6–3
Navratilova
6–1, 6–1

Seeded second and therefore at the bottom of the draw, Navratilova had climbed her way up the steep steps of the pyramid.

Stiff and slightly formal personalities and tennis games never win Wimbledon. Above all, winning Wimbledon requires suppleness, physical and mental power, quickness, and a delight in coming to the net. The Wimbledon grass requires that the winning player have the type of personality the English troops had in World War I: to win, you have to climb out of the protective bunker—the baseline—and rush forward instinctively across the grass to make the volley.

Ivan Lendl had proved a good, even an ardent learner, and Tony Roche was a great tutor on grass, but Lendl had started his course too late, and grass-court play went against his basic controlling nature. Like Agassi, Lendl had skipped Wimbledon the first two or three years of his career. In effect, Lendl was also two or three grades behind his contemporaries on grass. Agassi was repeating Lendl's earlier mistake. He was missing valuable learning time the way Lendl had in the early 1980s, when he was young and did not want to be humiliated on grass by John McEnroe and Jimmy Connors. But often, winning only comes through the front door of losing.

Now Lendl wanted the one thing that, historically, he had not been able to have. So deep was Lendl's commitment to winning Wimbledon on grass—the surface that least suited his nature because of its bad bounces and general uncertainty, its requirement that one rush forward into that land of reflex and chaos, the volley—that Lendl built a special grass court on his estate in Greenwich, Connecticut. No detail was overlooked. The court cost over $500,000 to build and the grass was the same sod used at Wimbledon, imported so that Lendl would practice with Tony Roche on the real thing. Lendl made manic preparations. He wanted each of his Japanese rackets to be at perfect string tension. In practice he used a new racket every eleven games, discarding the old frame, in order to simulate exactly what he did under match conditions. Lendl also purchased over a hundred dozen of the tennis balls used at Wimbledon, calling for new balls in practice after the equivalent of every seven games. Like Navratilova, who had become a metabolic perfectionist, Lendl left nothing to chance. The problem was that *chance*, risk, was part of what winning with the serve and volley at Wimbledon was all about. Lendl had been unwilling to practice following his serve to net at the Lipton on hard courts. Now, by skipping the French Open to concentrate on winning Wimbledon, which had always turned its back on him, Lendl was either going to produce a miracle through dedication or badly hurt himself trying.

After winning at Queens, Lendl was as dominant in the opening rounds at Wimbledon on grass as he once had been at Roland-Garros on clay. He needed just two more victories. But Lendl was tight in the first set with Edberg and lost it 6–1. Tony Roche, as loyal as the Australian summer is long, sat watching intently in the players' box with Ivan Lendl's attractive, black-haired wife, Samantha, pregnant for the second time in two years. Roche was quiet. He knew how far Lendl had come as a grass-court player. But Roche had been a finalist at Wimbledon in 1968 to Rod Laver, and he also knew that there were some things in life you could want with all your heart and never have.

Lendl had Edberg fully engaged in the second set. Ivan saved five break points with his powerful but highly formal-looking serve to go up 4–3 in the second set, and Lendl held break point on Edberg's serve in the next game. If Lendl had won it, he would have been serving at 5–3 to level the match at one set apiece. On break point, Lendl hit a forehand cross court with the snarl of a Doberman pinscher. The ball ripped down toward Edberg's forehand corner, a passing shot against anyone. But Edberg, lunging deeply to the right, his mouth nearly tasting the net cord, barely touched the ball with his racket extended like a sword but left it, dead on the grass, just on the other side of the net. Ivan Lendl's jaw dropped in disbelief. He thought he had broken Edberg's serve.

The second-set tie-breaker went to Stefan Edberg 7–2 on a series of forehand exchanges, the side where Edberg was supposed to be weaker. When the Swede had outplayed Lendl in the area of Lendl's greatest strength, the rest of the match was less difficult to win. The strong but stiff-moving Czech lost the semifinal to Stefan Edberg, the far more supple person and player by decisive scores: 6–1, 7–6, 6–3. In the green box seats, Samantha Lendl sat behind her Audrey Hepburn dark glasses. Tony Roche bowed his head. He was disappointed, too.

The Swede came to net and whispered a soft apology to Lendl with a bittersweet, understanding smile and turn of the head; Lendl, his dark eyes ringed with self-imposed pressure, stared up at the weird light coming over the low roof of the old English stadium.

In preparing for Wimbledon single-mindedly, in skipping the French Open, Lendl had set himself up for disappointment. He isolated his weakness and pursued it relentlessly, as if hoping to eliminate his last imperfection, like Ahab and the whale. The obsession was doomed to self-destruction. Lendl could not do it, and perhaps that would be his saving grace. Lendl would never be a great grass-court player—that is, a Wimbledon champion. The Czechoslovak American was at home on French clay and American cement—surfaces which had always been much more friendly to him—but he gave up Paris to fight for what always would be so unkind to him, Wimbledon. In that folly and pursuit of potential crushing disappointment, I liked him. The Duchess of Kent, her blonde hair spun like cotton candy, was probably never going to put the winner's trophy into Ivan Lendl's hand. She had never given it to Rosewall, either.

"Psychologically," said Lendl of his obsession, "I think I have come as far as I can with it."

Goran Ivanisevic took his warm-up serves first, and the English crowd was gasping at the speed. Her Royal Highness Princess Diana attended the semifinal, and although she had liked Boris Becker very much the year before, this year, when Becker was favored, Princess Di let it be known that she was rooting for the tall young Slav with the string of upsets and wicked unstoppable serves. She applauded both players enthusiastically as they bowed perfunctorily in her direction, but as the match progressed, the princess's body language showed she seemed more taken with the dark-haired newcomer than with the past winner.

With his jet-black hair, milk-white skin, and thin six-foot four-inch body, Goran Ivanisevic was dramatically handsome and could also really deliver the ball into the corners. Ivanisevic's serve was not only hard, it was incredibly quick. If he were a boxer, his knockout punch would be like Muhammad Ali's over Sonny Liston, very short and almost invisible. Ivanisevic's service motion was compact with a short toss and sudden hammer, the way many of the best tennis servers—Roscoe Tanner, Kevin Curren, John Newcombe—fired off their guns with a quick, short motion. With them, the service ace was over almost before the motion was finished.

Boris Becker, who had lost to young Ivanisevic at the exhibition match in Lausanne and at the French Open on red clay, looked thoroughly concentrated on his work as he dipped his muscular thighs and hit his own warm-up bullets, scattering the Wimbledon linespeople against the backstops. Becker did not have to play around in this one to keep his own attention. He knew he could lose, and he very nearly did. Ivanisevic, who outserved Kevin Curren in the quarter-finals, went wild with aces again. He hit seventy-eight aces in the tournament and twenty-six against Becker. His short left-handed backswing hammered serve after serve into the corners with tremendous skidding results. Becker could not guess which side to cover. The grass and limed lines were streaked with long marks. But Becker grew huge inside with the desire to overcome, and he held on, as Edberg had against Mansdorf, finally absorbing the young Yugoslav's willpower and strength by the margin of 4–6, 7–6, 6–0, 7–6.

"Will Goran Ivanisevic win Wimbledon one day?" the press asked Ion Tiriac afterwards.

"Goran will not only win Wimbledon once. He will win it five times!" declared Tiriac before he disappeared.

I chased after Tiriac as I had at the Lipton, when he said he would give me an interview the next day and then flew back to Europe. I wanted to ask him about the insides of Boris Becker, but after Becker held on by a string to beat Ivanisevic and Tiriac declared Ivanisevic the new Cinderella, the Romanian with the horseshoe mustache and hockey player shoulders disappeared into the changing rooms and never returned my calls.

The Romanian was elusive. As a businessman, he could be a finesse player as well as a power player. Tiriac rarely missed a trick. As regards Ivanisevic, his client's still young opponent, Tiriac was either right or his compliment would hang for years like a large stone around Goran Ivanisevic's neck.

Boris Becker and Stefan Edberg walked out together to play a final as they had so many times before, both as juniors players and as young men. The perfect putting surface of Wimbledon's first day had been reduced to a short, fast grass surface, hard and nearly bare around the service lines. Divots had been replaced. The grass had been rolled four dozen times. It was a flat, dry bed on which to dive.

The Royal Box was crowded with well-born men and women and elegant ladies in sun hats. The last row of the Royal Box was packed tight with actors, comedians, and handsome captains. New tennis balls were rolled out, and the two young champions began hitting at each other.

Boris Becker was still young but experienced beyond his years. After referring on the first day of play to the grass court as a "friend," presumably female, Becker added, "I have been away from for a whole year.

The grass here is faster than at Queens Club. They cut it shorter at Wimbledon."

Becker and Edberg. It was the first time that the same two players had met in three consecutive Wimbledon finals since the nineteenth century, when Renshaw beat Lawford three times in a row in the 1880s, twice in four sets and once in three sets. The two players knew the road they had to go down. "I know him blind," said Becker before the match. The red highlights in his hair had turned blondish red from all the sun.

It is usual for an audience to look for itself in the two players deciding a final. Becker's size, bulk, and country made him seem to many like the bully, but I felt the shape of my own body more in Becker's thick-set frame than in Edberg's slender, attractive, self-effacing strength. It was possible to like them both, but Becker was my favorite. I liked the way he dove for the ball. I liked his exuberance and his excesses, his interest in books, and his struggles to understand himself. But in the first two sets, Boris Becker played listless tennis, as if back in the match he lost to Edberg in the Masters final at Madison Square Garden in 1989; he seemed to expect fate and history to win this match for him, as a right, not from effort. It never works that way.

But a transformation took place during the great five-set match, which changed like the Circle Line of the London Underground through the personalities of these two great attacking players. The Swede's determination was fiercest at the start. The German had played Stefan Edberg twenty-three times as an adult and held a 15–8 edge going into the match, having beaten the Swede in seven of their nine finals. Edberg played that day as if he had to overcome his own ghost, the contented runner-up.

At the outset, Becker, the more natural bully or dominator in terms of physical strength, played as if power were the only answer, and as a result he could do nothing right. By contrast, riding his serve into net as if the kick serves were huge waves, Edberg banged his volleys away with a firm wrist and a steely Swedish will. Becker was forced into an uncomfortable defensive position. As the first two sets were swept away emphatically by Edberg, 6–2, 6–2, Becker began to look like a passenger on a sinking ocean liner who jumps overboard wearing an orange life vest, hoping a passing ship will spot him, pick him up, and take him in another direction. A shift in fortune did not look likely. Down two sets to love, the red-headed German with the blonde stubble beard stared at the worn grass near the net and, hesitating there as he thought about all that he had done wrong, gave the air above the immaculate English grass a kick.

Edberg was still going full steam ahead. The match with Amos Mansdorf in the round of sixteen had left the Swede sharp as a razor on his volleys, which continually hit the grass and skidded out of reach. Edberg was "unconscious," as the players say, and that was the only way to play tennis, setting a table for one in that quiet inner space. Edberg was so deeply inside himself that Becker, still bobbing and weaving on the surface of the event, could not penetrate him. Confident of himself at the outset, Becker now looked less and less sure of winning. And that was when he was most dangerous. His face changed. He became quiet. Becker was a wrestler on his back about to be pinned. And then he escaped.

Edberg had played like a champion for two sets, but in the third set, with victory so close at hand, the Swede could also smell its opposite— defeat. When a player is that close to something he wants, he gets the taste of both, victory and defeat, in his mouth, and sometimes he confuses them. Winning and losing should be kept separate because they do not mix well. But Edberg, hard and fierce at the start, but gradually gentler and ultimately less sure of himself than Becker, suddenly did what Paul Annacone had done in his five-set loss to David Wheaton: he tried to coast home on his merits. The fierceness of the boy from Västervik that had brought Edberg to the threshold of victory suddenly seemed pacified by the two-set lead. The fire began to die in the Swede. And Becker, instead of arrogantly banging his returns of serve with full swings, made very sure he acknowledged how well his opponent was serving by first more cautiously getting a few returns of serve back onto the court. No player will miss a ball that is not in. As Edberg finally began to miss one or two reflex volleys, Becker came to life. The role reversal, the transformation, was complete. Now Becker began to produce heat. It started with his return of serve and finally reached his own serve, the boiler room.

Edberg had won the first and second sets 6–2, 6–2. Becker won the third and fourth sets 6–3, 6–3.

They were capable of dominating each other, and neither looked happy with the realization. Edberg looked particularly distraught. As he sat low in his canvas changing chair, he glanced over his shoulder at Annette Olsen and Tony Pickard, who made a fist.

Edberg dried off his legs and went back out onto the grass stage where Becker was already waiting for him. It seemed to be the perfect comeback scenario for Becker. The romantic notion that the German boy pursued was that of the underdog who comes back against incredible odds—James Dean at the edge of the cliff. Becker often complicated things for himself. He was not the first tennis player to do so, but all the icing on the cake could have been Becker's with just a bit more killer instinct.

The English crowd was for the Swede who lived in London. Edberg lit the fire deep inside him, the fire of a Swedish policeman who never used his own violence unless he absolutely had to. The fighter in Edberg was tempered by his mother's gentleness, and it emerged heroically in Edberg from underneath all the weight Becker had put on him while winning the third and fourth sets. After nearly four hours the Wimbledon final went into the fifth set. Suddenly, Edberg's serve was broken.

The television sets in Germany were turned on to watch Boris, one of the few heroes the Germans had allowed themselves since Gottfried von Cramm lost three finals in a row, two to Fred Perry and one to Don Budge. Suddenly in the fifth set Boris Becker was rolling happily over the grass, a big, strong kid playing well within himself. At times, Becker displayed a maturity and sense of proportion unusual in a person so young. If he completed the reversal and won from two sets down, the resilient German would be the first player to do so at Wimbledon since the talented Henri Cochet beat the clever Jean Borotra 7–5 in the fifth set on the same Wimbledon Center Court in 1927.

When Becker broke the Swede's serve and went up 3–1 in the fifth set at Wimbledon, the comeback looked complete. Like German soldiers in the Second World War, Becker was most dangerous when forced to retreat. But when he won sets too easily, he sometimes became complacent, bored, even arrogant. The war metaphor was unfortunate, but watching Becker play in the light of a reunified Germany, you could not help but wonder if history is not the story of life captured in our bodies, and sport the peacetime battleground of those bodies.

The Swede would not quit. Less visibly determined than either of his countrymen, Borg or Wilander, Edberg said after the match that he was furious with himself after he double-faulted to give Becker the service break for the 3–1 lead. But Becker behaved curiously with leads. Sometimes, he was invincible when he got on a roll, gaining psychological and physical momentum. Becker was up a service break in the fifth set. But Edberg reopened the chink in the German's armor. Tiriac, Becker's coach, had said at the Lipton, "This loss has nothing to do with tennis!"

Becker's head had betrayed his body against the Frenchman, Fleurian, in Florida. At Wimbledon, the big German boy's mind again began to betray his body. It came down to a battle of wills. Something in Becker, some particle of self-doubt, made the German soften his resolve. The Swede, pumping the air when he broke back, hung on at 4–4, rebroke Becker's serve in the ninth game, and came home strong. Becker—like Navratilova, like McEnroe—was a great one and a strange one, so strong and so stubborn on the outside, yet vulnerable beneath it all.

Something about Stefan Edberg was like the man I imagined Raoul Wallenberg to have been: tall, thin, blonde, uncertain at times, but never a quitter. In England, at Wimbledon 1990, Stefan Edberg came back from the 1–3 fifth-set mire and won the match 6–4 in the fifth with five of the set's last six games.

The Swede lifted his arms in joy and belted the ball high into the old wooden stands where the pigeons, reporters, and fans have watched tennis for so long. Then, full of joy, Edberg took off his shirt the way Agassi had when Agassi beat him at the Lipton, and for the one and only time in his career, Edberg threw his wet shirt up into the English crowd to give them something, as he said later, for rooting for him. At different times, in different ways, Edberg and Becker had both been brave. In the moments when most people would have shown doubt, they each had continued to come forward. That was grass. That was Wimbledon.

The aftermath of the match was touching. Becker put an arm around Edberg and gave him a hug. For the tennis players, there was the match, the effort, the sensation of victory and defeat as it sank in through their sweat and feelings. Winning dries off after a shower, but losing seeps in for days. The two young champions had played each other since they were children. Edberg, twenty-four, was nearly three years older than Becker and he had always been the prodigy of the two, beating the young German phenom 6–3, 6–3 when Boris was fifteen in the quarter-finals of the Rolex junior tournament in Port Washington, New York. Edberg did not remember their junior match, but Becker, who lost it, did. Asked why he hugged Edberg when it was over, Boris Becker said, "My feeling was that I know how it feels both ways. With Stefan, we have been going through so many matches, some tough ones, some easier ones. We have played each other when we were both like children. I guess, you know, that it just came over me then."

They were not friends exactly, but the fight had brought them close. They knew each other's insides. "It is never good to come second," said Edberg, acknowledging Becker's hug in defeat. "I came second last year and many, many times. It is such a big difference between winning and losing a final. I took it quite hard last year when I lost, because I thought I really had a chance to win against him. I was very fired up, and maybe that is why I won today. I wanted so much to win that fifth set."

Edberg's determination had seen him through to the end. He had this to say about winning at Wimbledon and winning in general:

> I admit I save my big emotions for the tennis court . . . I think ordinary people are much more happy than the jetset and celebrity people. My parents, whom I respect as my greatest friends, taught me early that happiness is often a modest thing. It has nothing to do with money or fame.

Edberg's gray-haired English coach, Tony Pickard, limping into the interview bunker on his replaced hip like Alec Guinness in *The Bridge on the River Kwai*, hugged his pupil and had the final word: "Becker had him three–one in the fifth. Let's face it, he was gone. People think he's got no fire. I'm telling you he has!"

The survivors at Wimbledon—one man and one woman, Stefan Edberg and Martina Navratilova—had withstood two weeks of physical and personality slaughter. All the other bodies and minds had been beaten down after two weeks on the fast green English lawns until only those two names were left solitary on the diver's platform at the end of the draw.

BORIS BECKER

Leimen, West Germany

Boris Becker's hometown is an hour and a half south of Frankfurt by train and a half-hour south of Heidelberg by the old blue and white streetcar. Small modern suburban shops and homes had sprung up along the streetcar route from Heidelberg to Leimen so that I was almost in and out of town before I knew it. I asked the streetcar driver for an affordable hotel, and he pointed down a steep hill. The small modern hotel was surrounded by pale blue Opels and eight-year-old Mercedes. It looked affordable on American dollars.

"Hey," said the friendly American soldier with the Texas accent, getting off with me at the last stop in Leimen, "if you're looking for something to do, take that same *Strassenbahn*, the number three, back to Heidelberg and tell the driver that you want to get off at Bismarckplatz. They're having a fest this weekend."

The "fest" was a celebration in honor of Germany's reunification a few weeks away. I thanked the American soldier and went into the hotel on the outskirts of Leimen.

A small gold plaque on the stairwell announced,

> This building was designed by the
> architect, Karl-Heinz Becker,

father of the Wimbledon Champion,
Boris Becker

I smiled at the coincidence and pulled out my American Express card. The hotel designed by Boris Becker's father was well constructed and built to show a profit. The rooms were quite small but clean. The four-story hotel had a sparkling clean terrazzo marble staircase and entry foyer, a breakfast room with banquette seats and a cozy atmosphere, and, beneath it all, a rock-solid concrete construction with underground parking for four cars, a surprise for a hotel that small. This was the newer and less expensive of the two hotels in Leimen. At the front desk, the modern little small-town German hotel had three words printed on its business card: *kultiviert*, *behaglich*, and *gepflegt* ("cultivated," "snug," and "immaculate").

The hotel owner, a thin man who wore half-glasses at the end of a sharp nose, was dressed in a traditional gray wool jacket with green wool trim. He peered with concern for his guests over his glasses.

"Mr. Becker designed this hotel?" I asked in tourist German, thrilled to be there.

"Ja. Karl-Heinz Becker," said the hotel man solemnly with a precise smile. "Twenty years ago."

"Twenty years ago?" Boris Becker was three when construction began. The hotel building was well built. It looked newer than it was.

"Ja. Karl-Heinz Becker does not design much anymore," the Leimen hotelier continued with a not altogether friendly chuckle. "Now he has the Boris for a living."

A little touch of German envy. The hotelier's accompanying smile was *zer suce*, very sweet. The architect, Mr. Becker, was twenty years out of the deal, and the hotelier still had to get up for breakfast with his guests and serve them in his traditional jacket. The Leimen hotelier was a recognizable small-town German character, the type who refers to the young woman who serves the butter and jam in the morning for breakfast as "*mein Kollege*," my colleague.

I crashed into sleep that night after the long day's travel. Becker was relaxing in Kitzbühel, Austria, playing a small clay-court event before heading to America for the U.S. Open, skipping the hard-court events in Cincinnati, Toronto, and Indianapolis. He lost to Karel Novacek in the quarter-finals in Austria on the red clay. Becker was still unwinding from Wimbledon.

At 6:30 A.M. the next day, Saturday, I got up for a walk. Thick white mist sifted over the symmetrical houses of Leimen. There was not a soul yet on the streets. Up the hill, the town bakery was open for business, sweet smelling and spotless. I had a fresh peach danish. Gradually, children began to appear.

They climbed up from the valley on the soft slopes of the hill leading into town. A hundred years before, the children would have been coming out of the fields, but now they hurried up the hill on bicycle or foot, with large yellow school bags on their backs. By seven o'clock on a Saturday morning, all the young children in Leimen seemed to be heading in the same direction: school.

Leimen's town center is a small triangle down the cobblestone hill from the school. Two diesel Mercedes taxis are always waiting in front of the town's first hotel, Zum Baren, built in 1666. The old hotel, the *Rathaus* (town hall), and several other public buildings built in the seventeenth century have brown wooden cross-hatchings and bay windows that overhang the street.

The kids walked up the cobbled street past the old hotel to their grade school, the *Volkschule*, which Boris Becker attended for grades one to four. At fourteen, he took the streetcar every day to high school in Heidelberg, but he had started his education at the large brownstone grade school with its impressive black mansard roof, black roof turrets, and wood frame windows painted white. The cobblestone streets converging at the school were too narrow for the parents to park their cars as they let off their kids at the top of the hill. I watched the scene, the hurried kisses good-bye, the rush of children's feet up the school steps. The eighty-foot-wide brownstone elementary school, like many buildings in Leimen, dated to 1910, a year of big growth attributed to the birth of Leimen's cement industry. The German townspeople apparently valued education: despite their booming cement business in 1910, they used brownstone—a far more expensive material—to construct their grade school.

Inside the school, the old stone floors were scrubbed sparkling clean. Boys and girls held each other's hands as they walked from classroom to classroom behind their teachers that early Saturday morning. The German children were almost too well-behaved. Among all the cute blonde kids, a heavy redhead would have stood out like a sore thumb. I could smell the bakery across the street, and I imagined young Becker there, taller than the other children at the baker's counter. He was large and a bit overweight as a child.

Listening to him talk at the Lipton and at Wimbledon, I had sensed

Becker's intelligence. He was a little different, and that was part of Becker's appeal and the mystery as to why he self-destructed. He seemed destined for greatness. The interesting thing was that he might refuse that greatness. It was no surprise to me that Becker was so articulate and reflective when he spoke English. These little German kids were very well educated—they were all in school on Saturday morning by 7:15.

Before breakfast, I went looking in the heavy mist for Becker's home. The Beckers lived down in the valley at the very edge of town, facing the fields and low mountains outside Heidelberg. Some of the town's fields had been sold to build the local tennis club, whose architect, Karl-Heinz Becker, had designed it when his son was three. The Beckers lived not far away in a modest, square concrete-block apartment building that was four stories high. They rented two apartments and the ground-floor office at the side of the building. The apartment had its back to the town, so to speak, and its windows toward the fields. One sensed that many years ago, before his son ever played tennis, the architect Becker found exactly where he wanted to be.

The Beckers had lived in the same place for over thirty years, and the family remained very close; Becker's sister became an architect like her father. In a newspaper column that ran in over fifty newspapers across Europe in 1987—the German press was paying Becker up to $20,000 for a single interview, a price Tiriac still recommends—young Becker wrote, "Every year at Christmas time I go away with my family for a quiet vacation. This year we are going to a little Italian village. I'm looking forward to it. It's one thing that being a professional has not taken away from me."

After Becker won Wimbledon at seventeen, his father turned fifty. The son was playing indoors in Brussels at the time and phoned home to offer congratulations. That same night in Leimen there was a knock on the door and Boris walked in, unannounced, to surprise his father. He then flew back to Brussels the next morning and won the final. Later that year, still seventeen and while he was playing at the Wembley indoor tournament in London, the front door in Leimen rang again late at night. Boris was standing in the doorway light, grinning from ear to ear; he had flown back from England to sing "Happy Birthday" to his mother.

I was surprised by Becker's sensitivity. His competitive nature was less adamant than, say, that of Thomas Muster or Michael Chang. Becker had said as much to Arno Luik: "My opponents are human beings first, not opponents or enemies. I simply don't like it if someone is being destroyed like that. After a six–love, six–love match, you're exhausted, you've had your skin pulled up over your eyes and you're done for. That's below one's dignity. . . . I often am too nice to my opponents. That is why I shall never play as well as Lendl for so long a time."

Breakfast at the modern hotel Herr Becker had designed in Leimen was super *gemütlich*, very cozy. At eight-thirty, after the walk in the fog to the bakery and the school, "Moon River" was being piped gently into the breakfast room. Smiling to the Muzak, the wife of the lean Leimen hotelier served the morning coffee to each table of guests as the owner wandered around the breakfast room in his traditional jacket and short pants making sure everything was in order. The breakfast was bountiful: a large plate of Westphalian ham, cheese, black bread, and *schinken* lox. There was an entire table for muesli, raisins, milk, and croissants. I tried it all. I was in heaven. The breakfast Muzak bounced into a version of "In the Old Fashioned Way," and the fastidious hotelier shooed his wife around the room with her pot of coffee and looked on in horror as I went back for thirds on the Westphalian ham. The Leimen hotelier with the half-glasses and the unfriendly remark about Becker's father stuck in my mind. With the Muzak version of "In the Old Fashioned Way" still humming in my ears from the breakfast room, I headed off to the tennis courts, a five-minute walk away.

Like Steffi Graff's nearby and even smaller town of Brühl, Leimen was a combination of old and new Germany. When the tennis craze hit Germany in the late 1970s, there was still enough vacant land in Leimen to build tennis courts and a modern sports complex—and that is what the town wanted. Now there was an Olympic pool and sauna, soccer fields, and a gym where the Germans played their version of handball, a combination of basketball and soccer with passing, hand dribbling, and shots taken diving flat out on a wooden floor at a small goal. The Germans had several such indigenous games, and there were local teams and clubs (*Verein*) in Leimen for all the team sports. But tennis was an international sport and an individual sport.

In the 1960s and 1970s, tennis in Germany was quite different from what it is today. At that time, German tennis was like German politics—largely confined to its borders. Even in the late 1970s, when I was watching Wimbledon on TV in Kassel, where I was teaching American literature, German TV interrupted the 13–11 fourth-set tie-breaker of the classic Bjorn Borg–John McEnroe first match at Wimbledon to cut at 7–all in the famous 12–10 tie-breaker to thirty minutes of *Rundfunk* (local news). The Germans had nobody playing in that final, and so local news in Hessen took precedence over the Borg–McEnroe classic. Five years later, Boris Becker became the first German ever to win at Wimbledon. It was not so much that German tennis was different. Boris Becker changed it forever.

Tennis had been a wealthy man's game in Germany, at least since the 1930s and the days of its very talented (and homosexual) champion, Baron Gottfried von Cramm. Over the years, local tennis in Germany remained lucrative for a small number of German players and foreign ex-touring pros who chose to live in Germany and play in the local tennis leagues. Individual clubs were willing to pay the best German players and any available world-class talent a healthy salary to stay and play for the local tennis club once a week. Ilie Nastase, Ion Tiriac, Nikki Pilic, Tom Okker, and others played matches for German club teams when their playing careers were winding down. The rich Germans liked to watch good tennis and bet on the matches. Pride, especially local pride, was the impetus behind German sports at the time. The result was that the German players did not have to go beyond their own borders to make a fine living. This was good for the wallet, bad for the competitor. The endorsement of the number-one player in Germany was worth as much in the local German market as the endorsement of a Rosewall or Laver. The effect was that few German players traveled abroad and risked public losses outside their borders. Without taking the risk of losing badly, they never improved enough to compete well outside of Germany. After Wilhelm Bungert in the 1960s, Boris Becker was the first to really take the full risk. If he had been like the other German players, if the Romanian Ion Tiriac had not got hold of him, Becker could have made great money playing inside Germany and never leaving. The big redhead would have rotted on the vine. But with Tiriac's guidance and financial ambition, Becker took the big step out. He risked losing in order to get better. In 1983, he was ranked 563 in the world as a fifteen-year-old. In 1984, he was sixty-fifth. In 1985, he won Wimbledon and was ranked sixth in the world. He was seventeen. He had learned.

It was the Romanian Tiriac, stopping in Germany to land on his feet financially after his international tennis career was over, who saw young Boris Becker and recognized in this fifteen-year-old boy who liked the bakeries in Leimen a little too well that "there was something special, something extra that not everybody had, and it started with Boris's intelligence and his stubbornness, not his physical strength."

Above all, Tiriac saw that Becker could—and needed to—go beyond the local boundaries of Leimen and of Germany. Talent always needs resistance from other large talent. It rots if it remains unthreatened by potential competition. Before Becker, German tennis had rotted. But the small pond that provided such good incomes for the German teaching and playing professionals was not going to be big enough for young Becker. Tiriac had caught a huge red fish in Boris Becker and put him where he rightfully belonged—in the ocean of world tennis.

Becker had been taught first by Boris Breskvar, a local pro now in charge of tennis for the Bad-Würtemberg region. Breskvar eventually brought in a native of Romania with a German name, Gunther Bosch, who became the German national junior coach and in turn brought in his boyhood friend and Romanian Davis Cup tennis mate, Ion Tiriac, "Count Dracula," who eventually fired him. Tiriac was tougher than Becker, and tennis management, like horse training, is a tough business. Breskvar, who now coaches the rising German star Anke Huber, has renewed old business ties with Tiriac, who gives but also takes.

Like practicing scales on the piano, the tennis backboard is where all great players start. The wall sends back what you are at that moment, and in that way you gradually become what you can be. The red-clay tennis courts where Boris Becker learned to play were still wet with night rain and no one was on them, but at the rear of the club stood a pale green cement practice wall with a white line across it and a patch of red clay in front of it. It was the wall Becker learned on.

Having come at the tennis club from the back road, I sensed old-time Leimen with its country, not city, nature. Chickens and roosters scurried around the old "victory gardens" across the street. In the small field next to the Blau-Weiss ("Blue-White") Tennis Club designed by Herr Becker, two black goats munched grass and butted heads playfully. The Becker tennis club in Leimen was more a part of the fields than of the town.

Inside the indoor section of the club, large color photos of young Boris hung on the walls. Outdoors, the courts at the club were red clay, and the soft, slow European surface explained part of the mystery of why Becker, with his great serve and volley game, often hung back and tried to play from the baseline even on fast cement. The answer was simply what Clemson University's Chuck Kriese would call Becker's recall button. Boris was originally a clay-court player. An attacking serve and volley game was more suited to his size and natural power, but when Becker got into trouble it was usually because he insisted he could beat baseliners from the baseline. It went beyond stubbornness, which Becker had plenty of. When Becker got nervous, he was really just falling back on what he knew first, the slow red-clay courts at home.

The trick for Becker, the measure of his greatness, was to leave his past behind and become the player who, following his body's dictates and not his background, was most at home on the Wimbledon grass and the fast hard courts in New York City. Often Becker hung back, clinging stubbornly to his original game. But to be champion, to be himself, Becker ultimately had to overcome his early clay-court training, his first tennis memories.

Becker was not by nature conservative. The conservative response to a tennis court's open space, the response of Ivan Lendl, Michael Chang, or Mats Wilander, whose very beings seemed to have brought them to a tennis court to make a reply not a put-away, was an effort— as the chess champion Gary Kasparov described the play on a chess board—"to control chaos." Lendl's military tactics were the opposite of what Becker had to have. At his best, Becker, like John McEnroe, was capable of creating his own chaos, and a heavy offense was another way of creating a defense.

Tiriac, who interested me as a survivor and a shadowy figure who consistently eluded me, had recognized an American or Australian explosiveness in young Becker—a willingness to dive and get dirty, the big heart to rush forward to net and cross over the baseline as if it were not there. Lendl's attack was steeped in a ferocious yet fearful defense. Becker's attack was more like Tchaikovsky's "1812 Overture"—the full orchestra.

Far from being the stereotypical strong but cold German of the war movies, Boris Becker was outgoing, open, and casually warm-blooded. Except when he self-destructed, Becker played tennis with a great heart, and the town of Leimen and his family—father, mother, and architect sister—were deep in his heart. But after Boris won Wimbledon at age seventeen, things changed. He became as popular in Germany as the Statue of Liberty in America.

For tax-shelter purposes, Tiriac, whom Mr. Becker had hired, suggested that Boris move to Monaco. The son did move to Monte Carlo;

in fact, France, so different in so many ways from Germany, had always appealed to Boris Becker. He had wanted to win the French Open, though the French for Becker might always be out of reach the way Wimbledon was for Lendl because, despite Becker's red-clay upbringing and his particular love of things French, the German boy's six-foot four-inch, 188-pound body was a little large for the French championships. The Becker family trusted Tiriac but hated to see their son move to Monaco for tax purposes. Becker's father cried when he spoke about Boris after the first Wimbledon win, and he said, "We, the family, felt as if the world had gained a star and we had had our son taken away from us and Leimen."

The family remained exceptionally close, but life changed dramatically for Boris in the years between his first Wimbledon win at age seventeen in 1985 and the middle of the 1990 season, age twenty-two, three times a Wimbledon champion and just a 3–1 fifth-set lead over Edberg away from a fourth Wimbledon title. The German press, which Becker detested for its fickleness, was first-cousin to the English tabloid press. The German press first made Becker its hero and then its villain. In their eyes he was guilty, primarily of growing up. In Hamburg for a Davis Cup match in 1987, a young German woman got Becker's hotel room number wrong and slipped a note meant for Boris under the hotel door of an American photographer. The note to Becker from the unknown German girl read, "I want your tongue to meet mine."

While Becker had no girlfriend at the time, he has had several since. In 1988, after breaking three rackets in a match he lost in Australia to Wally Masur, and then firing his coach, Gunther Bosch, whom Becker accused of trying to turn him into a prisoner like Bjorn Borg, Becker flew to California and played a tournament at Indian Wells. He stayed in a butler-serviced $2,600-a-night villa with his girlfriend from Monte Carlo, Benedicte Courtin. Becker lost in the third round. Jay Berger beat Becker 6–1, 6–1 and called home to tell *his* folks.

Women came into Becker's life and had a strong effect on him. He particularly liked women who had nothing at all to do with sports, especially tennis. He considered such women to be more intelligent. Becker finished high school but possessed a mind that also needed a college. He craved learning about things other than the hermetic world of tennis. The gorgeous Mademoiselle Courtin eventually gave way to a young German woman a few years older than Becker, who taught Romance languages at a German university. In a sense, she *was* college.

She suggested books for him to read, and he read and admired them. He began to think about life. The days were over when the Romanian Tiriac could say to his hungry, innocent young ward, as he had after Boris Becker's first Wimbledon win, "Sloppy legs! Mr. Becker move like elephant. I tell you, Mr. Becker, the moment Wimbledon end, your life is over; you are born again with me. We go to run in Swiss Alps."

But a large part of what Boris Becker was inside—and also what he had consciously *avoided* becoming—was still in Leimen. The small, old German town was perhaps best reflected in the order and cleanliness of the town's public baths and sports complex. According to the schedule for the Fall, the steam bath would produce cleansing heat at 27 degrees Celsius on Tuesdays, Wednesdays, and Sundays, while cleansing heat of 30 degrees Celsius could be had on Fridays and Saturdays. Similarly, the sauna in the Sportpark Leimen offered a clear choice for every sauna need and desire:

Women's Sauna	Tues. and Thurs.	9 A.M. to 10 P.M.
Men's Sauna	Wed. and Sat.	9 A.M. to 10 P.M.
Mixed Sauna	Mon. and Fri.	2 P.M. to 10 P.M.
Family Sauna	Sundays	9 A.M. to 1 P.M.

In Leimen, the men had sole access to the sauna on the best days—Wednesdays and Saturdays—while those interested in the *gemischte* sauna (mixed nude public sauna) could join friends and strangers Mondays and Fridays from 2 P.M. to 10 P.M. The family sauna time was Sundays, just before or just after a church service, *natürlich*.

Back in town at Zum Baren, the 1666 hotel-restaurant, the *wiener schnitzel* was incredibly tender. There was a tall old man eating alone in the corner, pouring red wine out of a little pitcher. He had a look of such craziness in his eyes that even the older couples turned to stare at him. He looked like a veteran of the last war who badly missed his uniform. The waitress pointed to her *kopf*, her head, made a screw-is-loose motion with her finger, and shook her big change purse several times. The man gave the whole room the spooks. They served me an enormous dessert pancake with ice cream, chocolate sauce, and chipped nuts folded together, the best *palatschinken* I ever had, and the owner sent over a *schnaps*. They liked their sweets in Leimen. Food, drink, sport, and Friday nights at the mixed public steam bath. Leimen was quite a typical German town.

Boris Becker had an aura around him unlike any athlete in the world, and part of that aura was German. When the English tabloid press referred to the young German at Wimbledon as "Boom-Boom Becker" because his serves were as heavy as German World War II cannon shots, some of the English-speaking world laughed, but the seventeen-year-old German boy did not. He was more intelligent. His early reception in Paris hurt him at least as much as the English press had by calling him "Boom-Boom!" Boris said of France, "Paris—that's my dream. Paris is a thing by itself. They used to jeer me because I was a *Kraut*, a German tank. The past two years they supported me, which made me very happy. In Flushing Meadow, I have always been a favorite. I like playing in New York also. It has never happened that the public wasn't on my side when I played Lendl."

Becker, sensitive yet tough, could never shake the feeling that he was German and that the world always looked a little funny at the mere mention of his country. Thoroughly embarrassed by his country's violent past, sometimes Becker also seemed ashamed of his own physical power, afraid that the world would equate his abilities with the old German will to dominate. "To be German is not to be normal in international relations. To be German is to be looked at as something different in the world. Many people here feel responsible for everything in the world," said a prominent German female politician when it came out that German nerve gas had been sold in quantity to Saddam Hussein.

Every town has its surface and its underbelly, its present and its past. The brownstone school, the children going to class at 7:15 on Saturday morning, the quaint wooden cross-hatchings on the town hall, and the narrow cobblestone streets were not the entire story of Leimen's past, just as the mixed Friday night steam bath and the envious hotelier were not the entire present. Until you drink a few beers in Leimen or sip the sweet white wine, you cannot get beneath the surface into the deeper reality and know the town's past.

Sunday morning the monastery bells rang on Eisenbahn Strasse as the sunlight slowly burned off the early morning German mist, and nuns in full garb hurried into mass after gossiping for a while near the entrance to the old country church.

The hundred-year-old Berg Brewery, with its blue and white coasters,

was smack in the heart of old Leimen. The brewery's huge copper vats
sat in the showroom window, shined to a coppery glare. Its local *alt* beer
was particularly good, but the dark beer was much too sweet. This Sunday
the brewery was full of German tourists eating the small, delicious Nu-
remberger bratwurst. The better people from town also went there for
Sunday lunch, and one sensed here that the past was homogenized.

I walked back down to the Beckers' house. Across the street at the
edge of town was a rough old house with shutters that looked as if it
were occupied by the nursery-rhyme "old woman who lived in a shoe."
Leimen was a town of both rich and poor. Walking back from the fields
beyond the Becker house, climbing the narrow cobblestone street that
curved with its old streetcar tracks, I stopped in front of a dark restaurant
less than fifty yards from the Becker house. It was the kind of place I
normally would not go into except to use the bathroom in an emergency.
The windows were tinted yellow, and it was impossible to see the inside.
But there was a menu in the front-door window and, encouraged by a
place where they served food and beer on a Sunday morning, I went
inside.

The room was dark except for one wooden table over which a lamp
hung like a poker light. Five people—three men over seventy years old
plus the bar owner, a forty-year-old with a fancy black mustache and
sideburns, and the bartender's heavy-set wife—were seated at the
Stammtisch, the table for regulars. I wanted to talk to them about Leimen's history and what the people in Leimen thought of the Beckers,
who lived so nearby. Nobody spoke to me for about twenty minutes, but
after my third *pils* beer, I told the bartender I was in Leimen to learn
a little more about where Boris Becker came from, and I asked if I might
sit down with him and the old men at the *Stammtisch*.

"*Natürlich*," said the *kniepe* owner, pulling another *pils* into my tall
fluted glass.

The old men were friendly but wary. It was 11:30 A.M. on a Sunday
morning, and they had come in as if they were going to work, shaking
each other's hands at the start of the work day. There was an air about
them of office workers, dressed neatly in jackets and open-collar shirts.
In fact, the old men had worked in factories all their lives, and the huge
one, a giant of an old man, looked like he could still take care of himself.
Their drink was wine *Schole*, half sweet white wine, half water. Their
pleasure was gossip.

"You know," said the short, thick-set old man with the pink scrubbed face and a protruding chin, "the Boris doesn't live here anymore. Just the father and the mother live here. The sister became an architect like the father, and she went away. Karlsruhe, I believe. The Boris is somewhere in Monte Carlo, someplace like this. He has all his money on a Dutch island. Where? In the South Seas, I believe. All the money. Yes. He put it on a Dutch island. It was the idea of the manager, that Tiriac, not to pay taxes here in Germany."

"But," I pointed out, "Boris Becker is a champion."

"*Was*. Was the champion," laughed the old man. "No longer. He lost. Yes, he lost at the Wimbledon this year. To the Swede. He is no longer the champion, I believe."

"But whatever Becker has made in tennis," I said, trying to strike a sympathetic chord in these older working men for the player I thought was the most exciting right-handed player since Australia's Lew Hoad, "whatever Becker has made in tennis, he earned it with his hands and his legs and his back. He earned it all with his body and hard work. And his intelligence."

The three old men nodded in the bar's semidarkness, but they clearly did not approve of people, even tennis champions, who did not pay their taxes in Germany. These men had worked hard with their bodies, and it showed in their faces. The conversation turned to construction and to history.

"Is this building made of concrete or stone?" I asked, looking at the walls.

"*Natur Stein*," the old giant said. "Natural stone. The walls of this building are two meters thick. Cool in summer and warm in winter. House and cellar the same."

The giant, who was seventy-nine, was quite bald and looked like he could have played the big soldier in the movie of Erich Maria Remarque's World War I novel, *All Quiet on the Western Front*. The shorter one, red-faced and very stocky, wore a fresh shirt under his old jacket and looked more prosperous. In 1962, he had lived at Eighty-third Street and Second Avenue, the Yorkville section of New York City.

"You know what I liked about New York?" he asked.

"What?"

"All the streets were numbered. One after the other."

"Agh!" said the giant in disgust. "I like street names. To hell with numbers for streets."

The old men of Leimen spoke German very fast, in a local dialect, but when I had trouble understanding, the bar owner with the fancy black mustache and sideburns translated for me out of their local dialect into a more modern, simpler German.

"I saw a woman once in New York City," said the short, stocky man with the pink face. "She had an unbelievable platform."

I turned for a translation of *platform*. The man who lived once in Yorkville moved his hand out from his chest and smiled.

"What is the main business in Leimen?" I asked.

"Here in Leimen there are two main businesses for many years," said the old giant. "Concrete and asbestos."

It was no accident that Boris Becker's father was an architect. His profession was an artistic meeting between the town's material and a mind. "The asbestos business isn't doing so well anymore," said the giant.

"No," said the more prosperous old-timer, with a chin like a fist with a smile in it. "And you know, it was never the sheet asbestos fiber. It was the spray kind of asbestos. We used to apply it to the walls and ceiling with a fire hose. It's finished now, the asbestos business. But concrete is still big business in Leimen."

"Do the Beckers come in here often? They live just down the street."

The old men looked at each other, and one of them laughed. "Karl-Heinz Becker? In here? *Nay*. Never."

"*Nay*," said the bar owner. "Karl-Heinz Becker? *Nay*. He doesn't set foot in here."

They had a short laugh and another drink. The older men looked at each other. They were clean shaven. Suddenly amid the good-natured laughter the giant commented about the bartender's mustache. It seemed innocuous at first. But he said it again. The old men at the *Stammtisch* all laughed, but the bartender did not. The mustache was a little different. The bartender bore an uncanny resemblance to Leroy Neiman, the sports artist. The old men clearly did not like the bizarre mustaches or people who did not pay their taxes in Germany. They made another joke about the bartender's mustache and laughed some more. I had thought they were friends, but evidently they were not. Thus signaled, the bartender got up to get the old men another round of sweet wine *Scholes*.

"Fifty years ago," I said. "What was it like here in Leimen?"

The old men did their math. 1940. "Fifty or fifty-five years ago in Leimen? What was it like? Nineteen forty and before?" said the card player, an eighty-four-year-old fellow, sharp-as-a-tack, who had come in, shaken hands with the regulars, and sat down a few minutes before.

"There was a terrible time here in Leimen. Unemployment. No food."

"The great man," blurted out the man who had been to America. "The great man," he laughed derisively. "Adolf Hitler. He had us all working in the cement. Building the Autobahn. For eighty-four *pfennig* [cents] a day."

The card player looked over in surprise. "Did you work on that, too? I did also. Nineteen thirty-four to nineteen thirty-six. We built the Autobahn."

The men who helped build the Autobahn quietly took sips of wine *Schole.* "Thirty years ago in Leimen," said the card player, continuing the town history for me, "there was a big arrival of people from East Germany. Nineteen sixty. Too many people came here to Leimen and there were problems for work."

I paused uncomfortably, sensing in the air a fear of competition. "And now they are coming again?"

"Now they are coming again." He looked down.

"In general, what do people in town think of the Beckers?"

"The father of the Boris?" said the big bald giant, who had the warmest smile. "He is all right. Not like the father of the Steffi Graf. Karl-Heinz Becker? *Alles in Ordnung.*" "Everything in order," the old giant had said, trying to pay the ultimate small-town German compliment.

The old men of Leimen, who helped build the Autobahn for Hitler, sipped their wine *Sholes* and gossiped for another half-hour. They were the past, and they knew it. Boris Becker played a game they never dreamed of playing. He was the German present and the German future, so out of their mind's reach, such a symbol of the new prosperity. The old men resented Becker, the young star. He was the postwar prosperity. They were what Becker was not, the crueler past, but in that difference they were forever joined to him. And somehow Becker sensed this, and it made him unhappy.

"I have the impression you don't think highly of Boris Becker."

"No. He is all right," said the talkative, more prosperous one. "But the one thing we do not like, none of us, is the way he speaks German."

"How is that?"

"The Boris speaks a very low German. Like the poorest laborer," said the giant. "Like a bum. He speaks German very badly. Like he is stupid. Like he never went to school."

The old Leimen men all agreed. The quality of Boris Becker's German was awful. It surprised me, but it fit. The more they criticized him, the more I found myself understanding Becker and liking him. It all fit.

Becker in his press conferences was extremely polite and was so intelligent and articulate when talking to the American or English press. But
when the questioning shifted into German, Becker's voice and whole
attitude changed. He became a completely different person. The old
men in Leimen did not realize that Becker's low German was a put-on,
a disguise, like McEnroe's disguise as a rock musician. Some people
dreamed of being famous; Boris Becker dreamed of being normal. He
felt most relaxed behind the wheel of a car. Describing it, he did not
seem as inarticulate as the old men in Leimen said he sounded on German
TV: "The car is one of the few places where I can be undisturbed. It is
a place where I am somehow among people but yet can be alone. It's
the place where I think best. No one interrupts me; no one calls me."

Becker was one of the few tennis players capable of inventing himself—like an actor—as a person. He was proud to be German, except
when he was ashamed of it. He would never forget the thrill of his six-
hour Davis Cup win over McEnroe in Hartford in 1987, to give Germany
its first Davis Cup ever. But Becker, once happy to play the hero, had
grown uncomfortable in the role. Like many young Germans his age, he
felt ambivalent about the old images of strength. To be sensitive was to
be a little weak, and Becker did not mind showing his weakness. He
often said in both English and German that he did not mind losing, that
he could not expect to win everything all the time, and he meant it.
Losing, Becker implied, was what made him human, and that was what
he wanted to be. And yet he was being paid to win. It was not as easy
for him to balance as it looked. He was so different from Connors and
from the early McEnroe, who were so determined to win at any cost,
more like the older McEnroe, who also had doubts about the whole
process.

"There are many things about tennis I don't like that I simply must
do," Becker told Arno Luik.

It was odd sitting there with the old men of Leimen as they sipped
their wine *Scholes*. They were rough old men. Becker disliked the rigid
German conformity. Brought up around American soldiers in Germany,
even Becker's body language was very American. He perhaps naïvely
equated America with freedom. He liked American music and the devil-
be-damned attitude of American GIs walking German streets while on
leave. Becker liked to drive at night on the highway. He once walked
onto the road outside of Leimen and hitched a ride with a trucker going
to Berlin who had no idea who he was. Becker said he was so happy in
that moment of anonymity that he almost did not return.

The ultimate Becker dichotomy had to do with language. The old men in Leimen had got Becker wrong, just the way he wanted them to. They thought he was dumber than a day laborer. And yet, when Becker spoke to the American press after he won the U.S. Open in 1989, he told the press in perfect, soft-spoken unaccented English,

> It was quite tough on me after I won Wimbledon at seventeen. There was suddenly so much pressure. So many people were expecting me to go out and just overtake everyone. It was quite impossible, and I grew a lot in those years. A normal twenty-one-year-old doesn't have to do the things I do in some ways, and in other ways he has to do more. To call me twenty-one, it's wrong. In some respects I'm fifteen, and in some I'm thirty-five.

Becker was extremely self-aware. He understood himself in ways few other tennis players do. Despite his intelligence, the odd truth was that he was closer to fifteen in German and to thirty-five in English. When he spoke to the German press, he rebelled at its constant scrutiny, the myth making. Grunting his answers at the German press, Becker seemed to prefer identifying his tennis with America. A part of him was like an American or Australian player of the 1950s. He loved his country, but he had created another body memory, a different recall button. At times I sensed that Becker was not playing his opponent as hard as he was playing himself. Physically more like the big men of the game's past—Budge, Kramer, Gonzales—Becker's love of rebellion, of the underdog, was a reaction to his country's bullying past.

Of course, there was the other side of Becker: the killer. Tiriac knew that side was there from the beginning, or he would not have bothered, would not have picked this red-headed teenager out from the other prosperous and more accomplished kids in Germany. It was Becker the hunk, the thinker, the assassin, the player with an enormous heart that Tiriac liked on a tennis court.

In seven years on tour, Becker almost never lost to the same person twice in a row. A loss was like permission to go out and dominate fiercely next time. Boris Becker was of two minds. He liked to win, yet he had an intelligent malaise about winning, about being the victor, the German conqueror.

The old men in the Leimen bar stood up and shook hands with each other like postal workers. I said good-bye but we did not shake hands. Outside, the bright orange terra-cotta rooftops of Leimen were blackened

somewhat with age. Becker was both the best of the old Germany—
without its cruelty—and the symbol of the new Germany, which wished
it could correct the past. Tennis was a sport that reminded us that, though
the body had a memory of its own, there is a freedom attainable in effort
itself.

"You are not next to God if you win," Boris Becker wrote in a newspaper column, complaining about the German press. "And if you lose,
you are not next to the devil."

In a sense, Becker had to leave his past, his town, and his red clay–
court upbringing to uncover from inside his wonderful German *Lebens-
lust*, his "life delight," that was the key to the American and Australian
highlights in his explosive tennis game. Becker had almost outgrown
memory, but a bit of it was still there at the intersection of the young
German's stubbornness and his will. Boris Becker still had the potential
to be a champion as great as the chestnut race horse Secretariat.

Becker had been saving himself up for the next big effort. He skipped
all the tournaments between Wimbledon and the U.S. Open except for
the one, Kitzbühel, Austria, the mountain resort with soft red-clay courts.
The rest of the tour was already on hard courts in Canada (where Michael
Chang beat Jay Berger 7–6 in the third set of the Canadian Open Final)
or in Cincinnati (where Edberg crushed Brad Gilbert 6–1, 6–1 in the
final). But Becker, who loved to play in America, had just one American
goal: the U.S. Open.

I left Leimen in one of the two white diesel Mercedes taxis always
parked at the ready. It was night, two hours before dawn and my 7 A.M.
flight from Frankfurt back to New York City. The train platform in Heidelberg was cool for summer and crowded with street people passing
the night. I closed my eyes once I was on the train, thinking back on
Leimen. To win the U.S. Open on cement in New York, Becker had to
again be the aggressive, attacking serve and volley player that his body
and his deepest instinct, not his gentler intelligence, had created. Despite Edberg's great win at Wimbledon, I was convinced that Becker
was the best. The only person who might upset him was Becker himself.
As Andre Agassi said, "If Becker's playing great, sorry. You have no
chance."

YOUNG CHAMPIONS

The U.S. Open 1990

The first day at the U.S. Open was a great hot and steamy, sunny August day in New York. The air was like gauze. There was a bright, unhealthy gray sky over the city, and the ticket scalpers—more ambitious than their cockney counterparts in London—boarded the number-seven train several stops before the tennis stadium, marching through the subway cars shouting, "Tickets? Buying! Selling! Got any tickets?"

The number-seven was a subway train tight with silent, competitive American spirit. There was really nothing in London, at Wimbledon, to compare to the intense sensation of riding the Flushing local to and from the U.S. Open. The black, white, brown, and yellow faces of New York—never quite melting in that "melting pot" that children's history books said was supposed to exist—were streaming in and out of the air-chilled New York subways in steamy late August 1990, but most of the people who wanted to get off at the Shea Stadium–National Tennis Center stop to watch the tennis were white. American troops were pouring into Saudi Arabia to fight Iraq's Saddam Hussein. The track curved, and gradually, as I stared out the subway window, the tennis stadium loomed on the hazy blue horizon.

Like most modern sports stadiums, the Flushing Meadow Tennis complex began as a real estate deal. Negotiated in the late 1960s, the

"Flush" seemed at first like the original Manhattan real estate deal—the one in which the Dutch taught the Indians the value of land. Slew Hester was a real estate man who came from Mississippi, and New York City leased him some land. The discoverer of the Flushing Meadow site, like de Soto and Columbus before him, was not sure at first what he had discovered, but he had discovered quite a lot.

It was either a real estate folly or a stroke of genius. And this is why it happened. The West Side Tennis Club in Forest Hills was too small. It was not only too small physically to help tennis expand, but the private club was too "small" in other ways. Arthur Ashe was the first black to use the changing rooms; well into the 1960s Forest Hills refused membership to blacks and Jews. So a new site was needed for the national championships. Slew Hester and the United States Tennis Association were determined to open tennis to anyone who wanted to play.

The USTA wanted to build a national tennis center modeled on a public park, not a private club. The idea was that, in America, finally nobody would be excluded. On a tennis court at least, the son of a Chinese man was to be as welcome as the son of a Princeton man. The concept was idealistic and long overdue.

Slew Hester flew to New York to discuss possible alternative sites to the West Side Tennis Club, and as his plane circled La Guardia Airport for over an hour trying to land, he could not believe what he saw out the window: a stadium and lots of vacant land left over from the 1962 World's Fair. The land and Louis Armstrong Stadium were available, at a price.

The Mississippi real estate man was very pleased, and so was the USTA, on a per-square-foot basis. A deal was struck with the City of New York. Only one detail was overlooked: the flight patterns and noise of La Guardia airport. Throughout the negotiations, potential plane noise was never mentioned. As they tell the story today at the USTA, Hester, an innovator, did not hear any noise from the planes because he was *inside* one when he saw the site. The long-term land lease was soon termed "Hester's Folly" because of its lack of a "quiet enjoyment" clause. But like Seward's Folly, Alaska, the Flushing Meadow land deal looked better every year.

By 1990, New York City needed the tennis tournament at least as much as the U.S. Open needed the city. Suddenly the mayor was able to reroute planes from La Guardia, and the USTA was able to negotiate a second long-term lease under very favorable terms, doubling its space.

It all happened because Slew Hester, the man whose bronzed face and cigar greets you as you come through the stadium gates, a man whose social instincts were right, was stuck up in a plane circling La Guardia for an hour in the 1960s. Acquisition of the site for the U.S. Open was a good old-fashioned American land deal—sloppy, well intentioned, and full of unexpected good luck and timing.

The tennis crowd rushed from the train at the Shea Stadium stop, and I poured out with them into the sunshine and gorgeous August heat. Shea Stadium was on the other side of the tracks from the tennis stadium. Baseball was fun to watch for its slow, reassuring pace and distant spurts of beauty with a bat and ball. But tennis, with its emphasis on the individual rather than the team, was—for better or worse—the modern game.

In the world of sports, which is still a little purer than life itself, a major breakthrough happens only once every seven to ten years. A star is born and then a sport is never quite the same again. Fred Perry. Don Budge. Jack Kramer. Pancho Gonzales. Rosewall and Laver. Borg and McEnroe. Becker and Edberg. In tennis, most often the champions seemed to come in pairs, like stages of a rocket—after Tilden started it all alone. Tilden was the James Joyce *and* the Marcel Proust of tennis. The crowd was rushing along the boardwalk feeling the pre-match nerves, wondering who would be champion next. Would there be one star, or would there be a pair?

Adults were playing hookey from work. Schoolchildren were still on summer vacation. We were all late for Stefan Edberg's 11 A.M. first-round match, but we could probably catch the last few games. People on the boardwalk could not get there fast enough. It was a great tennis crowd, heading for a good look-see.

"There are no concessions this year on the boardwalk!" a balding fifty-five-year-old man in a madras short-sleeve shirt commented as we strode rapidly along side by side. It was all we needed as an introduction.

"I can't believe it rained yesterday. Look at the parking lot—it's steaming!" I said just as enthusiastically. "The pigeons down there look furious."

"You heard, of course, that the Swedish guy lost," said my instant New York companion. "I heard the scores on WFAN on the way out."

"Who? What Swedish guy?"

"The number one."

"Who? Edberg? No!"

"Oh, yeah. He got killed. First round. Straight sets. Six–three, seven–six, six–two. Edberg is finished. Out. He got beat by a Russian. But it wasn't Chesnokov."

"Was it Cherkasov?"

"No. That name doesn't ring a bell."

"And it definitely wasn't Chesnokov. He's seeded, and they wouldn't have met so early in the draw. I know who it was. Volkov. It was Alexander Volkov, the tall Russian left-hander. Volkov beat Stefan Edberg?" My heart sank. "I don't believe it. Impossible."

Edberg had been playing so well after winning Wimbledon, but like Borg, the Swede always had had trouble in New York. I had heard the supersonic boom of NATO jets flying low and upside down over virginal Västervik, where the red turreted church sat high on the hill that led down to the sea. This year Edberg could not blame the plane noise. Was the *thought* of the noise and New York itself enough to shake Edberg? Each tournament had its own sense of place, its unwritten relationship between the player who wins the tournament and the place where he wins it. McEnroe and Connors were made for Flushing Meadow. Borg and Edberg did not seem to be.

Stefan Edberg was drained before the tournament even started. The week before he made about $200,000 playing in the Hamlet Challenge exhibition tournament on Long Island. But it took Edberg five matches and a win in the final over Ivanisevic the day before the first round at the Open to earn it. Edberg had shot big-money dice and lost. Losing so early in New York was a shame for Stefan Edberg. He had just become the new number-one player in the world, finally replacing Ivan Lendl. But sometimes Edberg's results must have been a mystery even to him. He had shown tremendous heart at Wimbledon. But in New York, some guy named Volkov with a left-handed serve got hot on cement.

"That's it," said the New Yorker hustling along beside me. "That was the name of the Russian who beat Edberg. Alexander Volkov. The Russians are coming, the Russians are coming! How do ya like that? The top guy is out! You know, there are a ton of ticket scalpers out here today."

"At Wimbledon the touts were all over the place."

"I was at Wimbledon, too," said the New Yorker. "I saw Chang come back from two sets down on grass against the Australian, and I also saw *Miss Saigon*, the play. I thought they were both very good. My wife thought the play was great. I'd say it was *good*, but not great. But I can see why the director wants to bring that English actor over here in the lead role. That guy was great. Even if he wasn't Oriental. They pre-sold the production here. Let's face it. The director of the show could have gotten thirty million bucks for *Miss Saigon* with Mickey Rooney in the lead role, but he wanted to bring that English actor over, and I don't blame him."

"For future credibility."

"Very well put," said the man in the madras shirt as we neared the gates. "How are you getting in here?"

"On a press pass."

"Oh. So you're taken care of. I'm looking for 212."

"What's that, the area code?"

"No. The gate attendant. I used him last year. I'll show you how I get in." The man flashed a small, folded piece of white paper with the corner of a ten-dollar bill showing. He winked. "This year I'm looking for a front-row seat."

So was the rest of the city. Ticket prices ranged from $12 to $18 for an unreserved seat, day vs. night—$36 for the finals. Corporate boxes ranged from $7,000 to $20,000 for the two weeks.

Once inside, I looked around. The big concrete stadium seated twenty thousand people and the overhanging walkways on the back of the stadium looked down over the grandstand court, which seated only four thousand people but was linked to the stadium underneath by a single meandering pedestrian tunnel. If Wimbledon was once a small stadium like the Globe Theater and had become a complex more like the National Theater on the south side of the Thames, the Flushing Meadow complex was still a basic concrete tennis stadium, built more for dollar-per-square-foot functionality than the Tudor aesthetics of old Forest Hills, which had had a great charm that hid something not so charming. Beneath the two modern tennis stadiums, in the grandstand's underarm where T-shirts, Häagen-Dazs ice cream, and foot-long hot dogs were sold, the concrete walls were painted white and bright yellow. The tennis clothing and food booths were decked out like a political convention with bright red, white, and blue plastic bunting; they were doing a tremendous business, especially in hot dogs. The year before, eighteen thousand hot dogs a day were eaten during the two-week tournament. Something about competition makes Americans eat. I resented the New York hot dog prices for about three days, then found myself part of the orgy.

"FOOT-LONG HOT DOGS," the sign said, "$3.50."

"Hey," I thought as I hurried toward the press lunch for Michael Chang in the DuPont tent, "you got six inches for a buck seventy-five?"

Michael Chang, a baseliner by nature, a fighter by birth, had done surprisingly well on the grass courts at Wimbledon. After a great 1989 season when Chang won the French Open beating Edberg in the final, his good fortunes seemed to disintegrate, like the hopes that had risen, then were crushed in China. At the end of 1989, doctors operated on Michael Chang's right hip. He was only twenty-one. He had been recovering during the Lipton, and he lost in the first round in four of the first five tournaments he played on the red clay, trying to come back in Europe that spring and early summer. Getting to the fourth round on grass at Wimbledon reflected the toughness the Chinese-American boy had inside because clay, not grass, was his natural surface. Through it all, his ups and his downs, he kept his cool and stayed quiet. At his sponsor's lunch, I wanted to see in person if Chang's cool was coldness.

DuPont officials wandered in and out of the tent. It was a free lunch, and I was eating. Uniformed waiters and bartenders stood by in the heat. Chang's cousins, a young Chinese boy and his sister, showed up and said who they were, but the guard at the front of the tent would not let them into the reception until someone came out to identify them. Embarrassed and a little ruffled, Michael Chang's cousins sat down at a large round table at the back of the elegant green-and-white tent.

DuPont had seen something in Michael Chang that it liked. Out of five hundred international touring players DuPont had chosen Michael Chang, the son of immigrant parents, to be its media image. Chang was DuPont's Bo Jackson. Their three-year deal was in the neighborhood of five million dollars.

Suddenly, Michael Chang appeared. Chang's body was quite amazing. He was short, strong, and seemed incredibly light, like Peter Pan. Small lips of muscle hung over his kneecaps, and his body was incredibly low on fat. The skin on Chang's face was tight. His cheekbones were prominent; his face held two small black eyes that looked out at the world with nine parts intelligence and one part suspicion. There was something light and geniuslike about this Chinese-American boy. He could have been a Harvard student, but he was beyond that somehow, more like a chess player than a cellist, more like a math major than an English major. His aura was decidedly more science than literature. Chang liked the practical side of abstraction. Writing that did not have a demonstrable purpose, such as a law brief or a scientific report, held no interest for him.

Chang was a fast study on court and off. He had that elusive lightness of being—more Oriental than American—that gave him the patience to absorb the will power and ultimate unhappiness of larger men and heavier hitters. A small man, Chang loved to break down his opponents. He also loved to talk, and he did it well. But the press who traveled with the tour found him a little boring. Chang was the type of student who always had his paper in on time. There was a tremendous logic to his tennis game and his soul.

Carl Chang, the older brother, sat alone at one table as Michael, the prodigy, walked slowly around the corporate brunch. Much larger and heavier, Carl had been a good college tennis player but not a great one: too much power, not enough glide and instinct. Whenever he could, Carl traveled with Michael on the tour. At Wimbledon, a look of awe came over Carl Chang's face when he saw his younger brother do something truly incredible, on the run. It was an astonished look, both a tribute to his brother and an admission that he could not do the same. Talent is not always easy for brothers to understand, and it comes in different shapes. It wasn't so easy for either brother, but it was tougher on Carl.

Inside the DuPont tent Mr. Joe Chang, the father, looked more like Carl, only stiffer. By contrast, Chang's mother, Betty Chang, the daughter of a diplomat from Taiwan who fled to America in the 1960s, had an ease and self-assuredness more like Michael. Her husband had suffered all the immigrant's indignities and struggles in America, and it showed in Joe Chang's body language and personality. There was a certain irony in DuPont's paying Michael Chang over a million dollars a year, for Joe Chang was a chemist by profession but was never able to get a job with DuPont. With a Ph.D. in chemistry from Taiwan, the father bounced around at a variety of chemistry lab jobs from Minnesota to California, where he would drive three hours each way to work so that his sons could stay close to the complex the family had chosen for their tennis training. After twenty years in America, the closest Joe Chang had come to a DuPont lab was his son's visit there.

I went over to Mr. Chang and introduced myself. He looked nervous and a little distrustful as I shook his hand. He had thick thighs like his son Carl, and a sharp, almost pointed head. I told him why I wanted to talk to him.

"You want to write a book? Heh-heh-heh. Maybe we like to write this book ourself," said Joe Chang, smiling. He let loose nervous laughter and a strange smile. He had misunderstood what I was doing. He thought I wanted to write his son's life story, but I really wanted to ask Chang's dad a couple of questions about life on the tour. I explained, but he responded, "We don't want to give you the story. Maybe one day my wife going to write it." He cocked his head to one side. "Beside. How you going to tell our story? How can we control what you say we say?"

I nodded and backed off. Ju-Nie Shen, a writer for the *Chinese-American*, a daily published in New York City with a national readership of over two million readers daily, sat down with me a few minutes later to interview Michael Chang. A round-faced thirty-five-year-old Chinese woman with quick, intelligent eyes, Ju-Nie Shen knew Michael Chang better than any other American writer, and he opened up in front of us.

Talking to Michael Chang was refreshing. He was lean—not just in his body but in his mind. His intelligence radiated through his eyes and seemed fine, firm. There was no excess in him. No fat. No fear. And maybe not much fun. Chang looked directly into your eyes when he talked to you or when he listened. He was not afraid. He was thinking. He heard the question, and he responded to it. He saw what was there for what it was.

Michael Chang lacked the subjective in extreme. He seemed deeply afraid of only one thing—failure—and he was almost completely un-afraid. He was different from his brother and his father. He knew that he was somehow blessed, a gift of nature and of hard work. His confidence ran deeper than his self-doubt. Chang knew he was a miracle. Nearly two billion Chinese lived on the planet, and in a hundred years here was the only Chinese player who ever won a major tennis championship. Michael Chang was the Arthur Ashe of the Chinese-American com-munity, twenty years later. His Chinese fans loved him because he suc-ceeded with speed and tenacity where they had only barely been permitted to play at all. Michael Chang was not afraid to look into the eyes of a questioner—or into the eyes of the ball as it crossed the net coming at him with bad intentions from the other person. Chang's aura was not mere intelligence. It was fearlessness.

"I am not surprised where my life is now," he said. "This year, I think I got the toughest draw of all in the four years I have played here. This is cement, and you can't play clay-court tennis on cement. You've got to be offensive here in New York. Or someone will blow you away."

"What was breaking your hip like?" I asked.

"It was like a loud cracking noise," said Michael Chang. "I knew I had done something. It was loud. At first I thought it might have been my racket cracking. It happened in practice. I tried to tough it out and play a few more points, but I couldn't last. I could not stop limping. The X-ray told us that the hip was broken. It was a definite setback." Chang paused. "When I came back three months later, I had problems winning at first. I have learned to be more careful with my schedule. Jay Berger made the same mistake this year that I did last year. The appearance money in Europe is definitely a temptation, but I bet Jay has learned his lesson. Your body can only take so much pounding. It's difficult to perform well week after week, so I turned down the Hamlet and Forest Hills, and took the week off before the Open. It's our national championship, and I want to do well here."

"Did your parents make a lot of sacrifices for you?"

"Yes, they have. My father has a Ph.D. in chemistry, but that has not meant so much over here. One of the reasons I am so glad to have signed with DuPont is that my dad would have always loved to work for DuPont." Michael Chang paused again. "He hasn't had that opportunity yet." The sides of Michael Chang's high cheekbones narrowed intensely and so did his eyes. He had an anger in him.

"Do you think it's just a coincidence that so many of today's top American players come from families with first-generation immigrant backgrounds?"

Michael Chang shook his head. "It's no coincidence. It *is* pretty incredible. Everyone has their own different situation. Andre doesn't come from a wealthy family. I can't tell you about the other families. I come from a very close family. It is strange that the five best American players now all have that one thing in common. It's even more strange that we have all come through together in the same year."

Betty Chang walked by and smiled at her son. He did not say much after his mother's smile. The father had had the harder life. Carl was like the father—outspoken, blunt, a little bitter about being Chinese in America. Michael Chang was more like his mother, diplomatic if possible, savvy, strong, stubborn, giving the appearance of great gentleness but really tough when it counted. The Changs were in some ways an exaggeration of the Chinese family in America: triumph at a cost. The father was hungry to the degree that people are on the number-seven subway at 6 A.M. each morning in the darkness of Flushing, Queens. He had felt the corporate American boot and tasted the laces, too. Joe Chang wanted the American Dream, which, as he saw it, was larger than Taiwan, more powerful than mainland China. He had tried to figure out America. The wealth was there, but it was not always available. Unless you had a plan. Unless you were an artist. Or unless you were an athlete, a hero of some sort, a giant. And Michael was *that* miracle, the one in a billion,

the one who never took the subway. Joe Chang had suffered the quest
for the American Dream, but his son, the tennis player, had achieved
it, and more.

The boy's stomach muscles were hard as rocks down where it hurt.
When he played, Michael Chang liked to pick apart his larger opponent's
weaknesses. His broken hip had healed. But what of the boy's heart?
There was the Lord. The Christian Lord. The American Christian Lord
and Redeemer, the forgiver, the healer of thwarted ambition. Tennis was
part boxing, part chess, part body, part head game, and the Lord seemed
to have brought peace to Michael Chang, if not to his older brother or
his father, whose stomach still seemed to churn like broken glass, so
tense was he with ambition.

Betty Chang smiled again as her prodigy son went to sit with the
DuPont pubic relations man, who was about to introduce him to the
crowd. The mother's smile was free of tension. She was her son's touch
at the end of a backhand volley, the top of the bounce from his deep
kick serve.

"When we signed Michael Chang," said the trim but graying PR man,
"we had no idea Michael was going to be such a technician. But Michael
has spent quite a lot of time with us in the labs helping to design our
tennis-related products. The Kevlar tennis strings Michael uses are a
product we designed for Prince rackets. DuPont's Hi Evalay is utilized
for durability in Michael's Reebok sneakers. Michael actually helped
design the pump in our Reebok footwear, which uses DuPont fibers. If
you are wondering why we chose to sign Michael Chang instead of some
other tennis player, we'll tell you. After Michael won the French Open
in 1989, he said, 'It was exciting but also a *disturbing* personal time,
because I did not know how I would react to winning a major championship.' That impressed us at DuPont. We liked his *maturity*. We're
absolutely delighted to have Michael Chang with DuPont. Michael,
would you come up and say a few words?"

Michael Chang spoke with his chin up and his eyes darting brightly.
The young Chinese-American superstar's voice was slightly monotone
but sincere. "In the past I have had a lot of cramping problems due to
loss of water, especially at the French Open against Lendl. But the
DuPont Kumax fibers in my clothes keep me much drier in this kind of
heat. It may be worth two points a set in a five-set match. I am also a
fisherman," Chang added, breaking into a young, million-dollar smile.
"I use DuPont Kevlar for my fishing lines, too, and I haven't lost a
fish yet."

He dutifully posed for corporate photos for another half-hour, smiling quietly with each new DuPont executive group that wanted him in their picture. It took fourth-set patience, but Chang had it. For a million dollars a year, a lot was possible. Older brother Carl sat back with his cousins and his parents. Watching the tennis prodigy son quietly fielding questions and posing for pictures with DuPont's top executives, I could not help thinking that Michael Chang was an American miracle.

Michael Chang was scheduled to meet Andre Agassi in the quarterfinals, but he never got there. He was upset by the hungry little Russian, Andre Cherkasov, in three close but straight sets in the third round.

Boris Becker's second-round opponent was Yannick Noah. To say there was potential bad blood between the lanky mulatto serve and volley specialist from Cameroon and the outspoken young German was an understatement. The German *Wunderkind* had voiced what players like Wilander, Lendl, and Edberg may have thought for years but never said. Noah's talent was not wasted; it was just not as big as most people thought it was.

Noah had had a miserable year. At the outset, he hired Dennis Ralston, the former U.S. Davis Cup captain and number-one player, to help motivate and coach him. They started the season with a burst of good intentions, and Noah, trying for his new coach, reached the quarterfinals in Australia. He then lost in the first round of nine tournaments and the second round of two tournaments. His career was winding down. Noah was spectacular to watch, but talent was rarely the main barometer of success. Noah posed a curious problem. He was a classic example of a man who seems to have wasted his talent. Now thirty and just divorced, and badly missing his young son, Noah wanted to redeem his whole year in one match, the match against Boris Becker.

Becker attributed Noah's major problems to his ground strokes. Blessed with great touch and a grace of foot that no one else in tennis ever quite had, Noah had never bothered to really get down and work on his ground strokes—his weakness. He preferred to practice his serve and volley. As the years passed, Arthur Ashe, a prodigious on-court worker, the man who first saw Noah play as a boy in Cameroon, had less and less to say about France's adopted son.

Noah wore his emotions like a red bandana. He *looked* spectacular. But Becker and many of the other top players had felt for years that Yannick was a mime. Noah mimed effort. He mimed pain. He mimed

the guts of the game, having really spilled them only once, winning the
French Open in 1982. Noah appeared to go to his very psychic edge
every time he played, and when he won a big point, he roared in a
mixture of princely pain and triumph. But too often those mighty displays
of psychic victory were against players ranked a hundred places behind
him.

Noah had been badly insulted by Becker when Becker implied that
Noah's game was feared primarily because he was black and that Noah
did not deserve to be in the world's top fifty because technically he was
weak. But since then, Yannick Noah had not beaten anyone ranked ahead
of him. Asked about Noah before the Lipton, when Noah was number
twelve in the world, Becker said, "He's the most overrated player on
the tour." For a sensitive guy, Becker also had his hard, analytical side.
It was clear as they warmed up that the complicated half-black Frenchman
from Cameroon was finally going to play as hard as he could. His ranking
had fallen to forty-sixth.

By the luck of the draw, now they were meeting. Noah dug deep
into himself. Instead of miming effort, he was impressive again. He was
always beautiful to look at. His body exuded his old *joie de vivre* as he
flung himself around the court against Becker. Noah at thirty looked a
little older, slightly less fluid through the ball, but his serve was still a
major weapon when he hit it with bad intentions instead of kicking it in
three-quarter pace. But Becker's assessment was right. Behind his great
first volley, Noah had no ground strokes, at least none adequate against
a player who blasted the ball back on the return of serve. Becker stayed
back on the baseline as if he were playing on red clay. From years of
habit, Noah chipped and charged quickly up to net, unwilling to pay the
price from the baseline before trying to assume the position of domination
at the net. But the black Frenchman's reflexes and determination, the
combination that sparked in Noah in 1982 when he won the French Open
and the whole world seemed like it was always going to be his oyster,
were alive again. Becker won the first two sets, but they were much
tougher than the scores. When Becker went up 5–3 in the third set,
Noah called on his guts, and they were there.

Noah broke back to 5–all and fought into a tie-breaker with Becker.
There was no room for those two egos in the same tie-breaker. For a
moment Noah was his younger self—tall, smooth, handsome, strong,
and instinctive. He played everything pressed in on top of the net, the
area of greatest instinct.

But in competition, instinctive beauty without great technique is finally not enough. For a brief while, Noah showed more substance than style. But that was it. The New York crowd, which always appreciates physical beauty, continued to cheer for Noah, and he responded. But the harder Noah played, the more he struggled, and by the end of the third set the six-foot four-inch gap-toothed guy with Bob Marley dreadlocks was out of air. Boris Becker won 6–4, 6–2, 7–6(7–2). The match was much closer than the scores. Becker put a hand gently on Noah's shoulder by way of apology as they shook hands in the deep New York City heat. Noah smiled gently and turned away, disappointed.

Outside the locker room I caught up to Dennis Ralston, the former Wimbledon doubles winner, with Rafael Osuna. "When Yannick asked me to coach him, I was excited," said the Californian. "We did well in Australia at the start of the year. But when you take as much time off as Yannick likes to take off, it cannot be done. If you lose, you have to practice, not take time off until the next tournament. If you lose, you have to work harder," said Ralston. Fifty years old and red-faced, Ralston had raccoon circles of disappointment around his eyes.

Noah looked like he was going to die. He came into the air-conditioned interview room after playing Becker, like an aging race horse gingerly making its way back to the paddock after a loss. "I am disappointed," began Noah in his soft French-English accent. He spoke gently about missing his son very much and caring less about tennis. He was thirty. Twelve years on tour. He had probably just played the last big match of his career, but he was not quite sure of it. Admitting it was over would mean even harder work for Noah than tennis: trying to reinvent himself for life, never an easy task, but one every athlete has to address.

Noah was not the only player over thirty nearing the end of his career, but in spite of what Becker had said about him, Noah had had an immense talent. But talent itself is never enough. McEnroe, Connors, and Lendl were all over thirty, but their careers might burn on for a while fueled by their inner drive. Noah was a completely different soul, perhaps more beautiful to watch than to live with. Joseph Conrad's description of the prince in *An Outcast of the Islands*, written in 1896, might serve as a description of Yannick Noah and his talent:

And truly enough he had all the gifts of an exiled prince. He was discontented . . . turbulent. He was obstinate, but his will was made up of short impulses that never lasted long enough to carry him to the goal of his ambition.

When Boris Becker came into the interview room after beating Yan-nick Noah, he slung his large frame down into the chair and answered questions in a voice so soft, so gentle, and so matter-of-fact that nothing in life seemed too difficult for him to handle. He took a belt of water from a big plastic bottle, and the first word out of his mouth, said with a long sigh of satisfaction, was "Aagh!" Here was a race horse, and if he just ate his oats and drank his water he would be unbeatable. But Boris Becker in 1990 had the idea that he was James Dean, and winning was partly conforming.

"Boris, you made some rather personal remarks about Yannick Noah at the beginning of the year," said my Wimbledon pal, the writer from India. "What do you see as being missing from Yannick's game?"

"That's a difficult question really. Yannick has only beaten me twice in ten years. To beat me, he has to serve very, very well," said Becker softly, not trying to boast. "The court here is not that fast, but today his mind was a little better. The remarks I made? It was nothing personal. Just the truth I thought."

"Would you rather have had Edberg go all the way through to the final so you two could—" The young English reporter stopped.

"No. I prefer it this way." Becker frowned at the reporter. He did not suffer fools gladly. Players do not like to deal with hypotheticals. They play in a trancelike state of concentration, but the results are pure realism for even the best of them.

"Boris, the serve is the key to your game," said the older man from New Delhi. "But do you also feel confident in other areas?"

It was an innocuous question, but the answer would prove a clue to the increasingly complicated player Becker was becoming. Like Steffi Graf, who had too many different backhands to choose from, Becker got into trouble on the baseline.

"I can play from the back a bit," said the big German boy, sounding modest but challenged by the question. "I can slice a few backhands. It makes the game easier. Because you can't serve every time your best."

There was something modest yet perversely obstinate at the same time in the reddish blonde from Germany. Perhaps it was a streak of arrogance. Becker's greatest pleasure now, his "steak au poivre," was beating Ivan Lendl from the baseline. Becker was like a home run hitter who also wanted to be able to hit for average, like a singles hitter. The clay-court players were the singles hitters. In all of his modesty, in all of his pride, Boris Becker wanted it all, victory and defeat, love and struggle, in the same match, the same afternoon.

"Is the most mysterious part of tennis the serve, Boris?"

"Yes. The serve is a mystery. I have been trying for six years to figure out why it is coming sometimes and sometimes it is not." Becker smiled. "But I did not yet find out the answer."

"Boris. There's going to come a time, maybe soon, when Yannick will not be playing. Boris Becker, will tennis miss Yannick Noah?"

It was the sound-bite reporter from Texas. As Becker answered, a television camera clicked on, rolling tape for that night's evening news. Becker's answer was uncharacteristically false, for a moment.

"Oh, definitely, Yannick will be missed," Becker said, nodding and pushing his hair off his forehead. "I hope he plays another ten years to be quite honest." Then he added, "If he can."

"Are you still disappointed about losing to Edberg at Wimbledon?"

"Well. Here I am in the second round in New York. That is all. I cannot know more. And for Wimbledon? I can only say that you *cannot* win them all. You cannot win ten times in a row *all* the tournaments you want. That's how it was. That's how it's always going to be. I'm number two now." Becker spoke very calmly, shunning all tension. "That's pretty good, I think, or?"

"Questions in German!" shouted a young female American media rep. Most of the press in the room now got up to leave, but Boris Becker stayed and became transformed when he faced the German press alone.

"Ja," said Becker, changing the tone from his sensitive, soft-spoken, introspective Americanized English to his bold, direct, more guttural style in which the old men of Leimen said he spoke "low German." It was not "low German," just rough German. "*Abba curtz* [But short]," said Becker. "This is already enough now. Only two or three questions more."

Boris Becker must have had eyes behind his back. Only minutes before, when he was being interviewed on American TV, the German press people had crowded around the press television sets making fun of Becker in a dozen ways. They particularly mocked his soft tone of voice. The German press seemed to think Becker was rough, a macho boor, just another great athlete. The American press people knew better. They recognized Becker's stardom as the meat and potatoes of journalism. Becker and Chang were among the most articulate players on the tour, but Chang, though less talented, was fully centered and purposefully limited. Becker had the full orchestra and was interested in self-discovery. It would either cost Becker the race or carry him first across the finish line. The big boy from Leimen got up disdainfully after talking

to the German press for two minutes. Boris Becker was a German romantic with muscular, freckled thighs, a heavy serve, and a rebellious
nature. Both stubborn and gentle, Becker had recently developed the
unconscious habit of turning against his own talent. Like McEnroe but
gentler till provoked, Boris Becker could win or self-destruct, and people
marveled in either case.

All the winning and losing brought with it a sensation like dying. America's gritty Jim Courier followed Becker into the interview room. The
reporters fell deathly silent. No one had a question. Courier had got a
good draw, but it turned out badly for him. He lost a match he had been
expected to win against South Africa's Gary Muller, primarily a doubles
player, who got hot with his left-handed serve and blew the counter-
punching Courier off the cement court. After playing better at Wimbledon than he had expected, Courier was clearly upset to have lost in the
first round of the U.S. tournament he had hoped so much to win. Courier's talent was in his unorthodox strokes, his physical and mental
strength, and his heart. But for nearly ten months, while Andre Agassi
flirted with the top of the game, Courier struggled, ranked in the teens
and low twenties, ducking no tough tournaments—learning, competing,
but unable to break through.

"Is it the chicken and the egg thing, Jim?" asked one reporter finally.
"What comes first? Do you believe you can win the big match first, or
do you have to *win* one before you believe you can?"

Courier, who had won plenty of big matches around the world, sighed.
It had been a disappointing year, but sometimes a player has to live
through that to emerge on the other side of hell. "Well," said Courier,
"I think you have to *believe* that you can win the big match before you
can win it. I don't think you can ever win a match by going out there
not expecting to win. Today, Gary blew me away. He just served too
well."

Courier looked around for other questions, but there were none. The
room went silent. Courier had lost in the first round, and it was an Irish
wake. The press had no further interest in Courier's opinion. When the
press stopped talking to him altogether, just two questions later, Jim
Courier stood up abruptly and left, slamming the microphone head in
disgust. If he won, they could not get enough of him.

Throughout the season I had been after what it was that made some
of the players compete so well and others come up just short. Technique

is as much a part of the process as heart, because desire alone does not win tournaments. Playing with a severe Western forehand grip, Courier still lacked a top-flight volley. It was similar in golf and tennis. Technical proficiency as natural as the language you can sing in is what wins tournaments. Desire and great technique, combined, are what the champions have had. A disappointed but resolute Jim Courier went back to work.

Down in the bowels of the stadium complex I saw a short man with a square jaw and black hair pass by. He stopped quietly in front of the press door, but the tall black Pinkerton man would not let him through. The man looked too small to be a tennis player, but I recognized him right away by the square cut of his chin, now slightly wrinkled, and his jet-black hair, possibly colored. He was so famous to me, I shied away. But the young guard was giving him such a hard time that I leapt forward.

"Excuse me," I said to the Pinkerton guard who would not let the man in. "This man can go wherever he wants to here. This is Mr. Rosewall. He won this tournament twice."

The guard looked at him, checked my press badge, and nodded. Rosewall, shorter than ever, smiled and thanked me. The Australian had won the U.S. Open in 1956 and 1970. What a pair of bookends, fourteen summers apart. That was willpower. That was staying power. Here was a man who for fifteen years never hit a ball off center. He beat Stan Smith in the semis at Wimbledon in 1974 at age thirty-nine. He beat Rod Laver even after Laver had overtaken him. The little Australian never quit on court. He still played the seniors' tour, but not because he needed the money. In life after tennis Rosewall had made the best investments of all ex-players, and his contemporaries still kidded Rosewall about how tight he was with a dollar and a return of serve. Rosewall played so much bigger than his actual height. Awed the way someone might be meeting a movie star, I turned to go quickly, feeling awkward around a player whose greatness and competitive beauty had been in his smooth feet, his intense eye, and his quiet, blood-hungry guts. An English writer had once described Rosewall as the Fred Astaire of tennis, so perfect was his footwork, so well timed were his ground strokes. He had made it all look so easy. He beat Laver twice for money and pride in the WTC final in Dallas. I rooted for Laver in the marathon five-setter, but Rosewall had such tenacity. He never did drink.

"Mr. Rosewall," I said, coming quickly back to him, "would you have a minute?"

"Sure," said the Australian, ready to return the favor. He used to carve the heart out of his opponents with a fingernail, and yet the Australian in his gray flannels and blue shirt looked as friendly as Stan Laurel in the Laurel and Hardy shorts.

"What do you think of McEnroe?" I started.

"He used to be a great player," said Rosewall. "I don't know if he wants it anymore—or if he can have it."

"Harry Hopman coached both of you," I said.

Rosewall frowned. The Australian greats I had spoken to over the course of the season—Roche, Newcombe, and now Rosewall—were begrudging about Hopman, who had been both their Davis Cup captain and a working journalist. Harry Hopman worked the Aussie players hard like race horses, then played the journalist's side of the fence and wrote about them. The great Australian players respected him as a coach but few seemed to love him.

"I don't know why Hopman favored McEnroe," said Rosewall. "At one of McEnroe's very first Wimbledons, they were going to suspend him, and it might have done him a world of good. But Hopman cast the deciding vote that saved McEnroe. It was such a reversal. Out of character for Hopman really." Rosewall nodded, but he did not mention that Hopman had been John McEnroe's coach when he voted not to suspend him after that early Wimbledon. When Rosewall was eighteen, Harry Hopman had reprimanded him for getting out of a Morris Minor without going around to the other side of the car to open the car door for one of the top Australian women players who was riding in the front seat. The legendary Australian coach made the shy, young Rosewall run two dozen sets of wind sprints for not opening that woman's door. Rosewall never missed another car door or another forehand. Times had changed, but Rosewall had not. Rosewall was in his late fifties, but he still looked like he could scamper. He was a little Australian gentleman from the hard knocks school.

I asked Rosewall the same question I had asked at the Lipton to John Newcombe, who suggested that today's younger Aussie players still subconsciously felt the weight of the former Australian greats on their shoulders. But had Australia also gotten softer as a country?

Rosewall cocked his head, surprised. "Well, there may be something in that. When we were starting to play tennis in the late forties and early fifties in Australia, we had a lot less to distract us. Back then, none of us came from what you would call a wealthy background. Our fathers helped all of us get started in tennis. The courts were grass, but they got more like dirt after a while, so we all had to develop a good serve and volley instead of letting the ball bounce." A gentle wave of nostalgia traced through Rosewall's quiet Australian voice. "It may not be that Australia is getting soft," said the flat-stomached, square-jawed, black-haired fifty-seven-year-old. "But there are many more sports competing for the same people now in Australia. Now we even have basketball. There just are more distractions altogether. Back then, just after the war, we had just three choices on a weekend. You could play cricket, go to the beach, or play tennis." Rosewall smiled. "There really was nothing else to do."

Rosewall looked a lot like golf's Gary Player. Both are short, dark, and very strong for their size. In their time, they both simply *lived* to win. We shook hands, and Ken Rosewall disappeared under the massive concrete stadium.

The great Australian champion left me wondering if abstinence would win here. Rosewall had always brought a certain abstentious perfection to tennis. He was so tidy on court, so careful to give away nothing cheaply. If abstinence was going to help win at this year's Open, then Lendl or possibly Chang would emerge victorious. Laver had been a wilder talent than Rosewall. Maybe there was a touch of Laver or vintage McEnroe to be found in the draw.

Fast food was selling at an incredible pace. There was enough food at the Open for a Three Stooges food fight. The year before 250,000 hot dogs were sold in two weeks. In 1990, that record-breaking pace was being eclipsed. Soft drinks and American bottled water were selling briskly in the August heat. The bathrooms under the grandstand courts were overflowing. The stadium guards spitefully imitated schoolteachers by making the businessmen do the one thing they hated most—wait—while the women clinging to the cement-block corridor walls cursed the plumbing.

For many people living in nearby Astoria, the workday begins by traveling into Manhattan on the modern, brightly lit E train or the rattling old number-seven Flushing line. Tennis is not a game that Greek Americans who populate this part of Queens usually care about or played in America. But at Louis Armstrong Stadium there was one who did.

The Greeks in New York count among them the international financier Peter Peterson, but other modern-day Greeks still start their lives in America with steaming hot dog pushcarts or the crash of heavy plates accompanied by the call of "gimme whiskey down!"—New York coffee shop parlance for an order of rye toast. The coffee shops of New York City, many wallpapered with a Delphic temple overlooking a bright blue Aegean, are the warmest places in this bustling, jangling city. These oases of New York life are mostly run by Greek Americans. It is just such a small restaurant that Sotirios (Sam) Sampras owned in Maryland when his son, Pete, was a little boy.

Boris Becker was my choice to win, but Sampras was my dark horse, a long shot for following as a writer but not for a heavy bet. I had liked the Greek-American kid since I first saw him come from behind to win in Florida at the Lipton in the cold night wind. I even liked him when he got nervous at Wimbledon and lost to Cristo van Rensburg in that very disappointing first-round loss. I thought of what Clemson University coach Chuck Kriese had said about a player's recall button being formed young. The problem with Pete Sampras was that he was inconsistent.

The kid was fun to watch. Vic Seixas said Sampras reminded him of a young Pancho Gonzales. His technique was so good that it looked effortless. Like the young Rod Laver, Pete Sampras was as wild as a dart thrower in a balloon shop. Sometimes he missed, but sometimes he hit every balloon on the wall.

The Sampras–Jean Fleurian match at the Lipton was the type that is often forgotten, but it was a highlight of the season. If the Frenchman could have *imagined* winning, he would have won the match. A win like Sampras's in Florida was what I had been hoping to see when I set out on the tour in March. It showed strength of character. Rosewall and Laver, the Australians, would have won the same match. Rosewall would have won by releasing through the ball all that pent-up abstinence and honesty; Laver would have won by keeping his brilliant wildness willfully between the lines. Sampras won by hanging in there, winning from the baseline.

His mother in particular had kept the Greek-American boy's feet on the ground. Georgia Sampras said that "watching Pete play was wonderful," but she felt that "having his parents as spectators was not the best thing for Pete." She told her husband not to go to Pete's matches. "Let him alone," she told Sam. "He does beautiful."

So the Samprases had not come to Flushing Meadow. They stayed in California, fretting. What was inside the boy? What had he got from his parents? What was his own gift to the mix? Sampras's mother came to America from Greece in 1960, when she was nineteen years old—the very age her son Pete was now playing the U.S. Open in 1990. Georgia arrived in the country alone. Six years later, while working in the beauty salon of the Sheraton Park Hotel in Washington, D.C., she met her husband. Sam Sampras worked two jobs. He owned a coffee shop in Maryland and also worked for the Defense Department. He and his wife married a year after they met. Back in Greece, Mrs. Sampras had been one of eight children—five brothers and three sisters. "We grew up very poor in Greece," said Gloria Sampras. "It was hard."

Pete Sampras's draw at the Open was tough: Dan Goldie, who had gone five sets with Becker at Wimbledon; Peter Lundgren, a Swede with a two-handed backhand a bit like Gene Mayer's. Sampras's third round was tougher still, Jakob Hlasek, who had beaten Aaron Krickstein and held match point on Stefan Edberg at the Lipton.

Hlasek, the tall, muscular blonde Swiss-Czech with border guard good looks and a taste in literature for Stefan Zweig's story of madness, *Die Amok Laufer*, had three things to recommend him: he was tough, he had a beautiful game, and he never complained. Hlasek, like Brad Gilbert, was one of a handful of top players who were extra-tough because they rarely beat themselves. In Hlasek, Sampras faced a man, not a prodigy.

Jakob Hlasek had turned his season around by playing doubles. Paired with his friend Guy Forget, who was also honing his big game through doubles, Hlasek had found a way to take the pressure off himself and improve. Forget and Hlasek became a great doubles team. Doubles took Hlasek out of himself, and by the end of the year, Hlasek and Forget would win the one-million-dollar World Doubles Championships in Sanctuary Cove, Australia. By thinking less about themselves individually, Forget and Hlasek were each able to improve in singles as well as doubles. It was this Hlasek that Pete Sampras faced in the third round.

In Flushing Meadow that warm September night Sampras beat Jakob Hlasek 6–4, 6–3, 6–3, and it was much closer than that each set. The Greek-American boy was all concentration, no fooling around.

When Jakob Hlasek came into the interview room at ten-thirty at night, his powerful, angular face, sporting a full day's blonde stubble, was both relaxed because he had done his best and tense because part of him still wanted to play more tennis. But the match with Sampras was over. There were only three reporters in the room, and the young media woman got the normally polite Hlasek very upset. After Hlasek had answered just two questions from the three remaining reporters, she asked him to leave so she could bring on the next bunch of players for interviews. A defeated six-foot four-inch Hlasek sat there behind the microphones, staring straight ahead.

"But," Hlasek said finally, "I have not finished."

"I'm sorry," said the media person. "We need the room."

Hlasek was not used to being treated like a discarded sneaker. He had held match point against Stefan Edberg on cement and lost 6–7, 7–6, 7–6. He had played and beaten the very best—Lendl, Agassi, Connors—in singles and in doubles. "Well. I'm not leaving yet," said Hlasek into the microphone, turning back to the three of us. "I'll answer some more questions now."

"You almost beat Edberg down at the Lipton," I said. "You were number eight in the world two years ago. You played very well tonight, but Sampras broke your serve once in each set. How good is he? How would you compare Pete Sampras with, say, Goran Ivanisevic?"

Hlasek grinned. It was a question he had wanted. "There is no comparison," said Hlasek. "I have played with both of them. Goran is a very, very good player, especially from the baseline. But Goran needs more volley. So there can be no comparison between them. Ivanisevic is much more steady a player. And Peter is much more talented."

A hush fell over the room. Ivanisevic had been getting all the press since his win over Becker at the French Open and his awesome serving display at Wimbledon. "What are Sampras's chances at this tournament?" the Los Angeles reporter asked. "Can he get to the semis or the finals?"

Hlasek turned his strong blonde jaw and pondered. "Peter has the game for it, to win. But he can also be very inconsistent. Peter has to play seven very good matches. He has played *three*." Hlasek smiled and nodded. "Now," said Hlasek, looking at the three reporters and the media person. "I am finished."

He got up slowly, stiffly, and headed out the side door into the warm Flushing Meadow night. Down under the stadium, workers were picking up the day's garbage. Pete Sampras was ushered into the room. The three of us had a treat.

"That Hlasek is a good player," I said.

Young Sampras nodded. "He definitely is."

"Hlasek said that you have the game to win here," said the Los Angeles reporter.

"No." Pete Sampras dropped his head and shook it, embarrassed by the suggestion. "Maybe in a couple of years, but I don't think it is realistic right now. I'm just going out there and trying to win every match and see what happens. I can do it in a couple of years. I know I have the game; it's just a matter of putting it all together at one time and keeping my concentration at a high level. But it's very tough for the way I play at age nineteen to win a Grand Slam."

"Why do you say that you are too young to win here?"

"I think that it's the style of my game," said Sampras. "Chang stays back and is consistent without a lot of errors. I'm a little bit more up and down. I'm going to force the action, and if I don't play well, I am going to lose."

"Because of your age, do you anticipate playing Davis Cup?"

"No. I don't see playing this year. They will pick Agassi and whoever else is playing well. Maybe if Australia wins and it's on grass, they'll consider me. I would rather start against a weaker team. I don't know if I can handle the pressure of Davis Cup yet." Perhaps the French were listening.

"Do you have low expectations because you don't want the added pressure?" I asked.

Young Sampras thought about it and nodded. "I don't play well when there is a lot of pressure on me. My style is that I hit a lot of flashy shots, and if I'm tight I just don't play well."

"Will one of you young Americans become number one some day?"

"Edberg and Becker are very tough to beat. I think Agassi has the potential to be number one. Chang can certainly be close. And I'm going to go for it, and we'll see what happens. Wheaton is as dangerous as the others because of his serve. Wheaton is definitely a player to be watched," said Pete Sampras. He did not mention his friend, Jim Courier. Nobody did.

We broke up a few minutes later, and I corralled Sampras. We walked back and spoke as far as the changing rooms. It was late. After talking to Sampras, I spotted the reporter from WFAN, New York's twenty-four-hour sports radio station, coming out of the stadium as I headed back in a sugar daze toward the interview room after another Häagen Dazs and a twelve-hour day. The other reporter weighed 240 pounds, and he was covering his first U.S. Open. I waved "hello."

"It takes me a while to learn how to ask these tennis players questions," said the young reporter.

"I know," I said. "I've been learning, too."

"I used to come out here with my father as a kid, but we always sat way up in the stands," said the big fellow from WFAN.

"You're doing good," I said, as the stadium cleaner dragged huge see-through plastic bags out into the soft summer night. The night's matches were completed.

"Are you taking the subway back in?" asked the WFAN man.

"Not quite yet," I said. "Did you see Leila Meskhi go into the interview room yet?"

"Leila Meskhi? Never heard of her!" The reporter from WFAN grinned as I headed back down the neon tunnel to look for the short, black-haired Russian, a real comer.

But the Russian was not there. The only person left in the media room was a young Puerto Rican woman in her blue Pinkerton uniform with silver badge and matching hat. "I guess it's close-up time," I said, looking around for Meskhi. The big Sony TV monitor was turned to Tim Ryan's nightly CBS wrap-up of the U.S. Open. I looked at the Puerto Rican woman. She worked a ten-hour shift at a little above minimum wage. "Did you ever play this game?"

"I'd like to play," she said eagerly, but her mood grew sullen suddenly. "But I can't play nothin'. I got no time to play, I got nobody to play with me, and I got nothin' to spend to learn this game." The woman shrugged and looked disgusted. It was late at night after a long day's work. "You think one of the players will give me a lesson?"

"You know how you learn this game? First you get an old racket. Ten or twenty bucks, used. Then you shake hands with the racket, like this." I gripped my left thumb. "Wrap the fingers around it. Then you find a wall. That's how everybody who ever got good at tennis started. With a wall, not a lesson."

She smiled. "You think a player will give me a racket?"

Maybe they would. But the players, partly to concentrate, kept themselves strangely inside themselves. "See you in the morning," I said, and I went back out into the warm late-night air.

Outside again, the stadium shone brilliantly in the dark summer night. Across the tracks, Shea Stadium was an even bigger beacon of light. Vendors were still selling T-shirts on the boardwalk, and there were two policemen guarding the entrance to the subway platforms. It was a starry night.

New York was the city where I was born, the city that I had come back to ten years before—after five years in Europe—and it made me sad to see New York, city of cities, struggling still with racism. With my love of competition, I could not abide it. Was violence the inevitable cry from those for whom competition had become a sham? I did not know. But in August 1990, blacks and whites in New York were like distrustful adversaries poised on opposite sides of the net from each other, and nobody was winning, a long, ugly match in which neither side played well and both sides accused each other of cheating. The social match—the context in which the U.S. tennis tournament in New York was taking place—was almost out of control. A quiet fear ruled in some parts of white New York; disappointment and feelings of betrayal reigned in black and Spanish New York, and the number-seven train to and from Manhattan slung everybody together in bright neon silence, one group excited about the men and women's draws at the U.S. Open, the other group of riders contemplating the fact that at six in the morning and four-thirty in the afternoon there was no escaping the one hard truth of life in New York City: the harder you try, the more money you dream of making.

The number-seven train stopped at 70th Street and Elmhurst Avenue in Queens, and a pale black girl with glasses stepped off cautiously alone into the pitch-black night as the rest of the train swayed back and forth into New York City, its riders talking about the Mets' pitching and Steffi Graf's family.

Evelyn Krickstein, mother of the tall, hard-hitting American baseline player Aaron, was waiting for me with her sister the next day in front of the towering draw sheets. I had hoped to meet her husband, Dr. Krickstein, at the St. James Hotel in London and talk with him over a big English breakfast when I was at Wimbledon, but at the last moment Aaron Krickstein, seeded ninth, had to pull out with an injury, and Dr. Krickstein stayed in Michigan. The Kricksteins' son had been playing on the tour since he was sixteen and had been plagued with injuries. If Aaron Krickstein had not won more tight five-set matches in his career than anyone else on tour, one might have thought he was a hypochondriac. But Krickstein was resilient, and as I talked to his mother about him, I became interested in her as a tennis parent, as I had in her husband at the Lipton. Evelyn Krickstein was an extroverted woman with a smile that matched her husband's for warmth.

"Tell me about the ups and downs of the season from the mother's point of view," I began.

Mrs. Krickstein laughed. "Where should I start?" She had a worn paperback copy of Dostoyevsky's *Crime and Punishment* under her arm, a little light reading for a fifth-set tie-breaker? Mrs. Krickstein possessed an easy laugh and sense of humor. "Who did Aaron lose to at the Lipton?"

she asked me. "Jakob Hlasek? Oh. To tell you the truth, I don't know the names, I just remember Aaron lost the match. Herb knows. Herb remembers all the names, all the players. I go to the matches, but I'm just the opposite of Herb. I get too nervous. That's why you'll never see me on TV. You'll see Herb sitting in the box seat, but I'm sitting somewhere else. I can't take it. Yesterday against that Canadian boy [Andrew Sznajder], when Aaron went five sets, I was sitting way up high in the balcony by myself looking down. I don't like watching."

"You get more nervous than your husband?"

"Well," said Evelyn Krickstein, "Herb sits more sedately than I do. I fidget, and I don't want Aaron ever to look up and see me getting nervous for him and distract him. Herb is maybe not so sedate *inside*, but he *sits* very calmly." Evelyn Krickstein laughed. She had a round face, dark reddish hair, and cheerful eyes. She was full of life like a rubber ball. "I really don't enjoy the matches too much. I really don't. I like to go watch by myself. Then if I get too nervous, I can just walk away."

"Your son Aaron has a very calm, quiet demeanor on court. He behaves very well under pressure. But would you say the calmness he shows on court is not always what is going on inside him?"

"Well," said his mother, "I think he used to get much more emotional and upset inside, because you could see him begin to rush. If Aaron rushes on court, he is confused or emotional. But I think he's beginning to control that. And I think he gets that control ability from his father. Anything tennis related I think comes from his father." Evelyn Krickstein was underestimating herself. She had a solid Midwestern no-quit personality.

"How would you characterize Aaron's personality?"

Mrs. Krickstein thought a second. "A lot of people say Aaron's shy. But around his peers, kids his own age, Aaron's not as inhibited as he seems on court. He's just shy around adults."

"The thing people forget is that these guys are so mature in their abilities and in their moves around the court, but they are still *young*."

"Well, Aaron's even younger, because he didn't go through what most people do at fifteen, sixteen, and seventeen. Aaron never went to a high school dance, and he knows that. He was on the tour at sixteen."

"Do you think, Mrs. Krickstein, all this competition makes players more mature in some ways but socially maybe more immature?"

She nodded. "I think socially that's the toughest thing, especially for the young ones. The sixteen- or seventeen-year-olds. They have the ability tenniswise to play with anyone. But what do you do afterwards? You're there with your mother and father. The older pros have nothing in common with you. And I think Aaron went through a rough period like that. You feel like an outsider. That's what's tough," said Mrs. Krickstein. "When you're playing well, but you feel so all alone."

Aaron Krickstein's match with Australia's Pat Cash was a big match for both players, and it drew a big New York crowd. The once youthful Australian, recently divorced but in better physical shape than he had been in since his Achilles tendon tear the year before, was physically stronger than Aaron Krickstein but not as sound technically. It was an interesting battle of wills. The Australian's serve and volley had to overcome his own technical weakness, his ground strokes, which happened to be Krickstein's greatest strength. The round before, the mop-haired Krickstein had played the veteran's role and beat the rising Australian star, Jason Stoltenberg, in straight sets. But Cash, son of a trade union lawyer in Australia, was every inch a veteran, rough and ready to rumble. Krickstein refused to buckle. And in the end the return of serve brought down the server. Aaron Krickstein showed no signs of the rushing that his mother had feared for him. He was no longer tentative as he had been in the loss to Hlasek at the Lipton in March. Aaron Krickstein beat Pat Cash 6–4, 7–6, 7–6, and the twenty-three-year-old American shook hands with the muscular Australian as if the victory were as routine as chewing gum. Dr. Krickstein was sitting in the box seat right at courtside. Evelyn Krickstein was sitting alone halfway up to the top of the Louis Armstrong Stadium.

The Goran Ivanisevic–Jean Fleurian match was played on court nine, an outside court with a 700-person seating capacity under the shadows of the stadium and grandstand. Wilt Chamberlain, the tennis aficionado, was seated in the narrow players-press section of the stands, his legs cramped by the crowd. The atmosphere was electric. Ivanisevic was on a hot streak. The 161-pound Croatian was having a fight against the smooth Frenchman who looked quite good in high heels at the players' party in Nice and very good in a black Lacoste shirt and lime-green shorts.

Youth was a wonderful thing, but not necessarily if you had to coach it. This was a match to upset a coach's stomach. Balazs Taroczy, the young Croatian's coach, and 1985 Wimbledon doubles winner, kept wriggling nervously on his seat, and when he felt his player begin to get distracted or discouraged, the slightly balding Hungarian coach shouted out in his heavily accented English,

"Go-*on*, Goran! Fight! Fight!"

Wilt Chamberlain, seven inches taller than Ivanisevic, smiled and stroked his goatee. "The kid moves well for his height," said Wilt.

The week before the U.S. Open, Ivanisevic played five singles matches at the Hamlet Challenge. He had made nearly a hundred thousand in Jericho, Long Island, but like Edberg, this fighter had dried out. He won the first two sets with Fleurian, but he was pouring sweat in the New York heat and looked as thin as a bamboo pole. Goran's left-handed serves still exploded into the green backdrop, as they had against Berger at the Lipton and Becker at Wimbledon, but between points he looked tired and increasingly irritable, ready to go off like a Roman candle.

With Fleurian down two sets to love, Fleurian's coach, Mansour Bahrami, a dark-skinned Iranian with a huge black French grenadier's mustache, turned to Taroczy, grinned at Ivanisevic's coach, and said, "Ten dollars. Goran cannot win the next set. He will not win in straight sets. He cannot."

Taroczy nodded without looking at the ten dollars and shouted, "Go-*on*, Goran! Fight! Fight!"

It was a seesaw third set. The two players struggled to stay on top of each other, but after losing his own serve early, Fleurian finally won the set and the bet. Mansour Bahrami did not say anything, but he smiled and Taroczy stared straight ahead. When the match was over, and Ivanisevic had won in four tough sets, the two coaches nudged each other and laughed. They had both won and lost something. Fleurian shrugged to Bahrami when he came off. He had played well, and his expectations were lower. Ivanisevic also smiled when he came off, but he looked as thin as a marathoner and very tired. Taroczy had lost his bet.

The next day against Darren Cahill, Goran Ivanisevic went berserk. The young Yugoslav played and lost to the lean Australian in the weirdest way. Ivanisevic went up two sets to love. Cahill won the match 6–0 in the fifth set. By the fifth set the young Croatian was floating way out on a cloud of self-hate, immaturity, and talent come unglued. I had seen the fury before with another left-hander, McEnroe, but never quite like this. In a child's rage brought on by fatigue, Ivanisevic blasted the ball into the net and back fence and then applauded himself in disgust. The fifth set took about ten minutes. He was exhausted and too strong to realize how tired he was.

"I tanked," Ivanisevic said later. In tennis parlance, *tanking* a match means that you purposely throw it, out of boredom, anger, or because the plane to the next singles tournament was leaving and you were still stuck in the previous week's doubles match. It happened fairly often in doubles, but few pros actually tanked singles matches at major events, though Lendl did it once at Madison Square Garden against Connors in the round-robin Masters format, and Jimmy Connors called him "chicken————."

"It was pretty gutless of him," the Aussie, Cahill, said after the match.

That night in Manhattan I called Fabio della Vida, Ivanisevic's agent from ProServ's Milan office. It had been a long day for the agent, but he was still friendly. "Would you play Goran again in that Hamlet Cup tournament just before the Open? He looked like a piece of dried driftwood out there today."

"Probably," said della Vida, a quiet, easy-going Italian.

DuPont was not likely to sponsor Goran Ivanisevic instead of Michael Chang, so the agent had decided they should go for the money while it was definitely there. I thought it was a mistake. Race horses need to point to the big race. "What really happened to Goran out there? He didn't really tank, did he, Fabio?"

"Goran came back to the hotel and he said to me that Cahill played great. Goran felt he had been very lucky to even get the first two sets from Cahill, especially the first set, which was so close. Goran did not serve well today. Not like Wimbledon against Becker. But Goran did not mean *tank*. He does not really understand the word. He meant he gave the match away, yes, but not on purpose. One hour after the match, Goran was sorry. The storm had passed. He apologized to me and to Taroczy and said he felt he should have won the match. He felt very badly. When he came to my hotel room, we had quite a frank talk with Taroczy, who did not like it, either. But Goran can take a loss. He is very much hurt by a loss but he does not show it to them, not to the press. But he does not *tank*. He does not throw a match. Only sometimes," said the Italian manager with a sigh, "he goes a little crazy."

I saw it the way Fabio della Vida, the agent, saw it. Ivanisevic might have been temporarily "gutless," as the Australian had said, but he would not throw a match on purpose. Like Edberg, but more immature, Ivanisevic's match with Cahill was his eighth in nine days. The fiery Croatian was exhausted the way McEnroe had been when he got ejected in Australia at the start of the year. Ivanisevic was a Ferrari. And 1991 would not be a better year for him, with civil war breaking out between Croatia and Serbia. But Ivanisevic was special, even though he was down. Give me some emotion, even emotion out of control, run amok! The champions usually came from that soulful, unhappy source. Ivanisevic was a high-wire aerialist. He just missed the catch on the bar swinging back toward him.

"I am sad," said Goran Ivanisevic, "because I lost this match very stupid. If I am going to learn something, then it's okay. If not, then it's not okay."

Jay Berger, tortoise to many of the tour's hares, was still in the tournament. At the Lipton, Berger had beaten Ivanisevic by hanging in there and finally boring a path into the young Yugoslav's volatile brain. Ivanisevic had caved in, spitting angrily on the court at a line call. The season since then had been a seesaw for Jay Berger. He hit a wall in the rankings when he reached number seven in the world after the Lipton. In Europe on the red clay, he played fourteen tournaments in a row, but while that may have been a bad tennis decision for his ranking, which had slipped to thirteen in the world, it had seemed like a good business decision. Jay Berger was twenty-three, at the top of his ranking and game, and he had reasoned that the tournaments in Europe were going to offer him hefty appearance money only so many times in his life. Before going back to Plantation, Florida, the scrappy American had taken home nearly $400,000 in prize money and appearance fees.

It took a full month to get over the burnout. After putting himself out to pasture during Wimbledon, Berger came back strong. He was fresh, rested, and eager in Canada on cement in mid-August, beating Tim Mayotte and Jakob Hlasek before losing to Michael Chang 7–6 in the third set in the final. If the season was a business trip intended to provide maximum earnings and security for his future after tennis, Jay Berger had done extremely well. But if the season was also a search for a thrill or a moment in which you are able to snatch victory from the edge of defeat, Jay Berger knew he had to do well at the U.S. Open, which to an American with a topspin grip is Wimbledon on cement.

It would not be easy. Psychologically, Berger got nicked in Europe. By late August, he was playing well again, but the European players recalled his mediocre European season and once again were underestimating his abilities. That was their error. Berger was always vulnerable but never easy to beat.

In the first round Berger played the tough clay-courter from Haiti,

Ronald Agenor, who had lost 7–5, 7–6 to Berger in two close but straight sets in Estoril, Portugal, at the old Stadium. In New York, Berger beat Agenor in four long sets.

Berger's second-round match with the young Swedish colt, Johan Carlsson, was a marathon. It began at 8 P.M. in the grandstand and finished well after midnight. Carlsson's hard-hitting Swedish baseline game was just a little smoother than Berger's. They hit the ball very hard at each other and worked incredible topspin angles off the sides of the court with their two-handed backhands. Carlsson brought out the European in Berger. They played on the cement like two clay-court specialists, but not "pushers." At 9 P.M., the planes from La Guardia started up again, and then it was really Jay Berger time. Given a short overhead at net, Berger bunted it away for a winner with a drop shot overhead. The young Swede did not fold. They were so different physically as people—the thick-set, swarthy Berger and the beanpole blonde Swede—and yet they were almost identical in technique and in the utter fierceness of their determination. Johan Carlsson would stick out a long Swedish winter on the baseline. Jay Berger would stay back there himself as long as the New York City buses kept running. The match was obscenely long and good. They really clobbered the ball. Carlsson won the first set 6–3, and Berger look outclassed. When it was over, Jay Berger had won the match 6–2 in the fourth set. Carlsson looked like a stick of ice that had suffered a complete meltdown.

Berger was so honest in his interviews. "Do you hear the noise around the court?" a reporter asked.

"Yeah," Berger admitted. "Some people don't. But I hear the noise."

"Are you looking forward to playing Agassi in the round of sixteen?"

"I have no idea what is going on outside my little section of the draw," said Berger. "I don't look forward to anybody."

"Do you feel great, Jay?" asked the young reporter from WFAN. "Did it feel great to beat Johan Carlsson?"

Jay Berger shrugged, his eyebrows rising. "It's nice to win. It sure beats the alternative."

I went looking for Ion Tiriac in the players' lounge area, but the Romanian was not there. He had bamboozled me at the Lipton, hip-checked me at Wimbledon, and told me by phone through his secretary that if he could find a minute for me, he would talk to me about Becker at Flushing Meadow. Where—on the platform of the number-seven train? Tiriac would not be more specific. He had eluded me again. I paced back and forth underneath the huge draw sheets, looking for a sign of him.

"Have you seen Tiriac or Dr. Krickstein come through the front door?" I finally asked the guard, a large, sunburned, tired-looking man with a cap on.

"To tell you the truth," he said, "I know their names, but the only ones I know by sight are Becker, McEnroe, and Arthur Ashe."

I waited with the guard for a few minutes, and we talked. "What do they seem like to you?" I asked him. "The players?" The guard in the short-sleeve shirt and baseball hat shrugged. Before he had a chance to answer, a tall player who had just won a singles match came toward the guard's door with his heavy tennis bag slung over his shoulder. We held the door open, and the big-serving South African walked past us through the door without saying a word, without batting an eyelash.

"He didn't say 'thanks,' did he?" I asked. The player was thirty-two years old.

"I tell you," said the guard. "They're great athletes and all, but I've been holding this door open for about a week and so far no one's said nothin' to me."

"They're a little self-absorbed," I said. "They'll all get older soon enough. It's a temporary heaven."

Jay Berger was on court fourteen, halfway to Far Rockaway, for a night match. His opponent was an unheralded Italian qualifier named Cristiano Caratti, a player to watch. Caratti had beaten Derrick Rostagno, McEnroe's conqueror at Wimbledon, in a fifth-set tie-breaker to get there. Ranked thirteenth in the world, Jay Berger was supposed to be able to mop up the court with a qualifier. Berger could not. It was one of the most exciting matches in the tournament.

Caratti was a fair-haired northern Italian with a soccer player's deftness and coordination and a thin, determined face. For two and a half sets the Italian made Berger look incredibly bad. Jay Berger kept walking in semicircles, trying to work things out, but nothing helped. The young Italian was on fire. He was quicker than Berger. He had a better serve and volley than Berger, and his passing shots were fierce that day. Berger flipped his racket into the night sky in desperation. It was nearly a shutout. Jay Berger lost the first two sets, 6–2, 6–4, and the match was not nearly as close as those scores.

When the Florida native's serve was broken twice in the third set, the matter did not look optimistic. It was dark behind the court out where the old World's Fair Globe sat surrounded by its fountains. Maybe three hundred people were packed into the low aluminum stands. The court next to Berger and Caratti was empty. Down two sets and two service breaks in the third set with Caratti serving at 4–2, Berger could have called a cab and flown home to Florida. But he didn't. Jay Berger won the third set. He came roaring back with the strength and patience of a survivor.

There was only one service break in the fourth set, and Berger won it. Together as equals, the two players went into the enchanted area of a fifth set. It was beautiful.

Suddenly court fourteen at the U.S. Open was a public-park court again. The opponents played as if they were two juniors sent out to do battle without a referee on the last back court of a junior tournament that means nothing in terms of money or rankings but everything to the two players and their families. Caratti and Berger played their hearts out. The tension reached both players, but they rose above it. The nearby courts were bare. It was 11:30 at night and a lot of people had left. On court, flies whirled up into the jetstream of light.

When Berger broke Caratti in the first game of the fifth set, the Italian slammed a ball high off the green cement up into the starless sky, racing underneath to catch it before it fell.

"Cristiano caught it on his racket strings," said a New York woman.

"Yeah, but he's tired. Really tired," a black man in the crowd said of Caratti. "Look at him flex his legs. His legs are gone." But suddenly, the Italian caught fire again.

"This is *so bad!*" shouted Berger, whipping his right leg with his racket like a jockey taking a crop to his horse. Then Berger began to hit the ball with great lift from the backhand side, using his strong legs to lift his black Prince racket with a rising, scythelike stroke. Berger's ground strokes rose deeper and deeper into his opponent's court, pinning Caratti back behind the baseline. Court fourteen was great for a fan; you could see the faces of the competitors close up. A linesman missed a call on a deuce point.

"Oh, no!" moaned Caratti.

It did not matter. The match was so good a bad call could not touch it. The outcome was almost out of the players' control. They were two souls serving their rackets, their legs, and their hearts. They were not enemies. They were accomplices in a great competitive effort. It was brilliant. Serving at 3–2, Berger let a feeble country-club lob drop instead of smashing it, and the ball fell three feet in. The mood shifted. Berger looked vulnerable. Caratti hit two more aggressive topspin lobs, the most disdainful shot in tennis, to break Berger's serve and leave him hopelessly stranded between the net and the baseline in no-man's-land.

"Hang in there, Jay!" called a woman in the crowd.

"And you, too, Chris!" a New Yorker near me shouted out loud to Caratti. "I got a lot of cash on this one!"

Berger had gone from up 3–1 to down 4–3 in the fifth set with the other man's serve coming up. What could Jay Berger do to change his mood or his game during the fifth-set change-over? Berger sat down and changed his socks.

Still down 4–3 after the sock change-over, Berger walked back to the baseline. He bounced on his toes. The other guy was serving to go up 5–3 in the fifth set. Berger was in trouble and he knew it. The match was all but over. But the rising Italian star insisted on winning dramatically. Caratti, a baseliner for most of the match, suddenly showed how desperately he wanted it by racing in to net three straight times without working the ball around the court the way he had before. Berger passed him three times in a row. Berger was not giving an inch. He was as tight with points as Ken Rosewall.

"Take your time, Caratti," said an old New Yorker. "You look a bit lazy. Wake up!"

Berger knotted the fifth set at 4–all. Between points he berated himself fiercely to keep concentrating. It was as if Berger were overcoming his fear of losing by using anger at himself. He was frightening himself to do better, trying to make the dislike of possible failure greater than the actual sensation of fear. Berger blasted a cross-court forehand return of serve to break Caratti and go up 5–4 in the fifth set. After his second four-hour match in two days, Jay Berger was serving for the match— never a sure thing with the type of serve one could pull out of the trunk of a car like a retractable luggage stroller.

There was a huge moment of doubt in the final service game. At 30–all, Berger served what looked like an ace, and the linesman missed the line call. Berger's ace was called out. Instead of ad-in, match point for Berger, it was second serve, deuce.

Another player might have cracked with anger. The serve was definitely in. Caratti looked over at Berger, the server, waiting for Berger to say something to the umpire, but Berger looked down at the cement and said nothing. He was a pro. He put his second serve in play and won the deuce point. On the final point, Berger hit an ace up the middle to win the match.

Berger had won! He leapt up in the air, smiling from ear to ear. Caratti shrugged, and they hugged at the net, talking briefly to each other as if they had taken a trip together to the moon. Berger's smile was bright under his wavy black hair, and suddenly he blasted the remaining yellow ball high up into the Flushing Meadow night, way out of the court, above the trees, back toward the globe and fountains of the old World's Fair.

I identified with Jay Berger's victory. It reminded me of how at Wimbledon, and once in Philadelphia, officials nearly did not let me in and made a fuss about the color of my press badge, what I was writing, who I belonged to, what questions the players could be asked, what questions were not permissible to ask, who the "real" sportswriters were, who was allowed in and who was not. And in the end, as a writer, the only way to do it was to hang in there, to trust in your own ability, to not take no for an answer, to trust your heart means no wrong, to believe you can see what you can see, and to care, because these were the strugglers in life, the nonquitters, the hopers, and Jay Berger was that ever-lasting struggler, that nonquitter, a player of a certain talent who worked with all his heart to realize his abilities such as they were.

I felt like I had come through a test, too, and I was very happy to be there after the match with Jay Berger and his parents. I liked the way he handled himself.

"He was unbelievably tough," said Jay Berger, as he hugged his parents after the match.

His father, Paul, the dentist, was a lean, tall, handsome man with black hair—I had imagined him a little stockier—and Berger's mother, Carol, was shorter, blonde, and smiling. We had spoken at length by phone but had never met, and we huddled together in the darkness behind the stands. It was nearly midnight again. This was a tennis tournament in the old-fashioned way. The Bergers were thrilled with their son's win.

"This was worse than the five-setter Jay won against Ken Flach last year," said his mother. "The weather conditions helped Jay out that time. He got a rain delay against Flach, and it helped. But this boy Caratti just played so well. Jay went through three pairs of sneakers, five rackets [broken strings], and two pairs of socks. He's eating fruit out there. It was like he had set up house," laughed his mother.

"When it was four–love in the second set for the other boy, Carol turned to me and asked if we could get a seat for Jay on the plane home with us," laughed Jay Berger's father. "He was down two breaks in the third set and down two sets. He was down four–three and a service break in the fifth set. Not that many people could have won that match. We're so proud of him."

"Did Chang lose to Cherkasov?" Mrs. Berger asked like a mother at a junior tournament, except this was the big show.

"He was so far down, I think he must have," I said. "Cherkasov is a tough little guy, too."

"And Gilbert lost," said Mrs. Berger. "Wow! Mansdorf came through in the end. Five sets."

Jay Berger was tired but sat down after midnight in the interview room under the stadium. He knew how to compete. I asked, "What frame of mind did you have after you lost the first two sets?"

"You don't really think about that. You just gotta get into the match and win the next set. Then if you win that, you try to get back to even. For two and a half sets, this guy was basically just hitting winners off almost every single ball I hit. It was really tough."

"Did he stop playing great tennis? What changed?"

"I decided to start going for some shots myself," said Berger. "That's what I try to do when I'm losing like that. I try to find a secret or something. I try to find what is going to make this guy miss some balls. In the third set he went up a couple of breaks, and I just decided to move in a little bit on the court and start smacking the ball, not as hard as I can, but pretty damn hard."

"Did his level go down?"

"A little bit. It's hard to play as well as he was for three sets in a row. And I knew it. The way to beat somebody who is hot like that is just to hang on. I think that in almost every match you play, you always have one chance to get back into the match, and eventually I got my chances and took advantage of them."

Jay Berger was not the most talented player in the draw, but he had figured it out. He had a tough draw, but he made it into the fourth round. His next opponent was to be Andre Agassi. They went three close sets at the Lipton in Florida. This time it would not be as close. But Berger had reached the round of sixteen, and he was seeded thirteenth. He had done what was asked of him. Berger had had his ups and downs, but he made over $600,000 in prize money and appearances for the season, and he won the tough ones at the U.S. Open. Jay Berger and his fiancée, Nadia, who had been too nervous to watch him play Cristiano Caratti that night, made a happy couple. In two weeks their wedding party of thirty people would be floating on a chartered boat off the coast of Florida. Jay Berger had earned his success. He was exhausted but elated after the Caratti win: "It's hard to be objective when you're out there on court. Tennis players are pretty much perfectionists. We want to play so well all the time, but we can't always," Jay Berger tried to explain. "But I never gave up, which a lot of people do."

The next evening, a little after ten o'clock, Brian Watkins and his family from Provo, Utah, having watched the tennis earlier in the day, came out of their hotel and went down into the subway station at Fifty-third Street and Seventh Avenue in Manhattan, to ride to Greenwich Village for dinner. Brian Watkins never made it back aboveground alive.

There were eight other murders in New York City that night, but none was so publicized as the murder of this twenty-two-year-old assistant tennis pro, known at first in the New York City papers only as "the tourist," underscoring the publicity disaster for New York as well as the loss of a life. The Hispanic boys who committed the horror came from Jackson Heights, Queens, not far from the tennis stadium. When the Watkins family—tall, thin, and blonde—stepped down into the station, in an area slightly east of the hookers, pimps, and crack sales—an area where many people from out of town take a hotel room—there should have been no problem in the subway at that hour.

Brian Watkins had been a junior tennis player—not a great one—but he was competitive enough and skilled enough to teach others how to play. The family was close. Each year, the trip from Utah to New York to see the world's best play was the thrill of their year. The week's vacation was their trip to Aspen or Europe. They had watched Jay Berger play. They knew enough about tennis to appreciate the hard-fought match, the effort as well as the victory. The Watkins family was like 90 percent of the people who went to watch the tennis. They played the game and they loved it.

And so the murder of Brian Watkins in the brown subway darkness of the B and D train platform was a knife that went through the hearts of many Americans, but especially the tennis players and the great majority of New Yorkers who love their city, and sometimes fear it, too.

Tennis is a game that requires bravery. And Brian Watkins showed too much instinctive bravery. When the assailants cut open his father's back pocket with a box-cutter, took $200 in cash and the credit cards, and punched his mother to the subway platform for her handbag and jewelry, Brian Watkins reacted like an athlete and an older son. Instinctively, he leapt forward and made a reply, reacting not with his head but with his heart. He ran after the assailants. The Hispanic boy charged with the murder claimed that Brian Watkins ran right into his six-inch knife. The knife was still in Watkins's chest when help finally arrived.

The family from Utah did not have a chance, and no number of guilty verdicts would mitigate their loss. The Watkinses had come to New York to cheer on Brad Pearce, the young pro from Provo who had done so well at Wimbledon. You never believe something like that can happen to you. Nor could the Watkins family imagine that, as their son lay dying in their arms on the New York City subway platform, the eight assailants would run down the street to Roseland, the 1930s dance hall turned disco palace for the poor, while the Utah boy's mother was frantically making calls from a pay telephone down in the subway trying to get Emergency Services to send an ambulance, shouting to the 911 operator, "Oh, please. Please! My boy is dying!"

Thomas Repetto, a former New York City detective who was quoted in the *New York Times* the next morning, commented on the 2,450 murders in New York City during 1990, including Brian Watkins's death, saying, "Who shot whom and why and where—you can't keep track because there are so many. This is a hell of a way to live. Are we going to celebrate next year if there are only 1,983 homicides in New York City?"

Arthur Ashe, trim in a white Le Coq Sportif shirt and red warm-up pants with an American flag patterned over the zipper at the bottom right leg, was seated in the basement press lunchroom, a concrete bunkerlike space that was virtually empty. When I came in, the Andrei Cherkasov–Andre Agassi quarter-final was going on upstairs. There was quite a crowd in the stadium to see how the hungry little Russian who had beaten Chang would do against the American boy from Las Vegas via Iran. Neither Ashe nor I had heard of Brain Watkins's death, or if we had seen the headline the event had not fully registered. Ashe was having lunch alone, and I introduced myself and asked if I could sit down and ask a few questions while he ate. Ashe said, "Sure," and gestured to the empty chair across the table from him.

When the founder of the Shoal Creek Country Club, host to the 1990 PGA, said, "We don't discriminate in every other area *except* blacks," the repercussions were felt by golf and tennis clubs throughout the country. Prejudice—racial or religious—was an unspoken subject at many country clubs. The Shoal Creek incident, however, was resolved with the admission of one wealthy black businessman to the club.

Had so much really changed in the thirty years since Arthur Ashe burst on the tennis scene? Ashe spoke frankly about Shoal Creek, blacks in tennis, "Queen Victoria" and Andre Agassi—all subjects about which the pale, slender black survivor of two heart bypass operations felt strongly. His answers and opinions came from the heart and were spoken quietly in Ashe's measured, intelligent voice.

"Shoal Creek," said Arthur Ashe, "is very important. It has very little to do with sports. Golf just happened to be involved as the catalyst, but Shoal Creek goes way beyond golf. It got a ho-hum response from most blacks in the street. When asked about the Shoal Creek affair, they said, 'Who gives a——? I can't join that club anyway, and neither can my neighbor, so it's not a big issue for me.' Although they recognized the inequity.

"Of course," Ashe said, toying thoughtfully with his veal-and-rice dish, "there can be a very powerful tendency, human nature being what it is, if you are discriminated against for any length of time, to wallow in that, use that as an excuse for not getting what you want. But you can only play the victim so long."

I liked the way Ashe thought and spoke. " 'You can only play the victim so long'?"

"You can develop a dependency syndrome. In theory, I am very anti-affirmative action," the 1968 U.S. Open and 1975 Wimbledon champion continued. "I am against it because affirmative action means that I have been singled out to receive an advantage because of a disadvantage in past history. I don't really see my past history as being that disadvantaged. I mean, I like to be judged just like everybody else. But to the extent that society doesn't do that, well, then, yeah, affirmative action is necessary. But I think the country is worse off having to even go through the affirmative-action process. It's an admission of failure. It's an admission that things are so bad that you have to create special sets of rules or privileges that accrue to some people because you can't get the rest of society to treat everybody the same. Today in tennis, the U.S. Tennis Association is really going out of its way to do the right thing. Black kids certainly are getting special treatment. But blacks have been victims of unequal treatment for seventy years. That is tough to tell to a fifteen-year-old white kid who plays tennis. He just can't understand." Ashe sighed, clearly troubled by what he understood as an athlete to be true in life: that only the hardest workers, black or white, can turn their unformed talents into viable careers. America is a very competitive place, and tennis is that competition cleaned up some and made social.

"I was giving a lecture on affirmative action and reverse discrimination at Columbia University Law School," said Arthur Ashe. "The discussion got quite heated, and I finally said, 'Look. A lot of you people—white people—are sitting here at Columbia University Law because your parents had breaks. And my parents, specifically, legally did not have breaks. Some of you are legacies of a society that reserved certain places for people who are white. And if we'd had a chance to compete equally, we'd have ten percent of the seats in here, probably.' "

"That is what you meant when you said that 'structurally' there are still problems, not just economic problems, but structural problems in America—in tennis and in life?"

"That's right."

"And yet, we now see the American sons and daughters of recent immigrants doing so well in tennis—Andre Agassi, Pete Sampras, Michael Chang, Jennifer Capriati. Is the black situation really that different?"

"It is," said Arthur Ashe. "The immigrant brings a different mind-set over here. Most immigrants live for their children. Their entire adult actions and thought processes are guided by what is best for their children."

"So the difference between immigrant tennis families, who give so much to each other, and black families, where the family is often split up, is that the family itself is different? That the black family is not in a position to give?"

"Well, I have one other difference," said Arthur Ashe. "And that is, to the extent that an immigrant wants to become Americanized, one of the quickest ways to become Americanized, to be thought of as just another one of the boys, is to excel in something like sports. Or piano competition."

"Ballet. Gymnastics."

"Exactly. And tennis is *the* acceptance sport socially. Tennis and golf."

"Is the 'structural problem' for the young black tennis player still having access to the courts and to the rackets?"

"No," said Ashe. "There is no shortage of tennis courts in America. At the schools and the public parks, tennis is available."

"Not in Harlem or the Bronx."

"Well, you don't have the coaching there. And the competition is not there—not the kind that would attract the same degree of attention as a basketball court."

"I saw somewhat the same thing in England as regards tennis. The working-class athlete—white or black—is not getting the access to tennis over there. And as of 1990, I still don't see the flow of talent that could be coming into tennis from the black population in America."

"No. No, I disagree," said Arthur Ashe. "I disagree slightly with you. There are no more legal barriers. And if the black community really wanted to produce good tennis payers, it could do so in a minute—just as it is now part of our culture, part of our group ethnic will, to produce good basketball players. We are a little embarrassed if we don't. It's like the Canadians with their hockey players. Canada's very self-image is partially defined by its hockey players. Among black Americans, self-image—as repeatedly given to us by the media and by advertising—is defined by basketball. Black Americans just don't care that much about tennis. In fact, they don't care too much about anything that has to do with matters dealing with the upper socioeconomic classes. And that's definitely where tennis is."

Ashe nodded for emphasis. "That's the reason you get a ho-hum response from blacks in the street about the Shoal Creek affair. They recognize the inequity of the issue, but they can't afford to join the club anyway."

A Hispanic man with a cart full of dishes came rattling past our table just as Ashe got up to get some water. "The tendency is to blame things now on economics," Ashe continued. " 'Blacks can't join our club because they can't afford to join.' But what is or is not affordable can also be a reflection of discrimination. That's why Shoal Creek—and clubs like it— is not about golf, or economics. It's about structure."

Ashe spoke so calmly and intelligently. The Reagan years with their survival-of-the-fittest ideal, their competition-will-provide theory of government, widened the gap between the haves and have-nots. In social terms, the tennis net had been raised to the height of a badminton net.

"Try to put yourself in the position of a young black player coming up today," I said. "Would you see Arthur Ashe or Althea Gibson as an aid or a burden?"

"I don't think we're either," said Ashe. "Not anymore. Every day that goes by, Althea and I become less and less relevant. For some of the young black women players, Althea might as well be Queen Victoria. She's that far back from them in history."

I laughed. Ashe and Althea Gibson were clearly still the Rod Laver and Margaret Smith of black tennis, if not of American tennis. "I don't know about Queen Victoria. But I did think at Wimbledon that having Althea there on the final day was an added pressure that Zina Garrison did not need against Navratilova."

"I don't think it would have changed the outcome," said Ashe. "It was still a nice gesture."

"It was a beautiful gesture."

"It's a bit analogous—but quite different—to some player like Brad Pearce, the boy from Utah who got through to the quarter-finals at Wimbledon this year. Take a player like that," said Ashe, "and imagine. The parents are sitting at home, and they say, 'Oh. He's winning. Let's go over there and see him.' That's the worst thing parents can do if they are not there already. Absolutely the worst. Stay home!"

"Stay home! It's just added pressure."

"Right. If you don't, you're probably going to change this kid's traditional preparation for matches. He's going to worry about you if suddenly you're there. Better to stay home and watch it on TV," suggested Arthur Ashe. "Believe me. You don't need any added pressure."

"I guess, finally, I come back to you. How do *you* regard yourself—as a miracle or freak of talent, or as a reflection of possibility?"

Arthur Ashe paused to reflect. "No. I . . . I worked at it. I was not given. As I look back on it, I was not given any breaks that I did not deserve. The first really big break came when I was seventeen years old and was named to the U.S. Junior Davis Cup team. I *earned* that. And I had to earn it in only three of the five major junior tournaments because I was black. I couldn't play in the National Jaycees, and I couldn't play at the Louisville Boat Club."

"I played there. I played in both of those," I interjected. I had a different memory of Louisville. I remembered the party for all the players out on an old river boat. The players were out on the Mississippi River at night with the big paddle wheel turning. It was fun.

"So I made the Junior Davis Cup team on the basis of my sectional play," said Arthur Ashe. "At Kalamazoo. And the Westerns. Three of the five criteria. When I was offered a scholarship at UCLA—look—I was ranked fifth in the country. The UCLA coach called me and offered me the scholarship sight-unseen. He had never met me, had never seen me play. But I think I *deserved* it. I earned it. I got no breaks that I didn't work for."

"Are today's black athletes a little more pampered?"

"A *little* more?" Ashe's indignation almost made his voice squeak. Ashe had recently written an excellent three-volume history of the black athlete in America. "It *was tough*. I suppose it's easy for someone of my generation to say to a black of this generation, 'Wait a minute. You-all today are complaining, but things were worse for us. We got through it. Why can't you?' "

"Okay. They're more pampered. Is that why the black tennis player is still not getting through today?"

"No. I think it's easier in one way, but it's also tougher these days, too," said Ashe. "The overall competition is tougher. Much tougher. If I had to come through now, I don't know if I'd make it."

"Oh, yeah, you'd make it," I laughed nervously, still a fan. Ashe had had the most fluid timing and effortless first serve since Pancho Gonzales and before Pete Sampras. "Technically, you hit the ball so beautifully. That's really what counts. I don't see the same stroke ability from Zina Garrison. It was a different sensation when you hit the ball. Technically, I don't like the way Zina hits the ball."

"She has some stroke—ah—I wouldn't call them stroke *deficiencies*. I'd say Zina has some stroke *limitations*. There are some things that could help her, things that she doesn't do very well right now. But what she does, she does very well. It's just, Zina could use a little more variety. And it's not there. I will say this. The next black Grand Slam winner is more likely to be a woman than a man. I'm not saying anything negative about MaliVai Washington, but it will be a while before another black man wins a Grand Slam event. A woman will do it first. The best male black athletes are still playing basketball and running track."

"Do you think that when the black athlete—or the black person—is finally accepted into the country clubs, which still exist in America pretty much as they were thirty years ago, that when black people become members of the club, are part of it, then we'll also see a larger percentage of blacks competing in tennis—that is, participating in America itself at all levels?"

"I know what you're saying," said Ashe, who had never joined a tennis or golf club, though he had been invited to do so. "But country clubs just don't matter too much in tennis anymore."

I disagreed slightly. "I think club tennis is still the backbone of the sport—certainly for the people who watch and love it. But I know what you are saying. Country clubs generally don't produce the champions."

"Right. Jack Kramer, Pancho Gonzales, Jimmy Connors. Agassi. Sampras. All public-court players," said Arthur Ashe. "What is frustrating for me is that I realistically know that there is one hell of an opportunity going unrealized and literally wasted because we can't convince enough black kids to try this sport. If you're not in the sport, you don't realize that this opportunity, no matter how narrowly defined it may seem on the outside, is actually very much available. There are roughly thirty-three hundred college varsity tennis scholarships available in the United States each year. I would say black players—and I am being generous—get no more than two percent of those scholarships. And that is *not* the fault of the white coaches or the colleges. We're talking about millions of dollars of education available to any kids of anyone who want to put in the effort. And it's not really that much effort. We're not talking about competing with kids whose parents belong to private clubs. Most of those folks can afford to send their kids to college in the first place and don't take away the scholarship money. Unfortunately, we're talking about a black community," said Arthur Ashe, "whose focus is so concentrated on basketball that they forget everything else."

"Tennis is a skill sport."

"Exactly."

"But it's like reading, isn't it?" I asked softly. "If you don't start early, by the time you are fourteen or fifteen it's too late. Unless you get the coaching early, you won't have the skill level to get a scholarship."

"That's a good point," said Ashe. "Tennis is a skill sport. Coaching becomes a big factor."

"It just seems to me that if the country clubs had black members, if we were inclusive instead of being so exclusive, if we behaved the way America was supposed to be, there would be a broader range of possibility open to black kids and adults, not just tennis and golf players. My question is, 'Do people want their clubs opened up, or is part of the thrill of being a member knowing that someone else is not?' "

"It cuts both ways," Arthur Ashe replied softly. "The old kind of legal segregation is no longer there. I do think the Shoal Creek Country Club issue is a very important issue. And it is not just an important issue for golf or for tennis. It is an American issue."

Talking to Arthur Ashe, one had the sense that this slender man in his late forties was a bit frustrated. I could sense that he still loved tennis aesthetically, that he treated all people, black or white, fairly, but that he had not yet been able to convince the black community of the opportunity that tennis at the college level could provide for young blacks. Arthur Ashe is a man of manners and taste. And yet, Ashe had not been able through his shining, modest, and intelligent example to convince the white tennis clubs to beat the white golf clubs to the punch and truly open their doors to people whose sense of competition and ability to play sports was tremendous—but still separate and confined in terms of social access.

John McEnroe stood on the far side of the net calmly biting his upper lip, holding his racket lightly in his left hand as he waited for Spain's Emilio Sanchez to get himself together and serve.

It was 5–all in the fifth set. They had been playing on the brightly lit, packed stadium court for almost four hours. The baselining Spaniard, brought up with gritty red-clay instincts, and McEnroe, seeking redemption through excellence, had been throwing their personal styles and full hearts at each other for hours, looking for signs of weakness.

John McEnroe had finally come back home. As he told Robin Finn of the *New York Times*, "New York is like . . . me. L.A. is nice, but my motivation was kind of sapped away. Instead of getting the advantages, it seemed like I was getting the disadvantages, the unreality of the whole situation, the Hollywooding out, so to speak."

John McEnroe's presence in New York at "the Flush," as the Flushing Meadow Tennis Center was known to some of the inhabitants of the upper reaches of the stadium court, was greatly aided by the fact that nothing was expected of him in 1990. Most people thought McEnroe deserved the default in Australia. I did not. I thought Gerry Armstrong, the pleasant blonde ex-soccer goalie, and Peter Bellinger, the English tournament referee, had overreacted, paying McEnroe back for past behavior, not the situation itself. But by the time of the U.S. Open, McEnroe had accepted his punishment, and it had helped him. McEnroe was finally a little afraid of himself.

It had been a peculiar year for John McEnroe. A month after the default in Australia, an Avianca jetliner with over two hundred passengers crashed on Long Island, landing less than fifty yards from the McEnroe house in Oyster Bay's exclusive Cove Neck neighborhood. The McEnroe front lawn was used by the rescuers to land helicopters and for filling body bags.

By comparison, his personal struggles with tennis were easy, but McEnroe was not the type of personality for which anything ever was easy. Marilyn Fernberger, the long-time tournament director in Philadelphia, had tried to explain him by saying, "John is a perfectionist," which was probably why he kept screwing things up so badly. When McEnroe was in his twenties, people said that he was young, or that his parents loved him too much, or that his father protected him too much. But when you are thirty-one, it is time to do your own laundry. John McEnroe never much liked the box of Tide. If some other player had just once dared give John McEnroe a swift kick out behind a practice court, it could have helped him so much, but they all admired his talent too much. McEnroe, like chess master Bobby Fischer or poet Ezra Pound, had an odd aura of genius about him—and geniuses don't usually listen until it is too late.

By the start of the U.S. Open in 1990, no one really cared anymore whether McEnroe was a genius, and because of it he came back down to earth a better man. Undoubtedly, if tennis was the ultimate individual's game, McEnroe was a special case. He was too old to be scolded, and people were tired of his "raging bull" routine. McEnroe needed a new scriptwriter, but he had only himself, and at 5–all in the fifth set against Emilio Sanchez, he was quiet as a judge. McEnroe finally seemed to realize that for years he had been walking the plank of social opinion and using it as a diving board. Now a father and a husband, he had stopped smirking: time was no longer on his side.

Emilio Sanchez, whose younger brother Javier had lost to McEnroe in the first round, wanted the win in the round of sixteen match just as much as McEnroe. The heat in New York was Spanish, but they had scheduled McEnroe at night so it was a shade cooler. The Spaniard was twenty-five and at the height of his powers. McEnroe was thirty-one and slightly on the downside of his mountain. With McEnroe up 3–2 in the fifth set, they each had won 146 points, and the match hit the four-hour mark. It would be over in twenty-one minutes.

It was Age against Beauty, and McEnroe was Age. The handsome Spaniard was acrobatic and determined. But the New York crowd, which liked them both, breathed life into McEnroe's heart and legs. Sanchez's confidence had gradually been isolated by McEnroe over the course of the match, so McEnroe's message to the European was: "You are soft like red clay. I come from cement."

Sanchez cracked a kick serve into McEnroe's left-handed backhand, and it was McEnroe, not the Spaniard, who had to make the reply like a matador faced with the horns of a close-passing bull. Keeping his balance somehow, McEnroe blunted his bent-wrist backhand down at the feet of the oncoming Spaniard. And when Sanchez, having abandoned his baseline, volleyed up, McEnroe swept in and flung the backhand volley across Sanchez's face and away into the open court.

Jennifer Capriati, crushed earlier by Steffi Graf, was in the stands watching with her father and mother, and all three rose to cheer. Tatum O'Neal, John McEnroe's wife, leapt up and down. Her husband had broken the other guy. The Spaniard's marquee good looks, square jaw, five o'clock shadow, and brown eyes were deceptively innocent. John McEnroe, receding hair partly covered with a blue bandana, looked thin. His face was pale and lined with effort. But as they changed ends with McEnroe up 6–5 in the fifth set with the serve, McEnroe's feet again had that little bounce to them. Still, the Spaniard looked too young and too fit, waiting to return McEnroe's serve down 5–6 in the fifth set.

The week had started on a less sanguine note for McEnroe. It had been exciting to sit in the front row at McEnroe's crowded interview after he got through his opening match against Javier Sanchez, Emilio's slightly less talented brother. I had always loved the way McEnroe played. I had a love-hate relationship with McEnroe the person, recognizing an earlier, unhappy teenage me in him. I knew from experience that temper is a two-edged sword that can both create and destroy at almost the same time. I could see McEnroe creating and destroying through the years off the court, and I could imagine how it was with his family and his friends. I would criticize McEnroe, but a part of me would always sympathize with him, too. Unhappiness is not something you invent. Anger is the fire in the top of the forest. There are various ways of measuring success—one is by wins and losses, another is by turning a personal corner. By the end of 1990, John McEnroe seemed to have exorcised much of his demon. Ironically, that was what I was afraid of. I wanted him to win and silence his critics. But he would never silence them by losing.

We were all packed into the interview room, with its blue backdrop for television. The scene that first day would always stick in my mind. The McEnroe interview began with standard questions like "What do you think your chances are?" and "Realistically, John, how far do you think you can get here?" The luck of the draw had been kind but peculiar to McEnroe. To get to the semifinals, unseeded for the first time in ten years, he would have to go through the meat of a very tough draw. The reporters were jockeying for position around him. Since it was the first round, I wanted to ask McEnroe a question about Edberg, who just two days before at the Hamlet Challenge had beaten McEnroe in straight sets but now was already back in London after losing to Volkov. My chance came. John McEnroe looked at me. He had been friendly in Philadelphia, but I didn't think he recognized me this time. I wanted to phrase my question just right: "Two days ago, you played Stefan Edberg. And it was a pretty tough match. Now he's gone, and you're still in. Do you have any feeling of sympathy for Edberg? Any thoughts about what might have happened to him?"

John McEnroe thought about the question briefly, looked directly at me, sneered, and said, "What does that have to do with anything?"

The little bastard aced me. He caught me leaning in the wrong direction: compassion. In a sense he was right. Keep your mind on your own business and don't worry about what happens to anybody else. But the way McEnroe said it, the disdain in his voice was worse than what he actually said.

He did not know me and had no way of knowing that I had so often been his defender. He had an air of magic lightness about him that was his most attractive feature. The deftness in his hand was once matched by the lightness in his feet, and it formed a protective aura around him. That lightness was McEnroe's charisma, the part of John McEnroe I admired so much. But suddenly the other side of me wanted to meet him outside and flatten him. The entire room seemed to pause. There was a long silence in the interview room and I said nothing to him. A few minutes later, I knew what I felt: that McEnroe ought to think twice before he lashes out, because the person he insults might really be his friend, his defender and admirer.

When I was in England for Wimbledon, the English talked about McEnroe's uncle in Ireland, who apparently had the same type of temper on a golf course that John McEnroe once had on the tennis court. I understood the anger, the ferocity of it, the passion and disappointment of it. But what was his problem really? McEnroe seemed to have a Quasimodo chip on his shoulder, a humplike identity problem. His parents, Kay and John McEnroe, Sr., had braved the smallness of opinion, the awful, constricting limitations of religion, and through love the Jewish woman and the Irish man had thrown convention to the wind and married. They produced a champion. John McEnroe, their oldest son, born in Wiesbaden, West Germany, brought up in modest Queens, and finished in wealthy Manhattan, had a natural rage in him like jet rocket fuel. He was a thin, raging man, the Dylan Thomas (*"When I was a windy boy and a bit"*), not the Keats of pro tennis. Keats was for Edberg. Pancho Gonzales, also a champion, a Mexican American, had owned a gigantic rage that he could ride like a tidal wave to victory. McEnroe's anger came in smaller, tighter waves. I decided that my question was a clunker. But about ten minutes later, someone else asked McEnroe the same question about Edberg. This time he answered, but McEnroe had told me something far more interesting with his first answer, the kick: he had his game face back on.

Like a general, McEnroe soon couched his creative assault in modest goals and words. This was the right tactic. He had played a lot of tournaments—a fury of tournaments—since losing to Rostagno at Wimbledon. With that effort came self-awareness as well as better reflexes:

"Not playing and training off court was not going to get it done for me. I played all those tournaments to get the rust out, and there was a lot of rust to get out. I got to number four last year, but I wasn't into it. I had to get in there and take some losses. You can train hard off the court for being in shape, but that is a different kind of shape mentally and physically for tennis. There's no one out there who's going to help you. You have to work on yourself. I went out and played the tournaments and struggled. That's helped. I got some tough draws. If the results don't come, that will make my decision [about retiring] easy."

McEnroe paused. His pasty white, unshaven face was scruffy, calm but not contented. "It's not only if you let yourself win on the court. That's not as important at a certain point. You want to improve yourself as a person."

Platitudes for bad attitudes? I did not think so. McEnroe was talking now about tennis and happiness. Far from feeling like punching Mac in the nose, I now felt like standing up and cheering him on. McEnroe was finally going for the double victory, winning—and winning like a man, not a brat.

"John," said the reporter from the New York *Daily News.* "Did you

worry coming in here that you might not have gotten enough rust out?
That you might embarrass yourself competitively?"

"No," McEnroe said, suddenly defiant again, quickly proud and of-
fended. "I've won this tournament four times. I should never be embarrassed walking onto a tennis court."

He was right. McEnroe's second-round match with the dour baselining Russian Andrei Chesnokov, whose game had been modeled by
the Soviet coaches on Bjorn Borg, was a task for McEnroe. Chesnokov
had won in Nice, reached the finals of the Italian Open, and was such
a nightmare on red clay that he was seeded tenth at the U.S. Open.
Chesnokov looked nervous, though, when he took the court that night
against McEnroe.

John McEnroe waited for the huge American crowd still swarming
into the stadium to look at each other and sit down.

"Play," came the voice of the English umpire.

McEnroe bounced the ball four times and served a left-handed ace
off Chesnokov's forehand side of the court. Chesnokov reacted as if he
thought the ball was out, and McEnroe trotted lightly in a semicircle to
the backhand court ready to serve the next point.

The match with Chesnokov was very close but never in doubt. The
tenth-seeded Russian lost to the unseeded American in straight sets,
6–3, 7–5, 6–4, overwhelmed on the hard court, under the glaring lights
and the huge American crowd, by McEnroe's left-handed serve and
finishing volley. The Russian, who had had a better year than McEnroe,
was no match for him in the end—not because Chesnokov was physically
weaker, but because Chesnokov played as if he believed McEnroe was
the tougher man. McEnroe won all the love–30 points. The Russian
rarely smiled, but he did at the end of the match when McEnroe trotted
to the net and gave him his hand to shake. The Russian did not seem to
mind losing to a player of McEnroe's historic merit.

Now McEnroe's match with Emilio Sanchez, one of the best of the
entire two weeks, was nearly won. The most important set turned out
to be the first one, and McEnroe won it, 7–6. Sanchez won the second
and third sets. At 6–5 in the fifth set, McEnroe bounced the ball three
times before serving, and Sanchez stayed on his toes.

Mary Carillo, the engaging tennis commentator who won the French
mixed doubles in 1977 with McEnroe—one of the last times he ever
played mixed doubles—said, "Mac had a fantasy that he could come into
this tournament like Greg LeMond in the Tour de France without too

much preparation and win it. John's been up and down more hills than LeMond this week."

McEnroe was tough when the chips were down. In a close match, both players have a moment in which they can win or lose it. At 4–all in the fourth set, McEnroe double-faulted and then twice had to serve into the ad-out court. Emilio Sanchez had two consecutive break points to go up 5–4 in the fourth set and serve for the match, leading two sets to one. Faced with this kind of pressure, an absolute crisis situation, McEnroe stuck his hot sword in ice water and won both ad-out points, the second with an ace up the middle on his second serve. Love him or leave him, John McEnroe was New York's version of true grit.

The Spaniard, Emilio Sanchez, had dominated for much of the afternoon. But statistics sometimes reveal the truth: each player had a recall button. McEnroe was 9–1 in fifth sets at the U.S. Open, and Sanchez was 0–2. In the fifth set, McEnroe's delicately bunted forehand drop volleys began to take their toll on the legs and heart of the fleet but square-shouldered Spaniard. John McEnroe's younger brother, Patrick, leaped up in the family box to applaud his older brother's perfect drop-volley serving at deuce, 6–5. It was a touching display of loyalty that ran deeply through both brothers. In his way, the younger, slightly less talented brother was a champion, too. It was Patrick McEnroe who, in his unwavering love, had described his brother better than anyone else: "The man with the incredible hands."

In the end, McEnroe triumphed over Spain's superstar after four hours and twenty-one minutes of work. In a match that long, there is nowhere to hide. Sanchez eventually rushed net, but the tactic was desperate, for McEnroe had already exposed the European as essentially a baseline player. In the last game, McEnroe hit five left-handed overheads in a row, finishing the last of Sanchez's retrieving lobs off the side of the court into the box seats where McEnroe's wife, Tatum O'Neal, sat with two of his childhood friends from Douglaston, Queens. Bitter, strange to strangers and to himself, John McEnroe had loyalty deep inside him. It was his heart that brought him through in his greatest matches, and the match at Flushing Meadow with Emilio Sanchez was one of those.

David Wheaton offered McEnroe his first big American problem. The three earlier opponents—the two Sanchez brothers and the surly Chesnokov—were essentially European players, tough as nails in the case of Chesnokov and the older Sanchez brother, but finally unable to apply their red clay–court games and athleticism onto the unforgiving New York hard courts. David Wheaton, on the other hand, was a big American horse. But McEnroe, his New York face getting hard, seemed to have Wheaton next in mind when he said after beating Sanchez, "If I keep improving, I tell you. They're going to be scared again to play me. I hope people are scared of me. So that they feel my pressure. Not my words."

By the luck of the draw and the odd coincidences that often pit friends against each other, Wheaton—who squeaked by his doubles partner, Paul Annacone, and the highly coordinated Swede, Jonas Svensson, in five sets at Wimbledon—faced them both again in reverse order at the U.S. Open. The two great matches at Wimbledon were on David Wheaton's mind when he said. "I got a really tough draw here. But sometimes it's better to get a tough draw. It makes you concentrate that much harder. If you get what you think is an easy draw, that's when you really get in trouble."

Wheaton rose to the challenge of his draw, beating Svensson and Annacone in straight sets on hard courts. The Minnesota player carried a big stick: his towering serve. As they posed briefly for photographs by the side of the court as the national anthem was played, Wheaton looked like Jesse Willard standing next to McEnroe's Jack Dempsey. It was going to be a tough day for the big kid from Minnesota.

When Dr. Krickstein had said at the Lipton that McEnroe was tough, he meant it. McEnroe would fight for stones. McEnroe's fight was his greatest asset after his amazingly gentle hand. While he could no longer just sweep the court with his wide, angling serves and delicate bent-wrist backhand volleys, McEnroe still had the ability to isolate in his opponents the very thing they did not like about themselves. Sanchez and Chesnokov, baseliners, were proved lacking when they had to try to get to net. Like a dentist, McEnroe drilled right into Wheaton's cavity. After Wheaton's mechanical ground strokes were exposed, then his volley was proved lacking. McEnroe quickly reduced Wheaton to his big serve, and once McEnroe had established the serve as Wheaton's only dependable stroke, then the serve began to crumble around him. McEnroe still had the game and personality to isolate his opponent's deepest weakness, then set up a tent there.

After the Wheaton match, Tatum O'Neal gave her husband a big hug. But Tatum took no prisoners or lip from Big Mac, and McEnroe benefited from her presence. Tatum was a bad news bear. McEnroe, unlike Lendl, had not married a much younger woman he could dominate easily. McEnroe liked a good fight, and Tatum had the bloodlines to give him one. By the time the Open came around, the couple had left Hollywood behind and had come back to the dirt and daily New York toughness McEnroe came from and Ryan O'Neal, Tatum's father, liked. The old McNastiness was back, but quieter, thanks in large part to his wife. In Tatum O'Neal, John McEnroe had finally met someone who could absorb him, understand him, and give him a loving kick.

"He's here!" shouted a reporter when McEnroe came in after taking apart young Wheaton. McEnroe slumped down at the interview desk like Richard III being interviewed after the big night up in the castle tower. McEnroe rarely referred to his opponents by name. "He [Wheaton] played five sets of doubles yesterday night. That was perfect for me." McEnroe's eyes got intense, even a little cruel. "I lost my focus for a little while." He had won 6–1, 6–4, 6–4.

Wheaton came in still dazed from the fight. The crowd had been huge. The beautiful (and the not-so-beautiful) had been there. Ham Richardson, the former U.S. number one, had been in his box at the best angle to the championship court, dressed in his blue shirt with white starched collar, gold tie pin, and charcoal-gray business suit, doing a little box-seat Texas "bidness" in New York. Nick Bollettieri came up to visit in the Richardson box for a while. Real estate men with young women in flashy shorts trouped in, looking for a little recognition in a down market. Wheaton gave it all he had. But McEnroe had closed the door before the smooth-skinned Minnesota boy could get it open with his serve.

Blonde, tall, and incredibly square shouldered, David Wheaton loomed large but beaten over the microphones. He ran his hand through his hair, trying to understand what had happened to him with McEnroe, and he said, finally, "Experience is the one thing you can't practice."

There were only two big upsets in the women's play, but the depth of the women's draw was better than it had ever been. Steffi Graf, accompanied by both parents, was again playing so well she looked sure to repeat as the winner. Despite the presence of her father, Graf was feeling much better about herself in New York than she had been at Wimbledon. She could not forgive her father's indiscretion, or believe him when he said it had never happened, but she seemed to realize that she was completely innocent and that she had done nothing wrong other than be her father's daughter. Finally, Steffi Graf seemed able to turn her emotions toward the ball and the court, and once again she was devastatingly quick and accurate—the best woman player since Navratilova and Margaret Smith.

Graf's match with Jennifer Capriati was electric. The anticipation in the sold-out stadium was wild. The pair had played in Mahwah, New Jersey, the week before, and Graf barely squeaked by in three sets. But Jennifer Capriati was not yet up to beating a fully engaged Steffi Graf. The long-awaited rematch between the fourteen-year-old Capriati and twenty-one-year-old Steffi Graf was almost viciously one-sided, 6–3, 6–1 to Graf. Graf was too fast, too sharp, too good a volleyer; Capriati was still too young and a half-step too slow.

Capriati had changed quite a bit in the six months since the Lipton, where Nathalie Herreman sent a ball right over Capriati's head between points to welcome her to the pros. Jennifer Capriati was now both tougher and more tired; at fourteen, her smile was straining, and so was her game. In the first round, she struggled to beat the young German Anke Huber, just a year her senior, 7–5, 7–5. Two rounds later, Capriati was thoroughly exposed by Graf, and yet she took the loss so well, with such a big smile, one sensed that her day might come if her entourage, primarily her father, could keep it all in balance. Jennifer had no trouble keeping things in perspective herself, but she was not yet deep into adolescence, and the press had not yet fully turned on her or her father.

Monica Seles was my pick to win the women's tournament. I walked back with her to the changing rooms after she beat Ros Fairbank-Nideffer in the second round, 6–2, 6–2. Sixteen years old, she was tall now, almost six feet tall, and in her powder-blue warm-up outfit she talked and walked no longer like the giggly girl who had been uncertain about herself at the Lipton, where everyone poured attention on Jennifer Capriati until Seles won the tournament. The Lipton in March had renewed Seles's confidence in herself after all the bad publicity that arose when her parents quit Nick Bollettieri. The Seles family had been nomads and exiles, Hungarians who brought up their children first in Yugoslavia and then in South Florida. They had no margin for error.

As we talked, Monica Seles seemed already older, a girl fast turning into a young woman. "The tough part of the tour is the rain delays, the waiting, the thinking about getting the match over with," said Monica Seles. "Yesterday I was kind of waiting around to play the match until ten o'clock at night because of the rain. That's when they called the match off."

The sixteen-year-old blonde with red lipstick shrugged and laughed, shaking her head as if the tournament officials were a little crazy. "Every time I play her [Ros Fairbank-Nideffer], for some reason we are always canceled or rain delayed, always sitting around waiting to play each other. Today it was sunny, really so hot," she said in her Slavic accent, "I started to get a little headache out there. In the end it was all right. She has the kind of slow strokes that can put you to sleep very easily if you are not careful. I lost to her the last time I played her."

"Who are you playing tomorrow?"

"A girl called Linda Ferrando," said Monica Seles. "I think she's from Italy. I don't know much about my next opponent. I'll just go out and play her."

Seles's father usually scouted his daughter's opponents for her, but the Italian girl was ranked so low (eighth in Italy) that Mr. Seles did not bother to go out and scout the unknown Italian opponent. The Seleses had assumed that because Ferrando was from Italy she would have a baseline red-clay game. It turned out to be just the opposite. Linda Ferrando attacked Seles and came to net every time she could get there. Seles, totally unprepared for a battle, lost to Ferrando 1–6, 6–1, 7–6.

Talking with Monica the afternoon *before* her match with Ferrando, I found her extremely confident about herself and about life. She had delighted the press after her first-round win with her story about going to Bloomingdale's with her parents and getting lost in the perfume department for about thirty minutes, until the manager paged her distressed parents for her.

"I think what's happening in tennis is what's happening in gymnastics," Seles said as we stood near the women's changing room: "The players are getting younger and younger. Not just Jennifer and myself— Anke Huber, too. Rules say you can't be eligible under fourteen, but what can you do if you are playing so well? The technique in the kids is so good. But there are a lot of hard parts in tennis. Waiting around for the matches. Then going into a full stadium. Expecting everything from yourself. People don't realize this. It takes really a lot of maturity. The kids fourteen or fifteen in tennis really have this—much more than if you go to the classroom to see the children who don't do the sports. Steffi started—well, Tracy Austin was the first to be very, very young, I guess—but Steffi was the first in the modern era, and now myself and Jennifer.

"Each younger one is doing better and better. I don't know what age it will end now, maybe ten years old," Seles laughed. "Especially now that the Eastern Bloc countries are open. A lot of Russian girls will be good, of course, as they are good at any other sport. But if I was a parent," said Monica Seles, "I would restrict children to fourteen years old for tournaments and eight years old to start playing tennis. There would be too many things a child would miss before eight. I am glad now they did not give me a wild card at thirteen years old. Everything was still a play for me then."

"You had mentioned some girlfriends back home in Yugoslavia who are gymnasts. Are you still in contact with them? Are you all still friends?"

"The last time home I didn't have time to see anybody. But before, I was always writing them letters. The funny thing is that all of them are grown up. Before, we were little girls and had the interests in common. But now they all have boyfriends. They're just distant a little bit more from me. And you know, how big I have become in name. I mean, I have become very big, even home. And they're like afraid of coming to see me."

"A little bit in awe of you?"

"A little bit." Monica Seles shook her head. "It's really . . . tough. But then I was with them for two days in Yugoslavia, and we went to a night out, and then they realized it is the same person. Me. But the hard part is if you go to a nightclub or anything, people—boys—will come up and ask for autographs, and my girlfriends never knew that before and for them it's like, 'Oh! Why shouldn't you say no to these guys and tell them to go to . . .' " Monica Seles giggled instead of saying the word. "But I don't care. I signed the autographs for the boys."

"Do you miss anything from your life in Yugoslavia?"

"Oh, no. I still go back four times a year. Whatever I miss I can still get four times a year when we return."

We shook hands and Monica Seles climbed the stairs to the changing rooms. She was still sixteen when she lost to the very brave Linda Ferrando the next afternoon. The match was won 7–6 in the third set with Seles leading in the tie-breaker, just as Graf had led against her in the tie-breaker in the final in Paris. Sometimes confidence backfires. The Seles family had neglected to scout Ferrando, but I wondered in retrospect if that brief mention by Seles of a bad headache in the sun the day before in her match against Ros Fairbank might not have played just as big a role.

Martina Navratilova strode briskly along the tarmac outside the stadium. She was short and looked incredibly healthy—bronze as a gladiator in a Victor Mature movie. There were three large stadium guards in bright red shirts in a phalanx around her, leading her in her new white, aqua-blue, and leather triangular-design tennis outfit toward the stadium court. A female tournament official in a red jacket, speaking into a walkie-talkie in her left hand, shouted at the crowd to part like the Red Sea. The fans called out to Martina and waved to her as she passed. And behind her trailed her opponent, Federica Haumuller, a young Argentinian, who was soundly beaten before she got onto the court.

Navratilova was basking in the glory of her great win at Wimbledon. She could still dominate, still overwhelm the younger women on the court, but with her ninth Wimbledon victory, in that ultimate satisfaction, it was as if Navratilova had finally found the antidote for all her earlier fears and tears. One of the two greatest women players of all time (some would argue Margaret Smith was the greatest, since she had by far the most Grand Slam singles wins), Navratilova at times was as vulnerable on the inside as she was tough on the outside. Had she not been so human, Martina might have set records beyond belief. If the Czechoslovak woman had had Chris Evert's or Billie Jean King's tougher competitive interior, Evert for one would never have beaten Navratilova except on clay.

It was clear that Navratilova cared less about winning the U.S. Open than she had about winning Wimbledon, and although she won the women's doubles with Gigi Fernandez—beating the great team of Novotna and Sukova, who had won the first three Grand Slam doubles titles in 1990—in singles, Martina played the champion's role to the hilt and waited for her opponents to fold. This they did until the third round.

Manuela Maleeva-Fragniere, recently married to a French-Swiss man, was one of three short, spunky Bulgarian sisters who for years had been chaperoned by their ubiquitous mother to tournaments around the world. Marriage seems to have suited the elder Maleeva. She was both more relaxed and more tenacious at the same time. Most of all, she seemed to have Navratilova's number. The older Maleeva beat Navratilova three times in 1990. In the quarter-finals at the U.S. Open, Maleeva-Fragniere won 6–3 in the third set. At the conclusion, Martina pulled off her glasses and nodded with a wry smile as she trotted up to net to shake hands.

Zina Garrison, who fell to Navratilova on the grass at Wimbledon, survived longer than Navratilova at the U.S. Open. With great hopes for victory in New York, and accompanied by her loyal young husband, Willard, she twisted her ankle badly in an early round but hung on until the quarter-finals, where she lost to Arantxa Sanchez-Vicario, Emilio and Javier Sanchez's tough little sister, 6–2, 6–2. At the end, Zina could hardly run at all, and she burst into tears after the loss.

Navratilova had lost early, but that was not the player people would remember. Martina Navratilova was more like the woman who came into the interview room after her second-round win, 6–0, 6–4, over England's Clare Wood. She sat down behind the microphones, exuding the slightly bored ease of a district attorney forced to explain her latest case to the press, her blonde hair short on the top and long in the back. The dark circles around her eyes looked like beaten copper, souvenirs from her effort at winning against much younger players. Navratilova's face was still tight with tension, her mood a forced relaxed.

"Those lights are obnoxious," blurted out Martina as she sat down. She was wearing earrings and a gold chain. She related how her young English opponent had been too nervous in the first set, but Navratilova admitted that she had had a fit of nerves herself in the second set. "This is the U.S. Open," she explained. "There is still pressure, and I feel it. She played pretty lousy that first set, and I was playing nicely with good rhythm. Then I lost it, and I had a hard time finding it again. I had a few double faults here and there, and all of a sudden it was a very tight second set."

There exactly was the difference between Chris Evert and Martina Navratilova. It was a human difference, and that's what had always made their contests so close and so great to watch. Navratilova won on talent and overcame self-doubt. Evert's talent was flat, hard, and straight, generated by the toughness she had inside. Evert would have beaten the same girl from England 6–0, 6–1. Navratilova made it complicated and almost let the English girl get up and get back into the match.

" 'How come you get so nervous?' CBS just asked me!" Martina shook her head and half-laughed derisively because the television men once again had not understood her. "The more you do it," said Martina, "the more it means to you. When you're fourteen or sixteen or eighteen, you could have twenty Opens to go. I don't have that many left. Every one could be my last one, so it's precious. I do still get nervous. Her second serve in the second set was better than her first serve in the first set," said Navratilova. "When she was up four–three, serving for five–three, I knew I had to break her."

Martina Navratilova's voice was not quite shrill, but from the tightness in her throat, she sounded like a person who could never quite relax. Navratilova was a born fighter: she needed to hit something, and the ball would do. She seemed permanently tense inside, like a boxer who never knows when or where the next fight will be. Martina was a warrior. This was the understanding she shared with Chris Evert—they were both hooked competitors. The battle was for both of them the one sure thing in life, and the one thing they would have to overcome to find happiness and love. Lovers came and left, but the one real, deep emotional anchor was the fight itself. It was Martina's gift and curse. She suffered as a person from the competitor's disease. Until she won her ninth Wimbledon singles title, Navratilova kept having to prove that she was better, that she was stronger than someone else. Competition itself—the on-court struggle—was the only medicine Martina knew could cure her, relieve her drive, sustain her. Love had always come a close second, but now, with Judy Nelson and the last Wimbledon win and all those other accomplishments behind her, love seemed like it might finally overtake competition for first place in Martina Navratilova's soul.

Navratilova was a superb athlete. She physically needed the focus and fight of her sport. For the very best at any sport—Joe Louis or Muhammad Ali, Martina Navratilova or Bill Tilden—it takes a long time to stop competing *inside* after you have stopped competition on the outside. The mind's signal is trapped in the body's repetitive will: the instinct is always there to compete, to fight, to overwhelm in others what is overwhelming in yourself. It would be hard for Navratilova to stop, as it was for those three other great champions, for throughout her career so many people had said negative things about Navratilova's sexuality behind her back. Tilden put up with the same thing. Neither married; neither was tamed. Longevity at the competitive top was their reward and their isolation.

All those tennis balls struck. All those ad-out points fought for. A junkie has his needle. Navratilova, Tilden, Evert, Connors, and McEnroe had their contact with the tennis ball. Connors had had major problems with his father. Navratilova's absent father was still a source of fountain-like pain, as it had also been for Jimmy Connors, for Mike Tyson, and for Evander Holyfield; the latter had never met his father until the month before he won the heavyweight championship. The need to make contact, to overwhelm the overwhelming, was strongest in the great ones. Love could soften and absorb some of the competitor's disease but never all of it. Everywhere Martina went at Flushing Meadow in 1990, Judy Nelson was nearby, wearing sunglasses and a pale blue T-shirt that said, MARTINA IS MY ROLE MODEL, a reply to Margaret Smith Court's put-down of the thirty-three-year-old woman's sexual preference.

When it came to men and small-mindedness, Martina Navratilova did not suffer fools. She was fighting the old-fashioned men's world, and sometimes she played with that world on her shoulders. "Today I wore the Wimbledon headband," the tennis champion complained. "They said it was okay because it didn't have Herman Geist written on it like yes-terday. But then today, they told me that my water bottle wasn't ac-ceptable. I had already taped it over. They said it had to be more *neat*. Can you believe that?" Navratilova shook her head and chuckled in disgust. Officials. Men. She hated them for their pettiness. "So I put my bottle in a brown paper bag," laughed Martina. "I figured for New York that would be all right. They're used to that, no?"

The questions after her second-round win turned to Andre Agassi and clothing. Navratilova and Judy Nelson's tastes ran to blue triangles and leather overlays. Navratilova smiled. "My first reaction to Andre's oversize shirts and black shorts was that it would be very hot to play in daytime with all that black on his back. You wouldn't want to know my second reaction. . . ."

"Oh, please! Yes!" called out two reporters, necks craning like little birds waiting for their mother to feed them.

Navratilova smiled again. "Well, my second reaction was '*yuk*.' I guess someone must have designed Andre's clothes, but sometimes I think they just let a child loose with some crayons and that's what he wears. There seems to be no pattern or reason to his clothes. That's why Judy and I got into the clothing business in the first place. Most of the stuff out there just wasn't nice. Judy said to me, 'I can do better than that!' "

Someone asked Navratilova a question about Vitas Gerulaitis. The former U.S. Open runner-up, who had been an alleged cocaine connec-tion, had cleaned up his act. A Columbia University flop, Gerulaitis was a sharp broadcaster except for one major blind spot: women's tennis.

"Vitas is a dope," said Martina, and no one disagreed even though Gerulaitis once received an 800 score on his College Board math test before his one year at Columbia University. The strain of the day showed in the blue veins standing out on the side of Martina's coppery forehead.

"Vitas doesn't think the women should be paid as much as the men because they play five sets sometimes. He says women's tennis is basically lousy." Martina shook her head in disgust and the white headband on the very top of her forehead almost slid off her silk-blonde hair. "Why does he have to put down something? Why say men's tennis is great and women's tennis sucks?" Martina Navratilova asked the room full of male and female reporters. "Excuse my French."

The room was quiet for a moment. The women's champion was not long on tact. It took powerful pain to make someone that good, and Martina Navratilova carried around powerful pain. It made her a champion. It made her who she was.

"Was there ever any communication between you and Helen Wills Moody after you broke her record of eight wins at Wimbledon?" Navratilova's upper lip caught on her teeth. Helen Wills, the tall California glamor girl of the 1920s, who lost to but almost beat Suzanne Lenglen in Lenglen's "last hurrah," the famous match of the century in Cannes in 1926, won eight Wimbledon singles titles in ten years and dominated women's tennis in the mid-1920s and 1930s, the way Bill Tilden, Babe Ruth, and Bobby Jones dominated their games. Navratilova and Wills were in each other's league, but Wills—still alive—never called Navratilova to congratulate her on breaking the record.

"Was there any contact between you two?"

"No. She didn't call," said Navratilova quietly. "From what I understand, she's just not interested at all in talking to me. No. I didn't try to call her." Martina Navratilova, suddenly shy and hurt, shrugged and laughed nervously. "I guess I didn't want to be rejected."

The entourage of large male guards in bright red T-shirts and the short female official in the red jacket with the walkie-talkie in her left hand came to escort Navratilova through the concession stands to the changing rooms. Navratilova scribbled a few left-handed autographs on children's programs and beamed as the crowd called out her first name. Judy Nelson, tall and bronzed, followed the Navratilova procession at a short distance. She had a sultry, no-nonsense Texas voice. It was late when I introduced myself, but Judy Nelson was friendly although understandably a little rushed. Women's pro tennis was a not-so-glamorous high-profile life effort. Nelson put the women's-tour life in perspective. It was already past ten o'clock; most of the New York crowd was filing out of Louis Armstrong Stadium and going home to bed.

"We're a little rushed tonight," said Judy Nelson. "Martina has to get changed now and come back out for her doubles."

Steffi Graf seemed to have her mind back together. The German girl struggled once on her way to the women's final—against the South African Elna Reinach in the third round—but she was her beautiful moving, semiarrogant self in beating Jennifer Capriati, 6–1, 6–2. It was a lesson the young American would never forget, the type of loss it is healthy to have early in a career as long as it does not happen too often. Peter Graf stood up in his box and cheered his daughter. Mr. Capriati, a small bear of a man, looked ready to hibernate. When Navratilova and Monica Seles, whom Graf feared most, both lost, Graf seemed ready to forget if not forgive her father. She was in America, far from the European press. Part of her, like Boris Becker, longed for freedom, but while Becker hitched rides on trucks late at night in Germany, like a character from Jack Kerouac's *On the Road*, Steffi Graf was too close to her family to really rebel. She had posed for the German edition of *Vogue*, but although her legs were beautiful to watch on a tennis court—the way a female sprinter's legs are powerful to see move on a track—her father's alleged indiscretion with the young *Playboy* model made Steffi too smart to fall for that kind of vanity again. In that sense, her father's indiscretion may have liberated her. This was certainly the season when Steffi Graf ceased being a daughter and became her own woman.

The Graf father, a former used-car salesman in Germany, had hurt his daughter so deeply that Steffi's struggles endeared her to the American crowd, which has a big heart and always loves the underdog. The fair-mindedness of the American public touched Steffi. Each day at the Open, she became a little more comfortable with herself, a little more grown up.

After she beat Jennifer Capriati, Graf was asked to compare her own rise to Capriati's. She flicked the ponytail behind her and smiled. "I had a very different start," the slender young woman said, looking in profile like the Picasso women of the 1950s. "As a young girl, I played many ten-thousand-dollar tournaments. Many little ones. I went to the south of Italy. There are memories there I don't think she [Capriati] will ever have. She is playing the nice tournaments, and I sort of played some under conditions you wouldn't find anymore right now. I played many small tournaments, so it is difficult to compare both of us, Jennifer and me. She jumped right into the big, professional tennis and I started very small." Graf was shy about her large nose, and that shyness, beneath the surface arrogance, was part of what made her most attractive as a person.

"The first win I had was at such a small tournament," continued Graf. "I had to go through qualifying, then five regular matches. It was all in nine days. We played on a wood surface. It was a very, very big thing for me then. The hotel cost more than I got for winning the whole tournament. It was just good memories."

Spry after her win over Capriati, Staffi Graf crushed Jana Novotna, the doubles star, 6–3, 6–1, and beat the gritty Sanchez-Vicario in the semifinals, 6–1, 6–2. Going into the Saturday final with Gabriela Sabatini, Steffi Graf looked both physically and mentally resilient.

Gabriela Sabatini, like Pete Sampras, was in the enviable position of having been ignored for ten days. It is always easier to play when less is expected of you. And Sabatini, the cherub-faced Argentinian, had finally given the press the slip. She had a new coach, having dropped the notorious Betty Stove for Brazilian Carlos Kirkamayr. People had become skeptical about the Argentinian's game. Sabatini fans, perhaps even the woman in Florida who offered to buy Sabatini's wet tennis shirt for $500 from the guard at the Lipton, had almost given up waiting for Sabatini to shed her adolescence—which people of both sexes seemed to like physically—and become herself.

Sabatini had been in Steffi Graf's shadow for several years, and it looked in New York as if she would remain there. Sabatini barely squeaked by Mary Joe Fernandez, the tall, talented Miami girl whose father emigrated to America from the Dominican Republic. Fernandez was coached in Miami as a teenager by the dulcet-toned Fred Stolle, Roy Emerson's doubles partner and one of my favorite service motions to imitate when I was a mimic at nine years old. Fernandez always played well in the baking heat of Australia, but her attacking baseline game was vulnerable to pressure at net and pure speed, both of which Graf possessed. Mary Joe, who had started dating David Wheaton, was, like Wheaton, far better than just a hard worker, but the straight lines of her ground strokes locked her into a game that was seen easily in two dimensions, whereas Graf, Seles, Sabatini, and Navratilova were all players who, like McEnroe, Becker, and Edberg, had that elusive third dimension.

"Why the split with Gabriela in doubles?" a reporter had asked Graf two days before the final.

Graf put on her smirk-smile. "She wanted to play more doubles than I did. I would prefer to play whenever I want to, but Gabriela wanted to play more doubles tournaments, and I did not."

Doubles. The key and mystery of human relationships: how to coexist and win. The key also to the volley. Sabatini liked to play doubles. Graf was a singles artist.

Sabatini, the underdog, was relaxed as she took the court for the final. The Argentinian's foundation was still 100 percent topspin, but something had changed dramatically for her.

In the final, Steffi Graf's backhand split into many pieces, which was another way of saying that Graf could not cope with the pressure. She had seemed so newly confident during the two weeks, but at crunch time in the final the young German could no longer hide her emotions. Graf was still feeling defensive, and her state of mind simply came out in her play.

The Argentinian girl, the topspin artist, played magnificently. Sabatini's new coach deserved a lot of credit. Blonde, curly-haired Brazilian Carlos Kirkamayr had put a smile back on Gabriela Sabatini's face. For most of her career as a teenager, Sabatini had been a responder instead of an initiator. Margaret Smith, Martina Navratilova, and Steffi Graf were all initiators. Sabatini had been better at counter-punching. Not passive, but at times unsure, the Argentine had stayed back on the baseline for five years in a fair imitation of Guillermo Vilas, her legendary countryman whose topspin was so good he rarely came to net. Kirkamayr accomplished an amazing thing. He brought to the surface in Sabatini what Tony Roche had been unable to find in Ivan Lendl: an instinct to volley. Under the Brazilian's urging, the Argentine discovered her volley. Gabriela Sabatini found that not only did she have a beautiful volley structurally, but, more important, she uncovered the spirit of the volley, the inner fierceness and joy that lets a player throw caution to the wind and race from the back of the court into the oncoming speed of the ball, the way the graceful Maria Bueno had done so often in her prime. Sabatini, a South American by birth and instinct, discovered the thrill of intercepting the ball at its fastest point across the net. She not only liked it, she loved it and was good at it. Sabatini took to the volley and the race to get to net in a way that the more conservative Lendl and the more stubborn Vilas never could.

The women's final was both beautiful and touching. When Steffi Graf came onto the court in her fast-footed, dominant gait, Sabatini came on second, sauntering in her awkward side-to-side style. The relationship of their bodies on entering the court was the same as they showed when they were doubles partners as well as singles rivals. Graf, the dominant partner, looked eager to take control, but the match rather quickly became a surprise for Graf. Sabatini, not the former champion, dominated.

Now twenty, Sabatini applied the pressure instead of responded to it, and she enjoyed the role reversal. Her attacking game suddenly flowed naturally; it was like watching a defensive soccer team suddenly discover it is truly South American and capable of brilliant attack. Sabatini came to net every chance she got on a short ball, and Graf's backhand, mirroring her inner state, was increasingly undercut and self-doubting.

All the power and grace Steffi Graf had shown humbling Capriati, Novotna, and Sanchez-Vicario, with the loss of only ten games in six sets, now seemed to have been a mere cover. Monica Seles had created the monster Doubt for Graf on the red clay in Germany and France, but nobody expected to see her so uncertain on an American hard court, where speed had always been the fleet-footed Graf's greatest ally. Sabatini won the first set 6–2, and Steffi Graf looked miserable, upset that her parents were both there at courtside. *"Sentir mal dans sa peau,"* the French would say to describe Steffi, literally "to feel bad in one's skin." Even Graf's skin seemed to have an unhealthy pallor in the early September New York heat. Gabriela Sabatini, baking happily, looked untouchable.

Desperate, Graf tried to jog Sabatini's memory and push the handsome Argentine girl's recall button. Their relationship had always been based on Graf's dominance and Graf tried to remind Sabatini of the one-sided nature of their earlier relationship.

Graf began to return serve better. She broke Sabatini in the second set and led 5–4; the pattern of their earlier relationship began to re-establish itself. Steffi again looked to be the dominant personality—she was striking the ball briskly. But Sabatini stuck to her guns, and when the Argentine beauty nailed one of her incredible topspin backhands, the ball leapt up into the air, as if struck down at Tiera del Fuego and landing in Miami. The crowd in Flushing greeted Gabriela's reckless topspin passing shot with cheers of awe. The young Argentine bit a corner of her soft lower lip, held her racket gently in her left hand, and pumped her right fist as she shouted, *"Ahora mismo!"*—Spanish for "right now." Steffi Graf hung her head as if she had just finished a piano recital that had gone badly.

In the tie-breaker, tension became a factor again. Graf could sense her former doubles partner's Latino nerves across the net, and Graf felt she could win the match if she could just get through the second set. Probably 75 percent of the crowd, including myself, believed Graf was going to win, because, historically, Sabatini folded at the crossroads.

But the talented South American found herself. She had so often let Graf be the dominant personality, but now on the really big points Sabatini hit out. She felt what was on the other side of the net in the body of Steffi Graf, and it no longer scared her. She knew where Graf was vulnerable, the area of shaken confidence—Graf's backhand. Carlos Kirkamayr was behind Sabatini. Her sports psychologist, Jim Loehr, who had helped Sabatini immeasurably after Wimbledon, was behind her. And her family was back in Argentina, thus reducing the pressure on her, as Arthur Ashe would have suggested. In the players' box, Peter Graf in his bright, open-collar dress shirt, squeezed his wife's hand, closed his eyes, and leaned forward, praying that his daughter could pull off the second-set tie-breaker and then the match, absolving him of public guilt.

At the critical moment in the tie-breaker, Steffi Graf came up uncertain. Sabatini came up brave. Almost passed by a very snappy Graf forehand down the line, Sabatini lunged. Her backhand volley was an instinctive shot, the kind that only one man on the tour—Pete Sampras—made consistently when he was in the act of being passed. Sabatini hit the volley from behind her back and held the line of her arm as firmly as Sampras did, as firmly as a matador holds a cape, and the ball fell over the net. That volley broke Graf's spirit. On match point, Sabatini watched Graf hit the ball into the net.

Just six months earlier, when the season was beginning at the Lipton on Key Biscayne, Florida, I had watched Sabatini warming up in the pink gazebo off the side of the players' lounge, and almost bumped into her as the Florida policemen in brown uniforms and black boots had led her like Eva Peron out onto the green Florida concrete to play (and lose to) Conchita Martinez in straight sets. At Wimbledon, the young woman with the wavy black hair and soft pink lower lip had, like Steffi Graf, hurried away because the English and German press were having a field day over her well-intentioned but unrewarded romantic flings. But in New York, Gabriela Sabatini was finally all smiles. The Argentinian hugged her Brazilian coach for her volley and his kindness, and she thanked the New York crowd, first in English and then in Spanish, the language of her heart.

Gabriela Sabatini was finally a champion.

THE MEN'S SEMIFINALS AND FINAL

"If you have a five-year-old kid who will grow up to be like either Sampras or Agassi, who do you choose?" asked Ivan Lendl after losing his quarter-final match with Pete Sampras. "These guys represent different life values. I'm sad anyone can cherish Agassi. The kids see him as a rebel with his earring, hair, and no-shave look. They think they know better than their parents, and Andre is a model for them in that."

Ivan Lendl, Antonio Salieri in a sweatsuit, looked like an athlete who had trained so hard that he was a third thinner than he ought to be. He always had the fierce on-court presence of a concentration camp guard, but ten years near the top had whittled down the strong-willed Czechoslovak perfectionist. He suffered his biggest career disappointment in 1990, when he put all his eggs in one basket, Wimbledon, and failed even with Tony Roche's help. Lendl saw Agassi as a rebel. I saw him as the talented son of an Iranian immigrant, trying hard to conform to some idea of what America was supposed to be. Lendl, a first-generation immigrant himself, was more sympathetic as a loser than as a winner. He sounded as if he might become a strict father himself one day. Lendl's own dreams of tennis greatness had fallen slightly short, but he was still more fierce a warrior than the "Last of the Mohicans" Boris Becker had called him.

Pete Sampras—who had beaten muscular Thomas Muster, the gutsy left-hander from Austria with the lion's heart, before he upset Lendl in five gripping sets—finally sat in front of a packed crowd of reporters, as excited as he was. Ivan Lendl had once made Sampras pedal the exercise bike at his Greenwich mansion until the Greek kid almost dropped. The nineteen-year-old's voice was still shaking, his body pumped with nervous adrenaline, and he shook his head after beating Lendl to make sure it was real. The younger player had finally broken through against the player he respected and had feared. Pete Sampras had a shy grin, and the spaces between his teeth showed. "This is really the top of it. I played him in Milan. So I knew him. This time I wasn't overwhelmed. But my nerves and heart really got bumping. The crowd helped me out in the fifth set. I felt no pain in my body. But my feet were pretty cut up and now they're aching. The four–two game was crucial in the fifth set. Then he got a little tight. This is the top, my dream come true. I can't really believe what is happening to me right now."

Andre Agassi's march through the tough U.S. Open draw brought him to the semifinals quicker and easier than anyone else. In the round of sixteen, Agassi played Jay Berger. Their first set followed the precedent of their match at the Lipton that March. In Florida, Berger hit the ball unbelievably hard, actually outhitting Agassi on a hard court and winning the first set 7–5, before running out of gas. At Flushing Meadow in the heavy heat, after three long, hard night matches, Berger tried to go down blasting. But this time Agassi absorbed all his will and sent him running from side to side until Berger could stretch no more. The week before his wedding with Nadia and the wedding reception at night on a chartered boat off the coast of Florida, Jay Berger took a humbling straight-set loss on national TV. Maybe, coming prenuptial, it wasn't a bad thing. It was Agassi's wedding gift. As a tennis player, Agassi could be devastating.

There were many ways of judging success and failure. Berger was not a failure for the loss to Agassi. He never had that easy glide around the court that even some amateur tennis players can attain. But he did for himself what was most admirable of all: he got the most out of what he had. That is the way to judge a player and a person. Berger had the fight, the will to win, and without that inner fight—that life spirit—there is little hope for anyone.

"Andre," the press asked Agassi after the win, "you say on your Canon camera TV ad that 'Image Is Everything.' Do you really believe that?"

The Las Vegas twenty-year-old paused to consider the marketing phrase he did not fully understand. It was probably Agassi's image—or aura of lightness—that had kept Agassi from being defaulted against Petr Korda earlier in the draw when Agassi spat at the umpire's chair, then apologized and said he did not do it. Peter Bellinger, the tournament official who in Australia came onto the court with McEnroe, accepted Agassi's explanation and let him continue. Agassi now responded to the press, "I wouldn't say something that I could not believe in. Image *is* everything. I do believe in it. For the sake of everybody."

There were snickers in the press room. "For the sake of everybody?" Agassi had not quite meant what he said. He had not finished school, and he was living to regret it. He still annoyed the press. Agassi was accused of being ten million dollars dumb. In fact, he had begun to understand life a little better, but he still got flustered under pressure to be articulate. There were many types of intelligence, and many meanings of success in America. The athlete's instinctive intelligence, as specialized as an opera singer's, is vastly underrated. "Agassi doesn't *seem* smart," recent Wimbledon and

U.S. Open doubles champion Jim Pugh said. "But he is very smart on court, putting spins on the ball, changing pace, and hitting angles."

The press criticized Agassi so much, but Agassi was not a cruel kid, just self-absorbed and mentally lazy because of too much attention from others. Arthur Ashe spoke to Agassi's agent at IMG, Bill Shelton, to complain about Andre's behavior in the Korda match. The next morning the press used Agassi both as its lead story and its whipping boy. The remarks by some reporters were so scornful of Agassi as to sound childish themselves. Was everyone supposed to look and be alike in New York *Daily News* columnist Mike Lupica's eyes? As a child, Agassi had seen all the blonde kids playing at the wealthy country clubs where his parents could not become members. Maybe purple and green were the right colors for what the Iranian-American boy felt inside. Agassi wanted to please, but he had never been taught quite how to do it. He was easy prey for those sportswriters who preferred insult to imagination. But in other ways Agassi was generous and unafraid of the competition. It was the pressure situations and his own self-esteem that gave Agassi problems—rarely just the other players, because Agassi had beaten them all.

"Did you hear that Bjorn Borg is training in England and Italy for a possible comeback, Andre?" the sound-bite reporter from Texas asked after the victory over Jay Berger, and the TV cameras rolled.

"No. That's the first I've heard of it," said young Agassi. "I always thought Bjorn was so happy being away from the game. But Bjorn was such a great champion. Like a God. Sure. It would be great to have him back out there. I wish him all the luck in the world." (Borg would need it, but luck would not be enough. Playing with wooden rackets in 1991, Borg's comeback lasted just one tournament. Borg had abused his muse.)

As John McEnroe walked through the concession stands with his big racket bag over his shoulder, the crowd milling around the hot dogs, popcorn, and T-shirts started clapping their hands. He had that little bounce again to his step, that little smile. And so did Andre Agassi. Agassi's path to glory led straight to the boy from Leimen—Boris Becker. McEnroe's road back had intersected with Pete Sampras's road out. There were only four men left in the draw.

Aaron Krickstein almost made it to the semifinals, but in the end the slender boy from Grosse Point, Michigan, could not dent Boris Becker for more than the first set in a 3–6, 6–2, 6–2, 6–3 loss to the powerful but complicated German boy from Leimen. Mrs. Krickstein watched her son's season end from a general admissions seat three-quarters of the way up in the concrete stadium. Her husband, Herb—the doctor with the big shoulders, warm smile, and University of Michigan baseball cap—felt his heart rise in the first set, but his son's opponent started hitting the ball heavier and heavier and moving with that combination of power, determination, and flexibility that made him seem capable of greatness. But did Becker want to be invincible?

THE MEN'S SEMIFINALS

The last two days of play were a world unto themselves. The ticket prices and the tension were much different. From $12 for a full day's wander the first week, the seats for the three Saturday matches had risen to $26 each. The men's semifinals came after the women's final. The women did not consider it courtesy, because it made their final seem like a warm-up event. Becker and McEnroe did not like it either, because, they said, the format did not have the players in mind but rather catered to the almighty television. Since television was paying the lion's share of the bill, McEnroe and Becker—who wanted a day's rest between the semis and the final—were voices lost in the crowd.

Pete Sampras bounced the ball twice and looked up across the net at John McEnroe. The Greek kid with the shy smile and smooth-muscled but hairy legs had said after his win over Jakob Hlasek that he did not think he was ready to win a Grand Slam tournament because he was too young and because his attacking style was often accompanied by many errors. Now, just five days later, Sampras was ready. He was so smooth and effortless through the ball he seemed almost gentle hitting a serve 125 miles an hour. His jaw clicked quietly in satisfaction now and then, but that was the only outward sign Sampras gave that he was eighteen years old and in the semifinals of the U.S. Open. McEnroe was the heavy favorite. Sampras was such a colt. Like the young soldiers pouring into the Saudi Arabian desert, Sampras was brave and he did not know it.

In the locker room before their battle, McEnroe was lying on the vinyl floor, his head covered with towels. Sampras was seated in front of a television set, laughing at a feature on him that CBS was running. The younger boy was still not awed by the public persona the media might, if he won, continue to create. Sampras laughed at himself on TV.

McEnroe was stone silent, concentrating, putting on his game face, hooded by towels.

Dustin Hoffman was in the crowd. Robert DeNiro, the "Raging Bull," should have been there. Tennis was so much like boxing, but boxers and tennis players could hardly imagine each other. The key to victory for McEnroe was, as always, to harness his anger with concentration. Sampras flexed his handsome, square Greek jaw, but gave no other sign of inner tension. When they led the two players out onto the stadium court, McEnroe, U.S. champion in 1979, 1980, 1981, and 1984, was led onto the court first, followed by the challenger, Sampras.

McEnroe won the toss and hit his first serve flat into Sampras's chest. Jammed, Sampras netted a backhand. McEnroe arced his next serve off the side of the backhand court for another service winner. The crowd roared. Sampras hardly blinked. He was unafraid. He had something to say.

Boom! Sampras hit his first serve. (He would hit fifty-four aces in the fortnight.) He said what he had to say with such smoothness. Sampras had the timing of Muhammad Ali and Sugar Ray Leonard. He had a power that seemed invisible, almost unimaginable from a body that graceful. McEnroe, like Laver, peeled the tennis ball like an orange with his ripping, then gentle ground strokes. Sampras drew straight lines with a wand. Hands on his hips, John McEnroe scowled after Sampras came in and volleyed away Mac's break-point opportunity.

At a game apiece in the first set, McEnroe was surprised by Sampras's ability to pick which side Mac's serve was going to, and he served a double fault. McEnroe went down love–40 on his own serve. This was not Chesnokov or the Sanchez brothers. This was the fastest-hitting young player he had faced since Boris Becker in Hartford in 1987. McEnroe snarled and served an ace up the middle, 15–40. McEnroe scowled now, rocked back and forth leaning west, dipped his racket, tucked his chin under his right shoulder, and served a left-handed zinger that caught Sampras leaning the wrong way. Sometimes the biggest games come early; 30–40. McEnroe had saved another break point. And then came a thing of beauty. McEnroe's spinning left-handed serve was like an orange swung sharply into the court—heavy, twisting, fragrant. Sampras was jammed but put the ball in play. McEnroe, on top of the net with his forehand, hit a little drop volley with all the left-hander's feel and bad intentions. No one could get there. Sampras got there. He was there with a lounge chair and a book. McEnroe was gliding across the face of the net. At the last possible second, Sampras, on the full run forward, calmly played a backhand drop shot cross-court at a very tight reverse angle. Sampras had out-angled McEnroe—he halved a hypotenuse. The Greek kid had broken serve. Sampras looked grim-faced during the change-over; McEnroe sat down and draped a towel over his head.

Sampras's effort was so effortless, his contact with the ball, the moment of violence, so gentle. Sampras hit four nearly unreturnable serves to go up 3–1. Suddenly that score seemed as wide as the Grand Canyon. McEnroe, stoic, left-handed, Queens reared, scowled in respect. Sampras had the goods.

A statistic: Sampras was winning 90 percent of the points played on his first serve. McEnroe was winning just 20 percent when he had to hit a second serve.

Halfway to net behind a first serve clocked at 110 miles an hour, McEnroe was passed by a Sampras backhand, a six-inch backswing on the left hip—a rifle shot straight and deep up the baseline for an untouchable winner. McEnroe looked across the net at Sampras as if to ask, "Who are you, masked man?" Long shadows stretched across half the court. Sampras won the first set 6–2 in thirty-one minutes, and while McEnroe bristled, Sampras sat down to sip some Saratoga water.

When he was thirteen—five years before—Sampras had a two-handed backhand, a remnant of the Borg influence. His coach, Dr. Peter Fischer, after showing him the Laver tapes of matches against Rosewall, suggested that Sampras go to a one-handed backhand. The boy tried it, and for a while he began to lose to a lot of other boys his age. But Sampras stuck with the change. Fischer wanted young Sampras to find a playing style all his own, not be a Borg clone. Like writers who learn by reading their betters, Sampras had studied the styles of the best players before him. Pete Sampras's one-handed backhand was now the most beautiful in the world (with the possible exception of Edberg's), as straight and technically clean as any backhand had ever been struck. By contrast, McEnroe's backhand was a Frisbee (as Laver's had been), Agassi's was a vicious metronome, and Becker's a storehouse of all his inner excesses and doubts that emerged in the topspin and slice on his backhand side. Sampras's backhand, especially his backhand volley, was his great strength. It was simple and reliable, like a fine old watch. John McEnroe liked to "scare" opponents, but deep talent like Sampras's is never frightened by somebody else.

"Just a farce," muttered McEnroe on the change-over. He had lost another set.

Sampras hit twenty-one winners in the first two sets and had two unforced errors. He seemed like pure water. McEnroe, on the other hand, seemed like an old whore who had told and lived too many stories. McEnroe's beautiful sideways rocking serve was the only thing keeping him in it. Tatum O'Neal looked pale but calm in her sunglasses at court-side. McEnroe's parents looked ashen. Sampras continued to have the same answer to any problem John McEnroe tried to create: another ace.

McEnroe wanted to tell an old story that had worked for him in the past. He was a devilish Scheherazade. McEnroe looked up at the referee, Steve Ulrich, and said on the change-over, "Why of all people do you have to be here?"

Sampras got a little nervous and netted two easy balls. McEnroe walked the walk. On ad-out, McEnroe bent low at the waist, then rose to his toes as Sampras delivered. The serve was too big to return. Deuce. Sampras missed his next first serve and said to himself quietly, "I'm rushing." Then the Greek boy badly missed a backhand volley; ad-out again. Champions win the ad-out points. Sampras hit a serve 116 miles an hour that McEnroe could not return. As McEnroe started to go back to the deuce court, Sampras's serve was called out. McEnroe came back quickly to the ad court, ready to pounce on a second serve and come in to net. Sampras's brown eyes looked over at the referee, and there was neither anger nor tension in his look. McEnroe held a third break point, but Sampras won three points in a row with big serves and quiet reserves.

Elke Sommer, the blonde German actress, was in the crowd, perhaps for Becker. A man walking in the upper stands was wearing a white T-shirt that said on its back, "I Survived the Market Crash of '87." New York's Mayor Dinkins was there in a thin blue seersucker suit and a baseball cap. In August 1990, in addition to Brian Watkins's murder, thirteen black and Hispanic babies were killed in separate incidents of machine-gun cross fire. The mayor, a tennis fan, defended New York City by mentioning the coeds killed in Gainesville, Florida. It was all real. It was all America. And Sampras–McEnroe was the hottest ticket since Leonard–Hearns I.

McEnroe was never better than when his mouth was shut and his back was against the wall. No one ever played ad-out points better than McEnroe, unless it was Rosewall or Jimmy Connors. McEnroe came fighting back into it, silently, unbelievably.

It required all of McEnroe's intelligence, eye, hands, and instinct to break his younger opponent. McEnroe kept opening his mouth wide over his teeth, biting the air between points. Finally, McEnroe was nervous. Finally, he was lost in his subconscious. He could move again around the court. Sampras missed a key first serve, and on ad-out McEnroe rode the Sampras second serve to net like a wave. He played a brilliant touch cross-court backhand volley off his shoe tops, his wiry body still hesitating in the air as his left hand played the delicate deception. McEnroe pumped air with his left fist. Service break!

John McEnroe, Sr.—lawyer, father—sat watching from the players' box, wearing a Panama hat. He could see his son as no one else could. The father had kept his son balanced for years, but at a certain point the father was not strong enough to do it any longer, and John had to take over for himself. Now Mr. McEnroe's eldest son had another great moment—a great comeback tournament—but the father knew the real score. Chesnokov and the Sanchez boys were younger and stronger than John, but they were also baseline boys playing on a New York hard court. His son could take their pace all night. They allowed his son time. But Sampras was something else. He shortened time. He had ice-water veins and a strong immigrant's heart, flashing power and a handsome, combative nature. Sampras had uncanny timing on the ball—like no other American player since McEnroe. John McEnroe, Sr., leaned back quietly, watching his son and the passage of time.

Against this youth, life, and talent, McEnroe dropped so far down into himself he was playing from his toenails. It was Willie Nelson time, and Willie was singing, "*All of me. Why not take all of me . . . ?*" McEnroe was hanging on by a thread.

"You can't go against the machine?" McEnroe shook his head in disgust at referee Ulrich. "What do you think I'm asking about, the weather? Hasn't a machine ever been wrong?" Tatum McEnroe looked pale now. The gloss had worn off her lipstick. Her head remained still behind her dark glasses. The stadium lights burst on. Mountain lions die slowly.

After three hours and thirteen minutes of play, John McEnroe broke Pete Sampras's serve to go up 5–3 in the third set. McEnroe's face tightened with responsibility. He had to hold serve, and he did, grabbing the third set 6–3. Tatum grinned, sighed, and stood up, cheering McEnroe with the rest of the stadium.

The boy was suddenly nervous, nicked by McEnroe. Sampras started to miss his return of serves. He wanted so much to seem relaxed, but his body language became stiffer. The Greek kid looked at himself and his racket in hurt self-disgust. He was not passing well anymore. McEnroe was reducing him to a serve, ready to take him apart stroke by stroke as he did with Wheaton, like a spider does a fly. Sampras was out of synch. He just wanted to win and go home, that's all. Sampras's young face set hard. Then McEnroe hit his fourteenth ace. McEnroe wanted to take the boy out one step farther, out into the back alley where Edward G. Robinson left the Cincinnati Kid after the poker game, just one step farther. But the Greek kid hung tough. On Sampras's fourth break point on McEnroe's devilish serve, McEnroe watched Sampras rifle a backhand cross-court past his feet. He was broken, and one break was all Sampras needed.

Sampras won 6–2, 6–4, 3–6, 6–3. The sentimental journey was over for McEnroe. Antonio Palafox, McEnroe's Mexican coach from the old days—a stabilizing force in the comeback—said, "McEnroe is like a horn player who lost his lip." In the interview room, the press adored Sampras but asked serious questions of McEnroe, who had played his heart out.

Sampras was modest again, but not falsely modest: "Beating Lendl I was more stunned," the eighteen-year-old said. "But today I can't believe it. On the outside I look calm and cool. But on the inside my heart is really beating."

McEnroe experienced a kind of death in the afternoon, but in that death there was the glory of two weeks and the third set against Sampras. McEnroe was hard to love, but for those who knew him, he was hard to leave.

The crowd exiting the stadium that night was a swollen sea of humanity. The baseball game at Shea Stadium had let out just a little earlier, and now there was a large group waiting on the subway platform for the number-seven train back into Manhattan. There were only a few people on the eastbound side of the subway platform, heading out to Main Street, Flushing. I overheard something from the other side of the tracks. A fourteen-year-old Chinese boy, who weighed over two hundred pounds, was talking to a friend. It was the best explanation I ever heard of John McEnroe.

"Chaos," said the heavy Chinese boy. "He just liked to created chaos. Because he was comfortable with it. With chaos."

Boris Becker's agent, confidant, and Svengali, Ion Tiriac, had a face that Sergio Leone, the director of the Clint Eastwood classic, *The Good, the Bad and the Ugly*, would have used. It was a face that had lived. Tiriac's voice was gruff, very husky, and still thick with the charm of a Romanian accent. I had slipped inside the players' lounge to look for Dr. Krickstein, and talk about tension with the racket stringers, when I saw Tiriac burst through the swinging doors in an "important person" hurry.

This time I stuck to his verbal body check. Above his mustache, which was graying at the corners, Tiriac wore tear-drop, light-sensitive dark glasses. Tennis, his slightly pitted fifty-two-year-old face said, was a glamor business, and making a living for thirty years from a glamor business was a hell of a job. Next to Arthur Ashe, Navratilova, and Dr. Krickstein, Tiriac was the most articulate person I spoke to all season. I finally had him. Tiriac nodded quickly and led me into a quiet section of the players' lounge to the side of the stringing machines.

"I overheard you say something once about the difference between motivation and determination. You said that many players talk about motivation but that not all of them have the deep-down determination. How many players on the tour really have the determination to win?" I asked.

"There are two different things," said Tiriac. "How many players *show* determination and how many players really *have* it. There are more players than you think who have determination. To be in the top ten you must have it. But in the top five in the world, the determination is at another level. How you *show* it is also very important. Connors was really the guy who not only showed it but had the determination, and he made you feel it. That's a big advantage. It's not just to show for the sake of impressing your opponent. No. Determination is important because, like with Connors, like with McEnroe, you *feel* the pressure on you. There are a lot of them, like Borg, who never showed anything on the outside, but Borg *had* the determination anyway because he was always there—he never threw a gift to you. McEnroe, he had it. Boris has it if he wants it. Definitely, for the long picture, if you do not have determination deep down, you cannot succeed."

"Boris looked a little bored in the early rounds, but he showed some determination in the quarter-finals against Aaron Krickstein, when he came back from being a set down. I gather that you think with Boris the determination goes up and down."

"I think Boris can *buy* determination," said Tiriac, "meaning that Boris is beyond the average-level professional player. He is so secure that when he has to sprint—how to say—he can *use* that extra determination that he has. But Boris is not at the same level everywhere he plays. The difference between him and the other players is that he can pull out of his hat more determination and more power than other players in the important moments."

"Where do you think the fire in him originally came from? Some people said he was a fat kid, that he was a little unhappy back in Leimen. Where did the fire and determination in him, such as it is, come from?"

"I do not think it came from any unknown reason or any one thing. You have characters in life. Definitely he is a very strong character. Very stubborn. And with that stubbornness comes a determination."

"Was there anything in Becker that corresponds to the hunger that motivates the Eastern Bloc players—anything aside from his natural talent that made him want to fight really hard?"

Tiriac nodded. "He was for sure not the best junior when he was young. He had *many* losses. And *that* made him compete more. He had it inside, but we were not sure. We had to put him on trial. And I was right about him. He had more than average qualities. And then he took it on himself, once we took him out of the *system* in Germany."

"At the Lipton, after Becker lost to Fleurian, you said, 'That loss had nothing to do with tennis!' And you weren't too happy about it. You were mad. What did you mean?"

"I mean, I think that Boris didn't forget to hit the forehand or the backhand. I mean at the Lipton he didn't have the fire or determination that day. And when Boris doesn't have it, he's just a common player. Everyone can beat him." Tiriac's darting, competitive eyes behind his tinted glasses showed he meant just what he said. Becker could get him angry, but Tiriac had trouble getting Becker angry.

"You said that there are 'no *normal* superstars.' What do you mean?"

Tiriac nodded and paused. "There are a lot of players that hit a good tennis ball over the net. There are even some that win very important tournaments. But with that has to come the *personality*, has to come the temperament, has to come the *shining* of a human being. So that then, when he or she talks, even off the court, the people are listening. I don't think you have to be eccentric. You just have to have that extra personality for it."

"Charisma."

"Charisma? Almost. The *shining* of a human being. And that's what makes the difference between a great tennis player and a *superstar*. The great tennis player is also very good. But the superstar is *shining*."

"At the same time that Boris and the other young players are trying to play a very controlled game—keep the ball between the lines—they are discovering themselves sexually. Is that a difficult thing to balance?"

"I do not consider a tennis player different from any athlete. A tennis player is a normal human being," said Tiriac. "Everybody has to find his own dimensions, his own routine in life, and, ah, that's the reason this sex is not so much discussed."

"I sensed over the season when Boris went off the boil—like at the Lipton, when he had just broken up with his long-time girlfriend back in Germany, a young professor I think she was—I sensed his love life made a difference in his play on court. Am I right or wrong? Is it difficult to balance the personal life with the grinds of matches and travel?"

"I don't think so," said Tiriac quickly, flatly. "*Or* you have a life you accept with the good parts and the bad. *Or* you do another job, not tennis champion."

"What about Romania? What is the situation there since the change in the government?"

Tiriac paused. Of all the countries in Eastern Europe, Tiriac's Romania had broken most violently from its Communist past. At nearly the time of the French Open in 1990, the Romanian dictator Nicolae Ceausescu and his wife were stood up against a garden wall and executed by a partisan firing squad. Tiriac had known his country from both sides of the wall, from both sides of the net. Like Navratilova in Czechoslovakia, Tiriac had been able to get away to freedom.

"I don't think Romania is very different now from any other Eastern country," said Tiriac thoughtfully. "They are all new countries. New, reborn countries. That they stay for so many years in a system where you could not operate freely from every point of view is a fact. And *that's* the reason that they are going to have a very difficult time in the future until they find a real basis for a free society."

"Are they afraid of freedom?"

"I don't think they are *afraid* of freedom. I think they don't understand freedom. People in my country are very confused, not so much with the freedom but with the word *democracy*. They don't understand that, in my opinion, democracy *means* that you have even more responsibility . . . to respect the laws. They don't understand that only in a very well structured society, where you are obligated to respect your neighbor if you want to be respected . . . only then can you progress. In the new life in Romania, they all want to be the champion right away. Most of them, they confuse the term *democracy* with *anarchy*. And that's very dangerous."

"And sports?"

"In every country, sports are sponsored by somebody," said Tiriac matter-of-factly. "Might be government. Might be industry. Might be private companies." He shrugged. Sports were inevitable.

"Becker said that one has to *balance* a player, emotionally as well as technically and economically."

"I think that he is talking about control, and not trying to fight two opponents. It is enough you fight one. You don't have to fight yourself. In the cases where you fight yourself, what happens is what happened to Ivanisevic here at the Open."

"Why does Becker fight himself?"

"It's a temperament. It's a way of being. A way of living. On emotions."

"Is he too intellectual? Does he question too much and make things more difficult for himself as an athlete?"

"Put it this way," said Tiriac. "I don't think that all athletes are idiots. And I think that Becker is one of the most intelligent ones. And I think that is a fact and a big factor on the court. His life and his game are more cerebral than the others, except maybe McEnroe and Chang. They have different bodies. They are not as strong."

"And Goran Ivanisevic? You feel a bright future for him?"

Tiriac exhaled. "I think he is going to be a great player. No doubt about it. It depends, though, on him *how* great he is going to be. It depends on his determination. Also for Boris."

Tennis is the only sport where a middleweight can contend on an even footing with a heavyweight. Becker, six foot four inches tall and 192 pounds, came onto the court second, walking slightly nervously and sporting a light reddish beard. Andre Agassi, entering first, had a lot to prove to his critics. He had lost in the final of the French Open, where he was heavily favored to beat Andres Gomez. He had missed the Davis Cup against Czechoslovakia. But against Becker, Agassi was the underdog, and the pressure was on Becker to perform to expectations.

The Las Vegas boy was thicker through the chest and stronger physically from all the weight training with Gil Reyes, but Agassi had not gone to Wimbledon to take his lumps. Reports from the tournament in Cincinnati had to make you laugh. Arriving at the airport across the river in Kentucky, Andre called the Cincinnati tournament director to indicate that he and his large entourage wanted more security. Lynn Gottschalk, the tournament volunteer who took Agassi's call, gave him this response,

Andre. It's eleven o'clock in the morning and you're in Kentucky. Unless you've been on "Hee-Haw" recently, no one's going to mob you.

Andre Agassi might turn out a lot like Bobby Riggs, who had offered his coaching advice to Agassi but had not been contacted. At least Andre had a competitor's knowledge of his own worth. It was Agassi who had said, "Sorry. If Becker is playing well, no one can beat him."

Boris Becker started quickly against Agassi, breaking serve in the first game with a blasted topspin backhand down the line. Agassi took his characteristic little steps during the change-over. The night before, Agassi had had a call from Barbara Bush, wishing him good luck against Becker. Tiriac sat watching quietly in the players' box. Agassi broke Becker right back with a flurry of short backswing forehand winners.

Becker continued to play aggressively and confidently in the first set, attacking, coming up to net often. The Leimen rebel with the blondish-red goatee tossed himself down easily in the canvas crossover chair. He served and volleyed superbly just when it counted and won the first set 12–10 in the tie-breaker, after Agassi held and lost five set points. The first set was a tremendous ego battle, and Becker won it.

It was the network television anchorpersons' day to see and be seen at the U.S. Open. Tom Brokaw (NBC), Connie Chung and Peter Jennings (ABC), and Mike Wallace (CBS) were all at the Louis Armstrong Tennis Stadium in Flushing Meadow to watch Becker–Agassi, as were the television actress Linda Evans and actor Alan Alda, famous for the hit TV series "MASH."

Tiriac said, "The first set was one of the most intense I saw in my life. But Boris must take advantage of the geometry of the court. He must stay close on the baseline and always come in on Agassi."

Agassi's face was an unhealthy, pasty white under a scruffy dark overnight beard, and he looked scared to lose. He seemed uncertain and a little unhappy, both good signs with Agassi. Boris Becker looked happy and relaxed—James Dean after stopping his car at the edge of the cliff. Then somebody released the hand brake.

From the second set on, Becker played as if he were back in Leimen on a red-clay court. He stopped attacking and stayed on the baseline for the rest of the match. It was incredible to watch Becker change. True, Agassi was pinning him deep and blasting ground strokes from corner to corner, but Becker—stubborn, large, willful, and unintentionally cautious—ceased to force the issue of whose style and personality would be dominant. Becker's serve stopped being a weapon. It was a bit as if Becker were disarming himself. On first serves on a hard court, the big German boy spun in three-quarter pace second serves that Agassi ran around and hammered with his short, powerful forehand. When Agassi went up 5–2 in the third set, after winning the second set after two close line calls, Nick Bollettieri, in the players' box, wearing his green neon Ray-Ban sunglasses, smiled like the Cheshire Cat in *Alice in Wonderland.* In another twenty minutes, it was done.

Once again the big, friendly red-headed German young man from Leimen, who liked the pastries in the bakery across from his grade school, lacked the killer instinct. After losing 6–7(12–10), 6–3, 6–2, 6–3, Becker trotted to net, grinned as he had when he lost to Edberg at Wimbledon, put an arm around Agassi, and whispered into Agassi's ear in English, "You played unbelievable good."

It was beyond good sportsmanship. Something was wrong or right. To lose is human, but Becker embraced his conqueror.

After the semifinal loss at the U.S. Open, Becker was asked if he was disappointed, and he said mildly, "Not too much. I think this year I proved that I am a good tennis player. Of course I am disappointed to lose but I lost to a better player. I didn't give it away. I played good, but he just played better. I had to serve very good, and I only served good. Has Agassi changed his game since last year? He looks the same, doesn't he? No? I guess he is a bit tougher on the court than the years before. But that comes with age, I think."

Tiriac looked like he needed a Tums. Boris Becker was twenty-two, nearly twenty-three. He seemed genuinely at ease with himself. But in the long run, it was not ease that made champions. "To call me twenty-one, it's wrong," Boris had said the year before after he had won the U.S. Open. "In some respects I am fifteen, and in some thirty-five." Perhaps he had chosen to be fifteen again. His parents in Germany would understand.

After Becker left the interview room, some in the German press contingent again made fun of his soft-spoken manner in English. Here was the greatest player since McEnroe, the greatest player Germany had produced to date, a player soon to be the number-one player in the world, down for a moment—and the German press was kicking him when he was down. Some people love to tear down what is good and what is closest to them, and the German press was like that. But Becker, a champion inside—a player of strength, intelligence, and gentleness— would not let them tear him down. Becker measured victories and losses

in different ways from most other players. He was a German with a deep
memory and a sensitive soul.

Pete Sampras stood alone under the dark concrete stadium stands. It
was eleven-thirty the night after Sampras's third-round win over Jakob
Hlasek. There had been three reporters in the room after Sampras's win,
and the California boy explained to us why he was not yet ready to win
a Grand Slam event in 1990, least of all the U.S. Open. When the brief
interview was over, I followed him out under the stands. He was standing
there smiling in the semidarkness, shouldering his big red Wilson tennis
bag.

"Pete," I said, "would you mind if I walked back with you to the
changing rooms?"

"Sure," said Sampras, a first-round loser at Wimbledon. We started
walking out from underneath the stadium, up the steep steps past the
bar where they sold Velveeta nachos with whiskey or Campari, down
briefly past the hot dog and ice cream concessions, across the high chain-
link front entrance and the draw sheets illuminated from above and
below. His name was still on the draw, but neither of us had any idea
how long it would remain there. Sampras had an uphill fight, a very
tough draw. We walked around the side of the sponsors' courtesy tent,
through the kitchen to the locker room. He was still a boy that night
before his consecutive wins over Thomas Muster, Ivan Lendl, and John
McEnroe. Sampras did not think of ducking any questions. He was young
and still not afraid to talk.

"Where did your parents meet?" I asked. They were both Greek,
but his father was born in America and his mother emigrated from
Greece.

"They met on a blind date," said Pete Sampras. "In Potomac, Maryland, where I was born."

"Your dad had a small restaurant and worked for the government,
too. Why did your parents decide to move to California? Was that for
your tennis?"

"No. Not really. Not at first. My father had pretty much had it with
his job. He wanted to go away and try something new. So we went out
to California."

"You were about eight before you really started to play tennis?"

"Right. At Jack Kramer's club."

"And your father and mother were happier in California?"

"Right. And my brother and sister, too. We were all happier when we got to California."

"Your father is Greek American," I said as we reached the foot of the changing-room stairs. It was time for one last question. "Your mother is from Greece. What part of Greece is she from?"

"Sparta," said Peter Sampras.

I smiled. Sparta was the land of the warrior Greeks in ancient times. According to legend, Spartan parents used to chain their children to rocks and leave them in the sun for two days without bread or water. The ones who could survive did so—and lived to fight for the glory of Sparta. In a sense that was what all the tennis parents did. They put their children out on the rocks, hoping it would help them in life. It was a peculiar form of a deep love. The further the children went in the draw, the tighter the bonds to their parents, and the tougher the draw got.

"Do you remember the name of your mother's town in Greece?"

"I really wouldn't know," said Pete Sampras, nodding, as he tried to remember. "But my mother is from Sparta."

We shook hands, and the eighteen-year-old Sampras smiled, nodded his head a little formally, and climbed the changing room stairs. He was a colt. McEnroe said after their match, "He is so young, but he has ice water in his veins. Nothing seems to faze Pete." It was not ice water. Sampras had gentleness. Edberg had it, and Becker had it, and Agassi had it, too. Aaron Krickstein had it. Borg had it. Even McEnroe had it—lots of it—but he kept it well hidden. Gentleness. It was part of being calm. And Pete Sampras showed that inner calm that week in New York, when everybody else was more nervous. His mother came from Sparta.

"I'm tawkin'," said the lady with the New York accent as thick as a Whopper. "I'm tawkin' about where they make you go. To park the car."

Before the final between Agassi and Sampras, there was tension and lots of coffee and donuts in the press room. The press seemed to be picking Agassi (after his win over Becker) and rooting for Sampras. To break the tension, a New York reporter turned to a colleague and said, "When Yannick Noah hits a lob, do you call it Noah's arc?"

It was tough to pick Sampras over Agassi. Steffi Graf had said after she beat Jennifer Capriati, five days before she lost the final to Gabriela Sabatini, "You either lose to yourself or you get outplayed. Those are the only two ways you can lose."

I went to take a walk around the stadium grounds. Out in front of the stands, not far from where the large white draw sheets had filled up with names and numbers, I spotted Agassi's coach, Nick Bollettieri, standing almost alone. He had a racket in his arms and he was tucked up against the side of the stadium nearest the parking lot, talking to two admirers—parents of former tennis campers. Andre Agassi walked inside the front gate and a sixty-year-old woman with short gray hair and wearing a blue warm-up suit shouted, "Oh! Andre! Andre!" The bodyguard and strength coach, Gil Reyes, swarthy and goateed, chest like a bull, led the slender, tensely smiling Agassi through the front gate. He was dressed to play but headed into the changing area to wait. Bollettieri looked up but did not go in right away. It was too late for coaching. So I thought he might not mind talking for a minute.

"Nick," I said, as the parents drifted away. "We spoke at the Lipton in March for quite a while. I wonder if you had just a minute?"

"Were you nice to me?" Bollettieri asked, presuming whatever it was had already been written.

"Oh, yeah. Of course."

"Really. And now? Are you favorable?"

"More and more so."

"Oh. More and more so." Bollettieri grinned. The ex-Marine para-trooper, the little Italian man who had quit night law school in Miami thirty-five years before to do what he really liked to do—hit tennis balls for a living with his shirt off—smiled behind his fluorescent green sun-glasses. "Okay. I'll talk."

"It's a big day for you. Are you excited?"

Bollettieri kept grinning. "Yes. I'm excited. Are you?"

"I'm excited, too." I was nervous, too. "How do you think it's going to go for Andre? Any thoughts on it?"

"I just think Andre from the first point has to go for winners on the return of serve," said Bollettieri. "That's the key today."

"If Andre starts returning serve well, he might break the other guy's heart a little early on."

"That's what we hope," said Bollettieri.

"And if the other kid's serving that real big one?"

"Then Andre has to win his serve every time. He has to change his pace on his own serve and not try to outmuscle Pete. And there is one other thing we are going to do."

"What's that?"

"Pete likes the serve up the middle, because that's the lowest part of the net. That's where Pete likes to hit his aces. So what Andre is going to do is cheat over a little bit while Pete is in his windup and take away that ace up the middle. Okay?"

Bollettieri's voice was starting to crack with tension. He and his player were twenty minutes from their biggest match of the year—the biggest match of their lives. The crowd at the men's tennis final in New York was like the crowd there must have been when Jack Dempsey, the "Manassa Mauler," fought Gene Tunney. All the important people of the day seemed to be there. General admission was $35 and a box of Kleenex for the nosebleed. The front-row seats were for the high rollers. Pete Peterson the financier, Alan King the comedian, and Anthony Quinn the actor were all there. The acrobat in Fellini's *La Strada*, the Greek in *Zorba*, and a Mexican by birth, Quinn was wearing a wide gray suit over a rough blue shirt, his suit jacket draped casually over his shoulders as if he were in Rome. Quinn's left arm was wrapped tightly and warmly around his oldest son, who was two inches taller but not quite as tough looking as Anthony Quinn.

"We've got a true U.S. Open today," called out a smiling, thick-bearded black man selling small yellow ducks to the crowd still surging across the subway boardwalk to the tennis fight. "Two of America's boys. Two of America's finest today. Yes, sir!"

And it was true in its way: Agassi's forehand against Sampras's serve. Tennis, like boxing, was a battle of styles. There was tremendous excitement in the air. New York was the place for it—the pace, the Statue of Liberty, and the media. Before the players even stepped on court, the final would be a triumph of America's greatest asset, the immigrant. The son of Greek-American parents was meeting the son of Iranian-American parents. It was historic. The tougher the draw, the more likely they were to succeed.

At 3:55 P.M. sharp, the "Salute to America" began. The national anthem was sung by a man wearing white ducks and a blue blazer, who sang a B+ anthem, until the last ten bars. A flashy-looking blonde in a green miniskirt looked down at the CBS boxes courtside and then looked way up to the nosebleed section of the stands, where her boyfriend had a pair of $35 tickets. Actually, a little height gives you perspective. The armed forces color guard marched out onto the green hard court. At 4:11, as Lee Greenwood sang "God Bless the USA," Pete Sampras and Andre Agassi were led onto the court.

The "pomp and circumstance" reminded me of the first championship match I saw, at age seven, at the old Madison Square Garden with my folks, when Lew Hoad and Pancho Gonzales stood on the side of a court stretched over the hockey ice, as they put on a spotlight and raised the U.S. and Australian flags in the darkness. Tennis was a game of memories and families.

I remembered what Nick Bollettieri had just said about Agassi moving over toward the middle, the low point of the net, to cut off Sampras's aces. I got into my seat with a Häagen-Dazs just before the third point of the match, and started concentrating immediately.

Pete Sampras was serving into the forehand court. The score was 15–all in the first game. Sampras looked relaxed. Agassi looked nervous. Sampras bounced the ball twice before he served. Just as the Greek American went into his service toss, Agassi took two small steps over to his backhand to protect the middle against the ace, as planned. The dark-eyebrowed Greek kid tossed the ball into the air gently, and before we could move in our seats or Agassi could move on the court, Sampras aced the whole stadium, knocking the ball wide off the line on Agassi's forehand side at 115 miles an hour.

It was uphill for Agassi from there on. Agassi looked over the net in surprise, and the crowd roared at the first ace, the first mistake, the first stunning blow.

The loss for Agassi came like a verdict that could not be reversed. Sampras soared. On his shirt was pictured a large bearded Greek figure pulling back on a bow. Sampras could do no wrong that day. In an hour and a half, the shy Greek American became the youngest player ever to win the U.S. Open—the first Greek, the first Mediterranean immigrants' son ever to have his name and *winner* appear together in the morning papers. It was almost like getting elected president.

Jakob Hlasek, who had not wanted to leave the interview room after Sampras beat him, said, "To win here you have to play seven very good matches. So far Pete has only played three." By the end of the two weeks, Sampras had played seven great matches in a row.

The crowd filed slowly out of Louis Armstrong Stadium. The tournament was over, and I felt a tremendous exuberance that the right man had won. It was not that Agassi was not a great player. It was just that sports sometimes have a justice all their own, a reasoning, a monumental series of truths that sometimes are cruel and sometimes are so fine, so clean and wise that the event transcends the problems of the world. Wins and losses teach, and Agassi's loss felt like that. He needed schooling. In contrast, Pete Sampras's win in September 1990 felt right. Sampras had played so bravely, so unconscious of himself and all it might mean financially.

This was the year of the immigrant's child, the prodigy's chase toward the American Dream, the green light of desire at the end of the dock in *The Great Gatsby.* This was the year of Capriati and Sampras; it was when Michael Chang came back from a broken hip with a big contract from DuPont, but couldn't get his father, Joe, a job. The strength of the immigrant is the strength of America, and tennis clubs—like golf clubs— were very slowly opening their doors to newcomers. The tournament had always been won by the children of people who, generally because of birth, found themselves on the outside looking in. The tougher the draw, the better the competitor. This was the hard fact that united them all: Navratilova's stepfather drawing the court broom in sweeping circles over the red clay outside of Prague, the Beckers living on the edge of Leimen, Edberg's father serving as a detective in Västervik, Agassi's dad working as maître d' in a casino in Las Vegas, and Sampras, whose parents, like Michael Chang's, had experienced both the hardships and rewards of the American system. Tennis was that mysterious social game, that game of structure in America—and at the top, where Jay Berger had almost been and Pete Sampras was now—talent counted for nothing without the heart to keep trying.

As I walked out of Louis Armstrong Stadium with the happy, well-dressed crowd and headed back across the boardwalk to the subway, I thought of the night that the young tennis pro from Utah was killed defending his mother and father. I thought of Zina Garrison overcoming both bulimia and her parents' deaths to reach Wimbledon's final. I thought of the pink loft buildings for lease in Miami, the soft squeak the rubber wheels of the wheelchair competitors made at the Lipton, of Edberg's and Becker's bravery, and of my last conversation in the players' lounge.

"Dr. Krickstein," I said that fifth day, "you are an educated man. When you were getting into tennis with your son, what was it that drove you to want him to excel at such a game?"

"I guess I've always been interested in sports myself," said the big, burly man from Michigan. "My father was a rabbi, so I don't know what his athletic ability was. All we did was throw a baseball back and forth like in *Field of Dreams.*"

"Was he a competitive man, your father?"

"No," said Dr. Krickstein softly, letting out a little Michigan chuckle. "He was a total bookworm."

I smiled. Book people and competitive people in my experience were far from mutually exclusive.

"My mother *may* have been competitive," said Dr. Krickstein. "I don't really know. But I was always interested in sports, so I got all my kids into sports right from the beginning—first the three girls, then Aaron. He was always a competitor. Heck, he used to turn over the Monopoly board when he wasn't happy. I learned how to handle him from my girls. But never in my wildest dreams did I picture Aaron playing here at the U.S. Open. I just thought tennis was a real good sport."

"You're a pathologist. Do you think tennis is essentially a happy state of mind, or somehow a mirror of life with big swings of ups and downs?"

"Definitely the latter," chuckled Dr. Krickstein with his warm Michigan laugh. "No question about that. Certainly most of the top players are not really *happy* when they are out on the court. The nature of tennis is that you play so many points, many more than in baseball. You are playing in an atmosphere close to the fans. They are waiting for you to screw up, basically. You are swinging dozens of times at a small ball on each point, so you are going to miss a lot of balls, and that's tough to accept when you are trying that hard. It's just you out there, and the pressure in an individual sport is greater than a team game. Take a five-set match. There are so many mood swings. The players can never really relax. They know they can lose to each other every time they step out onto the court. Tennis is a big pressure sport. So it cannot be that happy down on the court. Not really. Not until the last point is over." Dr. Krickstein smiled. He loved it, loved the pressure. "If you can survive tennis, you can survive a lot. Not just as a player, but as a parent."

"Your son Aaron beat Pat Cash in three tough sets. He plays Boris Becker tomorrow. It would really be something if he won."

"Well, I wouldn't bet on it," said Dr. Krickstein, laughing, losing himself for a moment as he dreamed. "But wouldn't it be something if he did?"

MEDICINE MAN

The U.S. Open 1991

Jimmy Connors was magnificent. If Boris Becker was the moody, sensitive bull from the small town of Leimen, if Stefan Edberg was tennis's brave, quiet version of the lost Swedish diplomat, Raoul Wallenberg, then Jimmy Connors was a character so American, so raw and yet so courageous that the older generation could imagine him storming the beaches at Normandy and the younger generation could picture him telling off his parents.

There is a lovely, near-perfect symmetry to writing about a single season of a sport. The story benefits, if it is told well, from the theatrical unity of Time. The French dramatist Corneille felt that drama was a moment plucked from Time, which is made whole by the unities of Time and Place. But a book on tennis without Jimmy Connors would be like Samuel Beckett's *Waiting for Godot* without Lucky.

I also wanted to see what had become of all "my people." Jennifer Capriati had improved a lot, and so—incredibly—had Monica Seles. Edberg, Becker, McEnroe, and Courier had all traveled well. For me, 1990 and 1991 were inextricably linked in that strange, almost subconscious passage of time by which things change but seem the same. Only the match results tell us that things are different. But when a champion repeats, or an old star shines again, it comforts the part of us that wants things to stay the same.

I was not always a Jimmy Connors fan. When he was thirteen years old and playing in the sixteen-and-unders in the National Boys at Kalamazoo, Michigan, I envied him. He was so small yet he played so well. His mother, a woman of obvious strength, wore dark glasses and had her blonde hair spun handsomely up on her head. Wherever they walked, she lingered a few yards behind her son, trying to give him plenty of tether. Even for a tennis player, little Jimmy Connors looked incredibly cocky.

"Who's that little smart-aleck?" I asked.

"That's Jimmy Connors," answered my friend. "He's lefty."

I had never seen a face quite that full of twinkle and malarkey. Down on the Kalamazoo stadium court at age thirteen Connors had the same slightly undercut forehand going cross-court, topspin down the line, and vicious, hold-on-to-your-hats-boys two-handed backhand going for the corners. It was clear from the beginning. His talent was competing.

Jimmy Connors's grandfather had been a professional boxer in the lower-weight classes in the 1930s, and he had trained Jimmy to fight— as a boxer—when the boy was eight or nine.

Gloria Connors, his tall, attractive mother, had worked as a tennis professional in Belleville, Illinois. She gave lessons six to seven hours a day in the hot southern Illinois sun, raising her family of three boys with the help of her parents, not her husband. Stefan Edberg's mother introduced her son to the tennis courts, too, but Mrs. Connors was the only mother on the men's tennis tour who had taught her son how to play. Pancho Segura took over when he was sixteen, but Mrs. Connors was truly the source.

I had missed Jimmy Connors in 1990. In Philadelphia, where I fell in love with the way Pete Sampras played, before he won the Open and had to really face the media pressure, I was watching a fine match between Jaime Yzaga and Petr Korda. Four Philadelphia businessmen sat down near me at lunchtime in the upper deck of the Spectrum. The ball was being struck with great timing and beauty to the work, but so smoothly that there was no apparent struggle.

"You know," said one of the Philadelphia businessmen, "I miss Connors."

It struck me like a kick betwen the eyes. *That* is what they (and I) had missed so much in Connors. Life was a struggle, and Jimmy Connors was not an artist like John McEnroe; he was an impassioned struggler, more like the rest of us.

"The day I got back to Los Angeles from Monte Carlo last year, my surgeon was at the airport to meet me," Jimmy Connors said the day before the 1991 U.S. Open. "The doctor told me he was going to operate on my wrist the next day. 'There's really no risk involved,' he told me. 'If you don't have the operation, you're never going to play tennis again.' So I'm glad just to be here at all. This is like a second chance for me. Doc told me that if I could play for three months, I could play for the next five years."

Connors, now thirty-eight, had been back for six months. Ranked fourteen in the world before the wrist operation, by the end of his fallow 1990 his ranking had almost fallen off the unforgiving computer to number 936. In his first match back, indoors in Chicago, Connors lost to Jaime Yzaga 6–3, 6–0, and he said with ringing confidence, "I like some of the things I did tonight." In Japan in April, Connors nearly broke through. He had two good wins, then nearly upset Edberg, 4–6, 7–6, 1–6. Connors told the assembled Japanese press, "I am back in business!" The Japanese laughed and applauded the aging American star. A lot of the younger players thought he was crazy, too.

The two seasons had gone as follows:

	1990	**1991**
Australian	Lendl, Graf	Becker, Seles
French Open	Gomez, Seles	Courier, Seles
Wimbledon	Edberg, Navratilova	Stich, Graf
U.S. Open	Sampras, Sabatini	

There had been some notable changes in a year, but none more dramatic than the reemergence of Jimmy Connors. In Paris, the French stood cheering as Connors ran himself legless on the soft red-clay center court against Michael Chang, who at age nineteen was exactly half his age. Connors was leading 6–4, 5–7, 2–6, 6–4, and 15–love—a lead of one point after four hours—when he had to default because his body told his brain he was out on his feet. Jim Courier, who fought in the tour trenches for four years without most of the fanfare, or recognition, unexpectedly beat Andre Agassi, the bridesmaid for the second year in a row, in the French final, and when it was done, it no longer seemed like an upset. Courier's new coach, Spain's José Higueras, who had worked for Jay Berger during the red-clay European season the year before, had steadied Courier's competitive fire and shot selection. But Paris was aging too, and Connors was the real talk of the town.

There was so much rain in London in the summer of 1991 that for the first time in Wimbledon's 114-year history they played a rain make-up day on the first Sunday, which was usually a day of rest. The English, instead of giving tickets to the Wimbledon club members for the un-expected extra day, sold them at roughly $12 apiece to people who had queued up, rain or sweltering heat, along the dark brick wall that had stood between the club and the crowd since before Winston Churchill was born. Jimmy Connors, of course, was asked to play the match that broke with tradition, and he dispatched Aaron Krickstein on Center Court. The unusually raucous English crowd, sitting where the royals and swells usually sat, waved for Connors as if it were a football match between Manchester United and the Tottenham Hotspurs. Michael Stich, who had been a junior soccer star in Germany, upset Stefan Edberg in the semifinals, and then, still serving flawlessly, beat a surprised and nearly passive Boris Becker in three tight sets to win Wimbledon's silver and glory. But the three rounds that Connors played in England were what the English touts and the non–All-England Club members really loved. In a less malevolent way than McEnroe might, Connors embodied the break in form in a country where "form" does still count for so much.

Now, in August 1991, the thrill was there again as I took the subway from Manhattan to Flushing Meadow. It seemed as if everyone was rushing out to see the tennis competition. In the early 1990s, tennis had become modern theater for the sports cognoscente—expensive but a third of the price of a Broadway show. The players did not wear roller skates, and no helicopters whirred above stage to create the illusion of Vietnam. Nevertheless, the evening's match promised to be more fun— a verdict of Roman proportions. The games people would see from the stands were the dramas of two real lives clashing. Before a match was over, at least one player would be completely exposed as a person, naked in defeat, summed up for all to see, the way Corneille or Racine would have done it on the French stage: a win or loss—and why.

In 1991 most of the leading actors were still there from last year, but a few were missing. Yannick Noah had retired at the age of thirty-two— and was probably right to do so—because he had observed in his own personality a gentleness (Joseph Conrad would call it laziness) not suited to prolonged struggling. Noah grew his dreadlocks and formed a rock band in Paris. He played reggae and was enjoying *un grand success du moment*. Could he sing? It did not matter. He had a physical charm and at times a magical spirit. Noah was the only Davis Cup captain with a rock band, and he not only chose his team (Forget and Leconte) but inspired his French players, who were brave and more disciplined than their mentor, to a stunning post-Open Davis Cup victory over Sampras, Agassi, Flach, and Seguso.

As if locked in the memory of his 6–7, 7–6, 7–6 loss to Stefan Edberg at the Lipton the year before, Jakob Hlasek had what Chuck Kriese referred to as "getting his recall button rung by his opponent." The powerful Hlasek lost to the silky smooth Rostagno 6–7, 7–6, 7–6, 7–6.

In 1990 I had rushed out to the stadium on the first day and got there too late. Edberg had already been beaten in straight sets in the first round by the Russian left-hander, Alexander Volkov. Now I stood again under the big white draw sheets, dwarfed by all the names in tight black letters that would get larger as the tournament progressed. Steffi Graf was the women's first seed, more from computer memory than merit in 1991. Boris Becker, who had finally become the world's number-one men's player, was on top of all the other names. Buried inside the draw with a "WC" for wild card next to his name, Jimmy Connors was in the same quarter as Boris Becker. I nodded, sure Becker could win that confrontation.

The crowd plays a major role in a championship. The players have a will of their own, yet without the crowd pulling for them, it is so hard to win. Like a baseball crowd, the denizens of Flushing Meadow can turn the court into a homefield advantage. But they must love you first. When John McEnroe strode out onto the stadium court with Michael Chang, the New York crowd roared in anticipation of a battle to the death.

Michael Chang had never looked quite as tense. His skin was tight against his angular face. His eyes peered out with an intensity greater even than the roar of the crowd that had greeted the two American heroes, one a hero to his own people, one a hero to the memories of the crowd.

It had been a rough year for Michael Chang. Members of the press vilified his family for not cooperating with them, and this made the Changs draw even deeper into their shells. When Chang fell out of the top twenty, the family fired his Australian coach—big Phil Dent—and in his place hired Michael's older brother, Carl, a number-five player on his college team. The Changs even kept the coaching money in the family. David Wheaton took objection to the way he felt Chang snubbed the other players, not talking to any of them in the locker room. Wheaton, a devout Christian himself, also cried foul when Michael Chang stated he may have won a very close match because "I had a better relationship with Jesus Christ."

"He can't know that. Nobody can know that," said Wheaton.

Clearly Chang was grasping for straws in the larger world of competitive America. He had the powerful DuPont endorsement, but he remained an outsider to the other players, always a member of his family first. The pressure on Chang, as on Agassi, to live up to his multimillion-dollar endorsement contracts was enormous. Virtually the only person who still stood up for Chang was Boris Becker. "I'm one of the few people who can understand what he's gone through. I was seventeen when I won Wimbledon, the same age he was when he won the French Open. Your life stops being your own. Everyone wants something from you. People don't understand: this guy is very special."

John McEnroe seemed to sneer as he twisted into his left-handed serve and followed it up to net. McEnroe had never lost a match to Michael Chang, and he knew how to put the pressure on baseliners. But there were no baseliners like Chang, no reflexes as quick, no heart as hurt, no Chinese-American will as ready to burst to the surface. Chang's first return blew past McEnroe before he could get halfway up to net. McEnroe, a master of disdain, reacted as if the passing shot had not happened, but Chang slapped his thigh hard three times. He wanted this one as much as McEnroe ever wanted a match. Up above, the American crowd cheered, but Chang knew the majority would never *love* him—not the way they loved a McEnroe or a Connors or a Sampras or anyone who was not Chinese. Real or imagined, that was Michael Chang's baggage, and he carried it defiantly aginst McEnroe.

I tried to understand more by watching Chang's body as it moved. Chang was now much quicker than McEnroe, and that quickness was not just physical. The newspaper men disliked Chang. His father was the type of man who, if he owned a grocery store, would charge $7.50 for a pint of strawberries. It was Michael Chang's stinginess that the newspaper men detected and detested, but that was part of his speed, part of his leanness. I loved McEnroe, the attacker. I had never loved Chang, the defender, as well. But this night, Michael Chang threw off his fear and attacked the way Phil Dent had tried to get him to attack all year.

The looseness of the gut in John McEnroe's racket upset me. McEnroe's strings were not sufficiently taut, were not *now*. Chang's racket and being seemed strung tighter, and I thought somehow because of it he deserved to win. In the stands, Carl Chang looked leaner too, happier in his role as coach than in last year's role as brother. Michael Chang was so light but so strong mentally. He knew exactly what he had to do. His darting black eyes saw everything. He glowed like a star in the night. McEnroe was more human; he shouted and complained. The crowd roared in derisive sympathy. Chang consistently forced the crowd and McEnroe away, and just played. It was the new voice being heard. McEnroe was a bit like a painter or writer gone out of style, perhaps greater than Chang but now nearing a parody of himself. It would take people another ten years to fully realize how great John McEnroe was, but Michael Chang was also a kind of miracle, and he was *now*.

"McEnroe's a living legend. He'll win," insisted Alan King, the warm-hearted comedian and tennis aficionado, interviewed at courtside in his front-row box seat. But when you think of yourself as a maestro, a living legend, you never win. And McEnroe *knew* he was a maestro.

Down a set he could have won, McEnroe got brave, hard-headed, and beautiful. He was going to win this match after all. McEnroe's hair was short like Julius Caesar's. His face looked refreshed and honest. With maximum effort, John McEnroe regained purity. Chang was not impure; he just had met his match. McEnroe was another level up. By hitting harder, Chang could not go cross-court, and McEnroe, leaving small openings as traps, cut off all the down-the-line passing shots with angled volleys. Michael Chang heard the crowd roar for his blood, got nervous, and double-faulted away the second set. They entered the land of reflexes and recall buttons.

In the third set, a New York fan began to taunt McEnroe. "Shut the hell up!" hissed McEnroe. Chang stayed back on his baseline, glaring, waiting, never letting his concentration wane. He broke John McEnroe's serve six times in the first three sets and hit ten topspin lob winners. John McEnroe looked paste-faced, struggling to stay out of oxygen debt. Chang won the third set. McEnroe dipped deep into himself for the fourth. In the fifth set, Steve Ulrich, the referee, called a questionable Chang serve up the middle as an ace, and McEnroe said, "Words cannot describe how low I think you are." The crowd was with him. The ref had missed the call.

McEnroe began attacking Chang as if he owned the right to the land through inheritance, not hard work (Chang's method), and Michael Chang passed him again and again. McEnroe trailed 4–1 in the fifth set but the crowd nearly brought him all the way back to victory. His hair balding yet frizzy from defeat, his vanity knifed like Caesar's, John McEnroe slumped down behind the microphones to be interviewed at 1:00 A.M. after five sets and over four hours of tennis.

McEnroe knew he had been mortally wounded in this match. He was thirty-one and had lost to the nineteen-year-old Chang for the first time. A talent like his could always get hot, but now McEnroe had age, not temper, to contend with. In 1991, McEnroe finally brought his temper under full control. He would do so well at the Australian Open in 1992 that Peter Bellinger would tell the ball boys to emulate McEnroe's behavior. But Mac would fall in the quarter-finals in Melbourne, whereas in years past, if he was playing that beautifully, he would always have reached at least the semifinals. John McEnroe's triumphs had become exciting reversals of diminished expectations. His losses hurt more, because he really wanted again what he once had.

"I didn't play the big points well enough. That has been the story of my whole year," said McEnroe.

"Has anyone ever lobbed over you like that, John?"

"No."

Chang over McEnroe was not an upset. It was time coming due. Faced with McEnroe's persistent aggression, the force of a white street-tough, Chang had whipped a torrent of topspin lobs over McEnroe's head, turning a defensive position into a winning one by accepting briefly the very defensiveness of his situation, then punishing McEnroe for thinking he was more in control than he really was. As if to sum up the entire match, the state of affairs that made the American crowd cheer every move forward that McEnroe had made, on match point Michael Chang snapped off a final, defiant backhand topspin lob, leaving McEnroe glued to the court, an aggressor caught in the folly of his own aggression. It was the most humiliating shot in tennis, and Chang had caught McEnroe with it repeatedly. Michael Chang roared and shook his fist when the final point was over. Now in the interview room, McEnroe looked up. There was deep silence. The press sensed it. The loss to Chang was a loss McEnroe would feel for the rest of his life.

"This may sound like a stupid question, John," said a reporter. "But when you play a great match like that, is it harder to accept defeat, knowing it could have gone either way?"

"It is pretty disappointing," said McEnroe softly.

"The crowd really got behind you in the end. Did you think you could come back?"

"I always have a chance," snapped McEnroe. "And *not* because the crowd was getting involved. I could have won the first set. I had a chance for break point in the fifth set and broke my string on the return. It took a little time to get adjusted to that other racket, just enough to cost me a little bit."

There was always a certain karma to a match, a certain luck factor. Work creates luck, and Chang had worked against McEnroe like his life depended on it.

Michael Chang came into the interview room next. I was expecting to see a huge smile on his face, but he was grim from the effort of beating John McEnroe for the first time ever.

"Whenever you play John, it's very tough," Chang began, weighing his words. His voice was shaking with emotion. He was tired, and he had felt the intensity of the crowd's will as it rooted against him. "I don't know why I won. I don't know what made the difference."

The questions flowed. It was 1:30 A.M. Chang had won the match with great speed and tenacity. In effect he had beaten the stadium as well as John McEnroe. The reporters opened him like a coffin with a crowbar. Finally it was too emotional even for Chang. He asked the press, "Can I say one more thing?" His lips were trembling. "To my people back home," Michael Chang's chin shook as if he was about to cry, "thank you for praying for me."

And then Chang was gone.

The first-round match that intrigued me most in 1991 sent Andre Agassi against Aaron Krickstein. It proved to be a moment of redemption for Krickstein, who had been injured a large part of the year; a moment of joy for Dr. Krickstein, who deserved one; and a defeat as tough and unhappy as Andre Agassi had experienced since his Grand Slam final-round losses in Paris and New York.

Agassi had been so light, so fast, and so inspiring in the heat of the Lipton in Florida where he beat Stefan Edberg, in the final I will always remember for the wheelchair players who angled their vehicles up to courtside looking for unobstructed views of Agassi. But a strange thing happened. Having been proved a little weak during the three Grand Slam finals he lost to players he should on paper have beaten—Gomez,

Sampras, and Courier—Andre Agassi became so obsessed with "strength" that he became musclebound. Even Agassi's face looked thicker. But the more muscular Agassi *looked*, the more tentative he became. His natural speed, his angel-like quickness were gone. His timing was all off. Boxers and tennis players should not fool with weights. Run stairs, skip rope, do push-ups, frog leaps, and thousands of sit-ups like Stefan Edberg and Bjorn Borg. But for tennis, thick muscles are stupid muscles, and now Agassi had them. With his frosted blonde hair and thick chest, Andre looked like a miniature professional wrestler.

Tall and lean, Aaron Krickstein blasted Agassi around the court at Flushing Meadow, just as Agassi had often moved Krickstein around. For Krickstein, it was a great moment. Krickstein's serve, source of his father's angst over the years, was the stroke that most hurt Agassi. Krickstein won 7–5, 7–6, 6–2, and the scores were accurate. "Andre had a lot more to do with this than I did," admitted the victorious Krickstein.

After the match, Agassi was as quiet and disappointed as I had ever seen him. Perhaps the losses would teach Agassi the final lesson he needed to become a great player. Courier had faced the music Agassi had sometimes tried to avoid. He seemed stunned by what had just happened to him. The 1991 U.S. Open was to have atoned for his final-round loss to Sampras in 1990, but it did not.

"I don't know which hurts more," Agassi said softly, "losing first round or losing in the finals."

I hated to see great talents wasted. In the past, Agassi's manner, as squeaky-cute as McEnroe was belligerent, was in part to blame for how life (and the press) treated him. He had remained loyal to Nick Bollettieri, but now he needed to look hard at himself as a person, stop the weight lifting, and hire someone who had played the game at the highest level to coach him that last quarter-inch of the way.

Somehow, the rebel in the Canon camera ads had not yet fully met himself. The mirrors others held up to him were either too pretty or too grotesque. You cannot win a truly big event unless you like yourself and unless you are ready to die trying. Jim Courier, the French Open champion, had taken lots of lumps the year before, ducking no opportunity to compete—and to learn. Courier said toughly after the Agassi match in Paris, "Sorry. Somebody had to lose." The real Andre Agassi had roots as dark as Pancho Gonzales, and I hoped that one day Agassi might meet himself, accept that he was not the image of the blonde American teenager he portrayed in the television ads, but rather was the son of immigrant parents who had worked very hard for everything they had so their son could become a star in America. If Agassi continued to believe in his purely American image, he was finished.

Martina Navratilova had the biggest surprise of the 1991 season. Her lover and business partner, Judy Nelson, sued her for $10 million in palimony. Win or lose the U.S. Open, Navratilova was due in Texas to testify the Monday after the final. Just the year before, the Czechoslovak woman with the American flair for the immediate seemed to have found peace and lasting love with Nelson. What a difference a year makes. Judy Nelson now felt she was entitled to a major share of Martina's on-court as well as her off-court earnings. *Palimony!* Some pal. The circumstances would have brought down most players. Somehow Martina managed to make fun of herself and joke about having more trouble in one court than in another. Tennis players could be hurt in many areas, personal or professional, but the true champions—Tilden, Navratilova, Gonzales, Connors—never relinquish their first devotion and ultimate love, which is the tennis court and, often, by extension, themselves.

By contrast to the most public Navratilova, Steffi Graf was still in a precarious emotional state. She won Wimbledon in 1991, and no one ever won a major tournament unless the physical and mental were in balance. But Graf won Wimbledon in part because Gabriela Sabatini wanted to win the match so badly she self-destructed at the eleventh hour. Serving for the Wimbledon title up 5–4 in the third set, Sabatini forgot at the very last moment how to win, and Graf, playing from deeper memory, sensed Sabatini's hopes and growing nerves—dominated her within the last three games—and walked quickly away the winner.

Navratilova and Graf were on a collision course toward a confrontation in the semifinals. They had not played each other in two years, and the winner might with justice claim to be the greater player in the history of the game. Graf had speed, but Navratilova had reached an age, thirty-four, where she accepted herself more and had learned to control and use her nerves. On the way to her semifinal meeting with Steffi Graf, Navratilova had to overcome her old nemesis, Manuela Maleeva-Fragniere, who beat her three times in 1990. Martina did it the hard way, and then survived another three-setter, winning with her back to the wall against Spain's spunky Arantxa Sanchez-Vicario, 6–7, 7–6, 6–2. We were all a little surprised by Navratilova, but we should not have been.

"How did you do it, Martina?" asked my friend the Indian reporter.

"I've been watching Jimmy," grinned a tired but happy Navratilova. "I'm thirty-four, but next to him I'm a spring chicken."

Brothers in sport would make an interesting subject for a book. In tennis in recent years there have been the Gullikson twins, the Panatta boys, the Mayers, and any number of less successful brothers, one of whom makes it while the other remains unknown. If an older brother looks out too much for the younger one, the result eventually is resentment. Brothers who are athletes in the same sport must be as different as possible if they are both to survive with their skill and identity intact. And yet, as Patrick McEnroe took stadium court against Jimmy Connors, it was the similarities between the McEnroe brothers, not the differences, that people looked for.

Jimmy Connors, who had lost two U.S. Open semifinals 7–5 and 6–4 in the fifth set to John McEnroe, said, "Whenever I play a McEnroe, I try like hell to win."

The older brother was all sharp angles and lip. The younger was all rectangles and good behavior. But a McEnroe fire burned in both of them.

Patrick McEnroe was right-handed, and his entire personality and tennis game seemed to take off from that essential difference. He simply could not do the things his brother, seven years his elder, could do left-handed. But in 1991 Patrick reached the semifinals of the Australian Open, and John McEnroe lost in the second round. Patrick McEnroe had a win over Boris Becker at the Lipton, and a three-set loss to his brother in the final at Chicago—a match that was very close without being close at all. As Patrick McEnroe, ranked thirty-fifth in the world, warmed up against Jimmy Connors, it seemed there were really three players on the court, and the one who played the invisible third man least would win. Victory was a means of escaping the shadow of love.

Connors was not likely to take it easy on the sibling of his most difficult rival, but he looked old in the first set. Patrick McEnroe, the flip side of the nasty coin of his brother, looked calm and professional at his center. The crowd was skeptical of Connors at first. Its cheers rang more with hope than belief. Patrick McEnroe won the first set 6–4 and the second set went to a tie-breaker. Again the crowd tried to pull Connors through with the intensity of its favoritism.

Patrick McEnroe did not crack at first. He played in intense silence and won the second-set tie-breaker from Connors, 7–6(7–4). In the third set, Connors looked as if he was finished. Down love–2, he even started to limp. Patrick McEnroe noticed it, and it was the limp that first scared him. Connors was either hurt or acting. Sensing in the air the silvery presence of his brother, the tennis Richard the Third, Patrick McEnroe bore down even harder. Tight-lipped, unforgiving, refusing to be duped by act or actor, he went up 3–0 in the third set with two service breaks and prepared to serve to go up two sets and 4–0. And then it happened. The crowd left. Thousands of them started streaming out. The mayor of New York left. Mario Biaggi, the congressman back from doing time in a Texas jail, left. The chair referee asked people to remain seated, but the crowd had seen enough. They did not want to see their hero die. They preferred to get home and see the result on TV late news so it would hurt less. By the time Connors won a game, there were probably only six thousand people left in the twenty-thousand-seat stadium. It was like being at the Lipton: you could go wherever your emotions carried you. But what happened next was almost not to be believed. It was one of the great comebacks in sports.

I had seen Connors play a match in Boca Raton, Florida, eight years before against Claudio Panatta, the younger brother of Adriano. The young Italian star had led Connors on the green entouca 6–1, 5–0 and was serving for the match in the second set. I turned jokingly to a friend and said, "Match to Connors." Damned if Connors didn't win 1–6, 7–5, 6–1. Claudio Panatta started to limp when it became clear he could not close out the match. The hardest thing in tennis is to learn how to win the last two points of a match against someone who is better than you. It was a fact of life that Jennifer Capriati would have to face herself. The cruelest thing about winning is that most people have to pass through a valley; you have to have your heart broken at least once—and survive it—to become a true champion. Patrick McEnroe was about to have his heart broken.

Up in the stands, the crowd leapt to its feet and roared as Jimmy Connors held serve. It was championship pressure, the land of memory and instinct, unfakable and often frightening. Mr. and Mrs. McEnroe, Sr., sat silently together by the side of the court, and if their faces had ever suffered for their older son, the pain that came with all their hope and longing for their younger son was clearly etched on their weary faces. They knew even better than Patrick the flame that was James Scott Connors. But their son was winning 6–3, 7–6, 3–0.

A torch was lit. Suddenly Jimmy Connors was racing around the pale-green court like a hobo jumping off a freight train into the moonlit

Nebraska night, waving a piece of wood on fire. "Put it out! Put it out!" Patrick McEnroe's every response seemed to say. But he did not have enough water to put out Connors, or shut down the small crowd of people shouting at the top of their lungs as if their souls, their pent-up hearts, were all being released at once by this uppercut gesturing, this in-your-ear cussing, American original acting as if life itself was a question of victory and defeat and America was the promised land.

Connors was so low, so close to annihilation. It looked like a modern Horatio Alger story. Connors had fallen so far behind that if lost games were mortgage payments, the bank would have repossessed him. They could have lowered the prime rate to 2 percent, and *that* would not have helped him. Connors was two chips away from going bust at the crap table. His stock, once at 135, was down to 4¾, and the stockholders were demanding to know what had happened. Connors waved his racket hand in the air defiantly, and the crowd, his stockholders, believed in grand gestures and market miracles. Patrick McEnroe hung his head.

There is a vengeance to winning, and without it, as John McEnroe and Jimmy Connors knew, there is no fire, no hard ways win, no will to climb the mountain again. The third set slipped away, and the fourth set started to slide. Patrick McEnroe needed to step up. He needed to let the fire inside him ignite into flames, but to do that, to show the roaring strength and anger of his will, Patrick McEnroe would have to play-act at being his older brother, and this he would not, could not, do. Patrick McEnroe was dying to win, and yet he kept his emotions under strict control as if *they*, not Connors, were the key to the victory the younger brother was really seeking. He wanted to win, but he wanted more to be his own person, to be the McEnroe who would never boil over. A fine rage might win it. At two sets apiece, there was still a chance for victory, but there was no chance at all. I suddenly felt like shouting down to Patrick McEnroe, "This is not your fight. You cannot win it. Reinvent yourself. This is really your brother's fight you are fighting. Get off the court before they really hurt you."

But of course he could not leave. He was into it up to his neck. The New York fans felt for him the way they never did for his older brother. They liked him as a person. They were sympathetic to his predicament, and yet the crowd still wanted to see him executed. It was not enough to be nice in life. The crowd loved the knife in the night, the torch stuck in the heart. The Belleville, Illinois, hobo held them in his palm.

Patrick McEnroe had one final chance, one last moment of disappointment. Trailing 2–4 in the fifth set, he drew even. The rough remnants of the crowd, completely delirious with the miracle of Jimmy Connors's steadfastness and human toughness, fell silent. But Connors had found his killer legs; the limp was gone. It was now 4–all in the fifth set. And then like clockwork, as automatic as a Larry Bird free throw, Connors broke Patrick McEnroe's serve and held his own. It was over.

In the interview room, the remnants of the press corps did not hold Patrick McEnroe long. The claps, the roars of "Jimbo! Jimbo!" still echoed from high up in the stadium down into the back of the dead-quiet concrete room where the remaining media gathered as acolytes. The match had raced out of Patrick McEnroe's hands. The younger brother had tried to control what his brother would have let run wild. He just was not as good, not as wild in spirit or free in his strokes as his left-handed brother or Jimmy Connors. Despite this, Patrick McEnroe had played to the very outer regions of his ability. That is bravery. He looked neat but subdued as he came into the bunker in a fresh shirt. The two brothers did not look much alike, but the timbre of Patrick McEnroe's voice was uncannily like that of his older brother.

"Jimmy's a great player, and I can learn from him. But I wasn't nervous tonight," he said behind the microphones at 1:15 A.M. "I was pretty much able to block the crowd out. I didn't feel any particular kind of extra pressure tonight." We stared, nodded our heads, and let him go.

The match had lasted four hours and twenty minutes. It was 1:40 A.M. when a small group of us walked through the night, past the illuminated white scoreboards, and climbed the stairs to the locker room. In the semidarkness Jimmy Connors faced the press from on top of a desk, ice on one leg, blue tennis jacket closed over a bare chest. Some reporters stood on chairs to see him. From the distance of the stadium, Connors appeared to be so light and frail, but now he spoke with such firmness, such genuine feeling and love for his job that I felt I was in the presence not of a thirteen-year-old I had envied but of a kind of genius. Connors seemed like a railroad man. He seemed like he could get the train over any bridge, through any obstacle, to any destination. He spoke, and it was as if he were still on the court. The emotions of the moment poured out of his heart through his words. Both players had wanted the match in the desperate way a single child craves recognition from a parent. It took a permanent man-child or woman-child to be a great champion, and Connors, like Navratilova, was that.

"Did you at any point think you had lost it?"

"Well, it wasn't looking good. I will say that," nodded Jimmy Connors with a smile. "I just tried to get on the board. I played a good game to break him to go one–three down in the third set. Then the crowd just kind of lifted me. My racket started feeling better in my hand. My legs started moving. I wasn't on my heels as much, and I started coming forward. But in the beginning, Patrick didn't let me play like that. *He* was being the aggressor, and so I had to take that away from him. And it happened just in time."

"Does something like that match at Wimbledon, when you were down six–one, six–one, four–one against Mikael Pernfors in 1987, does the memory that this happened before for you help you now?" asked Mike Lupica.

"Memory?" said Jimmy Connors, looking sideways, dripping sweat. "In the old days, I used to win a lot because of my reputation. But I'm not twenty-two or twenty-four anymore. I'm thirty-nine in two days, and they all know it. But there's a pattern that has been set throughout my career from the very beginning, and the pattern is: you're going to have to kill me to beat me."

He did not say it boastfully, but he meant it down to his toes. Jimmy Connors was popular not only because he was a struggler. It was never a question in America or New York of just drawing even. The point of winning anything is to be more than equal. The New York crowd loved Connors not only for how low he could go but because, once the score was tied, Jimmy Connors got even with vengeance. A crowd's love is not all kindness. The spectators loved Connors at least in part because in battle he was a killer.

"And it holds true today." Connors continued. "I think a lot of guys understand that as far as me staying in there and doing what it takes to win up until the last minute, that is what I do best. It's for them to win. *I'm* not going to lose it. They have to take it from me. And if they can do that, then it's too good."

"Is your will exclusively yours?" asked a tired reporter. "Or did another athlete inspire you to have it?"

Connors paused politely. His will was not a tuxedo that was rented for a night's performance. "Naw. My will's just my own creation. It's something that can't be given. You've got to have it inside you. But when it's brought out, it has to be brought out in a way that makes you feel good about it. I was taught the game, and I started competing when I was very young. I *love* this game. I always enjoyed grinding it out in a bad situation, and I still really enjoy *grinding*. The people like it, too, and it keeps me in good shape and all the B.S. that goes along with that. But what I really love now is putting my game, which has been around for twenty years, up against these guys today and the way they hit with the oversized rackets. It's a new time for me. A second chance. And I'm coping."

"How much did you feed off the crowd tonight?"

Jimmy Connors had narrow, Budweiser-red eyes. "The crowd won it for me. I played some really good tennis in the last three sets, but the crowd was an awful heavy burden for Patrick."

"Did you ever doubt for a moment that you would win?"

Connors shrugged. "Patrick's had a very good year. I had to play my best. In the second set, I came from behind and got up there to six–all, and I get in a dogfight, and I lose it. He played me a good tie-breaker, and so I'm down two sets to love. But I'm not going to roll over and let things just go. I just have to stick in there. That's what they pay to see. That's what I'm *supposed* to do."

I loved the way he said "supposed." It was so workmanlike.

"How tired were you there in the fifth set?"

"It's not so much that I was tired. I wasn't cramping or anything like that. But playing anybody for four hours is tough. I had best take care for the rest of the night and get some sleep."

"To do this at twenty-two or twenty-three is one thing. You do this now, and other people walk around amazed. What do *you* have to say about it?"

Connors looked the reporter in the eye. "I'll do my talking when it's finished. Then I'll tell you how it's done." Jimmy's small red American face, creased with fatigue and honest effort, broke into a smile. His trainer, big Bob Russo, helped him off the desk, and Jimmy Connors sauntered sideways back to the shower room.

The reporters' bus was parked on the far side of the stadium. We straggled through the closed yellow-and-white hot dog, beer, and ice cream stands. I was so tired my eyes hurt, but I was happy. Each reporter and photographer still there was rewarded with a full seat on the bus trip home. The reporters were a strange and diffident bunch, but I liked every one on that bus because they, like Connors, had stayed to the end. The streets of Queens and the highway back to Manhattan were silent under the dinosaurlike heads of the neon street lamps.

"Football matches are much easier," said the bulky German sportswriter grinning in the seat behind the driver. "In football, you have only so much time, then a little penalty time, and the match is over. But this can go on *forever!* This is *madness!*"

"This is what we live for," agreed the elderly British writer from a famous London paper. "One of these comes along once a year and makes it all worthwhile."

"I've been taking pictures of Jimmy since he was sixteen," explained the photographer with camera bags and lenses slung across her chest like water pouches in a desert. "No *way* I was going to leave him early!"

Finally, I felt a sense of community. Happy to be with them, I fell asleep as the bus rattled into Manhattan.

"I should have known better than to leave," Ilie Nastase said the next day. Jimmy Connors's doubles partner and singles antagonist had left, with Connors down two sets and 3–0 in the third set. "I was hungry and it was getting late," explained the dapper Romanian. "But I should have known better. Jeemmy. You can never count him out."

The next afternoon, out on the practice court, Boris Becker, looking large but somehow thinner with his wispy red beard, stopped his practice and trotted across two empty courts. Jimmy Connors was there practicing. Becker walked over in that long, friendly loping stride of his, bent his head down to one side, and whispered soft words of congratulations. Connors nodded but hardly smiled.

That same evening, Boris Becker was out. He lost to the Dutchman whom Bud Collins had dubbed "the best little Har-hoose in Amsterdam." Paul Haarhuis was a player with great athletic ability and tenacity. A soccer player who did not take up tennis until he was seventeen, Haarhuis was 75 percent the player Becker *could* be, but on that day, in the heat at Flushing Meadow, the Dutchman's 75 percent was plenty.

"Were you surprised that Boris stayed back on the baseline so much instead of coming to net?" I asked him, thinking of the red clay of Leimen.

"Yes," admitted Haarhuis, "I thought he would be at net more."

Boris Becker revealed that his leg was hurt. He had trouble pushing off his right leg on his serve and volley. But a loss is a loss. It was a tough ending for Boris Becker. Earlier in 1991, he had become the number-one player in the world, but he had done it by consistently reaching the semifinals and finals of big tournaments, but not in his usual way, the beautiful, all-out win in the major finals. This time when Becker lost, I looked down at Ion Tiriac in the players' box, and the rough-edged Romanian—the guts to Nastase's glamor when they were a doubles team—no longer looked surprised. Injuries and luck and attitude are all somehow connected. You are what you are on a day when something happens. And the acceptance in Tiriac's face seemed to acknowledge for the first time that what he had had in Boris Becker might be gone forever.

The young, unthinking German athlete had been supplanted by a full-grown young man who loved tennis but also loved to reason and to question in the modern German way. There might be for Becker another hill, past this stage of his maturity—a hill where the notion of pure effort was once again equivalent to incredible fun. But as with Pete Sampras, for Becker realization of a certain dream seemed to have killed something of the dream itself.

Tennis is a game of individuality, but to be part of the tour is to belong to an incredible system, a corporate carnival that covers the world. Some players deal with that better than others. To Becker, it felt like caged individuality. Like the hunger artist in the Kafka story, Becker now felt himself paraded from site to site, and every chance he got he reasserted his individuality. He announced that he would not play Davis Cup for Germany against America. Becker said of German tennis's desire to win the cup back, "It almost means too much. It goes beyond the tennis match. They almost turn it into a war between countries, and I don't agree with that." Boris Becker, I confess, was still my favorite. He went beyond the wins and losses.

I checked the bulletin board in the reporters' lounge. Four TV sets were playing at once, and the cans of cold Coke, Sprite, and Saratoga water were almost all gone. It was hot. The referees had posted their "fine schedule" for the previous day, and I read it with a smile, because I always felt that being a referee said as much about the person doing that job as it did about the player getting the fine:

PLAYER	VIOLATION	FINE	CODE
1. Dimitri Poliakov	Audible obscenity	$1,000	J
2. Goran Ivanisevic	Abuse of racket	$500	N
3. John McEnroe	Verbal abuse	$1,000	O
4. Amos Mansdorf	Abuse of ball	$350	M
5. Goran Ivanisevic	Abuse of ball	$350	M

A large crowd had gathered around a side court. I could not see at first who was playing, but I squeezed in next to the high part of the fence.

It was not a match at all. It was practice. The McEnroe brothers were

warming up each other for their doubles match that night against Goran
Ivanisevic and Omar Camporese. The sight was quite beautiful. The
McEnroes moved so differently, and yet in the way the brothers, both
out of the singles, tried to set each other up, not beat each other, there
was gentleness, love, and understanding. John McEnroe practiced his
famous left-handed overhead, and his younger brother fed him lobs.
Then John called Patrick up to net and fed him some high forehand
volleys, as if to build back up his younger brother's confidence. That
night the McEnroes beat Ivanisevic–Camporese, 7–6, 6–4. It was a tough
business, but they were still brothers.

Goran Ivanisevic was my dark horse to win the tournament, while most
people expected him only to upset Ivan Lendl in the round of sixteen.
When Goran came into the interview room after losing his commanding
lead over Lendl in the third set and then the match like a Coke poured
down the drain, Ivanisevic threw his heavy blue racket bag down in
disgust and slipped behind the microphones.

"Ivan was *yust* controlling all the points!" said Goran Ivanisevic. The
young Croatian was breathing so hard after four sets with Lendl that his
slender shoulders were still rising and falling. "I played too defensively
to beat Lendl. I was looking for his mistakes, and this was *my* mistake,
because Lendl never misses. I did not come in. Why did I do this?
Because it was the wrong tactic. Why? I will tell you why! I did not
come in to net because I was not too confident. I was a little scared at
the back. He had more guts than me, and so he won."

Goran Ivanisevic got up and walked away mad but very beaten. He
was so talented, but he needed to fill out his frame and to grow up.
Against Lendl, he faded like a quarter horse matched against a champion
thoroughbred. The nineteen-year-old was not going back home to Split,
because his parents told him it was too dangerous for him to return, as
the fighting with the Serbs was fierce. Before the U.S. Open, Goran
declared he was a Croatian, and would no longer play Davis Cup for
Yugoslavia—the country no longer existed. He had the right kind of
pride, but he was not yet master of it. Yes, the world was splintering,
and some of the best players came from areas that had been independent
before the First World War. The anger Ivanisevic had shown the year
before losing to Darren Cahill now seemed to him a folly. But the fresher
fury of having Croatia destroyed before his family's eyes pained the
handsome Goran. For now, his rage at the war took away his heart for

tennis. But I still believed he would one day fulfill Tiriac's prediction of greatness—once Ivanisevic started playing like a man instead of a prodigal boy.

Ivan Lendl—who had left his country forever—smiled as he sat down to face the press wearing quite amazing three-quarter-length navy-blue bicycle pants over his tennis shorts. He wanted to seal in warmth during the interview. Lendl was an original, a truly strange and kooky guy, so disliked generally that I almost liked him.

"*J'aime pas son côté superieur*," a French reporter said to his French colleague; "I don't like Lendl's superior side." It was about as good a description of Lendl as I had come across in nearly two years of watching him up close.

"Goran said his back was bothering him," the French reporter started.

"Yes," said Lendl, smiling, taking the bait as he always did. "Personally, I think Goran got a little tired. That is all. His services were a hundred and twenty-five miles per hour on radar gun. *I* would like to have back pain like that." Lendl grinned, but there was irony, not warmth, in the smile. His face was older, leaner, chiseled by years of effort. His eyebrows looked bushier. Lendl was a competition freak.

"Ivan, do you think it will it be easier for Czechoslovak tennis players now that they have access to freedom? Or will they lose their motivation?"

Lendl frowned. He liked nothing about the question. It was both speculative and, by inference, personal. "Sure, it was nice to get out of Czechoslovakia. But that is not why you *start* to play tennis. You do not play tennis to escape. Money is not why you start, either. You start," said Lendl, "because someone is showing you. And you follow."

"In the first set, Ivan, you called the supervisor of referees out onto the court. What was that all about?"

"I was having trouble with the blimp," said Lendl. "It was bothering me above the court. I called the supervisor down to ask him to tell the blimp to make wider turns above the stadium. And they did."

I almost burst out laughing. Lendl could control the Fuji blimp from down on the court. I always admired Lendl's fierceness. Perhaps I was wrong to question the source of it and imagine it in a different context. I liked to think the deep bravery in Lendl's competitive fierceness would overcome his love of order. Lendl's next opponent was Michael Stich, the man who won Wimbledon in 1991.

Michael Stich pronounced his name like the last syllable in the word *mystique*—and no player ever won Wimbledon without a full share of it. Tall, loose in the knees, and slightly pigeon-toed like many great athletes, Stich almost looked uncoordinated, but his serve was clocked at 126 miles per hour. He had a great natural feel for the ball. The way he held the racket looked just right. Contact was so clean, so light to look at, so heavy to return. The year before, when Stich won Memphis indoors, he looked incredibly good but raw. In 1991, he grew into his awkward-looking body. Six foot two inches, another young European soccer star turned tennis player, Stich covered the court better than David Wheaton and approached Pete Sampras for sheer talent. After winning Wimbledon by beating Stefan Edberg and then Boris Becker, Stich had the aura about him—three parts confidence, one part aggression—that all the champions have. But Stich liked to emphasize his relaxed qualities. Wearing old purple sweat pants and a faint black 1950s goatee, Michael Stich looked a little like the title character in "Gilligan's Island."

At first, nothing seemed to bother the young German, but the champ was not long on diplomacy, either. "I don't like New York, not at all," said Stich in interview after beating MaliVai Washington in five sets. "I just don't feel comfortable here. All these buildings and noise. I prefer the country, America."

"Michael," said a young reporter from Hungary. "You beat Boris Becker in the Wimbledon final. But could you win in England without Boris winning there first in 1985?"

"Well," said Stich, fluent and at ease in English, "I am not *still* beating Boris at Wimbledon. That was one match, which I won. When he was winning Wimbledon at seventeen in 1985, I was home struggling in the juniors," said Stich, also twenty-three. "I do not compare myself to Boris, and that is because what he has done is so much more. He is better."

"Do you think you could connect with the crowd, like Connors?"

"There is no way," said Michael Stich. "Jimmy is a very large personality—like Boris in Europe. I think nobody except Jimmy and McEnroe can do this at the U.S. Open because these two are the heroes. They played so many matches here. *McEnroe and Connors.* You cannot compare these two guys to somebody else. They are alone."

I confess to rooting for Stich against Lendl in the quarter-finals. The scores were 6–3, 3–6, 4–6, 7–6, 6–1, and when it was over I had nothing but admiration for Ivan Lendl. Down two sets to one and a service break in the fourth set to the reigning Wimbledon champion, Lendl broke serve, won the fourth-set tie-breaker, and demolished his younger, perhaps more talented opponent, 6–1 in the fifth set. Lendl's mental pressure was almost as fierce as John McEnroe's serve. Michael Stich spun out of control in front of the noisy, New York crowd.

I missed Jay Berger. But fame is fleeting. Berger, master of the side court come-from-behind victory, was back in Florida. I had spoken to his father by phone and had got the news. Jay Berger had had two operations since January, the first to repair the lateral meniscus, the second to repair the repair. Berger's fourteen straight weeks on the tour the year before, his red-clay-court campaign, had eventually taken its toll. His good knee, not the one he wore the black patch on, needed repair when he came back from Australia. Knees are not like car wheels on race cars, but they are forced to cover ground on a tennis court as if it were the Indianapolis Speedway.

"I don't know what time the matches are," Jay Berger said the night before the semifinals. "But if you call me back at five o'clock we can talk tomorrow."

I winced. It might be match point for Connors, but I agreed. Berger was out of the draw, but he wanted to be called during the semifinals. Hell, he wanted to be *in* the semifinals. He wanted just that bit of loyalty, that trademark of his game, that stick-to-itness that made Berger so different from those who chased the neon.

I called Jay Berger, and I was glad I did. "I've gone fishing every day for the last four months. I've had time to myself for the first time in years, and I'm getting pretty sick of it. I've caught grouper, yellowtail, and bonefish off the Florida Keys. The first operation was pretty serious, and it hurt. It makes you realize how lucky you are just to be walking around. It's helped a lot being with Nadia. And now we have a baby girl, Alexandra, and that's great. I'm going to see Bo Jackson's surgeon next week. In tennis, you have to be able to come back at a hundred and ten percent. In most sports you could be just a little off your movement, but in tennis you can't lose even a quarter step. I think I'll be back." He would not be.

"What do you think of what Connors has been able to do?"

"Jimmy's probably my favorite player," said Jay Berger. "We practiced a lot together, and he really made a difference in my game. What did I learn from him? How things need to be done. He talked to me mainly with his actions. An hour of practice with Jimmy is like hitting three hours with somebody else. John McEnroe does it more with natural ability. Jimmy was a born worker. They're both great competitors," said Jay Berger.

And so, I thought, was he.

"Sure, I knew Jimmy," said Frank Hammond. "I umpired all the big matches. I once told John—I refused to call him Mr. McEnroe even though the rule book said we had to call him Mister—I said, 'John, I can be a son of a bitch or I can be a nice guy. Which do you want?' " The 250-pound referee chuckled. "I had bulk on my side."

As the names still in the draw moved toward that solitary line, I felt a need for historical perspective. Jimmy Connors was reducing some of the players to puddles. Karel Novacek, the tenth seed, a tough clay-court baseliner known for winning five-set matches, had lost to Connors 6–1, 6–4, 6–3 and afterwards blamed the super-cool air-conditioning unit in the players' changing rooms for giving him a cold and causing a complete meltdown against Connors. I had my opinion. How good *was* Jimmy Connors?

"McEnroe was brilliant, a genius with his hand and eye," said Frank Hammond. "But Jimmy Connors is the greatest tennis player who ever lived. Connors *ruled* tennis. He has the record for consecutive weeks at number one: a hundred and fifty-nine. That's from July 1974 to August 1977. Jimmy would have won the Grand Slam for sure if they hadn't banned him from the French Open twice for playing team tennis. That was pre-Borg. Borg was the greatest player ever on clay, but Connors was the best on all other surfaces."

"But at his best, wasn't McEnroe better?" I thought so.

"Not in my book. Connors won the U.S. Open on three different surfaces. He holds the all-time record for tournaments won—one hundred and nine! Jimmy's won here at the U.S. Open five times. That's more than anyone except Bill Tilden, Bill Larned, and Richard Sears, and two of them played before Teddy Roosevelt was president. No one has done what Jimmy has done in the last sixty years. I don't care how old Ken Rosewall was," said Frank Hammond. "Nobody *ever* beat Ken Rosewall the way Jimmy did at Wimbledon and Forest Hills in 1974. In the U.S. Open final, Jimmy beat Rosewall six–one, six–nothing, six–one." Hammond made a purring noise.

I had run into a Connors fanatic. I liked Laver, McEnroe, Gonzales, and Kramer in that order ahead of Connors on the best year of their lives. Tilden was like Proust or James Joyce—it was demeaning to rank him. I think Connors might have beaten Budge, the way Bobby Riggs did just two years after Budge's Slam, because Connors had the great return of serve. But Borg beat Connors when Connors wanted it most—at Wimbledon and Paris—and Connors returned the favor in New York. Don Budge would have beaten Borg on grass. History was such fun in sports. You were never wrong, as long as you had an opinion.

Despite Frank Hammond's opinion, part of me still needed to be convinced by the Belleville, Illinois, scrapper. Connors seemed at times like a sideshow. He lacked the power of Gonzales or Kramer. He lacked the touch and serve of McEnroe. He lacked the whippet speed and thousand sit-up strength of Borg. And for about five years he had lost to Lendl, whom he had once called "gutless." But by the time the two weeks were over, I too was shaking my head in amazement at the raw *inner ability* of James Scott Connors. I was always trying to determine where the inner strength came from in a champion, so I pushed Hammond where he really did not want to go: "But did you really know Connors?"

"Sure, I did. I knew Jimmy and Johnny Connors, and the third Connors brother who didn't play much. I forget his name. Lovely kids. I knew all the Connors brothers."

"When Jimmy was a kid, he was always with his mother at the tournaments, never with his father."

"That's right. His mother was the one."

"Were they separated? Or divorced?"

"No. I think they were Catholic."

"I read once that to thank you for refereeing his matches in Dallas, Connors said that he would do you one favor—whatever you asked—and you asked him to call his father."

"That's right. Jimmy's father was dying. It was 1974 or 1975. Jimmy had beaten Ken Rosewall at Wimbledon and at the U.S. Open, and we were doing some television matches in Dallas for the WTC. I asked Jimmy to call his father. They rarely saw each other. But Jimmy got mad and told me to leave *that* subject well enough alone. A week later, though, he said he flew out to see his father, and he did see him, just before his dad died."

"Where was his father? Had he left when Jimmy was just a kid?"

"Quite young. His father worked as a gatekeeper on one of those bridges in California."

"You mean a toll collector? On which bridge? Was it the Golden Gate Bridge?"

"I'm not sure if it was the Golden Gate Bridge."

"But his father was out there, and Gloria Connors and her three kids were back in Belleville, Illinois. She was giving tennis lessons to put her kids through school."

"That's right. The father just was not there. He was making change on the bridge. And then, of course, he died."

"I've had this growing feeling that a number of the top athletes—not just in tennis but also in a sport like boxing, where fighting is involved—have a gap of love they need to fill and never can because the person they are trying most to impress is not there now or maybe never was there. I know it sounds a little half-baked, Freudian, but I keep seeing it. The boxers Tyson and Holyfield never knew their fathers. Tyson was abandoned by his mother, too. And Martina never met her natural father, either. I think of the intensity of their drive. To me, it seems like they are all trying to impress this person who is not there. I *feel* it in them, Connors and Navratilova. They have something inside themselves to prove, and the world has no idea how deep it goes."

"I don't know about any of that," said Mr. Hammond, and I could almost see his big arm moving out horizontally as his big voice boomed "out." "But I can tell you this. Jimmy Connors is the greatest player I ever saw."

Aaron Krickstein slowly bounced the ball on the green cement court shining in the glare from the night lights. He looked across the net. He was up 5–2 in the fifth set, serving for the match against Jimmy Connors. Aaron Krickstein had always been popular in New York, but now the crowd cheered like it would lynch him if it meant pulling Connors even. It was like playing a Davis Cup match in Paraguay, Krickstein would say later. The crowd was vociferous when he missed a first serve, and Connors swayed from side to side like a cat with a green fluorescent stick between its paws. Louisiana Senator Huey Long would have liked the scene—the crowd was so one-sided. I was seated in back of an English woman who had been covering tennis for twenty years for London papers.

"Is there much cheering in England when someone misses?"

"No. We don't often applaud errors in England."

"It's not very attractive, is it?"

"No," the black-haired English woman said softly. "Certainly not when a player serves a fault."

It was not fair to Aaron Krickstein. And yet there was something powerful about what had transpired. Connors came back again, back like Lazarus from the dead. He stole the second set. He won the fourth convincingly, and in the fifth set, Connors trailed 5–2, 5–3, 5–4. The stadium—the great globe of light—began to roar. It was almost demagoguery. Connors was a marvel, a bona fide American original in a time of too many superior foreign products. The crowd loved this son of Illinois with the hobo's smile because he did not run away from his work. James Scott Connors was the Connors who stayed. He did not run from the hell of the moment, from the three kids screaming, from the bills to be paid, from the whole damn American thing. He did not run from his responsibility and spend the last years of his life taking tolls on the Golden Gate Bridge. He was the land and the bay, not the bridge. He was not change; he was fierce constancy. He stayed and fought the battle that all of us sometimes feel like quitting. He was superb.

Jimmy Connors gave back to you more than McEnroe, the tortured, self-absorbed modern soul, gave back. Jimmy Connors was an American throwback, the vaudevillian, the circus barker, the medicine man who sold his magic elixir from the back of a covered wagon. And we bought it from him because what he had, we wanted. And even if you did not believe this substance could be bottled, you'd buy it from him anyway, because you did not mind being taken in this way, did not care that the magic elixir worked mostly for him. By the time his pitch was over, 7–6 in the fifth set, people were ready to swear by whatever the medicine man was selling. The Nuprin people got the Connors and Chang ad on the air almost the next day. And in a sense, that is what Connors's colossal struggles did: they eased pain, they made people feel great to be American.

Dr. Krickstein looked stunned in the low, dark tunnel between the court and the interview room, where Connors again held court. "It wasn't right," said Dr. Krickstein. The father watched his son surrounded by a group of reporters and shook his head. "The crowd was even swaying the referee. But what can you say? Aaron played great. But Jimmy just kept coming at him."

Young Pete Sampras came into the interview room after his quarter-final loss to Jim Courier, and there was not a seat in the house. The year before there had only been two reporters in the same room with us. Now he was the defending U.S. Open champion. In tennis, that is a bit like being president. The Greek kid was nineteen and did not want all the responsibilities of public office.

I was still unabashedly a Sampras fan. He had won a lot of matches and money, but glory did not make him tick. In December 1990, playing at the Compaq Grand Slam Cup in Germany, Sampras—the youngest player ever to win the U.S. Open—also became the first player ever to win a first prize of $2 million for a single tournament. That was more than Rod Laver made in his entire career. The runner-up in Germany, Brad Gilbert, got $1 million, nearly as much as Ken Rosewall made in his thirty-year career. The money was swollen all out of proportion, but the Germans were paying it. The moment Pete Sampras was handed his check, he announced that he was giving $500,000 to charity, in the name of a family member who had died. The nineteen-year-old made the gift with such decency and honest good-heartedness that I was touched. It did not matter if he won another Grand Slam event. His parents were lucky. Their son of Sparta had humble beginnings and a noble heart.

But Sampras was not ready to wear the mantle of champion. Jim Courier, whom not even Arthur Ashe had picked for the world top ten, was made of stronger, more focused, if less brilliant, stuff. Perhaps the inconsistent pattern of play from Sampras's junior years had returned, as Coach Kriese had suggested it would. Pete Sampras's climb in 1990 had been straight up, but 1991 had been an up-and-down year so far. Pete Sampras had two flaws as a champion: he was modest and he had self-doubts. But greatness is partly natural ability. When he lost in the quarter-finals of the 1991 U.S. Open to his best friend from Bollettieri's tennis camp, Jim Courier, Sampras said simply, "I am no longer the reigning champion. I kind of feel how Chang felt when he lost the French Open. The bag of bricks came off his shoulders. Maybe things might calm down a little bit around me now. The monkey's off my back."

"That's disgusting," Jimmy Connors would say of Sampras's remark the next day. "He's in the wrong business. What are we here for, if it is not to win?"

I knew what Connors meant, and what his entire being stood for. I could admire that, too. But the Greek kid's nature was more gentle. It was the irony of all this competition: what made Sampras such a decent person might turn out to be his flaw as a long-term champion.

"Pete," someone asked, "who do you pick now to win your title?"

"Lendl is a possibility," Sampras said softly, annoyed how quickly the vultures were ready to settle elsewhere. "Jimmy, too. But, you know, I think Edberg is the strongest of everyone in the draw right now. This summer has been tough for him. But he's due. I think Edberg will probably win this tournament."

Stefan Edberg's quarter-final match with Michael Chang was the key in determining the outcome of the tournament. Before meeting Chang, Edberg had struggled. He went four sets both with Bryan Shelton, the black serve and volleyer from Alabama, in the first round and Jim Grabb, the doubles specialist, in the fourth round. Edberg's match with Michael Chang was a test of styles and wills.

Michael Chang showed such prolonged flashes of speed and brilliance that if Edberg had not risen to the occasion, had not leapt for and covered the topspin lobs that left McEnroe frozen to the court the match before, Chang would have slipped through even the narrowest of psychological or physical openings. Chang played 30 percent better than he had in beating John McEnroe.

They played on a cool, clear night. Chang's return of serve against Edberg was like a gunslinger's draw. Edberg kept riding his serve into Chang's body, but Michael ripped return after return past the best volleyer in the game. Chang was moonwalking. He ran as if he was on air. So clean were Chang's passing shots, so fast his feet, so keen his mind, he played too well to be beaten by anybody that night.

Edberg played from no finer instinct than Michael Chang, but he played to the very depth of his instincts. D. H. Lawrence wrote in "Apropos of Lady Chatterley":

> While we are in thought we can not really act, and while we are in action, we can not really think. But the two conditions should be related in harmony.

It was not greater will, it was greater harmony with which Stefan Edberg beat Michael Chang. If the Swede had been two degrees off in a hundred, Chang would have prevailed. But Edberg was in total control of himself—part aggression, part glide, all serve and volley.

"Did you try consciously to volley behind him so he could not run them down as easily?" I asked Edberg after the incredibly close three-set victory.

"I tried to mix it up," said a happy Edberg. "Sometimes I volleyed in front of him, sometimes behind him. I tried never to give him the same pattern."

Edberg's ever-loyal coach, Tony Pickard, was hidden behind a column. I caught him as Edberg prepared to leave. "He's never won here. Can he do it, can he win the whole thing?"

Pickard exhaled nervously. "Well. We're still here."

Michael Chang looked crushed when he first came in. To survive against McEnroe and to finally hear the crowd cheer for him against Edberg was a momentary thrill, but he had lost. What hurt was knowing he had never played that well and lost before.

"Michael," said an older gentleman from a London paper. "Do you realize what a great match you have just played?"

"Yes," said Chang, and his face relaxed into a smile.

Arthur Ashe told me the year before that it is best for players to stick to the routine they know best. Steffi Graf was accompanied again in America by her father and mother. Graf was twenty-two now. Even after the alleged affair her father never admitted to, she wanted her parents right next to her. I thought she was wrong. She seemed to be the kind of young German woman who was afraid of leaving her family and becoming her own person. On the surface, Graf could be bold, but her confidence, once seemingly indomitable, now was what perhaps it always had been, a coverup of something less secure.

At her best, Steffi Graf was one of the six best women players ever to play the game. (In my order, they are: Navratilova, Margaret Smith, Steffi Graf, Chris Evert, Helen Wills, and Billie Jean King.) I believe the modern era has produced the greatest women players. Their bodies and minds are that much freer. At the U.S. Open in 1991, the women would have stolen the show had it not been for Connors. Steffi Graf and Althea Gibson were the best natural movers. Graf, even Navratilova would admit, would be the greatest if she had the instinct to come forward and volley off her serve—the fearlessness to rush like Navratilova, Smith, Gibson, and King headlong into the area of greatest instinct—the net. Like Borg, Graf had such pure speed. But like Lendl, something in Steffi Graf's personality—some fear or sense of order—left her on the baseline unless the volley was absolutely certain of being put away.

Graf did not lose a set in the early rounds, but she lost a lot of games. The other women sensed a weakness in her. Graf played her best match in the quarter-finals, crushing Conchita Martinez, the victor over Zina Garrison, 6–3, 6–1. She faced Navratilova next in one of the women's semifinals. It was a dream match. They had not played since Graf won the final at the 1989 U.S. Open, beating Navratilova 3–6, 6–4, 6–2. On paper, she was favored. At anything like full confidence, Graf was the most beautiful player I had seen since Maria Bueno.

A convincing win by Steffi Graf would dispel her family demons and set her free to resume her reign and grip on historic greatness. But Navratilova wanted one more chance to prove her historic superiority. The loser of this semifinal would feel a low like Napoleon's retreat from the Russian winter.

It was Graf who lost. She played well enough to win only one set and have a convincing lead in another. It was nearly a complete reversal of the final in which she beat Martina in 1989. Two years later, Martina had control of her nerves. Navratilova was at an age when she accepted herself. Steffi Graf was at an age when every discovery still hurt. Graf wanted too much to erase the memory of her tribulations about being her father's daughter. At the very point at which Graf had dominated Navratilova two years before, now Navratilova stepped up the pressure and snuck home with her third straight three-set win, 7–6, 6–7, 6–4. Graf could have won the match in the second-set tie-breaker, but Navratilova, sensing the window ajar just a bit, knew how to get through. She eased past her own nerves and got onto Steffi Graf's.

It was a younger woman who really stole the 1991 show, however. Before the tournament, I picked Jennifer Capriati to win the women's title. She was fifteen, but she had improved so much in the last year and a half that my doubts seemed no longer founded. I had underestimated not her will but her ability.

Capriati was much faster around the court in 1991. Her legs were trimmer, and she had spent hours just working with a footwork coach. She played a hundred matches and sat through all those interviews. The young girl had truly gotten tough. She now hit the ball harder than anyone else, and Nathalie Herreman would no longer dare to blast another ball at Jennifer's head between points. Capriati seemed poised to me, ready to win it all.

Television sensed the American teenager's value and tried to cash in on it the day before the U.S. Open began by staging a $100,000 match between young Capriati and the previous year's Open winner, Gabriela Sabatini. The public tuned in to Jimmy Connors's real tournament matches, which were near the top of any sports TV ratings, watched in over 3 million homes, according to the Nielsen ratings. But people ignored the exhibition match. Capriati took home the appearance money and lost the match 6–3, 6–3. "It was just an exhibition," she grinned afterwards.

By the luck of the draw, which no longer seemed like such luck to me, Capriati and Sabatini met again in the quarter-finals. Jennifer Capriati played as if she were possessed. Now five foot seven inches and 135 pounds, the fifteen-year-old tore into Sabatini. Capriati cracked her first serve at over one hundred miles an hour, the only woman player consistently to serve that hard since Margaret Court. She drilled her ground strokes like Chris Evert but harder, because Capriati, having harnessed the new Wilson racket technology, not only hit the ball, she rode it. In the end, Sabatini, less sure of herself from being passed so often, shrugged her wet black hair to one side, squared her shoulders, and trotted to net to shake hands, having lost 6–3, 7–6. "She used to be able to control me," Capriati said, smiling, "but not anymore."

The Capriati–Seles semifinal was thrilling, as good or better than the Connors–Krickstein. Seles liked to play angles, but the more orthodox right-handed American girl took Seles's sharp left-handed angles and put a straight American line through them with such pace that even Seles could not cope. Capriati dominated the first set, 6–3, and even when Capriati lost the second set by the same score, it seemed almost a tribute of respect to Seles before Jennifer Capriati was going to close out the Yugoslav player. Nearly everyone was pulling for Capriati in the third set. Serving for the match, Jennifer Capriati stood so close to victory she could almost hang it on her wall at home.

But what did victory look like? It was twenty thousand fans sitting in a stadium watching two people and roaring encouragement to one. It was a clear, sunny late summer day with the evening shadows falling across three-quarters of the court, so that each ball passed through light and shadow a dozen times before the roar of the crowd confirmed each moment's verdict. Jennifer Capriati was up 5–4, deuce. She was two service points away from the match. At Wimbledon that year, she had beaten Martina Navratilova, and so she was not only two points away from the match, Capriati was probably two points away from the championship. It was so sweet it would taste like icing. The fifteen-year-old bounced the ball and cracked her serve. Monica Seles grunted.

Greatness is often strange. Monica Seles's backhand, each time she hit it, was a strange and beautiful shot. The crowd booed her, but the unorthodox Eastern European and the spunky young American kept pounding away until Capriati missed.

"*C'est nul*," said an unimpressed French reporter.

I disagreed. It was one of the most exciting matches I had ever seen.

The crowd cheered every move young Capriati made, and still Seles kept bending to the ball, trying to find a way to win, looping high lobs to break the American's third-lane pace—buying time, trying to change to European time if she possibly could. There was a moment's hesitation. To win, sometimes you have to leap off a cliff. But with Capriati at the precipice, Monica Seles grabbed her ankle.

Jennifer Capriati never left her feet again. Their effort was so full-out, the goal so obtainable for both of them, that their two hearts beat as one. But only one could win. The fifteen-year-old from Florida lost the match twice, once serving at 5–4, deuce, once serving up 6–5, deuce—twice just two points away from victory. Seles played the tie-breaker brilliantly, but the match was already over when Capriati hesitated on the cliff of victory. McEnroe, Gonzales, Navratilova, Borg, Sampras, and Courier all had to pass through the hell of losing big matches before they could become a champion. Capriati thought for one moment that she had already broken through, but Jennifer Capriati had only had basic initiation into the champions' club.

The Florida girl took nearly an hour to get back to the interview room to answer the press's questions, and when she arrived it was clear from her red eyes what she had been doing. Her father, Stefano, stood at the side of the room wincing. His fifteen-year-old daughter had wept her heart out, on his shoulder, and they were not the tears of some spoiled, undeserving little rich girl. They were the tears of a prodigy whose young life was the spirit of competition itself.

"Jennifer," a reporter began to do his thing, "how tough is this loss for you?"

Capriati was wearing long white pants and a white V-neck tennis sweater. Her chin started to tremble. "Well. It was all in my hands. And then it slipped away."

"Did the crowd help you today?" asked Bud Collins, who was consistently kind to the players who had lost.

Capriati managed a smile. "Yeah. They always help me."

But the gentle questions were over. "Jennifer," the Texas TV sound-bite man asked, "when did this loss hurt worse, on the court or right now?"

"Now." The fifteen-year-old picked up a towel and held it tight to her face. Composed, she said, "Last year I didn't come close against her. It hurts worse when you could have won it."

Twenty minutes later, Monica Seles came into the room all decked out in the No Excuses blue-jean fashions she had been advertising since she became friends with Donald Trump and Marla Maples (who had plenty of excuses to make to each other). Seles was wearing lots of lipstick and huge triangular earrings. If it was not high fashion, it certainly was high adolescence. It looked like teen night out in Dubrovnik.

Seles, a young woman virtually without a country, handled herself under pressure with a skill way beyond her seventeen years. She had won the first two legs of the Grand Slam, then skipped Wimbledon because of injury, mysteriously hiding out at Donald Trump's mansion in Palm Beach, Florida. In the ways that counted, though, she was wise beyond her years.

"Monica, how did you feel when Jennifer served for the match twice?"

"I did not get so nervous. Last year, I prepared everything before the tournament and got the totally opposite result. For this one, I didn't prepare as much. You never know which way will work."

"Did the crowd reaction, when they booed you on the close calls, and when you served faults, did that bother you just a little bit, Monica?"

She answered with absolutely no rancor. "The crowd did get a little more behind Jennifer. But, I think, that is normal. Because, I mean, what she has done, being the youngest, is like the same that Jimmy Connors has done, being oldest. Players like them only happen once in a while. Definitely everybody would love having Jennifer in the finals more than me, but that is so normal. When I watch Connors, I feel the same way. I pull for Jimmy. It is what people feel. They are both exceptional."

And so was Monica Seles, who at seventeen was able to make an answer like that.

"Do you think you were stronger mentally than Jennifer was at the end?"

"I don't think so," said Monica Seles. "I really don't think that Jennifer is fifteen or I am seventeen or Martina is thirty-four. They are both very good players and we are all mature and young in different ways. Today, I think it was a little luck. You can say the same thing with Martina's match with Steffi today. Just that little thing."

Navratilova's win over Graf in the semis was not a prelude to a win over Seles in the final. Seles played beautifully and won the one-sided women's final 7–6, 6–1, and the match was not that close. No, the image of Martina that stuck in my mind was her comeback earlier in the tournament to beat the gritty twenty-two-year-old Spaniard Arantxa Sanchez-Vicario, who spoke English with a Castilian accent and was willing to stay on court all day. The score was 6–7 (6–8); 7–6 (7–5); 6–2. Martina had been an inch away from dying, and instead she broke young Sanchez-Vicario's heart. After that match Martina Navratilova was beaming, her mind never as happy as after a win.

"Martina. What has allowed you to play this long?"

Navratilova did not hesitate. She grinned: "My body."

Despite Jimmy Connors's miracles, not everyone was his fan. When Connors got a questionable call against Patrick McEnroe, he charged the referee's stand as if food were being taken off his plate, shouting, "Turn that damn Cyclops machine off. It's worthless. And so are you." During his match with Aaron Krickstein, he shouted at the referee, "You are an abortion!" The next day he was taken to task by the press, that exemplary group of nonswearers. "Jimmy, how would you like it if you were called an abortion?"

"Well," said Connors, thinking about it, "I've been called worse."

He undoubtedly had been. At least part of this piece of American tumbleweed was from Roseanne Barr country. And yet he consistently went beyond his limitations. He loved what he was doing, which was part entertainment, part plain struggle.

Jimmy Connors's amazing string of wins ended with a thud in the semifinals against the player in the draw who most reminded Connors of his younger self, Jim Courier. It was close for a set, but the freckle-faced redhead from Dade City, Florida, who might have been distracted by Connors the year before, now played like a complete pro—one who had honed his skills by being unafraid of losing. The crowd was shifting toward Courier but still hoping for Connors. The old Indian reporter, who had been my pal at Wimbledon, turned to me with a knowing smile and said, "The crowd is running with the hare and hunting with the dogs. I have observed this in visiting your country for many years. The crowd here likes to root for the underdog but go for the winner."

The Indian reporter was usually right, but when it was over, the American crowd rose to its feet to loudly applaud both Courier and Connors.

In the other men's semifinal, Stefan Edberg was too strong and graceful for Ivan Lendl. Edberg's will was like a rock, but he smiled softly when he had won. The shot of the match came after Lendl, in an unusual moment of arrogant desperation, hit a ball behind his back. Two games later, Edberg stood on the baseline and whipped his racket behind his back, hitting an outright winner at incredible speed.

"Anybody can do that," Lendl shouted at him on court.

"Yes," Edberg said later. "But I guess I did it better."

There is a magical scene in Fellini's *La Strada* in which Anthony Quinn, playing a one-man traveling circus strong man, bursts the chains across his chest and Giulietta Masina applauds wildly. For me, Pancho Gonzales always possessed something of that brooding strong man.

When I was young, Pancho Gonzales was on a par with Pablo Picasso in painting, Pablo Casals on the cello, and Isaac Stern on the violin. Gonzales *was* tennis. And yet even as a child, I sensed there was something more—something dark, angry, and troubled about the force that was Gonzales.

I had seen Pancho Gonzales in the crowd two days in a row, and nobody approached him. He rarely spoke to the press, but I thought he might have some insights. Gonzales in his sixties was still tall, dark, and handsome, more like a native American than a Mexican American. I wanted to speak to him in the worst way, but he disappeared. His friend George McCall, the former U.S. Davis Cup captain, said he would try to arrange it for me, but he was not overly optimistic. "Richard leads his own life. He's not quoted much because he doesn't like to talk much. I'll see what I can do, but don't count on it. To give you an example, a few years ago Gatorade contacted me. They wanted Pancho to be the spokesperson for their television ads. It was quite a nice contract, too. Pancho said, 'No thanks. I don't like to drink the stuff.' " McCall chuckled. "Pancho is never going to be a millionaire, but he doesn't care. He's a free spirit, and I think that is great. Pancho goes where he wants to go. I hear from him maybe every two or every three weeks, whenever Pancho feels like returning my call."

"Mr. Gonzales," I said when I reached him one night at home in Las Vegas, "do you remember playing Lew Hoad at Madison Square Garden, on a court set up over the hockey ice? During the warm-up you bounced your overheads into the hockey nets."

"I remember the hockey ice. Not the other business."

His voice was neither unfriendly nor friendly, and I realized I was talking to Pancho Gonzales, champion. He clearly did not like loose talk. His voice was lean, slightly dark, and in its timbre I sensed a general dissatisfaction, as if Pancho had seen too many short lobs in his lifetime.

"Mr. Gonzales. What makes a champion? What ingredient do all of them, the real ones, have?"

"Sacrifice," said Gonzales. "Giving up enjoyment of life for the sake of practice."

"What about inner drive?"

"You don't always start with inner drive," said Gonzales. "You create it. You create a feeling that you don't like losing. You think of something that hurts. Take Edberg, for instance. He's always been up and down. This year he's a whole lot stronger. He has made himself that way. Edberg probably was not aware of what was missing for two or three years. You create that inner feeling when you realize what is missing."

"Did you feel any extra drive because you came from a Mexican-American background at a time when tennis was pretty much a country club sport?"

"No," said Pancho Gonzales. "I felt no discrimination. Most of the players in my day played for the feeling of enjoyment as the motivator. Today they want to make money. Check the newspaper clippings in 1947 and 1948. They were saying I would never be any good, because I was too easy-going."

"You got pretty intense as a pro."

"Well, as a pro, at eighteen, I became a different person. I was intense," said Gonzales, "because I didn't have any school knowledge of things. That lack of knowledge made me intense and dissatisfied off the court, and it carried onto the court with me. I just didn't have the knowledge of things."

"And the others did?"

"To some extent. What got my attention was not just having to play tennis with Bobby Riggs and Jack Kramer, but having to do business with them. The business side of it really gave me the drive to beat them."

"How do you rate Connors and McEnroe among the champions?"

"Very high. Their desire to win is very high. More than sixty to seventy-five percent of the players in a tournament do not have the heart to gut a match out. One fella will say, 'Oh, my stomach is hurt, or my shoulder is hurt.' They don't realize how much the person across the net is also hurting. But McEnroe and Connors made the sacrifices."

"What about Boris Becker?"

"Not sacrificing enough," said Pancho Gonzales. "He carries too much weight, so he gets hurt. Look into horse race handicapping. The horses are twelve to fourteen hundred pounds, and they handicap them with five or ten pounds in weight. Becker is two hundred pounds. He can't do it carrying five to ten extra pounds. I'm about the same height as Becker is. I liked it around a hundred and eighty pounds. You just don't go out and play, even if you're tops. Becker has cut corners."

"What is right and what is wrong about Andre Agassi as a player?"

Gonzales, who had been married to Agassi's older sister, hesitated. "I really had nothing to do with his tennis. I will say this. Andre has to get some knowledge of how to get to net and finish the point. Up to that stage in a rally, he's probably the best person playing today."

"What do you think of the involvement of parents with their children's tennis? Is there too much of it?"

"When I was thirteen, I was hitchhiking all over California to tournaments. Today they drive the kids around in quality cars. I survived and learned to play. The parents today don't give the kids enough credit. By the time a kid is thirteen or fourteen, they know more than a parent ever will about tennis. The parents are wasting their breath unless they just want to hang around and be a shoulder to cry on."

"You played Connors and you beat him. How old were you?"

"I beat Jimmy in the final of the Pacific Northwest in 1970. I was forty-one or two. Jimmy was seventeen or eighteen."

"Laver said you had his number."

Gonzales paused. "I beat Rod Laver in five sets at the Howard Hughes tournament at Madison Square Garden in 1969, but Rod beat me plenty, too."

"Would you have been able to hit a topspin backhand playing with today's rackets?"

"No problem. The rackets today are so light you can swing them like a Ping-Pong racket. We used wood rackets two or three ounces heavier so it was harder to flick over the ball with your hand and wrist."

"Mr. Gonzales, is there a player playing today who reminds you of you?"

"No. There really isn't."

"Pete Sampras?"

"No. No way. He has a different attitude. He's a big hitter. I like his first serve. But I think I could mix things up more. He hits everything hard. I was more a thinking player."

I sensed I had been talking to someone unusual and large, someone whose game was so original in 1950 it had only been surpassed rarely— if at all—in either half of the century. Pancho Gonzales was a little bit like Anthony Quinn—just as direct but a little less happy. He was not an actor. He was a champion.

"I hope you got what I said right," Pancho Gonzales said. "Because mostly they don't, and that's why I'm not too interested in talking."

There are matches, big and small, that are won because a player is brave or lucky or physically strong or faster or mentally more tough or hungry. Stefan Edberg's tournament final against Jim Courier was all of these. It was earned magic. It was the type of match, if one is lucky, that comes once every year, as pure an effort and victory as any player can imagine. Edberg's serve was like a series of huge waves that battered the coast. Few reporters had seen as incredible a display of classic serve-and-volleying in many years. Edberg's attacking instinct was beautiful to witness. His volleys were put away with such suddenness and inner strength. His serve was so deceptively light to look at yet so powerful that Edberg could ride it to net again and again. His back bent on his serve like a pole vaulter's fiberglass pole, then suddenly he was on top of the net. Edberg's reflex volleys were part will, part absolute inner balance. Even when Courier stepped up and hit his baseball-bat two-handed backhand at the Swede's feet, Edberg made winning volleys from his shoe tops.

Courier had beaten Edberg at the French Open, and they always had close struggles before. Perhaps the cool summer weather at the 1991 U.S. Open was more to the Swede's liking than Courier's. But all day, Edberg was insistent. His volleys were like frozen ropes. The gliding Swede won as the late afternoon sun glazed the stadium court with a yellow light that reminded me of the old court by the side of the railroad tracks leading into Västervik. Edberg's face looked so unassuming and gentle in the interview room afterwards. "I was very disappointed last year and very lucky this year," he said with joy on his face. "We did not go into the city this year but stayed on Long Island in a home, not a hotel room, and that made a big difference. How was it for me playing today? It was almost like a dream. The tension did not come at all. It feels like a relief now, but I was so relaxed the whole time. It was a feeling like the first two sets against Becker last year at Wimbledon. I could do nothing wrong. It is a very unusual feeling. The backhand volley I made? That was a nice little shot. How I got it back, I do not know. I was one step ahead of him thinking all day. My strategy was to attack at every opportunity. What does that feel like? Well, you are reacting very fast without having to think too much. You just react and go and knock it off. Things just worked out better for me this year. You want to struggle in the first week, and if you get through it, then things get better. With Chang I got my rhythm back. That was the key match for me. He made me play. He made me think. It was like my match at Wimbledon last year with Amos Mansdorf. I survived it, and it picked me up. I'm just a happy guy now. I have tried to keep a positive mind, and I have managed to do so all the way through.

"Is my father a detective? Yes, my father knows every crook in Västervik." Stefan Edberg smiled proudly. "I am sure my father was watching me at home in Sweden."

The match had been so pure on Edberg's part. Jim Courier, as good a competitor as we had, shook his head philosophically and said, "I've taken whoopings before." It was a bit like a country-and-western song alongside Sibelius's violin concerto. But it wasn't yet time for a country song.

"Today is one of those days that I have worked for very hard," said Stefan Edberg, "a day that comes from concentrating even when you practice on your day off. I just got it at the right moment. This is probably the best match I ever played. I don't want to take anything away from what Jimmy has done here, but," smiled Edberg, "in a few years when they look at the record book, it will be my name that is there."

Tony Pickard made a fist. Stefan Edberg had beaten Jim Courier, the French Open champion, 6–2, 6–4, 6–0. "But the real drama was three nights ago," said Bud Collins softly as the interview room cleared.

The night of the Jimmy Connors–Paul Haarhuis match, I took my wife to Flushing Meadow. My press pass entitled me to one or two guest tickets during the tournament, but I could not sit with my guest. Part of the fun of watching a tennis match is sitting next to someone you really want to be with in those seats. So I took a chance. Well before the tournament had begun, I bought two tickets from Ticketron for the night-session quarter-finals.

The good news was that Connors was playing the night for which we had our tickets, and my wife—like half of America—was dying to see Connors. The bad news was where our seats were located.

"Do we go up?" my wife asked, looking toward the flags flapping above the stadium.

"I think so," I said, looking at my ticket stubs. Corporations had bought all the seats remotely near the court. IBM was in the second row. Infiniti and Fuji Film were front-row-center. I was prepared to climb a little. But let me put it this way: when we started the climb up the nearly vertical stadium steps, we were at sea level in Holland, and when we reached our destination we were in Switzerland.

"Do you have to know somebody to get these?" laughed my wife.

"Nice seats," I said. "For yodeling."

There were two scoreboards at the very top of the stadium. We were not under the scoreboard, we were behind it. If we stood up, we would hit our heads. There was only one row behind us. And behind that, for people like myself who grab onto walls when they see *Vertigo*, there was air. There was a certain comedy to watching other men and women dressed smartly in business suits, as they came up the concrete mountain, staring hopefully at their ticket stubs, then watching their faces like ours turn to disbelief, embarrassment, and then determination as they kept climbing up, up, up into the sky. The players were already hitting down on court.

"Which one is Connors?" asked my wife, wishing she had opera glasses.

"He's the one with the green fluorescent racket. Gee. Thirty bucks a ticket."

"I ordered my seats in July," I overheard the man in the row behind us say, and I felt better.

Bob Uecker never had it so good. The night Connors played Haarhuis they could have sold seats on top of the scoreboard. The air was electric. It was a cool night, and a light breeze was blowing. Two hot dogs and a beer later, we were rapt. We had the aerial perspective.

It was like being part of a photograph of the crowd watching the Jack Dempsey–Jess Willard fight outdoors in Ohio in 1917. Except this was New York City outdoors, in the night of 1991.

People on the streets were talking about tennis the way they talked about the World Series when I was a boy. People in office buildings had turned on little television sets during office hours to get a peek at what was happening to Jimmy Connors. A young guy in an elevator told me the day before, "I never really liked tennis, but I was in a bar yesterday with about a hundred people. And that Connors! We were all cheering."

I could see things that night I had not been able to see before. I was far enough away now. Down on that distant court the two players moved each other like chess pieces. The Dutchman was far too fit and young for Connors. Jimmy kept trying, but he had met his match. Haarhuis won the first set easily, 6–4.

"Haarhuis is just too good for him," I explained to my wife. "He's just too young."

A man in a blue suit, sitting with his wife, was clapping his hands every time Connors missed. Not everybody liked Connors, but I had to root for him. I was out of the press box, where neutrality is supposed to be maintained. There came a point of such importance that you could feel the whole match swinging on it while the point was still going on. This was the setup: Connors's serve had been broken at love to let Haarhuis go up 5–4 and serve for the second set and a two-set lead.

Jimmy Connors knew he had to have the next game, and as they changed ends to let the Dutchman serve, Connors made a gesture of defiance to the crowd, and the crowd roared. It was their roar that gave him any chance at all. Connors had become more than just a player for them. He was one of them but out of reach. His defiance was the crowd's defiance. The lean Dutchman went down 30–40 on his own serve, and again Connors exhorted the crowd. Connors was a method actor, up to anything Brando and DeNiro could do. Give Connors a stage, and he could find the method.

Haarhuis attacked when he was down, so it was a brave point all the way around, but the one point changed the entire match. It was the point of the tournament. Connors put up one lob, and Haarhuis smashed it to one side of the court. Racing wide, Connors put up another lob, a little deeper, a little higher, and Haarhuis hit that one, too, but now the lobs from Connors came higher and higher, almost reaching the top of the stadium. Haarhuis, through fear or some misguided sense of combative pride, would not bounce the overheads. As the lobs hung in the air, the crowd screamed and Haarhuis swung. Connors kept retrieving like a dog, until finally Haarhuis hit one short. This time, instead of lobbing, Connors raced in, drilled a forehand right at Haarhuis's chest, and then at full run crushed a flat two-handed backhand that merged completely with the backhand line. He had broken back!

The roar of the crowd almost took off the top of the stadium. Connors went on to win the set 7–6, and Haarhuis was never the same. Connors sold the crowd his complete line of elixirs. The medicine man working out of the back of his covered wagon ran Haarhuis through the heart and trotted to net victorious. The entire stadium rose to cheer the Connors effort.

"His head dropped at the start of the fourth set," Connors said. "When I saw that, I said, 'Okay. Come on. Let's get out of here.' "

For the fourth time in four tries, Jimmy Connors had pulled an upset.

He did not have enough for Courier, and Courier did not have enough for Stefan Edberg. But the draw was a stepped pyramid, and each step had its own moments of beauty. When Stefan Edberg won, he shook hands and ran straight to the box seats to embrace Annette Olsen, the girl from Växjö. There was summer in their hearts.

But in those two weeks in 1991, the crowd's heart belonged to Connors. He gave back to the people what they wanted, and what they longed for was an American who tried, who hung in there, who fought each match like his life depended on it. Jimmy Connors was from the heart of the country, and he had that raw, pulsating American desire to win—James Cagney in joy, Roy Orbison in sadness.

Jimmy Connors was a Yankee Doodle Dandy, Cagney dancing up the side of a vaudeville wall. The allure of Connors for so many people was not just his fighting American spirit—the way Americans were supposed to be made in the good old days—but his face and attitude, if too much alley cat for a Norman Rockwell cover, displayed a tough Midwestern American spirit. I could imagine Connors fighting in the Civil War.

I asked my wife to wait for me in the press room while I went down to hear Connors hold court one last time.

"He's like the Music Man," said my wife. He had turned the whole country on its head.

"In the third set I started seeing everything as big as a basketball," Connors said. The thirty-nine-year-old from Belleville, Illinois, was still part-boy, part-man. He was like Huck Finn but not as naive.

Jimmy Connors was a lasting myth from the heart of America—young forever, irreverent, loyal, and tenacious. And talented. In the end, his dream was everyone's dream: a streak of golden sun spreading over the court at the end of the afternoon. The families of the top players all walked toward that sun. And if in later life the players who had once been great still seemed like children, perhaps it was because they all had been so fierce and brave, men and women before they had been children.

"This summer has surpassed my wildest dreams," said Jimmy Connors. "Playing that second Sunday at Wimbledon because of all the rain this year, and having the crowd they let in do the wave for me. And before that, the French crowd cheering me during the match against Chang. And now this, here in New York, where through the years I have had my biggest wins and disappointments."

The prizes were given, the trophies were held aloft. Stefan Edberg, still shy, could not stop smiling. I felt now that my goal to pursue the nature of tennis competition was over. I wondered what Boris Becker was thinking; I was not sure he would ever win a big one again, but I hoped he would. I liked so many of the players, the winners and the losers—the risk takers, the ones who gave their heart and soul out on the court. This final day belonged to Stefan Edberg, as the day before had belonged to Monica Seles, but a large part of the tournament still belonged to James Scott Connors.

I thought about the walk back to the reporters' bus at 2 A.M. after Jimmy Connors had defeated Patrick McEnroe.

I thought of Wimbledon and its green lawns and requirement that the winners charge forward over the baseline. There were no echoes as the stadium cleared—only memories of the beauty, skill, and madness of the bouncing ball, the pursuit of victory and that tortuous footpath to the end of the draw.

INDEX

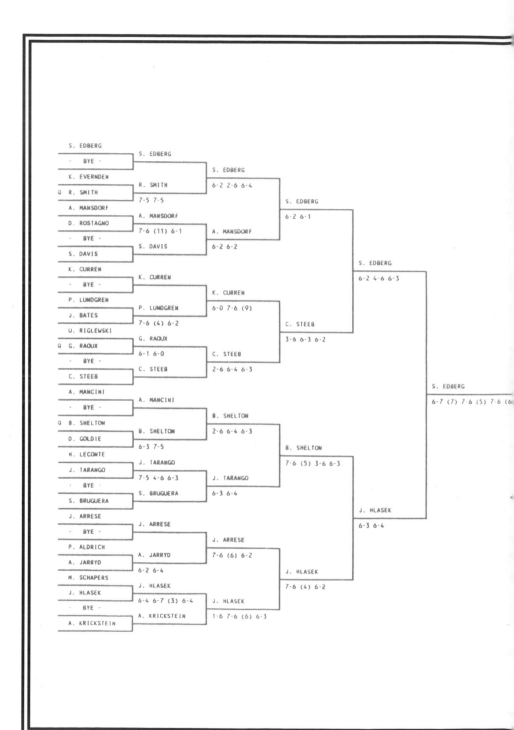

S. EDBERG
- BYE -
       S. EDBERG
K. EVERNDEN
Q R. SMITH
       R. SMITH
       7-5 7-5
               S. EDBERG
               6-2 2-6 6-4

A. MANSDORF
D. ROSTAGNO
       A. MANSDORF
       7-6 (11) 6-1
- BYE -
S. DAVIS
       S. DAVIS

K. CURREN
- BYE -
       K. CURREN
P. LUNDGREN
J. BATES
       P. LUNDGREN
       7-6 (4) 6-2

U. RIGLEWSKI
Q G. RAOUX
       G. RAOUX
       6-1 6-0
- BYE -
C. STEEB
       C. STEEB

A. MANCINI
- BYE -
       A. MANCINI
Q B. SHELTON
D. GOLDIE
       B. SHELTON
       6-3 7-5

H. LECONTE
J. TARANGO
       J. TARANGO
       7-5 4-6 6-3
- BYE -
S. BRUGUERA
       S. BRUGUERA

J. ARRESE
- BYE -
       J. ARRESE
P. ALDRICH
A. JARRYD
       A. JARRYD
       6-2 6-4

M. SCHAPERS
J. HLASEK
       J. HLASEK
       6-4 6-7 (3) 6-4
- BYE -
A. KRICKSTEIN
       A. KRICKSTEIN

S. EDBERG
6-2 6-1

A. MANSDORF
6-2 6-2

K. CURREN
6-0 7-6 (9)

C. STEEB
2-6 6-4 6-3

B. SHELTON
2-6 6-4 6-3

J. TARANGO
6-3 6-4

J. ARRESE
7-6 (6) 6-2

J. HLASEK
1-6 7-6 (6) 6-3

S. EDBERG
6-2 6-1

C. STEEB
3-6 6-3 6-2

B. SHELTON
7-6 (5) 3-6 6-3

J. HLASEK
7-6 (4) 6-2

S. EDBERG
6-2 4-6 6-3

J. HLASEK
6-3 6-4

S. EDBERG
6-7 (7) 7-6 (5) 7-6 (6